The Agrarian Question
and Reformism in
Latin America

THE JOHNS HOPKINS STUDIES IN DEVELOPMENT
Vernon W. Ruttan, Consulting Editor

ASIAN VILLAGE ECONOMY AT THE CROSSROADS:
An Economic Approach to Institutional Change,
by Yujiro Hayami and Masao Kikuchi

THE AGRARIAN QUESTION AND REFORMISM
IN LATIN AMERICA,
by Alain de Janvry

THE AGRARIAN QUESTION AND REFORMISM IN LATIN AMERICA

Alain de Janvry

The Johns Hopkins University Press
Baltimore and London

338.18
D32a

This book has been brought to publication with the generous
assistance of the Andrew W. Mellon Foundation.

Originally published (hardcover and paperback), 1981
Second printing (paperback), 1983
Third printing (paperback), 1985

The Johns Hopkins University Press
701 West 40th Street
Baltimore, Maryland 21211
The Johns Hopkins Press Ltd., London

Library of Congress Cataloging in Publication Data

de Janvry, Alain
The agrarian question and reformism in Latin America.

Bibliography: pp. 303–6.
Includes index.
1. Agriculture and state—Latin America.   2. Land reform—Latin
America.   I. Title.
HD1790.5.Z8D4   1981   338.1'88   81–4147
ISBN 0-8018-2531-8   AACR2
ISBN 0-8018-2532-6 (pbk.)

m.R

Alain de Janvry is professor of agricultural and resource economics at the
University of California, Berkeley.

Contents

**Chapter 8.   The Agrarian Question and Change
in Latin America: Conclusions**   255

Figures

Tables

Preface

While in the field in Latin America as well as in the classroom teaching courses on economic and agricultural development at Berkeley, I have repeatedly been impressed by two frustrations that are widely shared by others and that thus motivated me to write this book. One is that practitioners of economic development—policy makers, project directors, international donors and lenders, and political activists—lack a global interpretative framework that would allow them to give consistency to the variety of actions they undertake. As a result, the practice of economic development has been reduced to the evaluation and implementation of disconnected projects. Underlying these projects is a dramatic paucity of understanding of how they fit into the broader economy and what their political implications are. Most particularly, there is a general incomprehension (or neglect) of the state as a social phenomenon and of its logic, role, and limits in the management of reforms. In terms of the practice of development, a crying need thus exists for a unifying framework that is both sufficiently comprehensive to explain the multidimensional facets of underdevelopment and sufficiently simple to provide a broad set of guidelines that can in turn be made more specific in particular historical, geographical, and ideological contexts to serve as a basis for policy formulation and political action. This book is consequently written principally for practitioners of economic and agricultural development who have been preoccupied with finding a consistent theoretical framework in which to interpret the situations they observe and want to transform.

The other frustration that has recurrently perturbed me is that the global interpretations that have been developed—in the context of modernization theory as well as in that of political economy—have remained at very general and abstract levels. This, while pleasing to academic scholars of world economic systems and armchair revolutionaries, has left the practitioners of economic development, from policy-makers to political activists, in a vacuum: the global frameworks have provided only sweeping directives that can hardly be translated into pragmatic programs, and specific projects can be fitted into the global frameworks only in a rather distant and artificial fashion. In this book, I consequently attempt to show that this vacuum need not exist; a global interpretative framework is indeed essential for policy and political action, and it can serve to give very pragmatic directives for the definition and implementation of "what is to be done." Not only should the test of a theory's relevance be its ability to guide social action; conversely, a concern with the practical exigencies involved in changing the existing social reality is essential for developing a meaningful social theory. Consequently, this book is also written for scholars and students of economic development in an attempt to further our understanding of the global phenomenon of underdevelopment in the world economic system and to show how this knowledge can be used in the analysis and design of specific projects.

I am of course aware that by standing thus between two powerful traditions in development economics—pragmatic project design and abstract studies of global frameworks—I expose myself to critiques from both flanks. The practitioners may lose patience with the generalities that will often appear to them to be rhetorical and gasp for immediate guidelines for action. I believe that these guidelines are there but that they can be deduced from the global framework only through historical and conjunctural studies of the infinity of concrete situations—a task that is left to each practitioner and that is forever undertaken anew. The scholars of global systems may also lose patience with the specificity of the analysis of particular projects, such as land reform and rural development, which inevitably brings us to the level of the concrete, such as farming systems in peasant fields on the Altiplano. It is my hope, however, that both practitioners and scholars will admit that the problems of world underdevelopment, and especially the dramas of widespread hunger and massive rural poverty, are some of the most pressing we face today and that an essential first step in moving toward a solution is to bridge the existing gap between global interpretations and pragmatic policy and political guidelines. Even if modestly, this study attempts to move in that direction.

The writing of this book took several years and involved extended periods of stay in Argentina, Chile, Colombia, and Peru as well as frequent visits to Ecuador, Mexico, the Dominican Republic, and Brazil. My main indebtedness goes to my students at Berkeley, who provided both a constant opportunity for joint learning and invaluable assistance. I want in particular to acknowledge the contributions of Carlos Garramón, Luis Crouch, Margaret Andrews, David Runsten, Carmen Diana Deere, Lynn Ground, Ramón Crouch, Marilyn Skyles, Ednaldo da Silva, William Gibson, Frank Kramer,

Jean Jacques Dethier, and Curtis Dowds. I am also indebted to my companions in Latin America, and especially to Efrain Franco, Reed Hertford, Richard Dye, Lowell Hardin, Peter Bell, and Darryl Fienup, who made most of my fieldwork possible. Because we share the same preoccupations, if not necessarily the same opinions, I have also received essential encouragement and criticisms from Irma Adelman, Vernon Ruttan, Albert Hirschman, Edward Schuh, and Carlos Benito. Finally, much credit goes to my wife, Barbara,and my sons, Marc and Laurent, who shared patiently in the uncertainties and discoveries of frequent traveling.

Abbreviations

APRA	Alianza Popular Revolucionaria Americana (American Popular Revolutionary Alliance, Peru)
CEPAL	Comisión Economica para la America Latina (see ECLA)
CEPLAES	Centro de Planificación y Estudios Sociales (Center for Social Planning and Research, Quito, Ecuador)
CIAT	Centro Internacional para la Agricultura Tropical (International Center for Tropical Agriculture, Bogotá, Colombia)
CIDA	Comite Interamericano para el Desarrollo Agrícola (International Committee for Agricultural Development)
CIDE	Centro de Investigación y Docencia Economicas (Center for Economic Education and Research, Mexico City)
CIMMYT	Centro Internacional de Mejoramiento de Maiz y Trigo (International Wheat and Maize Improvement Center, Mexico City)
CIP	Centro Internacional de la Papa (International Potato Center, Lima, Peru)
DANE	Departamento Administrativo Nacional de Estadística (National Statistical Administrative Department, Bogotá, Colombia)
DRI	Desarrollo Rural Integrado (Integrated Rural Development program, Colombia)
ECLA	Economic Commission for Latin America, Chile
FAO	Food and Agriculture Organization, United Nations

FLACSO	Facultad Latinoamericana de Ciencias Sociales (Latin American Faculty of Social Sciences)
ICA	Instituto Colombiano Agropecuario (Colombian Agricultural and Livestock Institute, Bogotá)
IFPRI	International Food Policy Research Institute, Washington, D.C.
IIA	International Institute of Agriculture, Rome
IICA	Instituto Interamericano de Ciencias Agrícolas (Inter-American Institute of Agricultural Sciences, Bogotá, Colombia)
ILO	International Labour Organisation, Geneva
INCORA	Instituto Colombiano de la Reforma Agraria (Colombian Agrarian Reform Institute, Bogotá)
IPE	Instituto de Pesquisas Economicas (Institute for Economic Research, Brasilia, Brazil)
NACLA	North American Congress on Latin America
OAS	Organization of American States
OPEC	Organization of Petroleum Exporting Countries
PIDER	Programa Integral de Desarrollo Rural (Integrated Rural Development Program, Mexico)
PREALC	Programa Regional del Empleo para America Latina y el Caribe (Regional Employment Programme for Latin America and the Caribbean, ILO)
SARH	Secretaria de Agricultura y Recursos Hidráulicos (Secretariat for Agriculture and Water Resources, Mexico)
SINAMOS	Sistema Nacional de Movilización Social (National System for Social Mobilization, Peru)
UNCTAD	United Nations Conference on Trade and Development
UNESCO	United Nations Educational, Scientific, and Cultural Organization
UNRISD	United Nations Research Institute for Social Development
USAID	United States Agency for International Development
URPE	Union for Radical Political Economics

Introduction

This book is a case study of the uneven nature of capitalist development and of the role and limits of the state both in implementing a set of reforms directed at the contradictions of uneven development and in re-creating another set of contradictions in so doing. The dialectic of this sequence of contradictions and reforms is used to analyze the agrarian question in Latin America: its origins in the social class and economic structures of peripheral nations in relation to international forces, its economic and social dimensions and the dynamic of its transformation through time, and the implications it has for the design of political programs.

By nature, capitalist development is taken to be combined and uneven: (1) combined because capitalism forms a system on a world scale, with the result that all its component parts are organically and dialectically interrelated; and (2) uneven because development is not linear, homogeneous, and continuous but, on the contrary, is marked by inequalities over time, space, and individuals. Over time, accumulation occurs through a sequence of periods of expansion and stagnation. Growth creates barriers to growth, and the overcoming of these barriers both makes growth possible again and re-creates new barriers. Over space, development in particular regions and countries is associated with deformed development in other areas. Development and underdevelopment thus constitute a single dialectical unity and are the joint outcome of accumulation on a world scale. And over individuals, accumulation is accompanied by social differentiation into classes and by the transformation of social classes. Competition in the economic and political spheres also constantly jeopardizes established individual positions within classes.

Uneven development is the direct consequence of the inherent nature of capitalism as both a class society and an unplanned economy. Its class nature implies interclass contradictions between capital and labor over the control of the process of work and the appropriation of the economic surplus; its unplanned nature implies intraclass contradictions among individual capitals in the generation and use of the surplus. One of the implications of uneven development is the continuous reoccurrence of crises that are both the symptoms of unevenness and the mechanisms by which the system adjusts its component parts and attempts to reproduce itself. The history of capitalist development can thus be written as the history of a succession of periods of expansion and crisis that both continuously transform the system and restore its dynamic while at the same time re-creating new contradictions.

Once the neoclassical automatism of free-market adjustments and Say's Law—according to which supply automatically creates its own demand—are rejected, the understanding of crises appears as the principal subject matter of political economy. Crises are extraordinarily complex phenomena that have been conceptualized differently by classical, Marxian, and Keynesian political economists.

In general, crises can be classified into two categories: (1) crises of accumulation, or objective crises, which materialize under the form of inflation and recession; and (2) crises of legitimation, or subjective crises, which enhance class struggle and eventually question the reproduction of the social relations of capitalism. Each of these crises can result from a variety of causes that give it its particular historical form. Obstacles to accumulation have been associated with decreasing profitability of investment (resulting from declining returns for Ricardo, gloomy expectations for Keynes, and rising organic composition of capital for Marx); underconsumption; rising wages; the contradictory role of the state; and disproportionality between investments in different economic sectors. Similarly, crises of legitimation have been associated both with accelerated development of the forces of production and with economic stagnation. The essence of all crises, however, is to be found in the fundamental characteristics of the capitalist system, in particular its class and unplanned nature.

Attempts at overcoming crises originate at two levels: at the level of decentralized adjustments by individual capitalists, whose initiatives propagate via market mechanisms, and at the level of the state, through reformist policies. Individuals thus react at the same two levels, and these reactions are both complementary and contradictory: (1) as lone actors in a highly competitive (even under monopoly capital) and, hence, selective environment that pits members of the capitalist class against each other; and (2) as members of a class that can partially coordinate its global interests through use of the state apparatus.

The state thus appears as a social relation that is both the object and the instrument of class conflicts. This social relation establishes a process for the exercise of power via institutional arrangements directed at the management of both objective and subjective crises. In the first case, accumulation must be sustained in spite of systemic constraints; in the second case, legitimacy of class dominance must be maintained in spite of class struggle. And while both are necessary, they are also contradictory. On the one hand, there are trade-offs between effective management of objective and subjective crises; on the other hand, there are inherent limits to the capacity of the state to manage crises due to its limited fiscal means, administrative capacity, and its own legitimacy.

In this book, I use the dialectic of uneven development on a world scale to provide an interpretation of the underlying causes of the agrarian crisis in Latin America, identifying against this background the logic of public reforms in agriculture and observing the achievements and limits of state management of this crisis.

The agrarian crisis is characterized in its objective and subjective dimensions—that is, in terms of sharply uneven development among farms, crops, and regions and in terms of massive rural poverty and political tensions. Objective and subjective agrarian crises have induced the states in Latin American countries and international agencies to promote a sequence of reforms. As part of the cold war, these efforts started in the 1940s with a definitely political purpose under the banner of *community development* programs. The objective of the programs was to mobilize rural people on a community basis in order to stimulate democratic forms of government that would prevent internal revolutions and undertake development activities. During the 1950s, reforms centered on promoting agricultural development through *diffusionist* models transferred from the United States. Extension agents were sent to the countryside to diffuse the backlog of technological knowledge presumed to be available through international transfers. In the early 1960s, in response to the political shock waves of the Cuban Revolution, legislated *land reform* programs were initiated with the principal purpose of eradicating remnants of feudalism in the *latifundios* and *fazendas*. By the mid-1960s, as the world food situation was becoming tighter, agricultural development was again the dominant policy, but this time on the basis of *new technologies* specifically developed for the ecological conditions of Latin America. As the Green Revolution accelerated the development of capitalism in the context of production structures that had been modernized under the impetus of land reforms, social contradictions resulting from the rapid transformation of the peasantry became dominant. To counteract rising subjective forces among peasants and reduce migrations to the urban slums, integrated *rural development* was introduced in the early 1970s. Through these programs, the apparatus of the state was being mobilized to induce the diffusion of Green Revolution technology through the ranks of impoverished peasants with the expectation of preserving the peasantry and thus enhancing the production of cheap food and reaping a harvest of legitimating results. As the limits of dealing with poverty via rural development became increasingly evident, the strategy of *basic needs* was put forward as an instrument to improve welfare among the masses of dispossessed peasants and the rapidly rising numbers of rural workers.

The economic crisis of the late 1970s, however, placed narrow limits on the capacity of the state to sustain this type of reform. As a result, peasant demands were increasingly suppressed and rural poverty was largely abandoned to the fate of migration and proletarianization. At the same time, balance-of-payment requirements and a new international division of labor for agriculture led to massive integration of Latin American agriculture into the activities of *transnational agribusiness* firms.

In Chapter 1 of this study, the forces underlying the agrarian crisis are established in terms of the laws of motion of capital in the center-periphery structure. To do this, the evolution of thought on unequal development is retraced from Marx, Luxemburg, and Lenin through the *Monthly Review,* dependency, and development-of-underdevelopment schools to the modes-of-production approach. The contradictions of accumulation in the periphery of the world capitalist system are then established in terms of that system's particular social class structure, the logic of disarticulated accumulation, and the nature of imperialism. This leads us to take a position in a number of current debates, such as those on crisis, imperialism, and unequal exchange. Then, in Chapter 2, we proceed to characterize the agrarian crisis in terms of stagnation of food production and sharply uneven development of the forces of production and in terms of "functional dualism" between capitalist and peasant agriculture. Functional dualism is characterized both as a source of primitive accumulation through cheap semiproletarian labor and cheap food and a contradictory process that leads to the destruction of the peasantry. The principal manifestations of this contradiction are the demographic explosion, ecological collapse, increasing landlessness under competition for land with capitalist agriculture, and urban migration.

The debate on the nature and future of peasants—from Chayanov, Lenin, and Kautsky to articulation of the modes-of-production approach—is then reviewed in Chapter 3 for the purpose of establishing the mode and class position of peasants. This permits us to locate peasants under the capitalist mode as an unstable fraction of class that ranges from the petty bourgeoisie to the semiproletariat and that differentiates along a variety of roads—junker, farmer, and merchant. We use this to construct a typology of social classes and farm enterprises in Latin America and to follow the dynamics of its transformation.

We turn in Chapter 4 to an interpretation of the agrarian crisis based on the laws of motion of capital and the social class structure in Latin America. This is done by identifying a number of fundamental contradictions in agriculture: between rents and profits in the period of transition to capitalism and in the posttransition period; between cheap labor and balance-of-payment requirements; between cheap food and development of the forces of production in capitalist agriculture; and between use and reproduction of the peasantry as a source of cheap food. We also attempt to locate Latin American agriculture in the new international division of labor that emerged in the late 1970s and to trace out the evolution of these contradictions in this new order.

In Chapter 5 these contradictions are then taken to the level of the state and to reformism as the attempted management of crisis. We first characterize the capitalist state and identify some of its specific functions in the periphery. We then identify the limits of reformism in relation to the legitimacy, fiscal, and administrative crises of the state itself. Finally, we introduce the chronological history of agrarian reformism in Latin America before turning to a detailed study of land reform and integrated rural development in the subsequent two chapters.

In Chapter 6 we look at the sixty-year history of land reform in Latin America starting with the Mexican Revolution. A typology of land reforms is developed using the concepts of mode of production and social class, and seventeen land reforms in ten countries are thus classified. This permits us to contrast reforms that seek to (1) redistribute land to peasants within a precapitalist or a capitalist agriculture, (2) induce a transition from precapitalist to capitalist agriculture along either the junker or the farmer road of development, or (3) promote a shift from junker road to farmer road. While these reforms have been successful in inducing a rapid elimination of precapitalist social relations in agriculture, and in some cases in eliminating the landed elites from control of the state, their impact has been severely limited by the constraints of disarticulated accumulation. The permanence of these constraints, which reproduce the objective and subjective dimensions of the agrarian crisis, implies that the solution to the agrarian crisis increasingly lies outside the domain of agrarian reformism.

With the end of land reform in the early 1970s, rural-development and basic-needs programs assumed a key position in the strategy of agrarian reformism. In Chapter 7 we discuss the political and economic purposes of these programs and analyze in detail three specific projects in Mexico, Colombia, and Peru in order to identify the achievements and limits of this type of reform. These studies permit us to refute many of the traditional myths about peasant agriculture and to show that rural-development programs are highly contradictory, for in fomenting the development of capitalism among a rural petty bourgeoisie, their economic means tend to negate their dominant political ends. The strategy of basic needs proposed by reformist states thus appears as the most recent attempt to reproduce functional dualism, even though it runs into narrow limits because of legitimacy, fiscal, and administrative crises of the state.

In Chapter 8 we discuss the policy and political implications of the theses advanced in the previous chapters regarding the mechanisms of dependent-disarticulated accumulation in the periphery, the nature of the agrarian question and the problems of unequal growth and rural poverty, and the reformist role of the state in managing land-reform and rural-development programs. We do this by surveying a number of recent policy proposals on growth with equity and by developing a critique of these proposals. This permits us to advance an economic program for equitable growth. Specifically, we argue that the social articulation of economic systems, whereby the final-goods market for the modern sector is located in the expenditure of wage and peasant incomes, should be the key objective of structural transformation; and that the rapidly emerging rural semiproletariat and landless labor are the fundamental progressive political forces in agriculture, even though they are fraught with all the ideological contradictions that their peasant roots and continued linkages to subsistence agriculture imply.

1

Laws of Motion in the Center-Periphery Structure: The Underlying Forces

There has been a tendency to look at the problems of agricultural production and the welfare of rural populations as separate issues that can be understood within the realm of the agrarian sector or even at the village or farm level. This approach characterizes the two major prevailing interpretations of the production performance of Latin American agriculture. The monetarists have exposed the detrimental effect of market distortions on supply response without explaining their origins in the broader political economy.[1] And the structuralists have concentrated on land tenure and farm size without questioning the broader class structure and economic systems in which they are inserted.[2] Similarly, rural poverty has been rationalized as a phenomenon *sui generis,* a problem associated with the stubborn resilience of traditional culture and with dualism and marginality.[3]

We reject this approach and start our analysis of the agrarian question in Latin America from the postulate that the problem is but a symptom of the nature of the class structure in the periphery and of the particular process of capital accumulation it undergoes.

The other approach, which has dominated American social science in the field of development since the 1950s, is that of the modernization school. Rooted in neoclassical theory, modernization theory has segmented wealth from poverty, growth from stagnation, development from underdevelopment, and present from past. Following the traditions of Locke and Hume in liberal philosophy and of Newtonian physics, this school has atomized society into rational self-seeking individuals whose actions are impartially reconciled into social optimality by the "invisible hand" of the market. Social relations are

7

reduced to relationships through things in the process of exchange, a phenomenon that Marx labeled ''the fetishism of commodities.'' It has thus created the norm of a world of social harmonies where, in the context of *laissez faire,* each individual (each factor) is remunerated according to his or her participation in production. The relevance of social classes and of power relations in understanding economic phenomena is in this way negated. And so is the relevance of exploitation, racism, sexism, militarism, and imperialism. Social and political problems are confined to the irrational category of ''distortions'' or attributed to ignorance and mistakes. And the state is reduced to an institution that is presumed to arbitrate impartially the conflicts among individuals and interest groups. By accepting Western capitalism as the unique norm, all countries are ethnocentrically thrown on the same axis of ''normal patterns of growth,'' although temporarily located at different stages.[4] Development is reduced to a process of diffusion of innovations.[5] The history and specificity of the less-developed countries are thus effectively negated, and their only possible future is predetermined by the history of the more-developed countries.

We reject this approach as well, and rely instead on the methodology of dialectical and historical materialism to develop a dynamic theory of society that provides a framework within which the agrarian question and reformist state interventions can be understood. The dialectical approach implies centering the analysis on the emergence of contradictions as the basis of movement and social change. The materialist approach implies placing the key contradiction in the conflicts that emerge among social classes in the process of production and appropriation of social surplus. Consequently, the concept of exploitation replaces the neoclassical premise of social harmony. And while, in this approach, the process of production and circulation of material goods is the basis for understanding social systems, it by no means reduces them to economic phenomena. On the contrary, it stresses the existence of a constant dialectic between objective and subjective forces wherein the former characterize material production while the latter characterize class conflicts.

The accumulation of capital is the objective force that guides the historical development of capitalism, and the exploitation of labor by capital is the mechanism by which this accumulation occurs. This process is, however, characterized by unequal development between firms, sectors, regions, and countries. While virtually all Marxists thus call on ''the law of unequal development'' to explain the joint occurrence on a world scale of development and underdevelopment, there is strong disagreement both on how this law operates and on the nature of its impact in the periphery. From Marx and the classical theories of imperialism to the ''radical structuralist'' and ''neo-Marxist'' interpretations of underdevelopment, the law has been widely reinterpreted. To take a position in this important debate, it is useful to retrace the evolution of the idea of unequal development. However, each particular conceptualization of unequal development must be approached not in the abstract but by specific reference to (1) the particular historical epoch of imperialism to which each was applied—from Marx in 1840 to today; (2) the particular understanding of the contradictions that characterize the process of capital accumulation in the dominating countries; and (3) the particular ideological purpose of the theory. The evolution of the idea of unequal development shows that there have been two major reversals on the interpretation of its implications for the relative development of center and periphery. The first reversal occurred with Kuusinen at the Sixth World Congress of the Comintern in 1928 in opposition to the formulation of the law of unequal development by Marx and the classics of imperialism. This reinterpretation of 1928 has been at the core of the theories of dependency, "the development of underdevelopment," unequal exchange, and, in general, the *Monthly Review* school. The second reversal, which is associated to some extent with Amin but more consistently with writers in the *New Left Review,* opposes this reinterpretation and restores many of the classical ideas on the law of unequal development.[6] The debate on the law of unequal development and the positions assumed through these successive reversals are far from only semantic and academic: they correspond to major differences in the understanding of underdevelopment, and they have sharply constrasting policy and political implications.[7]

EVOLUTION OF THOUGHT ON UNEQUAL DEVELOPMENT

It is well known that Marx did not devote significant attention to the problem of unequal development on a world scale. His observations on India and South America were principally aimed at identifying the barriers that colonialism and the internal class structure in those countries created for the expansion of capitalism. His analysis of the laws of motion of the capitalist mode of production was, however, essential to an understanding of the impact on a world scale of the development of capitalism: he stressed the *expansionist* drive of the capitalist mode of production, which results from its competitive nature. Since not only the surplus product is alienable, as in all class societies, but also all the means of production are as well, a surplus expropriator must compete with other appropriators in order to reproduce his social position, since he has no extraeconomic right to his property.[8] It is this condition for survival—which exists even under monopoly capital—that creates the drive to maximize profit and to accumulate, not some inner behavioral ethic. And it is this condition that, in the context of secular downward pressures on the rate of profit and recurrent economic crises, throws capital beyond national boundaries and beyond the confines of capitalist production. This inner expansionist dynamic thus universalizes the capitalist mode of production and homogenizes social relations. While colonization, with the associated presence of merchant capital and mechanisms of primitive accumulation, temporarily prevents the penetration of capitalism in the sphere of production and results in high profits for the industrialized countries through plunder and trade, it also becomes an instrument of development of modern industry. All noncapitalist modes are ultimately destroyed, not dominated and functionalized and thus reproduced, as others were later to argue. In comparing Germany to England, Marx then made the well-known prediction that "the country that is more developed industrially only shows, to the less developed, the image of its own future."[9] Irrespective of its origins—endogenously created or externally imposed—capitalism was to re-create autonomous patterns of growth similar to those of Western Europe.[10] Unequal development was then in no way expected to imply a sustained growing income gap between the early and late industrial countries and between imperialist centers and colonies.

Like Marx, Rosa Luxemburg derived her theory of the world expansion of capitalism from the contradictions of accumulation in the center countries under competitive capitalism.[11] To do so, she used Marx's equations of reproduction, to which she added two new postulates: the continued occurrence of capital-using technological change in production and constant real wages for workers. The logical consequence of these assumptions is an increasing deficit in the production of capital goods and an increasing surplus of consumption goods relative to the effective demand that originates in wages; in short, they lead to the occurrence of underconsumption crises. Self-sustained capital accumulation in the center is thus impossible. Capitalism needs to continuously expand its sphere of circulation by incorporating additional precapitalist areas in which part of the surplus production of commodities can be realized and from which cheap raw materials can be imported for the production of capital goods. Imperialism, with its associated doses of violence and interimperialist wars, was thus seen by Luxemburg as the process of conquest of precapitalist markets.

While the assumptions Luxemburg tacked onto Marx's equations of reproduction have been widely criticized for introducing an illogical mix of dynamic (technological change) and static (constant wage) specifications,[12] as well as for contradicting history (especially the rise of wages in the center), Luxemburg's analysis of the penetration of capitalism in the colonies by merchant capital offers an insightful description of the process of destruction of precapitalist spheres.[13] In terms of unequal development, the impact of merchant capital on the periphery is to temporarily postpone the development of capitalism by competing with local industry and reinforcing precapitalist social relations, but it is eventually also to spread capitalism in the sphere of production as well. The dominant capitalist mode absorbs all precapitalist modes and tends toward exclusivity, but in so doing it also exports to the periphery the tendency for overproduction of consumption goods. As a result, the crisis in the center is only postponed until all precapitalist spheres have been absorbed. Here again, after a transition period in which merchant capital dominates in the sphere of circulation, unequal development on a world scale implies a process of catching up between periphery and center.

Twenty years after Luxemburg, Lenin and Bukharin also centered their analyses of the world-wide spread of capitalist relations on the contradictions of accumulation that exist within capitalist areas.[14] But twenty years after Luxemburg, the structural conditions in the center were markedly different. Competitive capitalism, which exported commodities on a world scale, had been replaced by monopoly as the dominant form in both industry and finance. Without developing an underconsumptionist theory of crisis as Luxemburg did, Lenin also located the origin of the limit to capitalist accumulation in the center in the underdevelopment of individual consumption capacity: "the necessity for exporting capital arises from the fact that in a few countries, capitalism has become 'overripe' and (owing to the backward stage of agriculture and the impoverished state of the masses) capital cannot find a field of 'profitable' investment."[15] It is, however, possible for the capital-goods sector to grow relatively autonomously from the consumption-goods sector: this offers domestic investment opportunities for capital but also leads to the accumulation of enormous masses of capital that drive down the rate of profit. The fall in the rate of profit and the consequent accumulation of a financial surplus are thus the forms that capitalist crises assume under monopoly capital. Surplus capital then seeks "young areas" external to the capitalist sphere: "In these backward countries profits are usually high, for capital is scarce, the price of land is relatively low, wages are low, raw materials are cheap."[16] In the phase of monopoly capital—"the highest stage of capitalism"—imperialism thus assumes the form of the export of finance capital (industrial and financial) in search of high profit rates in contrast to Luxemburg's export of commodities in search of new markets. But the export of capital also stimulates the export of capital goods and all sorts of commodities. Because it is necessary for overcoming the contradictions of accumulation in the center, the export of capital leads to severe rivalry among colonialist countries for access to and control over external territories. Lenin used this interpretation to explain the "second" colonial period, which started in the 1890s with the sharing of Africa and eventually led to the outbreak of World War I.[17]

Thus, through finance capital, imperialism spreads capitalism to the periphery, where it implies accelerated growth: "The export of capital affects and greatly accelerates the development of capitalism in those countries to which it is exported. While, therefore, the export of capital may tend to a certain extent to arrest development in the capital-exporting countries, it can only do so by expanding and deepening the further development of capitalism throughout the world."[18] There is a consequent tendency toward unimodality and homogenization on a world scale under the capitalist mode as "capitalism is growing with the greatest rapidity in the colonies and in overseas countries."[19] For both Lenin and Bukharin, the law of unequal development thus implied that capital is transferred from center to periphery and that the periphery consequently grows faster than the center.

It was with the adoption of Otto Kuusinen's thesis at the Sixth World Congress of the Comitern in 1928 that the idea of unequal development on a world scale was reversed from a theory of accelerated growth in the periphery to one of stagnation. Observing that British imperialism was hindering the industrial development of India, Kuusinen inferred: "It is characteristic of capitalism that the development of some countries takes place at the cost of suffering and disaster for the peoples of other countries . . . . the colonization [of backward areas] made possible the rapid development of capitalism in the West."[20] Not only was capitalist penetration in the periphery under the aegis of imperialism a source of surplus extraction to the benefit of the center but it also created a bottleneck to industrialization and resulted in stagnation. This reversal was later to acquire theoretical legitimacy with Sweezy's work on underconsumption crises and the counteracting role of the state[21] and with Baran and Sweezy's work on imperialism.[22] From the reversal also emerged the "development-of-underdevelopment," "dependency," and "unequal exchange" schools of thought on the issue of backwardness, although the political implications of these theories were to be sharply at odds with those put forward by Kuusinen.

Kuusinen's analysis of the obstacles that imperialism created in the process of industrialization was based on the alliance that foreign capital, in search of social support in the colonies, was believed to have sealed with the feudal oligarchies. This "feudal-imperialist alliance" blocked the emergence of a national bourgeoisie and cancelled the historical progressiveness of capital in the periphery. The political implication of this thesis, which was to become the doctrine of Latin American communist parties, was that the struggle against feudalism was a necessary stage in any progressive strategy. This implied the formation of broad alliances to promote "national bourgeois revolutions" in Latin America.

Sweezy and Baran's theses (often referred to as the *Monthly Review* School) were developed in the 1940s and 1950s in a historical context that was markedly different from that of Lenin and Bukharin. The United States had recovered from a major recession and was going through a sustained period of economic growth under strong government intervention; a continued succession of violent and cold wars absorbed a high fraction of the labor force and of the public budget; the United States had replaced England as a world hegemonic power; and monopoly capital was exporting industries on a world scale in the form of multinational corporations. Sweezy and Baran rejected Lenin's semiautonomous growth of the capital-goods sector as a source of demand and went beyond Luxemburg's crude underconsumptionist thesis based on the fixity of real wages at subsistence level. Their theory of underconsumption was based on the tendency for the production capacity of consumer goods to expand faster than the consumption capacity of rising real wages. Monopoly capital implies the tendency for a financial surplus to rise in the monopoly sector: on the one hand, productivity gains can be retained as extra profits instead of transferred via falling prices, since firms now have the capacity of controlling prices; on the other hand, surplus value is redistributed among firms from the competitive to the monopoly sector. Lack of investment opportunities due to insufficient expansion of effective demand and to the defense of monopolistic positions implies that part of this surplus sits idle and drives down the rate of profit on the global mass of social capital. However, a number of counteracting forces are brought into play by individual entrepreneurs (capitalists' consumption and investment and the sales effort) and by the state (Keynesian public expenditures and, in particular, military spending). By means of these interventions, and especially that of the state, the surplus is "burned," and the problem of circulation can be resolved within the center itself.

For Baran and Sweezy, imperialism consists of the export of industrial capital in the form of multinational corporations. It provides an ideological rationale for military expenditures at home and permits the capture of profit rates in the periphery which are higher than those in the monopoly sector in the center.[23] The surplus thus captured is repatriated: the periphery is drained of its investable surplus, which blocks the development of the forces of production; and this surplus enriches the center, where it contributes to a further advance in the development of the forces of production, even though part of it will again be "burned." As Baran and Sweezy argue, "Indeed, except possibly for brief periods of abnormally high capital exports from the advanced countries, foreign investment must be looked upon as a method of pumping surplus out of the underdeveloped areas, not as a channel through which surplus is directed into them."[24] The world expansion of capitalism, while not theoretically necessary to maintain the rate of profit in the center, has historically been an integral part of the resolution of contradictions in the center. Imperialism has thus simultaneously created growth and stagnation. Following the lead of Kuusinen, the law of unequal development on a world scale has been inverted relative to the formulations of Marx, Luxemburg, Lenin, and Bukharin: unequal development is development of the forces of production in the center and their underdevelopment in the periphery. "Far from serving as an engine of economic expansion, of technological progress, and of social change, the capitalist order in these countries has represented a framework for economic stagnation, for archaic technology, and for social backwardness."[25]

While Kuusinen's revision of the law of unequal development was based on the feudal-imperialist alliance, Baran and Sweezy's focused on surplus extraction from the periphery. These approaches were followed by Frank and the Latin American "dependency" school's[26] attempt to explain the historical process of underdevelopment in Latin America and, in particular, the "failure'' of import-substitution industrialization after World War II.[27] According to Dos Santos, for example, the task of dependency theory is to reformulate the classical theories of imperialism in order to explain stagnation, not growth.[28] As Frank explains it, "the metropolis expropriates economic surpluses from its satellites and appropriates it for its own economic development. The satellites remain underdeveloped for lack of access to their own surplus and as a consequence of the same polarization and exploitative conditions which the metropolis introduces and maintains in the satellite's domestic structure.''[29] The internal dynamic of dependent economies is fundamentally determined externally by their insertion in the world economic system and the resultant ties between the internal and external structures. Import-substitution industrialization merely redefines the nature of dependency and enlarges surplus extraction. Development and underdevelopment are thus partial but joint processes of one world system.

In keeping with the approach followed by Sweezy in his debate with Dobb on the transition from feudalism to capitalism, Frank defines capitalism as a world system where production is oriented at the market and where the purpose of production is profit-making.[30] This allows him to neglect the characterization of social class relations and to characterize Latin America as capitalist throughout, since it has been tied to merchant capital from the dawn of colonization.

With capitalism (not Kuusinen's feudal oligarchies) everywhere, and with dependency relations blocking the development of the forces of production through surplus extraction, Frank thus "proves" the need for socialism as the only objective solution to underdevelopment. The political implication of this interpretation was to dominate Latin American revolutionary thinking after the galvanizing success of the Cuban Revolution. The misery of the workers and peasants was seen to have created the objective conditions for armed struggle. Since the national bourgeoisie was either nonexistent or tied to the interests of imperialism, tactical alliances with the bourgeoisie as suggested by the traditional communist parties were impossible. The insurrectional *foco,* a small group of determined individuals willing to make sacrifices, was enough to create the subjective conditions for catalyzing the revolutionary potential of the masses.[31] The doctrines of Che Guevara were thus to draw a generation of idealistic young people into hopeless warfare rather than political organization and the task of developing socialist consciousness.

The development-of-underdevelopment approach was recently used by Wallerstein to analyze the development of capitalism on a world scale.[32] By similarly defining capitalism according to the existence of commodity production, instead of in terms of social class relations, he identified the developmental dynamic of world trade and the consequent world division of labor that it created. This world system is, however, characterized by unequal power relations among nations, with the result that the division of labor leads to accelerated accumulation in the center and stagnation in the periphery.

The surplus-extraction approach to underdevelopment gained major theoretical status when Emmanuel explained the determination of international terms of trade using the labor theory of value.[33] In so doing, he went beyond the attempts of Prebisch, Singer, and the Economic Commission for Latin America (ECLA) to show that international prices have deteriorated against the periphery in the postwar period—a proposition hampered by great empirical difficulties.[34] Emmanuel located the source of unequal gains in trade in the wage differential between center and periphery—a proposition for which empirical evidence was easy to find.

Emmanuel opposes the Ricardian theory of comparative advantages by assuming perfect international mobility of capital, and hence equalization of rates of profit on a world scale at equilibrium, while assuming immobility of labor, and hence the persistence of differences in wage rates. According to Emmanuel, an international gap in wages between center and periphery leads to terms of trade that favor the higher-cost products exported by the center and devalue the exports of the periphery. Unequal exchange in trade thus becomes a factor of surplus extraction even with fully capitalist production relations in the periphery, equally high labor productivity, and perfect free trade. This, in turn, is taken to explain stagnation in the periphery.

Emmanuel's analysis—in spite of the attractiveness of its theoretical purity—is, however, fraught with serious theoretical and empirical difficulties; and it is fair to say that the debate on unequal exchange in which Bettelheim, Amin, Braun, Mandel, Kay, Weeks and Dore, and others have participated is far from settled, in spite of the claims made by some contributors.[35] Some of the most serious objections that have been raised are (1) that the periphery cannot be characterized by capitalist social relations throughout, for significant low-productivity, noncapitalist spheres of production remain;[36] (2) that wages cannot be taken as exogenous variables if unequal exchange is to be seen as an integral element of a process of accumulation on a world scale;[37] (3) that unequal exchange does not apply to exported goods that are produced by both center *and* periphery when such goods in fact constitute a majority of the commodities traded internationally;[38] (4) that unequal exchange assumes equilibrium in the capital market, which implies that capital movements have already resulted in a world equalization of the rate of profit, an assumption that seems to contradict observed facts and that, if true, would contradict perpetuation of a wage gap between center and periphery;[39] and (5) that international capital movements would, in fact, imply faster growth rates in the periphery—an interpretation of unequal development that is contrary to Emmanuel's very perception of the process of underdevelopment.[40]

It was Amin who brought to their most elaborated forms the development-of-underdevelopment interpretation of backwardness and the associated interpretation of unequal development as a pattern of homogeneous growth in the center and stagnation or highly uneven growth in the periphery. To do so, he developed the concept of peripheral capitalism to characterize the nature of accumulation in the periphery of the world system and relocated the mechanism of unequal exchange within the theory of historical materialism to make surplus extraction the key element of his model of underdevelopment. According to this model, wages are no longer an exogenous determinant of unequal exchange but are determined by both objective (capital accumulation) and subjective (class struggle) forces.

In Amin's analysis, the center economies are characterized by an articulated (or autocentric) pattern of accumulation whereby a portion of the productivity gains in the labor process translates into increased real wages, thus permitting a dynamic equilibrium to obtain among sectors and between production and consumption. The consumption capacity of the economic system expands in relation to the development of its production capacity. The underlying tendency of central capitalism is, however, toward underconsumption and the resulting emergence of an idle financial surplus that depresses the rate of profit on social capital. As in Baran and Sweezy, state intervention can counteract this tendency through the squandering of surplus value in the center. The social basis of this intervention is found in a presumed "social contract" between capital and labor, a contract which empowers the state to manage conflicting wage and profit demands in relation to productivity gains in order to sustain expansion without crises. "The monopolization of capital, on the one hand, and labor organization on a nationwide scale, on the other, have made possible 'planning' so as to reduce conjunctural fluctuations."[41] A self-sustained process of accumulation is thus possible in the center. Writing in the late 1960s at the end of a long period of expansion characterized by only mild fluctuations under the guidance of Keynesian public policies and attenuated labor militancy in the center economies due to rapidly rising real wages, Amin does find empirical support for his postulated model of articulated accumulation. As it appeared, the major contradictions of accumulation were no longer located in the center economies but emerged in the stagnating or dualistic peripheral economies with their large, impoverished masses.

While an internal solution to the maintenance of a dynamic equilibrium is thus possible within the center itself, an external solution also exists that functionalizes the periphery in the maintenance of this dynamic equilibrium on a world scale. Because this external solution has historically been available to the center and because the "social contract" in the center has not been sufficiently effective in fully overcoming declining-rate-of-profit tendencies, it has been utilized, even though it is a secondary equilibrating mechanism for the center. But its implications for the periphery have been devastating.

For Amin, the periphery has had two functions in the development of the world capitalist system: on the one hand, it has offered an expanding market at the expense of precapitalist areas; on the other hand, it has increased the average rate of profit. And this dual role has been redefined over time as the center evolved from competitive to monopoly capital:

In the age of competition it was the first of these two functions that was vital, because keeping wages at the center at relatively low and stagnant levels (down to about 1860, at any rate) came into conflict with the objective requirement, in the model of autocentric accumulation, of a parallel growth of the reward of labor and the level of development of the productive forces. External extension of the capitalist market was therefore of prime importance as a means for realizing surplus value.[42]

This interpretation is analogous to Luxemburg's, for during this period wages were at subsistence levels in the center. But Amin goes beyond Luxemburg in identifying the role of trade as also to maintain the rate of profit in the center, which results from the import of wage foods and raw materials that are cheap either because no rent is paid in production (American wheat) or because of natural comparative advantages. Yet, there was no unequal exchange through trade during the period, since wages were equally low world-wide.

The role of the periphery changed with the rise of monopoly capital and subjective forces that pushed wages upward and internalized market expansion in the center:

After 1880 the monopolies created the conditions needed, first, for wages at the center to rise with the rise in productivity, as required for autocentric accumulation, with competition between firms no longer proceeding by way of price cuts, and, second, for the export of capital on a large scale to the periphery to become possible. The first of these changes reduced the role of the periphery in the mechanism of absorption. At the same time, however, it reinforced the second function, that of raising the level of the rate of profit, which was tending to decline faster at the center. This became possible through export of capital, which enabled forms of production to be established in the periphery which, although modern, nevertheless enjoyed the advantage of low wage-costs. It was then that unequal exchange appeared.[43]

Unequal exchange and the repatriation of profits sustain the rate of profit in the short run but further aggravate the rise of a financial surplus in the center in the next period. Squandering of this surplus through state intervention, as in Baran and Sweezy's model, and new capital exports to the periphery, however, again permit maintenance of a dynamic equilibrium on a world scale. In the periphery, unequal exchange and the outflow of profits block accumulation, even though rapid growth occurs in specific periods and sectors: "The dialectic of this contradiction between the tendency to external deficit and the resorption of this deficit through structural adjustment of the periphery to the center's needs for accumulation explains why the history of the periphery consists of a series of 'economic miracles'—brief periods of very rapid growth while the system is being established—followed by periods of blocked development, stagnation, and even regression: miracles without any future and take-offs that have failed."[44]

With expansion of the market for the world system as a whole located in the center and in the consumption of luxuries by the periphery's elites, the periphery is fundamentally reduced to the dual function of providing cheap exports and high rates of profit on expatriated capital—both on the basis of cheap labor. This function is developed by maintaining in the periphery a process of extroverted and disarticulated accumulation where high labor productivity in the modern sector is accompanied by cheap labor and where semiproletarianization in the noncapitalist spheres cheapens the cost of maintenance and reproduction of labor power.[45] With a functional articulation between capitalist production and noncapitalist modes enhancing capital accumulation, the periphery is thus highly dualistic. Unequal development implies that the growth sectors, with their short-lived "miracles," are concentrated in the capitalist production of exportables and luxuries, while the production of mass consumer goods remains noncapitalist and stagnant and that of capital goods is essentially nonexistent.[46] And it is principally in the noncapitalist modes that the impoverished masses bear the social cost of unequal development.

Central to the line of thought on unequal development running from Sweezy and Baran to Amin is the idea that the center appropriates a large part of the periphery's economic surplus. This surplus extraction tends to block sustained accumulation in the periphery while it enhances that in the center, and thus unequal development means, as it did for Kuusinen, growth in the center and stagnation in the periphery.

The whole development-of-underdevelopment (or radical-structuralist) school has recently come under severe criticism from within the Left itself on several issues, and several critics have reverted the law of unequal development back to its classical formulation. By the early 1970s, the world economic situation had, of course, changed dramatically: sustained expansion in the center had given way to crisis; rivalry among center countries had increased for access to both raw materials and markets; and the social-democratic basis of state legitimacy in center countries had become increasingly strained as the economic slowdown and inflation implied higher unemployment levels and stagnating or declining real wages. In the relations between center and periphery, the terms of trade had turned largely in favor of the latter, and the center's capacity for external determination had been severely weakened by the outcome of the Vietnam War, the rise of the OPEC cartel, and successful revolutions in postcolonial Africa and Nicaragua. In the periphery itself, the stagnationist vision of underdevelopment was shattered by the observation that many countries were in fact industrializing rapidly. Moreover, the Nicaraguan Revolution had demonstrated that a national bourgeoisie does exist, after all, and that it can be mobilized in broad progressive alliances.

A few statistics serve to dismiss the crucial postulate of stagnation. As Table 1.1 shows, whereas the annual growth rate in GDP was of comparable magnitude in center and periphery until 1968, it was 79 percent higher in the periphery than in the center over the period 1969–76. The difference between Latin America and the United States was even higher, reaching 164 percent in the latter period. While growth rates in manufacturing and gross fixed capital

Table 1.1.   Average Annual Growth Rates in Gross Domestic Product, Manufacturing, and Gross Fixed Capital Formation

	Percent								
	Gross domestic product			Manufacturing			Gross fixed capital formation		
Region	1950–60	1960–68	1969–76	1950–60	1960–68	1969–76	1950–60	1960–68	1969–76
Developed market economies	4.0	5.1	3.3	4.5	6.5	2.6	4.2	6.5	2.0
Developing market economies	4.6	5.0	5.9	6.8	6.6	7.7	—[a]	6.4	9.2
United States	3.2	4.8	2.5	2.9	6.4	1.6	1.8	5.8	0.3
Latin America	5.0	5.1	6.6	6.6	6.3	7.6	—	5.4	8.3

Sources: United Nations, *Yearbook of National Accounts Statistics, 1966* (New York, 1966), tables 4A and 4B; idem, *Yearbook of National Accounts Statistics, 1977* (New York, 1977), vol. 2, table 4A.

[a] — = data not available.

formation fell precipitously in the center economies from 1960–68 to 1969–76, they actually increased in the periphery. In the 1969–76 period, the growth rate in manufacturing was 196 percent higher in the periphery than in the center and 375 percent higher in Latin America than in the United States. Gross fixed capital formation was 360 percent higher in the periphery than in the center and more than 26 times higher in Latin America than in the United States. Even on a per capita basis, the growth rate was higher in the periphery than in the center. In spite of a population growth rate of 2.8 percent in Latin America compared to only 1 percent in the United States, the growth rate in per capita GDP was 124 percent higher in Latin America than in the United States.

While there is no unanimity among the critics of the underdevelopment school—whom we generally characterize as "Neo-Marxists"—and while there is a tendency to create a straw man in promoting the critique of an opposing school of thought, the threads common to any such critique can be summarized as follows:

1. Several members of the underdevelopment school define capitalism in reference to the sphere of *circulation*. Hence, the world capitalist system, whose parts are related via the capitalist market, is capitalist throughout and has been so since the origins of Western mercantilism in the sixteenth century. Consequently, underdevelopment in the periphery can only be blamed on capitalism.[47] On the issue of the determinants of the transition from feudalism to capitalism, the market is similarly taken to be the driving developmental force.[48] For the opposing school, by contrast, capitalism is defined by a set of

social relations that imply commoditization of both labor and the means of production and by the accumulation of capital on the basis of the appropriation of surplus value. The transition to capitalism and the subsequent development of the forces of production obtain when surplus value is captured on a relative rather than an absolute basis.[49] The concepts of mode of production and social class are thus essential to the analysis of backwardness.

2. For the underdevelopment school, the *external factor* conceptualized through surplus extraction by the center from the periphery is the prime determinant of backwardness and a significant source of accumulation in the center. Surplus extraction occurs via plunder;[50] the repatriation of superprofits on merchant, financial, and industrial capital;[51] deteriorating terms of trade;[52] barriers to trade that are unfavorable to the periphery;[53] and unequal exchange.[54] The opposing school of thought does not deny the existence of international transfers of surplus to the benefit of the center but rejects using them as an explanation for underdevelopment. As Brenner states, ". . . neither development in the core nor underdevelopment in the periphery was determined by surplus transfer."[55] For critics such as Weeks and Dore, Brenner, and Kay, underdevelopment results from an internal class structure that blocks the development of the forces of production.[56] This implies that the productivity of labor remains low and surplus value is produced to a large extent on an absolute basis. Thus, Kay goes so far as to claim that "capital created underdevelopment not because it exploited the underdeveloped world, but because it did not exploit it enough."[57] For other critics, such as Warren and Phillips, capitalism can rapidly develop the forces of production in the periphery, but such development is based on an internal class structure that reproduces dependency and dissociates growth from the satisfaction of the needs of the masses, thus perpetuating underdevelopment in a qualitative sense.[58]

3. By focusing on the external factors, the underdevelopment school tends to replace the relations of exploitation between social classes with those between *geographical areas*.[59] Class conflicts in the center are seen to have been overcome via a "social contract" between capital and labor under the aegis of the state.[60] Center workers benefit from imperialism and are bought off: The calls for an international workers' alliance consequently lack an objective basis. The overexploited masses of the periphery are left as the only weak link in the world capitalist system and hence a likely source of socialist revolutions. For the opposing school, the rate of labor exploitation is in fact greater in the center than it is in the periphery because the difference in labor productivity is greater than the difference in wages. Consequently, the objective basis for class struggle is more acute in the center. However, the key feature of capitalism is antagonistic class relations on a national and a world scale, and thus an objective basis for international workers' solidarity does exist.[61]

4. Because stagnation in the periphery is seen by the underdevelopment school to be the inevitable corollary of growth in the center, capitalism is held to be *incapable of developing the forces of production* in the periphery because the periphery is being robbed of its surplus.[62] Peasant spheres and semiproletarianization are sources of primitive accumulation that increase the rate of profit in the modern sector.[63] Noncapitalist modes of production that are articulated to and dominated by capitalism are thus functionalized to the requirements of capitalist accumulation and reproduced in this symbiotic position.[64] For members of the opposing school such as Warren and Phillips, the penetration of foreign capital and extroverted accumulation accelerate industrial development to levels of growth rates that are eventually superior to those of the center, thereby reestablishing Luxemburg and Lenin's interpretation of the law of unequal development on a world scale.[65] As Warren writes: "The view that exploitation caused by foreign investment can be equalled with stagnation is absurd. Whatever imbalances such investment may cause, it is still true that under capitalism exploitation is the reverse side of the advance of productive forces."[66] Cardoso, who was formerly identified with the underdevelopment school,[67] has also recently observed that "associated dependent development" in the periphery need not entail economic stagnation. On the contrary, "development and monopoly penetration in the industrial sector of dependent economies are not incompatible."[68] The moving forces behind this type of capitalist development are the state and multinational corporations, which are usually associated through joint ventures with local capital. The classical interpretation of the law of unequal development is also endorsed by the other critics of the underdevelopment school as a necessary long-run outcome, even though they stress stagnation in the short run resulting from the stubborn persistence of precapitalist social relations. As these critics postulate, precapitalist spheres—beyond a phase of primitive accumulation—represent a hindrance to capitalist development because the low productivity of labor in the production of wage goods maintains high labor costs in spite of low real wages.[69] In the longer run, consequently, capitalism also penetrates the production of wage goods, displacing peasants and artisans, even though expansion of a market for wage goods is severely limited by low wages and unemployment.

In the following section, we will develop a model of capital accumulation in the center-periphery structure of the world capitalist system that permits us to identify the roots of the problems of agricultural production and rural poverty in Latin America as well as to understand the basis for reformist attempts on the part of the state to solve these problems. The model derives from Marx's conceptualization of the laws of motion of capital in terms of a set of interrelated dialectical processes between productive forces and social relations, between objective and subjective forces, between production and circulation, and between internal and external factors—all of which come into play in the process of reproduction and transformation of social systems. The model greatly relies upon Amin's concepts of peripheral capitalism and accumulation on a world scale, and hence upon a number of concepts of the underdevelopment school, but introduces some key modifications that correspond to the incorporation of several aspects of the above Neo-Marxian criticism into the main postulates of the underdevelopment school.

1. Capitalism is defined as a type of social relation, the reproduction of which implies a dialectical relation between production and circulation and not supremacy of one over the other. Hence, the concepts of modes of production and social class are the key instruments of analysis. Here I side with the critics of the underdevelopment school.

2. Internal and external factors are dialectically interrelated, and attempts at establishing the superiority of one over the other in explaining underdevelopment are superfluous. The essential analytical approach is instead the analysis of classes and the contradictions between them. The external factors can both transform the internal class structure and create possibilities for the reproduction of hegemonic internal class alliances. Capitalist development in the periphery can sustain rapid but uneven development of the forces of production. On these two points—the primacy of class analysis over surplus extraction and the possibilities of growth instead of stagnation—I again side with the critics. However, I concur with the underdevelopment school on the persistence of surplus extraction from the periphery, although I reject unequal exchange as the principal explanation of this transfer.

3. Patterns of articulated or disarticulated accumulation are not geographically determined, exclusive, and stable structures, but are only the reflection of the hegemonic dominance of particular class alliances. Peripheral capitalism and the associated pattern of primitive accumulation is not a *sui generis* reality with its own distinct laws of motion, but is only a phase—however historically exceptional and prolonged—in the development of capitalism in particular areas of the world system. This, again, is consistent with the critics. However, as I will show, the underdevelopment school's position that the rate of surplus value is higher in the periphery is correct. This is what explains the conjunction of surplus extraction and high growth rates.

4. In the phase of peripheral capitalism, peasant and artisan spheres both sustain accelerated (if unstable) accumulation in the modern sector and are being destroyed by being so used, even though the time span over which they remain in existence may be considerable. Thus, unequal development is a process whereby growth of capitalist production in the periphery feeds upon the stagnation, impoverishment, and destruction of the peasant and artisan spheres. This process is consistent with the classical interpretation of the law of unequal development and its restoration by the critics of the underdevelopment school.

THE DIALECTIC BETWEEN PRODUCTION AND CIRCULATION

The basic postulate from which we start is that capitalism is a world system and that consequently a single process of capital accumulation is taking place on a world scale but in a heterogeneous structure composed of a center and a periphery having unequal relations of dominance. This single process of accumulation can be understood in terms of the fundamental law of motion of capital that was so lucidly unraveled by Marx in *Capital* and *Grundrisse*.[70] This law of motion derives from the dialectical unity of production and circulation, the two processes that together sustain the accumulation of capital.[71] It explains (1) the inherent contradictions of capitalist society that originate in its class and unplanned nature, (2) the mechanisms through which these contradictions create growth and barriers to growth, and (3) the essence (if not the form, which has historical specificity) of the recurrent crises that characterize the history of capitalist development.

The dialectical unity of production and circulation derives from the fact that after the act of production, surplus value is embodied in the value of commodities that must circulate (i.e., be sold) in order for surplus value to be realized as money and for capital to grow. Thus, the capacity of the economic system to consume must be continuously expanded in order for its production capacity to grow and hence for sustained capital accumulation—capital's "historic mission"—to occur. This drive to accumulate is not an inner or acquired trait of the capitalist but is an inescapable systemic force that derives from the class and unplanned nature of capitalism and the resulting competitive pressures it creates. As Marx said:

The development of capitalist production makes it constantly necessary to keep increasing the amount of capital laid out in a given industrial undertaking, and competition makes the imminent laws of capitalist production to be felt by each individual capitalist as external coercive laws. It compels him to keep constantly extending his capital, in order to preserve it, but extend it he cannot except by means of progressive accumulation.[72]

In this competitive context, the *necessary* relation between production and circulation is also *contradictory:* circulation is the negation of production, and production is the negation of circulation. The *essence* of economic crises is found in the contradictory nature of this relationship.

The class nature of capitalism implies the existence of interclass conflicts regarding the generation and distribution of the economic surplus and, in particular, regarding the determination of profit versus wage levels. The unplanned nature of capitalism implies the existence of intraclass conflicts as capitalists compete over the appropriation of the means of production and of effective demand. Competition and the consequent quest for higher profits imply two sets of reactions at the level of individual capitalists that are contradictory at the level of social capital: (1) introducing new technologies and new rationalizations of the work process in order to increase the productivity of labor, and (2) holding down labor costs by restricting wages to the minimum allowed by prevailing subjective forces. Increased labor productivity implies that the production capacity of the economic system increases, that there is more product per employed worker. Restricted wages and labor-saving technology imply that development of consumption capacity tends to lag behind development of production capacity:

Contradiction in the capitalist mode of production: the labourers as buyers of commodities are important for the market. But as sellers of their own commodity—labor power—capitalist society tends to keep them down to the minimum price.[73]

Capitalists and capital are in conflict. "To each capitalist, the total mass of all workers, with the exception of his own workers, appear not as workers but as consumers.[74] This contradiction was also identified by Kalecki:

One of the main features of the capitalist system is the fact that what is to the advantage of a single entrepreneur does not necessarily benefit all entrepreneurs as a class. If one entrepreneur reduces wages he is able *ceteris paribus* to expand production; but once all entrepreneurs do the same thing—the result will be entirely different.[75]

Moved by the profit motive and the law of survival of the fittest, capital is thus driven to expand in the sphere of production and simultaneously encounters a barrier in the sphere of circulation. The contradiction between production and circulation results in the periodic emergence of unsold commodities and in the increase in circulation time (materializing under the form of involuntary inventory investments, reduced cash flows, etc.). The consequence of increasing labor productivity in the sphere of production is an eventual tendency for the organic composition to rise and for the rate of profit to fall.[76] More importantly, constraints in the sphere of circulation result in a periodic tendency for the rate of profit to fall under atomistic capitalism and for the financial surplus to rise under monopoly capitalism.[77] The *essence of crises* and the laws of motion of capital derive from the periodic tendency for the rate of profit to fall. To overcome this barrier, a set of reactions is induced at the level of individual capitals in the spheres of production and circulation and at the level of social capital through the state. The particular historical nature of these reactions and the specific contradictions they create in turn determine the *forms of crises*.

By reproducing the essence of crises, even if the form is overcome by historically specific reactions, capital necessarily re-creates new forms of crises. This indicates that while a theory of the *essence* of crises can be deduced from the defining characteristics of the capitalist mode of production, there can be no abstract theory of particular *forms* of crises. The study of the forms of crises demands the study of history.

In summary, the class and unplanned nature of capitalism, and the consequent contradictions between individual rationality and systemic needs, materialize in the contradictory nature of the necessary relation between production and circulation. This contradiction results in the tendency for the rate of profit to fall, which creates a barrier to accumulation. The set of reactions induced by the quest to overcome this barrier determines the dynamics of capital and, in re-creating historically specific contradictions, the forms of crises.

This single process of capital accumulation occurs in a world economic system that is structurally *heterogeneous*.[78] Heterogeneity is the outcome of unequal development whereby some areas of the world capitalist system have achieved industrial revolutions—from England in the mid-eighteenth century to Russia and Japan in the late nineteenth century—while the rest of the world has fallen under their domination through colonialism and the imposition of free trade. Within the context of this center-periphery decomposition of the world capitalist system, we will conceptualize the structure of center nations as socially and sectorally articulated and that of peripheral nations as socially and sectorally disarticulated.

In a structurally heterogeneous world economic system the single world-scale process of capital accumulation creates markedly different contradictions (both objective and subjective) in each part of it (center and periphery). The contradictions of accumulation at one pole—say, the center—create the *necessity* for external relationships with the other pole—the periphery—in order that barriers to accumulation in the center may be overcome. Reciprocally, the contradictions of accumulation in the periphery and the drive of capital to transcend them create necessary external relationships with the center. At each pole, a necessary external relationship is eventually met by a *possibility* that arises from the occurrence of a corresponding external necessity at the other pole. Reciprocal necessities create mutual possibilities that shape the laws of motion of capital on a world scale.

While the structures (center and periphery) of the world economic system have an organic solidarity which they derive from the existence of a unique world-scale process of accumulation, one structure—the center—is *dominant* over the other. The dominant structure thus attempts to subject the other structure to the requirements of the resolution of its own contradictions. That is, the center attempts to mold the dominated periphery so that the internal contradictions of accumulation in the periphery will create the external relationships that are consistent with the necessities of the center. This process of domination and transformation of the internal conditions in the periphery is fraught with antagonisms and has met with resistance because it is highly contrary to the normal process of social change. As Mao Tse-tung explained in his study of dialectics:

Changes in society are due chiefly to the development of the internal contradictions in society, that is, the contradiction between the productive forces and the relations of production, the contradiction between classes and the contradiction between the old and the new; it is the development of these contradictions that pushes society forward and gives the impetus for the supersession of the old society by the new. . . . External causes are the condition of change and internal causes are the basis of change, and the external causes become operative through internal causes.[79]

Through domination and the resultant change in internal causes, external possibilities are induced to meet the necessities of the dominant center. In this fashion a single, world-scale process of capital accumulation is able to produce development in the center and underdevelopment in the periphery.

In summary, the starting points from which to identify the laws of motion of capital in the center-periphery structure are: (1) the *unity* of the process of capital accumulation on a world scale, which is characterized by necessary and contradictory relationships between production and circulation; (2) the *heterogeneity* of structures conceptualized as socially and sectorally articulated centers and socially and sectorally disarticulated peripheries; and (3) the *dominance* among structures that molds the external necessities of the periphery into possibilities for the center to overcome its barriers to accumulation and growth.

Analysis of the laws of motion of capital in the world economic system thus requires the study of a double dialectical process: the dialectic between production and circulation and the dialectic between center and periphery. To do this we will proceed to: (1) identify the contradictions that arise in the process of accumulation in socially and sectorally articulated structures that characterize, in an abstract sense, the economies of the center; (2) similarly identify the contradictions that arise in the process of accumulation in socially and sectorally disarticulated structures that characterize the economies of the periphery; (3) explore the mechanisms of surplus transfer between periphery and center; and (4) identify the laws of motion of capital in the dialectical unity composed of dominant articulated centers and dominated disarticulated peripheries. In this dialectical whole, internal contradictions create external necessities that are met by possibilities according to relations of dominance among structures and internal contradictions in the other structure. The laws of motion of capital in this dialectical organic totality provide the scientific basis for a theory of unequal development. As a method of exposition, we will start with the abstract concepts of articulation and disarticulation and derive the corresponding laws of motion of capital. We will then use these concepts in the context of historically specific social formations to explain the concrete phenomena of unequal development.

CONTRADICTIONS OF ACCUMULATION
IN ARTICULATED ECONOMIES

The structure of a sectorally and socially articulated, closed capitalist economy is schematized in Figure 1.1. In this economy, sector I produces capital goods, and sector II produces wage goods for final consumption.

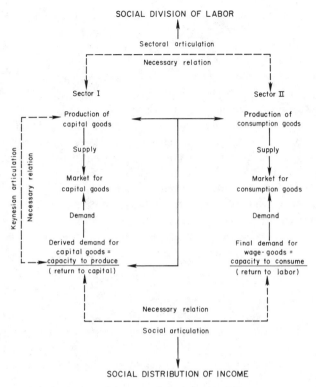

Figure 1.1. Structure of an Articulated Economy

On the supply side, the economy is *sectorally articulated,* for linkages exist between productive sectors. An increase in the production of consumption goods creates an increase in the derived demand for capital goods. As Hirschman, Rosenberg, and others have argued, sectoral linkages are essential to create investment "accelerators" and to induce the implantation and modernization of other sectors of economic activity.[80] This articulation is the objective determinant of the social allocation of labor among sectors of production. In the process of growth, maladjustments in this allocation determine business cycles that arise from *sectoral disproportionality.* These business cycles have been analyzed in the context of the equations of reproduction by Tugan Baranovsky, Kautsky, Luxemburg, and recently by Harris.[81] They have also been conceptualized by Samuelson, Hansen, Kalecki, and Kaldor through the accelerator principle in the Keynesian multiplier model: small changes in the rate of growth of final demand are translated into large changes in investment demand.

On the demand side, the necessary relation between the development of production and consumption capacities (i.e., between derived demand for capital goods and final demand for wage goods) implies a *social articulation* between capitalists and laborers. This results from the fact that production capacity is determined by the return to capital, while consumption capacity is determined by the return to labor, since sector II is devoted to the production of wage goods.[82] Social articulation thus implies the existence of an objective relationship between the rate of profit and real wages, between development of the forces of production and the rate of surplus value, and between the rate of growth and the distribution of income.

The concepts of social articulation and of the necessary and contradictory relation between production and consumption capacities go beyond other formulations in explaining the nature of the relationship between economic growth and income distribution. In the static neoclassical model of general equilibrium, prices are fully determined by exogenous consumer tastes and technology. Prices and the prevailing (unexplained) personal distribution of factors of production establish the personal distribution of income. By not distinguishing between physical and financial capital, one can make income distribution fully endogenous to the economic system.

In the neoclassical growth models and in the Harrod-Domar model (where input-output relations are specified in terms of fixed coefficients), economic growth increases with savings and hence with inequality.[83] Here, the distribution of income is fully exogenous. Growth, however, presumably creates employment and wages, which in turn later permit the benefits from growth to "trickle down" throughout the population. Inequality is thus seen as necessary for accelerated growth, which later leads to greater equality, but this process remains unexplained by theory.

In the Sraffian model, which is static, technology is exogenous.[84] Equilibrium conditions imply a continuum of feasible combinations of wages and interest rates that constitute the "wage-profit frontier." Which combination will apply on this frontier and, hence, which distribution of income will prevail cannot be determined in the realm of pure economics but is subjectively determined by the nature of class relations.

By formulating the problem dynamically and in the context of political economy, Marx was able to call on both objective and subjective elements in the determination of *both* economic growth and the distribution of income. The necessary relation between production and consumption capacities provides the objective element (the condition for reproduction of capital on an expanded scale without crises); the contradictory nature of this relation, which results from the class and unplanned nature of capitalism, provides the subjective element. Both economic growth and income distribution are thus endogenous and inextricably interrelated.

In the process of growth, periodic maladjustments of this necessary relation create business cycles and structural crises due to *social disproportionality* in the distribution of income. Business cycles are short-run downturns that are self-limiting and that generate endogenously the conditions necessary for a subsequent recovery. By contrast, structural crises are not self-correcting and, to be overcome, require either fortuitous external events or structural changes.[85] The *premium mobile* of the dialectical relation between production and consumption capacities originates in the tendency for the rate of profit to fall (under competitive capitalism) or for the surplus to rise (under monopoly capitalism) and in their interplay with the countertendencies that result from the reactions of both capitalists and capital to these tendencies. It is the historically specific nature of these reactions and the particular contradictions they recreate which determine the particular *form* that crises of "social disproportionality" will assume.

Individual capitalists react to falling profit rates in the spheres of production and circulation. In the sphere of production, falling rates of profit spur technological change, the centralization and concentration of capital, and the export of capital to the periphery, where high profit rates can be captured (financial and industrial imperialism). Each of these reactions is in turn contradictory and re-creates both growth and barriers to growth. Technological change tends to increase the organic composition of capital; monopoly power leads to higher prices of capital goods and to inefficiencies; and repatriated profits increase the investable surplus.

In the sphere of circulation, falling rates of profit associated with increased circulation time induce the creation of new products (diversification) and new wants (advertising), the advancement through time of effective demand via consumer credit, the organization of unequal exchange and unequal trade with the periphery, the quest for external markets, and also the development of markets for capital goods and for luxuries originating in the consumption of profits. Each of these reactions is in turn both growth-promoting and contradictory: the sales effort increases circulation costs; the creation of new wants induces subjective forces and stepped-up union pressures for higher wages; consumer credit implies increased buying costs and reduced future effective demand; and unequal exchange and trade increase surplus repatriation to the center. In particular, an increase in real wages that was more rapid than the increase in productivity throughout the 1960s led to a squeeze on profits in the 1970s.[86] This form of crisis is thus partially created by the very reactions to underconsumptionist tendencies through the sales effort and the creation of new wants. That consumer tastes are not exogenous—the doctrine of consumer sovereignty not withstanding—but are manipulated by business firms has been forcefully evidenced by many, including Fromm, Packard, Galbraith, and Slater.[87] The resulting gap between wants and satisfaction levels determines the subjective acceptability of income earned. Increasing this gap through the sales effort induces stepped-up wage demands that are particulary difficult to resist after a sustained period of expansion when the unemployment level has been greatly reduced. As a solution to realization crises, the external market is severely limited by subjective pressures within the center which, as Amin convincingly argued, forced a geographical relocation of market expansion principally within the center after 1880.[88] Similarly, market expansion through increased demand for sector I—Tugan Baranovsky's "merry-go-round" solution, where a realization problem can never exist due to social disproportionality, since an expanding demand for new and more capital-intensive machinery (machines to produce machines) can always be created—cannot be a solution, even though it is an important component of total demand and can have countercyclical effects.[89] While theoretically correct in terms of the equations of reproduction, this solution neglects the importance of subjective forces in defining the ultimate end of the process of production, which is to produce commodities for human consumption.[90] Development of the consumption capacity for final goods out of the return to capital is also potentially significant as a countercyclical measure, but it is ultimately contrary to the competitive nature of capitalism, a system where reinvestment of profits is obligatory for survival.

Reactions to falling profit rates at the level of social capital obtain through interventions of the state—Keynesian expenditures, Baran-type surplus burning, and O'Connor-type social capital expenditures.[91] These expenditures also tend to re-create new contradictions in the form of inflationary pressures, increased production costs, and higher tax burdens, and eventually translate underconsumption tendencies into a profit squeeze. Moreover, state management of social disproportionalities through reforms has its limits—this time in both the fiscal and legitimacy crises of the state.

Beyond the crises that originate in sectoral and social disproportionalities, a third type of crisis can be located in Figure 1.1—the Keynesian-type crisis that results from disproportionalities between aggregate income (on the supply side of the market) and aggregate expenditure (on the demand side of the market). At the production level, costs of production are incomes for other firms, individuals, and regions; costs determine wages, profits, exports, and tax revenues. Equilibrium obtains if, at the expenditure level, wages are spent on consumption, profits are spent on investments, exports are compensated by imports, and taxes are matched by government expenditures. If, however, expenditures lag behind incomes—in particular, because uncertainty of knowledge and foresight imply increased liquidity preference and hence a gap between savings and investments—insufficient demand leads to unemployment, falling production and wages, and underconsumption. The government can then be called upon to borrow or tax away excess savings and create an effective demand without increasing the productive capacity of the system, and in the process will re-create full employment again. Operating better than Tugan Baranovsky's merry-go-round, the military-industrial complex can create such a demand for sector I without producing machines that must breed more machines; it can produce machines that are simply stored or dumped somewhere in the world. Keynesian policies, however, are only effective as countercyclical measures for slowdowns originating in underconsumption as a form of crisis. When the crisis results, as in the early 1970s, from underproduction of surplus value, Keynesian instruments become inflationary and tend to aggravate the crisis. The crisis itself must then assume the form of an assault on wages and on state expenditures.[92]

Two major implications can be derived from the laws of capital accumulation under social articulation, and they provide fundamental contrasts with the case of social disarticulation.

1. Labor being both a "gain" and a "loss" for capital,[93] the laws of accumulation embody the long-run objective need for real wages to increase in relationship to increases in the productivity of labor. The exercise of subjective forces to achieve higher real wages and *distributive* income policies thus has an objective basis. And so does the rise of populist social-democratic political regimes, since labor militancy for material gains can be exercised without questioning the existing economic system, at least as long as the productivity of labor keeps on rising and employment levels are high. Income distribution for market creation does not, however, occur automatically, but requires crises and class struggle. Neither does it imply the elimination of poverty: wants are always re-created beyond satisfaction levels and reproduce subjective poverty; and unequal development (among economic sectors, regions, and individuals) implies the localized persistence of objective poverty.

2. The dual need to reduce labor costs (an objective necessity for each capitalist if he is to maximize profits and survive competition) and expand consumption capacity (the objective necessity for capital) leads to full *proletarianization* of the labor force. With proletarian labor, it is not the worker who is changed into a commodity; it is his labor power, the time actually sold on the labor market. Labor power is thus transformed from a fixed cost under precapitalist social relations into a variable cost. This makes it possible to tailor labor costs to labor needs in the face of fluctuating production (weather and seasonal patterns) and market conditions. Simultaneously, proletarianization implies the decomposition of the precapitalist economy and the full monetization of payments to labor, which thus create the home market for both capital goods and wage goods.[94] As a result, all noncapitalist modes decompose and are incorporated into the dominant capitalist mode of production. There is a rapid tendency toward *unimodality* and ultimately only two social classes.

The key objective contradiction of accumulation in an articulated economy is thus the tendency for the rate of profit to fall or for the financial surplus to rise—a result of the essential contradiction between capitalists and capital, which itself results from the class and unplanned nature of the system. Like any barrier that can be overcome within the context of the dominant social relations, two mechanisms of adjustment are available: (1) adjustments made by individual capitals in the spheres of production and circulation and (2) management by the state through public reforms.

Individual adjustments and reforms can assume two dimensions relative to the nation-state. One consists of overcoming the barrier to accumulation through changes internal to the center nation-state itself. At the level of reforms, this will logically imply the need for an enhanced planning capacity of the state to deal with sectoral and social disproportionalities and increased state expenditures on social capital to increase the rate of profit in the private sector. This solution thus leads to a steadily increasing intervention by the state in economic and social affairs that goes beyond mere post-World War II Keynesian policies.

The second dimension consists of overcoming the barrier externally through a redefined division of labor between center and periphery. While the role of the state is also important here, capital, in seeking external solutions, transcends the territorial boundaries where the nation-state is most effective. Adjustments made by individual capitals in the world economic system and pressures on peripheral nation-states are part of this external solution. Inasmuch as possible, external solutions are sought over internal solutions because they minimize the need to redefine class positions and the role of the state within the center. In this case, the necessary external relationships that this contradiction creates correspond to the quest for opportunities to sustain the rate of profit or to absorb the financial surplus.

CONTRADICTIONS OF ACCUMULATION
IN DISARTICULATED ECONOMIES

Sectorally and socially disarticulated economies can be of two broad types: (1) export-enclave economies and (2) import-substitution economies. The first type is schematized in Figure 1.2 and includes instances where the exporting

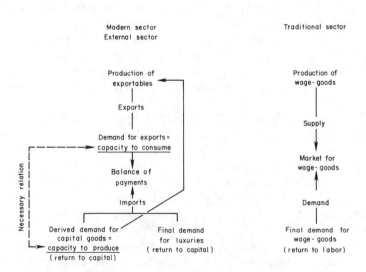

Figure 1.2. Structure of Disarticulated Export-Enclave Economies

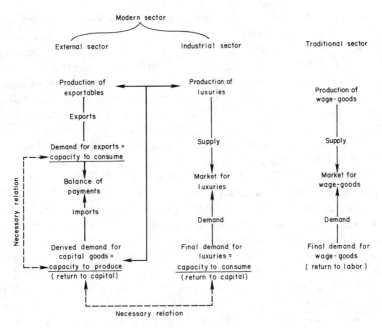

Figure 1.3. Structure of Disarticulated Import-Substitution
Industrialization Economies

enclave is a plantation, a mine, or an export-oriented industry. Figure 1.3 depicts the structure of an economy in which import-substitution industrialization has taken place and in which the luxury consumption items previously imported by the local bourgeoisie (out of the return to financial, commercial, and industrial capital) and by the landed elites (out of rents) are now produced locally behind protective tariffs.[95] These types of fully disarticulated economies are highly simplified theoretical abstractions that are not meant, as such, to describe historically specific social formations. However, their laws of accumulation provide fundamental contrasts with those of articulated economies. First, we will derive these laws. Then, we will gradually move from the abstract to the concrete in incorporating the concept of disarticulation into more complete and hence historically relevant models of the Latin American economies.

Under *sectoral disarticulation,* forward linkages in the production of raw materials (plantation and mining) and backward linkages in industrial production (outward- and inward-oriented) do not exist. Industrialization under sectoral disarticulation thus implies external dependency for the import of capital goods and technology and places equilibrium in the balance of payments as a necessary constraint on the capacity to produce. The performance of the export sector and the nature of the terms of trade on the international market are determinants of accumulation in the modern sector.

The necessary relation between production and consumption capacities does not imply a relationship between return to capital and return to labor: the economy is *socially disarticulated*. In export-enclave economies (Figure 1.2), the modern sector's capacity to produce is determined by the return to capital that creates the derived demand for capital goods for the production of export-ables; the capacity to consume is developed externally by the demand for exports. The return to capital (and to property in general, including land rents) also sustains the import of luxury consumption goods. And equilibrium in the balance of payments establishes the necessary relation between the capacity to produce and the capacity to consume.

In import-substitution economies (Figure 1.3), the modern sector's capacity to produce is created by the return to capital; the industrial sector's capacity to consume also derives from the return to capital, while that of the external sector is created by the demand for exports. Satisfying the necessary relation between production and consumption capacities thus now implies (1) creation of a *home market* for industry through consumption of part of the surplus value (the other part sustaining the development of the capacity to produce) and (2) satisfaction of the *balance-of-payments* constraint by expanding the production of exportables to sustain the development of the capacity to produce. In both export-enclave and import-substitution economies, the return to labor creates the final demand for wage goods that are assumed to be produced exclusively by the traditional sector in this purely disarticulated model.[96]

The key difference between social articulation and disarticulation thus originates in the sphere of circulation—in the geographical and social location of the market for the modern sector. Under social articulation, market expansion originates principally in rising national wages; under disarticulation, it originates either abroad or in profits and rents. The implications of accumulation under social disarticulation contrast sharply with those identified above for articulated accumulation:

1. Labor being only a "loss" (cost) for capital, the exercise of individual capitalist logic in the context of competition implies the perpetuation of low wages. The objective contradiction between individual capitalists and social capital regarding the level of wages has disappeared; the development of both production and consumption capacities is maximized by minimizing labor costs. Insofar as social control permits, surplus value can be extracted on an absolute rather than a relative basis. Beyond this, a rise in labor productivity need not translate into wage increases. The contrast shown in Figure 1.4 between the United States and Brazil in the relation between labor productivity and real wages in manufacturing is quite revealing. Between 1966 and 1974, the productivity of labor in the United States increased by 17 percent while real wages increased by 5 percent. In Brazil the productivity of labor increased by 91 percent while real wages dropped by 12 percent.

Social disarticulation creates an objective basis for the excercise of subjective forces that are unfavorable to workers' economic gains and that justify

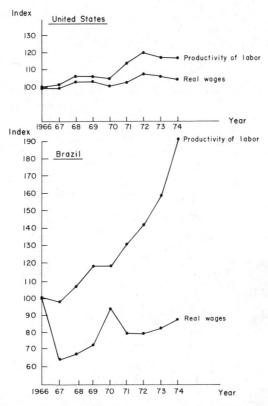

Figure 1.4. Productivity of Labor and Real Wages in
Manufacturing, United States and Brazil, 1966–74

regressive and repressive labor policies. Thus, the distribution of income has almost systematically worsened in all Latin American nations in spite of generally high growth rates in GDP, especially in industry. As Table 1.2 shows, the share of income received by the poorest 20 percent of the population declined or remained constant between 1960 and 1970 in all Latin American countries for which data are available except in Colombia, where the change observed is virtually insignificant.[97] In Mexico, even though the share of income received by the lowest 20 percent remained constant at about 4 percent between 1960 and 1970, it had deteriorated from 5.6 percent in 1950 and declined to 3.3 percent by 1977.[98] For Brazil, the most reliable data on income distribution have been elaborated by Langoni.[99] They indicate that the share of the lowest 20 percent of the income-earning population declined from 3.5 percent in 1960 to 3.2 percent in 1970. These data also show that the relative income position has deteriorated for all income strata except the top 10 percent. It is likely that absolute poverty has increased for a significant fraction of the population. Real minimum wages have declined by 45 percent

Table 1.2.   Growth and Income Distribution, 1960–70

| Country | National income received by poorest 20 percent | | Average annual growth rates (1960–70) | |
	1960 (1)	1970 (2)	Gross domestic product (3)	Industry (4)
Bolivia	—[a]	4.0	5.2	6.5
Colombia	3.0	4.0	5.1	6.0
El Salvador	6.0	4.0	5.9	8.5
Honduras	—	3.0	5.1	5.2
Dominican Republic	—	5.0	4.4	6.2
Ecuador	4.0	3.0	5.9	7.6
Paraguay	—	4.0	4.3	5.5
Jamaica	2.0	—	4.5	5.3
Costa Rica	6.0	5.0	6.5	9.3
Brazil	5.0	5.0	8.0	9.7
Chile	—	5.0	4.2	5.0
Uruguay	—	4.0	1.2	1.1
Venezuela	3.0	2.0	5.9	4.5
Argentina	7.0	5.0	4.2	6.0
Mexico	4.0	4.0	7.3	9.3
Panama	5.0	3.0	7.8	10.1
Peru	3.0	2.0	5.4	5.5
United States	4.0	6.7	4.3	4.9

Sources: (Cols. 1 and 2) World Bank, *World Tables, 1976* (Baltimore: The Johns Hopkins University Press, 1976), pp. 515–17.

(Cols. 3 and 4) World Bank, *World Development Report, 1978* (Washington, D.C.: World Bank, 1978), pp. 78 and 79.

[a] — = data not available. Countries for which income distribution data are not available have been omitted.

in Rio de Janeiro and 50 percent in São Paulo in the period 1960–70.[100] And there has been a close association between median wages paid in manufacturing and minimum wages.[101] This objective logic for regressive and repressive labor polices implies that, except in the case of a small workers' aristocracy, labor militancy will tend to be directed not toward social-democratic settlements but rather against perpetuation of the existing economic system.

2. Of the two motives for proletarianization of labor that exist in articulated economies, the first (reducing labor costs), but not the second (creating a home market out of rising wages), applies to disarticulated economies. As a result, labor costs can be further reduced by perpetuating the subsistence economy that partially assumes the cost of maintaining and reproducing the labor force. *Functional dualism* between modern and traditional sectors thus makes it possible to sustain a level of wage below the cost of maintenance and reproduction of the labor force—a cost that would determine the minimum wage for a fully proletarianized labor force.[102] Here, wage is only a complement between the subsistence needs of the worker and his family and net

production in the traditional sector. From the standpoint of the employer, labor is "free" and fully proletarianized; labor is a variable cost paid in cash. But from the standpoint of the labor force, labor is only *semiproletarianized*, since part of the laborers' subsistence needs are derived from production for home consumption. Functional dualism thus provides the structural possibility of meeting the necessity for cheap labor that derives from the laws of accumulation under social disarticulation.

Growth of the modern sector does not create a tendency to eliminate peasants in response to the need for market creation. However, over the long run, peasants are outcompeted for access to the land by capitalist agriculture and are increasingly proletarianized: unimodality eventually occurs by the back door, and with dramatic social costs. Functional dualism is thus only a phase of the development of capitalism in the periphery; it is being destroyed over time by being used today. It does not have its own stable laws of reproduction as Amin and Bartra suggested.[103] Hence, peripheral capitalism is not a distinct mode of production with its owns laws of motion, but is only a historically specific stage in the development of capitalism in the periphery. It is this extended period of primitive accumulation, in which a surplus is extracted from the traditional sector via the labor and wage-foods markets and in which the traditional sector gradually decomposes while sustaining rapid accumulation in the modern sector, that can be properly labeled the development of underdevelopment.

Some further implications of accumulation in socially and sectorally disarticulated economies are:

1. The claims of disarticulated accumulation on surplus value are multiple, for profits and rents must simultaneously sustain: (1) the extraction of surplus to the benefit of the center via the repatriation of profits, payment of royalties, interest payments on debts, unfavorable terms of trade, and the outflight of domestic capital; (2) the formation of savings to be invested in the replacement and growth of the modern sector; (3) the creation of the domestic capacity to consume industrial luxuries; and (4) the costs of repression, corruption, and co-option in reproducing the social relations of peripheral capitalism. Thus, in no case can backwardness in the periphery be attributed—as Bettelheim, Brenner, and Weeks and Dore recently argued—to lack of surplus generation. A *high rate of surplus value* is generated on the basis of (1) high labor productivity in the modern sector and (2) low wages permitted by (*a*) functional dualism with subsistence agriculture and the urban informal sector, (*b*) repression of wage demands in the industrial sector, and (*c*) the import of cheap wage foods from the center (internationalization of the value of many staple foods) and the imposition of price controls on wage goods.

Empirical evidence on relative wages in modern industry in center and periphery is available from the International Labor Office (ILO). In 1973, the average wage in the manufacturing industry in the United States was eight times higher than that in Brazil, ten times higher than that in the Philippines, fourteen times that in South Korea, eighteen times that in Morocco, and twenty-four times that in India.[104] For Latin America as a whole, this wage gap is 5 to 1.[105] At the same time, the productivity of labor in modern manufacturing and in the export enclaves of the periphery is not markedly different from that in the center.[106] And the length of the workday is also essentially the same in the modern sector of the periphery as it is in the center.

Empirical evidence on the relative magnitudes of the rate of surplus value in center and periphery can be obtained from national accounts data.[107] Surplus value can be approximated in the price domain from the value added by resident firms plus indirect taxes minus consumption of fixed capital minus compensation of employees minus subsidies, and variable capital can be calculated from the compensation of employees. In 1972 the average rate of surplus value in the center (fourteen European countries, the United States and Canada, Australia and New Zealand, and Japan) was 0.68. By contrast, it was 1.83 in the periphery (fifty countries of Africa, Latin America, Asia, and the Middle East, and Greece and Portugal). According to these same data, the rate of surplus value was 0.45 in the United States and 0.62 in Canada versus 1.23 in Venezuela, 1.47 in Argentina, 1.51 in Colombia, and 1.66 in Brazil. These data support Amin's statement that "the proletariat at the periphery is being more severely exploited than the proletariat at the center."[108]

Even though the rate of surplus value is high in the periphery, the multiple and competing claims on surplus value there imply a low *rate of saving,* which tends to curtail the rate of accumulation based on national income. Thus, the average national rate of saving between 1960 and 1973 was 19 percent in the periphery and 23 percent in the center. In 1973 it was below that of the United States in seventeen of twenty-two Latin American nations.[109] These lower rates of saving can, however, be supplemented by calling on foreign investment and loans that thus eventually sustain rates of industrial growth above those in the center. But each of these mechanisms is in turn contradictory: the call on foreign capital increases the future flow of repatriated profits, and increasing indebtedness raises the cost of servicing the foreign debt. As a result, Latin America's foreign debt was almost three times greater in 1975 than in 1969.[110] In 1975 the average external public debt for Latin American countries was equal to 18 percent of their gross national product and 74 percent of the value of exports.[111] Half of the foreign-exchange earnings from exports in Brazil, Mexico, Chile, and Uruguay were absorbed by servicing the foreign debt and repatriating profits; the figure for Panama was 55 percent, while that for Peru was 60 percent.

2. Creation of a home market for industry out of the partial consumption of profits and rents periodically limits *market size* to the point that it constrains industrial growth. Both bottlenecks—rate of saving and market size—can be relaxed by means of increasingly regressive income distribution patterns. In this fashion, the concentration of income and the consequent social narrowing

of the market become conditions of growth rather than sources of stagnation. The size of the domestic market and popular resistance to further regression of the distribution of income remain recurrent limits to growth. As Tavares observed for Brazil, "Although we reject the stagnation thesis and do not see any limitations to the potential for Brazil's capitalist expansion in the current stage of its development, we do believe that it presents constant and recurring problems related to the realization of surplus."[112] This pattern of market creation in turn negates the possibility of a "natural" evolution from social disarticulation to articulation as a product of growth, even though accumulation in industry proceeds at an accelerated pace.

3. Import-substitution industrialization under sectoral disarticulation tends to imply an increasing need for the import of capital goods and technological knowledge. The resulting structural *deficit in the balance of payments* also acts periodically as a bottleneck in industrial expansion.[113] This deficit can be reduced by boosting the performance of the external sector and calling on foreign capital. In agriculture the deficit induces the shift of land away from the production of food for domestic consumption toward the production of exportables.

4. The objective logic for cheap labor requires *cheap food,* which as will be seen in Chapter 2 can be met in one of three ways: (*a*) through "cheap food policies" that suppress the price of food; (*b*) through concessional imports; and (*c*) through technological change and the development of capitalism in agriculture. Each of these is in turn contradictory: cheap food policies imply the stagnation of domestic food production as modernization of agriculture is made unprofitable; food imports increase the stress on the balance of payments; and the development of capitalist agriculture marginalizes peasants and accelerates the liquidation of functional dualism.

5. The rate of profit in commercial agriculture is maintained by compensating for cheap food through the hiring of cheap agricultural labor. The hiring of semiproletarian rural workers at wages below subsistence costs is secured through *functional dualism with subsistence agriculture.* Subsistence agriculture thus becomes the ultimate embodiment of the contradictions of accumulation in the disarticulated economies. There, the peasant household constitutes an articulated-dominated purveyor of cheap labor and cheap food. However, subsistence agriculture slowly disintegrates under this domination as it performs its essential structural function under disarticulated accumulation. It is destroyed by the demographic explosion that occurs (children being an essential means of production and protection); by migration, ecological destruction, and the expropriation of land; and by increased submission on the labor, product, and factor markets.

6. Even though peasants are eliminated as food producers and transformed into a labor reserve, functional dualism is re-created in other forms in the course of its ultimate elimination. Thus, as the population of Latin America becomes increasingly urban, while employment in the modern sector remains

a relatively fixed share of the total labor force, the *informal urban* sector becomes a new source of subsidy for the maintenance and reproduction of labor power. As recent studies of the myriad productive activities that occur in the informal sector evidence, that sector serves as a source of cheap wage goods and services for the economy.[114] Its activities are closely integrated into those of the modern sector, and the informal sector thus also subsidizes part of the costs of the formal capitalist firms.[115] As Alejandro Portes concludes, "The presence of the urban informal sector makes possible a condition of high surplus value extraction by compensating for concessions made to the organized segment of the working class with the continuing exploitation of unorganized informal workers."[116] Under the present circumstances of extraordinarily rapid migration to the cities and labor-saving technology in the modern sector, the informal sector shows no sign of disappearing and hence appears to have its own laws of reproduction in functional association with the modern sector. Yet competition with capitalist industry and the increasing commodification of the household create the same use-destruction contradiction that pertains in the case of the peasants, though it evidences more varied and stubborn forms of resistance.

Thus, the dominant objective contradictions that periodically create for the disarticulated economy the need for external relationships are weak financing capacity, limited market size, a deficit in the balance of payments, and stagnation in food production. Each of these is also the source of cycles and crises for the periphery. Since the periphery is, in addition, strongly affected by economic cycles and crises in the center, as the demand for raw materials and hence also the import capacity fluctuate violently, the growth pattern in the periphery demonstrates substantial instability, even though the growth trends tend to be superior to those in the center.[117]

DEPENDENCY, CLASS STRUCTURE, AND SOCIAL DISARTICULATION

The emergence of a structural pattern of disarticulated accumulation in a peripheral country is the outcome of a complex and unstable social process. The key dimensions that condition this process are the class structure in the particular peripheral country and the subjective contradictions that characterize it, the type and acuteness of the prevailing objective contradictions, and the pattern of insertion in the international division of labor and the external possibilities that it offers at a particular historical moment. Analysts of the world economy and the joint phenomena of development and underdevelopment have tended to overstress the effect of the domination of center over periphery—through colonialism, forced free trade, and imperialism—to the neglect of objective and subjective phenomena existing within the periphery itself. This criticism generally applies to the Latin American "dependency" school and to the development-of-underdevelopment school, in spite of their invaluable contributions to the understanding of underdevelopment. As Brenner pointed out:

Frank . . . and his co-thinkers such as Wallerstein . . . followed their adversaries in locating the sources of both development and underdevelopment in an abstract process of capitalist expansion; and like them failed to specify the particular, historically developed class structures through which these processes actually worked themselves out and through which their fundamental character was actually determined.[118]

In using the concept of disarticulated accumulation, care must be taken not to misunderstand it as an externally imposed and permanent structure or as a structure whose internal contradictions, while creating needed external possibilities for the center, cannot bear on the transformation of the structure itself. While brilliant, Amin's use of the concept of disarticulation is in this sense inadequate. His analysis of the functionalization of the periphery to the center's needs is based on the presumption that "the economies of the system's periphery . . . are without any internal dynamism of their own,"[119] and this presumption makes it impossible for one to understand political and economic instability in the periphery or the role of subjective and objective forces in its transformation.

Establishment and reproduction of a structure of socially disarticulated accumulation implies powerful conflicts among fractions of the bourgeoisie. It would clearly be useless to attempt a global schematization of the process through which disarticulation develops, since this process obviously assumes specific forms in different countries and time periods. However, a general characterization of the social class structure in contemporary Latin America can be used to identify the types of class alliances that will favor disarticulated or articulated patterns of accumulation. Such a characterization is given in Figure 1.5.

There has been tremendous confusion about the definition of fractions of the bourgeoisie, in particular about the difference between national (indigenous) and dependent bourgeoisie.[120] However, the concept of social disarticulation provides a rigorous and operational definition of these two groups: the dependent bourgeoisie is involved in the trade (*comprador*) or the production of exportables and luxuries; by contrast, the national bourgeoisie produces and trades (as merchants) wage goods.

Given these definitions, it can be said that two types of class alliances tend to exist. One will dominate over the other and thus gain control of the state and redirect the process of accumulation toward the structure that it favors—articulated or disarticulated. Dominance of the alliance among international capital (metropolitan bourgeoisie), dependent bourgeoisie, and landed elites (fundamentally involved in the production of exportables, inputs for industry, and luxury foods) implies that the logic of disarticulated accumulation—and hence of cheap labor and cheap food—prevails. Foreign capital and multinational corporations are pervasive. The proletariat is in open

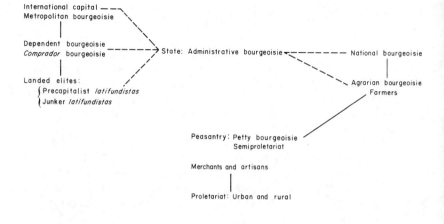

Figure 1.5. Social Class Structure and Alliances

opposition, and the state thus needs to assume a repressive role. Most Latin American countries at present fall into this category.

Dominance of the alliance among national bourgeoisie, agrarian bourgeoisie (those fundamentally involved in the production of wage foods), peasantry, and proletariat creates the logic for a socially articulated pattern of accumulation. The proletariat is incorporated into social-democratic arrangements legitimized by the ideologies of state planning, welfare state, and corporate democracy. State interventions can be directed at seeking a balance between the development of production and consumption capacities. The Peronist "social pact" of 1973, the Peruvian "bourgeois revolution" of 1968, and the Lara government in Ecuador are all recent—and unsuccessful—attempts at establishing the dominance of the articulated class alliance in Latin America.

Which class alliance and hence which structural model of accumulation becomes dominant depends upon internal and external factors. The key internal factor is the position of the bourgeoisie vis-á-vis the proletariat.[121] If the peripheral bourgeoisie is weak relative to the proletariat, it seeks alliance with the landed elites and foreign capital against the working class. Alliance with foreign capital in turn depends on the particular contradictions of the center and on the need it has to seek external possibilities of resolving them. When both this internal need and external possibility exist, the peripheral bourgeoisie will tend to be dominated by the dependent fraction. If, however, the bourgeoisie is strong, the national fraction can seal an alliance with the workers and peasants against the landed elites (thus eliminating absolute land rent) and against submission to foreign capital. The articulated alliance then tends to be dominant.

The dominant class alliance in Latin America from the period of liberal reforms in the 1850s to the Great Depression in 1929 included the export-oriented agrarian oligarchy, the commercial bourgeoisie (*compradors*), and foreign capitalists. During this period, development of the export sector and promotion of trade liberalism were priorities, while expansion of the internal market was largely irrelevant to the interests of the hegemonic alliance. Several countries such as Argentina and Uruguay thus became actively integrated into a world division of labor dominated by England (a food-deficit country) and experienced rapid economic growth. When this international order collapsed in 1929, most Latin American countries engaged in a process of import-substitution industrialization, a process which developed in a relatively autonomous manner, at least until 1945, because the center countries were plagued by recession and war. Industrialization was, however, initiated in a social context that preserved the social hegemony of the landed elites and *compradors*, who in turn became the new industrialists. As Hirschman observed:

> The fact that import substituting industrialization can be accommodated relatively easily in the existing social and political environment is probably responsible for the widespread disappointment with the process. Industrialization was expected to change the social order [i.e., permit the rise of a national bourgeoisie] and all it did was to supply manufactures![122]

In the initial phases of industrialization, a market was created not only for luxuries (formerly imported) but also for wage goods, through rapid creation of an urban proletariat. Thus, the potential for either articulated or disarticulated development was present. Because the internal market was important, many countries saw the rise of populist governments—Getulio Vargas in Brazil (1930–45), Bétancourt in Venezuela (1945–48), and Perón in Argentina (1946–55)—that engaged in liberal reforms. Industrialization without social redefinition, chronic deficits in the balance of payments, limited financing capacity, and food crises, however, forced increasing orientation of the industrial sector toward the production of luxuries and exportables and imposition of the merciless logic of accumulation under social disarticulation. Throughout the 1950s and 1960s, as the world economy became increasingly dominated by the expansion of center capital and the penetration of multinational firms, attempts to establish the hegemony of the articulated alliance became increasingly difficult. The dismal collapse of the Chilean, Argentine, Ecuadorean, and Peruvian attempts undoubtedly established this fact.

Of course, strong conflicts do remain regarding dominance of one alliance over the other, even if the disarticulated alliance has historically obtained the upper hand. In no case could one consider the disarticulated model to be monolithic and without contradictions either between or within classes. In its management of crises, objective as well as subjective, the state will always have to deal with the contradictory demands of these two alliances.

Evidence of this contradiction is most obvious in Brazil.[123] There the state is the guardian of the interests of both the hegemonic dependent bourgeoisie and the dominated national bourgeoisie. At the level of the state, the key contradiction is the irreconcilability of simultaneous demands by both alliances for market creation: the dependent fraction requires cheap labor and regressive patterns of income distribution to boost the demand for luxuries, while the national fraction requires wage increases in relation to gains in labor productivity to create a domestic market for wage goods. And yet, it is the dependent fraction which, needing wage increases the least, can best afford them, while the national fraction, which needs wage increases the most, can least afford them. High labor productivity and superior profitability conditions in the disarticulated industries permit an increase in wages in response to subjective demands and thus create a small, stable, and politically docile workers' aristocracy. And, indeed, the multinational sector tends to offer the most attractive wage opportunities. By contrast, low productivity and high levels of competition force the national bourgeoisie to oppose wage increases vigorously and thus to contradict its class interests in the sphere of circulation. Overcoming this contradiction by state spending, however, re-creates another contradiction—the fiscal crisis—which is evidenced, in particular, by high rates of inflation and an enormous and growing foreign debt.

O'Donnell explains the instability of Argentine politics between 1956 and 1976 in terms of the conflicts and contradictions between two class alliances, the "defensive alliance" (articulated) and the "governing alliance" (disarticulated), which reduced the state to nominal relative autonomy. The political and economic crises that accompanied the victory of the defensive alliance led to the implantation of a new bureaucratic authoritarian state in 1976, strict government control over the articulated alliance, and an unrestricted opening of the economy to multinational capital.[124]

Increasing dominance of the disarticulated over the articulated alliance, and hence increasing subordination of the periphery to international capital, is consequently not a mechanical process, nor is it harmoniously accepted in the periphery. Precapitalist forms resist the encroachment of capitalism, and the national bourgeoisie opposes the rise of the dependent bourgeoisie to hegemony. The ideology of nationalism often becomes a form of organizing resistance.[125] Under this banner, the petty bourgeoisie and the proletariat can be mobilized by the national bourgeoisie in an effort—which can take fascistic expression—to resist subordination to the disarticulated alliance.

A similar caveat must be made regarding social articulation in the center. Like disarticulation, articulation is not a geographically determined, exclusive, and stable structure, but is only the reflection of the hegemonic dominance of a particular class alliance in a complex social structure. Thus, no economy is ever perfectly articulated, and articulation is never free from severe contradictions. Large social groups remain excluded from sharing in productivity gains (segmented labor markets maintained by racism, sexism, etc.) and areas and sectors benefit unequally (unequal development). Crises are not eliminated by social articulation as long as the essence of capitalism (and crises)—its class and unplanned nature—remains. Elimination of crises would require both a fully effective "social contract" (class harmony) *and* total planning—two requirements that do not necessarily imply socialism but that certainly no longer correspond to capitalism. Capitalist exploitation of the production process through surplus value extraction and class struggle in the spheres of production and circulation remain the inherent features of capitalism under social articulation and hence the basis of its laws of motion.

MARKET-WIDENING AND MARKET-DEEPENING

In the theoretical explanation of disarticulation, a simplified model of import-substitution industrialization under social disarticulation in which the modern industrial sector produces exclusively luxury goods was discussed. This is clearly an excessive simplification since the modern sector does produce wage goods, both because hegemony of the disarticulated alliance does not eradicate a national bourgeoisie and because a number of luxury goods—e.g., some textiles, processed foods, construction materials, and simple household appliances—are simultaneously wage goods. A more realistic model than the one presented in Figure 1.3 is thus one in which the modern sector has three branches of production: the external sector, the luxury-goods sector, and the wage-goods sector.[126] The traditional sector also produces wage goods.

The distinction between luxury and wage goods in the modern sector is important not only because there is a fundamental difference between them in the relation of productivity to wages, as previously discussed, but also because of differences in the relation of productivity to profits. Since luxuries do not enter into the determination of the value of labor power, an increase in the productivity of labor in their production leads to temporary extra profits for innovative firms (differential rents for these firms) but not to a sustained increase in profits in the long run once the innovation has been diffused throughout the industry. A modern sector producing luxuries is thus characterized by cutthroat competition and productivity increases, but not by a sustained rise in profit. Consequently, there is a strong incentive to develop monopoly positions because they are the only way to capture high profits in the long run. Not surprisingly, strong monopolies are a familiar characteristic of the structure of luxury production—such as that of cars and electrical appliances—in the periphery. In Mexico, for example, 75 percent of industrial production originates in noncompetitive sectors, and the degree of concentration of a particular industry is directly related to the presence of multinational firms.[127]

Productivity increases in the production of wage goods lead, on the contrary, to increased relative surplus value as the value of labor power is reduced and to increased profit rates. Indeed, beyond the stage of primitive accumulation, in which the value of labor power is only partially insured by the capitalist sector, increasing productivity in the production of wages goods is the dynamic mechanism of increasing profits. Since use of primitive accumulation (functional dualism) tends to negate the reproduction of artisan and peasant spheres as sources of wage goods, development of a modern industrial and agricultural wage-goods sector becomes increasingly imperative for high profit rates. As Bettleheim and Weeks and Dore have argued, in contrast to the development-of-underdevelopment school and the idea of articulation of modes of production, wage-goods production becomes increasingly capitalist, and the excessively slow penetration of capitalism into the wage-goods sector is itself a factor of underdevelopment.[128] The traditional sector is increasingly transformed into a mere reserve of cheap labor.

The domestic market for the modern wage-goods sector can increase in two ways: (1) through structural shifts whereby the rural subsistence economy is eliminated and employed workers rely on wage earnings for access to the means of subsistence (we call this process of increasing the domestic demand for wage goods via proletarianization "market-widening"); and (2) through wage increases, which not only augment total effective demand but, following Engel's law, also shift the qualitative composition of the wage basket away from mere essentials and increasingly toward technologically demanding durable goods (we call this process of demand expansion via rising wages "market-deepening"). The differences between the two processes in the implied relation between productivity and distribution of income are sharp, for only in the latter process is there social articulation.

In the center, domestic market-widening and export on the international market were the principal spheres of circulation until the 1880s. As Amin argued, it was only with the rise of monopoly capital and workers' strong revolutionary pressures that market-deepening subsequently became the principal source of market creation. This shift did not occur in the periphery, where market-widening remains the primary source of demand for the wage-goods sector. Clearly, destruction of the peasant and artisan economies, urban migration, and proletarianization, which all create market widening, have proceeded at an extraordinary pace. Between 1965 and 1970, the urban population of Latin America (in localities of over 2,000 inhabitants) increased at a rate of 4.1 percent a year, while the rural population growth rate for the same period was 1.4 percent.[129] Between 1960 and 1970, the urban sectors of Argentina and Chile absorbed 100 percent of all population growth while Mexican cities absorbed 71 percent; Brazilian cities, 68 percent.[130] Consequently, the market-widening effect was substantial, especially in the early phases of industrialization, which to a significant extent was aimed at the production of wage goods.[131] Subsequently, however, the penetration of foreign technology dampened employment creation,[132] in spite of eventually very high growth rates in industry, and the suppression of real wages atrophied effective demand, thus severely limiting the market-widening effect.

In our disarticulated model, with market-widening for capitalist wage goods, technology and the distribution of income determine the return to capital.[133] Profits then fully determine both the production and consumption capacities of the luxury-goods sector. The level of output of luxury goods in turn determines employment levels in luxury-goods production and in wage-goods production, the latter to sustain workers engaged both in luxury-goods production and in the production of wage-goods to sustain luxury-goods employment. Employment then determines the effective demand for wage-goods. With wages maintained at a minimum that is compatible with subjective forces, the wage-goods industries grow at the rate of employment creation. Thus, social disarticulation implies that the dynamic of growth is confined to the luxury-goods and external sectors, while the wage-goods sector is modernized under the constraint of creeping market-widening.

A 1976 study of the distribution of consumption by income strata shows clearly that there is a direct relationship between a greater share of demand originating in upper income levels and higher sectoral growth rates (Table 1.3).[134] Growth in production was slower in the wage-goods sector than in any

Table 1.3. Share of Different Income Strata in Total Consumption, 1974, and Growth Rate of Production by Type of Commodity, 1967–68 to 1975–76[a]

	Percent					
	Income strata, 1974					
Commodity Consumed	Lower 20 percent (1)	30 percent (2)	20 percent (3)	20 percent (4)	Higher 10 percent (5)	Annual growth rate of production, 1967–68 to 1975–76 (6)
Wage goods						
Food, beverages, and tobacco	5	18	14	29	29	3.2
Meats	2	10	11	34	41	3.0
Cereals	8	24	25	24	19	3.1
Beverages and tobacco	5	17	19	29	30	3.1
Wearing apparel	2	12	12	32	42	5.2
Clothing	2	11	11	32	44	
Footwear	3	13	16	32	36	
Luxuries						
Durable goods	1	5	8	26	61	10.8
Motor vehicles	0	1	1	13	85	12.0
Electrical appliances	1	4	8	37	50	9.1
All commodities	3	12	14	28	43	

Sources: (Cols. 1–5) Anibal Pinto, "Styles of Development in Latin America," *CEPAL Review,* 1976, p. 114.

(Col. 6) United Nations, Department of Economic and Social Affairs, Statistical Office of the United Nations, *Yearbook of Industrial Statistics, 1976* (New York, 1976).

[a] Averages estimated on the basis of data from Argentina, Brazil, Chile, Colombia, Honduras, Mexico, Paraguay, Peru, and Venezuela.

other sector, and a larger fraction of the demand for wage goods originated in the lower income strata. Thus, production of food, beverages, and tobacco grew at a rate of 3.5 percent between 1967–68 and 1975–76, while 23 percent of the demand for these goods originated in the poorest 50 percent of the population; for clothing and footwear, the rate of growth in production was 5.2 percent, while 14 percent of the demand for these goods originated in the poorest half of the population. These figures contrast sharply with those for durable goods, where the growth in production was 10.8 percent and the share of the poorest half of the population in consumption was only 6 percent. The fastest-growing sector was motor vehicles, where only 1 percent of the demand originated in the poorest 50 percent of the population and the growth rate of production was 12 percent. Market expansion in the dynamic sector consequently requires either export growth or concentration in the distribution of income to create an expanding demand for luxuries. The same ECLA study thus concludes that "the more dynamic elements of the productive apparatus are interrelated and depend mainly, and sometimes entirely, on the demand of the groups situated at the peak of the distributive structure. In other words, given the level of average income in the region and the individual countries, if the present style of development is to work and progress, then income must be concentrated in those strata, so as to sustain and increase demand for the favored goods and services."[135]

Similarly, data for Mexico show that for high-growth sectors, demand is located principally in the upper income group. Lustig analyzes how the distribution among income groups of a 1 percent increase in total income would affect the demand for particular products.[136] Her results, given in Table 1.4, indicate that for traditional wage goods such as food, beverages, and tobacco, the greatest demand effect is obtained by distributing income toward the lower income levels. By contrast, the greatest market expansion for durable goods is obtained by concentrating income in the upper groups. Hence, for the dynamic sector, market expansion requires income concentration. In turn, the dynamic sector requires the greatest share of imported capital, is least employment-creating, and has the highest rate of participation by multinational capital in production.

In the case of Brazil, Oliveira observes that the production of wage goods is increasingly insured by the capitalist sector, even though growth of this industry was severely curtailed by the fall in real wages during the 1960s and early 1970s.[137] Market expansion fundamentally proceeds under the pull of urban growth. Yet, slow-growing markets do not prevent the penetration of high-productivity enterprises and multinational capital. Dias thus shows that in spite of a constant rate of per capita consumption of textiles during the last twenty years, modern technology has been extensively adopted, production has been increasingly concentrated in larger firms, and foreign interests control more than 17 percent of productive capital.[138] However, the dynamic of

Table 1.4.   Mexico: Distribution of Income and Consumption
in Urban Households, 1968

		Percent					
		Share of total consumption			Redistributive effect[d]		
		Traditional			Traditional		
Income bracket (pesos)	Share of families	I[a]	II[b]	Modern[c]	I	II	Modern
0–3,000	74.6	48.7	34.6	18.6	1.2	1.1	0.5
3,000–6,000	18.0	30.3	32.8	22.7	0.6	1.0	1.2
More than 6,000	7.5	21.0	32.6	58.7	0.3	0.7	4.5
Growth rates, 1960–76 (percent)		5.1	7.3	11.5			
Participation of multi- national corporations in production, 1970 (percent)		28.4	20.7	53.6			
Import coefficient, 1970		0.06	0.12	0.25			
Capital/labor ratio, 1970		75.1	67.9	89.0			

Source: Nora Lustig, "Distribución del Ingreso, Estructura del Consumo y Características del Crecimiento Industrial," *Comercio Exterior* 29, no. 5 (May 1979): 535–43.

[a] Includes food, beverages, and tobacco.

[b] Includes textiles, clothing, footwear, furniture, books, and chemical products.

[c] Includes durable goods (automobiles and electrical appliances).

[d] Percentage change in consumption when a 1 percent increase in total income goes to one particular income bracket.

industrial growth remains based on consumption by the upper income strata and on the international market. Thus, Arroyo concludes his study of income and consumption from 1965 to 1975 by saying that "the worker does not weigh decisively in the sphere of circulation. In this way, the capitalists find themselves to a certain extent free of the necessity to consider the proletariat as a consumption factor."[139] As for Brazilian exports stimulated by foreign-exchange, fiscal, and credit incentives, they increased in value terms at an average annual growth rate of no less than 31 percent between 1967 and 1977.[140]

The pattern of industrial growth is thus locked in a process in which market-widening (proletarianization) sustains the slow growth of wage-goods industries, while income concentration sustains the rapid growth of luxury industries (fundamentally durable goods). As a result, growth under hegemony of the disarticulated alliance does not evolve per se into market-deepening. The transition from social disarticulation to articulation is not an automatic outcome of economic growth as Kuznets and Chenery claim in their identification of unique "normal patterns of growth." It is a social option that can be achieved only through class struggle and social change.

MECHANISMS OF SURPLUS TRANSFER BETWEEN
CENTER AND PERIPHERY

Having used the concepts of articulation and disarticulation to identify the contradictions of accumulation in the center and periphery, we now turn to an analysis of the mechanisms of surplus transfers between these two types of economies.

The center's necessary external relationship in overcoming the cyclical tendency for the rate of profit to fall is made possible via two mechanisms of surplus extraction that correspond to external necessities for the periphery and originate in the relationship of domination that exists between center and periphery. The first mechanism results from industrial and financial imperialism associated with foreign investments and loans. The second is associated with international trade and can materialize through three specific mechanisms of different relative importance: unequal exchange in trade, unequal trade, and unequal rewards in the formation of international prices. Through these mechanisms, center and periphery are integrated into a world economic system within which the necessary relation between production and circulation obtains. The history of domination of center over periphery and of hegemonic dominance of the disarticulated alliance in the periphery has created these external possibilities for the center.

Industrial and Financial Imperialism (Differential Profit Rates)

This most transparent form of surplus extraction occurs both directly as returns on foreign investments and loans and indirectly through interest payments on an external debt incurred in particular to maintain equilibrium in the balance of payments. Center capital—primarily embodied for the last twenty-five years in multinational corporations—is invested in modern enclaves and industries in the periphery, where it captures high rates of profit and repatriates a large fraction of them.[141]

As seen in Table 1.5, the evidence supports the existence of a net surplus transfer toward the center. If remitted profits on foreign investment are deducted from the capital inflows into external areas, the balance of capital flows to and from the United States between 1960 and 1972 is negative for all regions of the world except Western Europe. For all regions, profit remission exceeded the net inflow of U.S. capital by 154 percent; for Latin America, one of the oldest areas of penetration of U.S. capital, the net outflow during the same period was 319 percent of net capital inflows.[142] Magdoff similarly estimated a figure of 297 percent for Latin America between 1950 and 1965.[143]

This massive repatriation of profits is made possible by the capacity of U.S. manufacturing subsidiaries to finance new investments in the periphery using locally generated capital. Newfarmer and Mueller show that, in the period

Table 1.5.   Flow of Funds Related to Direct U.S. Investment, 1960–72

Area	Million U.S.$		
	Net capital account inflows	Repatriated dividend income	Inflows less repatriation[a]
All regions	38,533	59,408	−20,875
Canada	7,058	9,195	− 2,137
Western Europe	16,954	11,709	5,245
Latin America	4,188	13,343	− 9,155
Other	10,333	25,161	−14,826

Source: Richard Newfarmer and Willard Mueller, ''Multinational Corporations in Brazil and Mexico'' (Report to the Subcommittee on Multinational Corporations, U.S. Senate, Washington, D.C., 1975), p. 11.

[a] A negative sign indicates that income returned to the United States was greater than the flow from the United States to the recipient areas.

1958–68, only 20 percent of the funds used by U.S. subsidiaries in Latin America originated from net capital inflows from the parent corporation.[144] The remaining 80 percent was generated internally by the subsidiary itself or was borrowed locally: about 40 percent came from retained profits and depreciation, while about 40 percent was borrowed principally from sources in the host country.

For the center, export of capital is part of the search for counteracting forces to the tendency for the rate of profit to fall. For the periphery, the call on foreign capital and foreign aid originates in the periodic need to make up for a deficit in the balance of payments and for weak domestic investment capacity. These needs create the internal possibility for industrial and financial imperialism to occur.

For foreign capital to be attracted to the periphery, the rate of profit (after due adjustment for differential risks) to be gained there must be greater than that in the monopolized sector in the center. As Kalecki and Baran have argued, monopolistic superprofits in the center originate in a biased redistribution of the surplus value from the competitive sector to the monopoly sector.[145] The tendency toward equalization of the rate of profit that characterizes competitive capitalism thus disappears, and monopolistic superprofits can occur without necessarily decreasing the relative participation of labor in the social product. In the periphery, by contrast, lack of an established competitive sector implies that superprofits on foreign investment originate elsewhere: in the joint occurrence of high productivity and low wages, wages that are kept down through suppression of workers' demands, functional dualism (cheap semiproletarian labor), the internationalization of value (imports of cheap wage foods), and the increasingly efficient production of wage goods (development of capitalism in response to market widening).

The industrial products obtained through foreign investments find an expanding market either in exports to the center or in the limited internal market of the periphery, which consists of both luxury-goods consumption out of surplus value and market-widening through proletarianization. In the first case, a new international division of labor is established whereby the center exports capital goods, technological know-how, and financial capital and the periphery exports raw materials, finished industrial products, and a financial surplus. Countries with a relatively docile and skilled labor force tend to be recipients of labor-intensive, resource-intensive, and polluting industries. The international division of labor implies the development of the bulk of the capacity to consume in the center and of part of the capacity to produce—under higher profitability conditions—in the periphery.

In the second case, import-substitution policies create the structural conditions for the exploitation of a limited internal market. Deterioration of the participation of labor in the social product, which is structurally possible with accumulation under social disarticulation, increases the surplus value that is distributed among foreign capital, associated national capital, and the supporting bureaucracy. The last two social groups create a home market for luxury consumption goods produced by the modern sector. This market is limited by competition for the surplus value between foreign and domestic recipients and, among the latter, by competition between consumption and investment expenditures (including capital outflight). Regressive income-distribution policies are promoted to overcome these contradictions since they result in an increase in both market size and investment capacity. In the upper classes, income, and hence consumption levels, are similar to those observed for the bulk of the population in the center. The demand profile thus created in the periphery replicates that of the center, but with one key difference: the commodities that are wage goods in the center are luxuries in the periphery.[146] Internationalization of consumption patterns in turn creates attractive investment prospects for multinational corporations, which can ship to the periphery the same technology already employed in the center.[147]

Industrial and financial imperialism is thus the materialization of the mutual need for external relations that arises from the contradictions of accumulation in the center and periphery. The tendency for the rate of profit to fall in the center is partially counteracted by the center's high return on exported capital. Deficits in the balance of payments and in the investment capacity of the periphery are temporarily counteracted by the periphery's call on foreign capital. Overcoming barriers on a world scale allows capital to grow. And growth re-creates new barriers in a continuing contradictory process.

Surplus Transfer Through Trade

International trade is another mechanism by which the periphery contributes to maintaining the rate of profit. The import of cheap raw materials by the center reduces the cost of constant capital while the import of foods and industrial wage goods reduces the cost of variable capital; thus, imports increase the rate of profit. Participation in international trade is a necessity for the periphery in order for it to create the capacity to import: sectoral disarticulation implies the need to import capital goods and technological knowledge for the modern sector; and social disarticulation and the consequent food crisis imply the need to import food. The three mechanisms by which international trade can result in surplus extraction to the benefit of the center are (1) *unequal exchange,* whereby equilibrium *production prices* imply a transfer of value from disarticulated (cheap-labor) economies to articulated economies; (2) *unequal trade,* whereby domination of the international market by the center results in a monopolistic rent to its benefit, an advantage that materializes in a discrepancy between production and *market prices;* and (3) *unequal rewards* to labor owing to differences in productivity in internationally traded commodities.

Unequal Exchange (Differential Production Prices)

According to Emmanuel and Amin, unequal exchange in trade results from the transfer of value that occurs at equilibrium in the exchange of commodities between countries characterized by unequal rates of surplus value.[148] In the transformation of value into production prices, the gap between value and price—due to unequal organic compositions of capital—is modified in favor of the economy with the lower rate of surplus value. The result is that in trading according to relative production prices, the economy with the higher rate of surplus value receives relatively less labor in its imports than it gives away in the products that it exports.[149] With the internationalization of the price and value of wage goods in the world economic system, real wages become an unambiguous indicator of the value of labor power. And there is no question that real wages in the exporting sectors of center and periphery are markedly different. As a result, the rate of surplus value is many times higher in the modern sector of the periphery than in the center. The logic of this discrepancy lies in the contrasting laws of accumulation that obtain under social disarticulation and articulation: in the center, development of the capacity to consume blocks upward adjustments in the rate of surplus value at the same time that it reinforces a fundamental contradiction, the tendency for the rate of profit to fall and for the surplus to rise in the monopolized sectors; in the periphery, social disarticulation reconciles individual capitalists and social capital by perpetuating cheap labor and hence high rates of surplus value.

Unequal exchange is thus seen as a mechanism of surplus transfer via trade that does not result from higher rates of profit in the periphery, monopoly pricing, investments by foreign capital, or plunder. Surplus transfer occurs even in trade carried out according to equilibrium production prices. It is the direct outcome of exchange between center and periphery in a world economic system characterized by (1) the international mobility of products and capital (and hence by the formation of international values and an international average rate of profit), (2) restrictions to the international mobility of labor, and (3) accumulation under social articulation in the center and under social disarticulation in the periphery.

While the mechanism of unequal exchange provides a theoretical understanding of the unequal benefits derived by the center and periphery from the international division of labor and international trade, it is a mechanism that requires equilibrium in the capital market. It is also clear that the international movement of capital toward the periphery that is required for this equilibrium to obtain is bound to have an effect on peripheral wages. Consequently, wages cannot be taken as an exogenous variable.[150]

As noted earlier, we prefer to omit the concept of unequal exchange for the purpose of our analysis: underdevelopment is fundamentally a disequilibrium situation, and accumulation on a world scale is fraught with serious "imperfections" in the capital and product markets that are the reflection of structural heterogeneity and relations of domination. The concepts of industrial and financial imperialism and unequal trade, as well as the concept of unequal rewards, are more useful in conceptualizing actual surplus transfer between periphery and center.

Unequal Trade (Differential Market Prices)

A transfer of surplus value to the center results when in trade transactions the center uses its power to directly impose price distortions on the world market via quotas and tariffs on imports from the periphery[151] and through monopolistic pricing by merchant capital.[152] Due to the essentiality of imports of capital goods, technology, and food from the center, a fall in the international terms of trade to the detriment of the periphery will logically force it, at least in the short run, to increase its exports, thus generating a backward-bending supply curve of exports.[153] The center can then capture increasing volumes of exports at lower prices—a phenomenon denounced by Prebisch and the ECLA some twenty-five years ago. Through this mechanism, the transfer of surplus value that occurs assumes the form of a monopoly rent that creates a discrepancy between the production and market prices of peripheral exportables. By contrast to unequal exchange, the mechanism of unequal trade operates at the level of market prices, not production prices.

Unequal Rewards in the Formation of International Prices (Differential Productivities)

Most of the products of the modern industrial sector of the periphery are not specific to the periphery but are identical to those of the center, although sometimes they are produced through different labor processes. With nonspecific goods, if the average productivity of the periphery is lower than world-average productivity, a unit of product originating in the periphery will require more embodied labor than the world-average embodied labor consumed in the production of that commodity. On the world market under competitive conditions a unique price is established that corresponds to the world-average embodied labor required to produce that commodity. Individual products are exchanged on the basis of this world price regardless of how much labor was expended in their production. The result is that "on the world market, the labor of a country with a higher productivity of labor is valued as more intensive, so that the product of one day's work in such a nation is exchanged for the product of more than a day's work in an underdeveloped country."[154] On the world market, unequal quantities of labor are exchanged in trade. The effective devaluation of embodied labor that originates in the periphery under conditions of lower productivity leads to lower wages. By contrast to Emmanuel's unequal-exchange argument, in this case it is not lower wages that lead to unequal exchange; it is lower productivity that leads to unequal rewards and hence creates the objective basis for lower wages.

This nonequivalence of embodied labor is, of course, a reflection of the normal functioning of the law of value in the formation of market prices. Exactly the same process penalizes low-productivity firms and rewards high-productivity ones, resulting in elimination and concentration in the industrial structure. Thus, higher profit rates are captured in the center than in the periphery as a result of international trade, even without international movements of capital, in contrast to industrial and financial imperialism, where surplus extraction results from the internationalization of capital.

Since in Latin America the productivity of labor in the modern sector that produces nonspecific goods tends to be approximately as high as that in the center, unequal rewards in the formation of international prices are a secondary factor of surplus extraction. This leaves industrial and financial imperialism and unequal trade as the principal mechanisms through which surplus is transferred internationally.

ACCUMULATION IN THE CENTER-PERIPHERY STRUCTURE
AND THE CURRENT CRISIS

Center and periphery thus constitute a dialectical whole whose organic unity is provided by the fundamental, necessary, and contradictory relationship that exists between production and circulation. The specific contradictions between the center (downward pressure on the rate of profit and associated forms of crisis) and the periphery (structural deficit in the balance of payments, limited market size, low investment capacity, and food crisis) are both met and reposited by three mechanisms of surplus extraction: industrial and financial imperialism, unequal trade, and unequal rewards. Through historical relations of domination that act via the national class structure, the peripheral economy has been partially molded by highly conflictive and unstable processes to provide the external possibility for the resolution (and re-creation) of the center's contradictions. This structuralization takes on the aspect of social disarticulation that obtains under hegemonic dominance of the disarticulated class alliance. Accumulation of capital on a world scale thus produces simultaneously development (growth and rising real wages) in the center and underdevelopment (eventually rapid growth and stagnant real wages) in the periphery.

This process of accumulation occurring on a world scale in the center-periphery structure—which we have characterized in terms of unity, heterogeneity, and dominance—is, however, highly contradictory and tends to negate the perpetuation of growth and rising real wages in the center. The increasing *integration* of the world capitalist system on the basis of a highly unequal world economic structure is the fundamental condition that both insured growth in the center and precipitated a structural crisis of capitalism in th 1970s. Sustained economic expansion from the 1940s to the late 1960s and the growing internationalization of capital in that period created the conditions for both the destabilization of center economies (and initiation there of a long process of selective *dedevelopment*) and the rapid acceleration of accumulation in a majority of the countries in the periphery.

In this fashion the reversion of the law of unequal development to its original classical formulation, brought out in the early 1970s by critics of the development-of-underdevelopment school, was increasingly confirmed. Reinforced unequal development was to create new forms of contradictions, but would not eliminate the fundamental structural characteristics of the world economic system—its unity, heterogeneity, and relations of dominance.

Emergence of the crisis was fundamentally rooted in two phenomena that were created by the very process of growth: first, the increasing internationalization of large segments of social capital beyond the stages of multinational and transnational corporations to the development of *metanationalization,* which is the ultimate divorce between capital and nation-state. While the multinational corporation repatriates profits to the home-base country and the transnational corporation returns profits to the group of mother-countries, metanational corporations accumulate a large fraction of profits in offshore banking centers. Thus, there is no longer a one-to-one correspondence between imperialism and surplus extraction to the benefit of the center; while both imperialism and surplus extraction continue unabated, the accumulation of surplus no longer need entail economic benefits for the center countries.

Second, sustained economic growth (reinforced in the United States in the 1960s by military expenditures in Vietnam and stimulation of the domestic economy by Keynesian instruments) led to an increasing *squeeze on profits* as low unemployment levels pushed wages to unprecedented highs while antipollution, work safety, consumer protection, and social welfare laws increased production costs. Thus, while the rate of profit on U.S. corporate assets was on the average 8.1 percent between 1951 and 1959 and 8 percent between 1960 and 1968, it dropped to 5.8 percent between 1969 and 1976.[155]

The joint occurrence of these two phenomena—the metanationalization of an important fraction of social capital and the squeeze on profits in the center—was the root cause of the structural crisis of capitalism that began in the 1970s. Both phenomena implied a sharp decline in the repatriation of profits to the center states. In the center, this led to a slowdown in industrial growth, stagnant real wages, increasing inequality in the distribution of income, inflation, deficits in the balance of payments, and enhanced conflicts among fractions of the bourgeoisie and among classes. It also implied a process of selective dedevelopment and a redefinition of the role of the state in both its objective and subjective functions. In the periphery, it led to sharply accelerated industrialization, while disarticulation remained the social image of the engine of growth. And in the offshore financial markets, it implied the massive accumulation of a financial surplus that was the concretization of underconsumptionist tendencies on a world scale. Let us now return to each of these elements in more detail.

The squeeze on profits at home and reduced repatriation of foreign earnings (metanationalization) led to a marked divergence in the rates of industrial growth and fixed capital formation between center and periphery (Table 1.1). Thus, while the yearly growth rates of manufacturing were nearly equal in the United States and Latin America in 1960–68, in 1969–76 Latin America's growth rate was 4.8 times higher than that of the United States. Similarly, the rates of gross fixed capital formation in Latin America and the United States went from being nearly equal in 1960–68 to an impressive twenty-eight times higher in Latin America in 1969–76.

Reduced investments in the center, a consequent stagnation in labor productivity, and a continued rapid increase in demand and production costs resulted in major inflationary pressures and growing deficits in the balance of payments. While the productivity of labor in private U.S. business sectors increased at an average of 3.2 percent per year between 1950 and 1959, and 3.3 percent between 1960 and 1968, the rate of increase fell to an average of 1.4 percent between 1969 and 1978 and specifically to 0.4 percent in 1978.[156] Simultaneously, monetary wages continued to increase and effective demand rose enormously by means of the boom in consumer credit that displaced forward in time future consumption capacity, thus counteracting the effect of relatively stagnant real wages. Thus, while real median after-tax family income increased at an annual rate of 2.8 percent between 1950 and 1968, it declined between 1969 and 1976 at an annual rate of −0.3 percent.[157] Yet consumer debt increased by over 50 percent between 1975 and 1978, reaching the staggering figure of $1,031 billion.[158] Demand was further increased by a 50 percent rise in the debt of the federal government over the same time period to some $798 billion in 1978. Adding to these sources of demand was the partial repatriation of foreign profits for consumption purposes, a more rapid growth in productive services than in the production of commodities, and a massive increase in food exports fomented by dollar devaluations and export subsidies. Demand-induced inflation was reinforced by a cost squeeze on firms and the monopolistic capacity of many sectors of the economy to translate higher costs into higher prices to protect profit rates. These higher costs originated in wages and benefits, energy and raw materials, and land values. The result was a major spurt in the inflation rate, which reached 12.2 percent in 1974 and again rose to 9 percent in 1978.[159]

The growing deficit in the balance of payments could also be explained by the conjunction of a profit squeeze at home and the metanationalization of capital. Increased domestic purchasing power created a growing demand for imports—in particular, the import of oil for private transportation—while foreign demand for manufactured products was increasingly met either by U.S. firms producing abroad or by European and Japanese exporters who had by then firmly established their competitive position vis-á-vis the United States on a newly reconstructed technological basis. Thus, in 1976, while U.S. manufacturers' exports totaled $76.6 billion, sales of overseas subsidiaries of U.S. firms reached $212.8 billion, of which $37.7 billion were exported to other countries. As Magdoff observed, "The US. balance of payments deficits would soon disappear if the $37.7 billion of the export activity of the multinationals abroad, let alone a portion of the $161 billion they sell in the countries where they are located, were replaced by exports from the United States."[160]

A squeeze on profits and the spread of metanationalization imply a process of selective dedevelopment in the center and an attack on wages that includes selective disarticulation of segments of the labor force. Dedevelopment is associated with the fact that particular branches of industry leave the center and fall under the aegis of metanational capital, thus increasing the regional and sectoral unevenness of development. As this process occurs, competition between the national bourgeoisie (whose economic fate is tied to the nation-state) and the metanational bourgeoisie is enhanced. The defense mechanisms of the national bourgeoisie include an increased rate of exploitation of domestic labor and improvement in the efficiency of social capital through greater national planning. The first implies an increasing segmentation of the labor force, in particular through the hiring of cheap Third World labor (especially Mexican and Caribbean illegals), the psychological preparation of workers to accept lower wages (Neo-Malthusian campaigns like the Report of Rome), the downgrading of work and education, a further shift in the tax burden away from corporations and toward the working class, and exercise of the repressive capacity of the state. Thus, a new locus for class struggle is created that originates in the conflicts between national and metanational bourgeoisies and materializes in those segments of the working class of the center that bear the cost of increased exploitation and dedevelopment.

In the periphery itself, accelerated industrial growth occurs on the basis of cheap labor and high profit rates—i.e., on the basis of the disarticulated model of accumulation. While the U.S. corporate profit rate on total assets was on the average 5.7 percent between 1970 and 1976, the profit rate on foreign assets was 13.6 percent.[161] And direct private U.S. investments abroad doubled between 1970 and 1977, reaching a total of $149 billion.[162]

The result of this decentralization of industry on a world scale is a sharply increased pattern of unequal development within both the center and the periphery. This pattern leads to a relocation of class conflicts away from (principally) the periphery, away from the antagonism between center and periphery, and toward increasingly local conflicts within both the center and the periphery. It also leads to an increasing reincorporation of several socialist societies (including the Soviet Union and China) into the world capitalist system through a new alliance between metanational bourgeoisies and revolutionary elites. Transnational capital finds access to cheap and docile labor and stable markets in these societies, and for the sake of this goal is able to transcend ideological differences among nation-states.

Development of offshore banking centers is the institutional form this metanationalization of capital assumes, and these centers become the receptacles of a financial surplus accumulated on a world scale. Thus today the Eurodollar market is valued at $350 billion and the Eurobond market is worth $50 billion, more than the total money supply in the United States. And growth in the offshore capital markets is fundamentally demand-determined because the Eurocurrency market is free from reserve requirements. As a result, domestic monetary policies are less efficient because domestic firms and governments have direct access to these uncontrolled offshore capital markets. These markets also substantially weaken and destabilize the U.S. dollar as the ratio between offshore dollars and U.S. gold reserves continues to increase.

The growing divorce of nation-state from metanational capital implies that the world structure based on the center-periphery dichotomy will be increasingly difficult to maintain. The center is becoming locally disarticulated and hence conflict-ridden, both among fractions of the bourgeoisie and among classes, while articulation for the majority of the working class is reduced to implying a linkage between increasingly stagnant labor productivity and stagnant real wages. The periphery is incurring high growth rates, but it remains essentially disarticulated and hence based on cheap labor and cheap food and on the use and destruction of the functional dualism that exists between commercial and peasant agriculture. The resulting accumulation of a financial surplus in offshore financial markets is the symptom of a structural crisis of underconsumption on a world scale.

In the periphery, the cheap labor–cheap food and functional-dualism relationships remain the essential determinants of the two problems addressed in the present study: the stagnation of food production and the dynamics of rural poverty. Before developing an interpretation of the causes of these problems, we turn in the next chapter to a factual characterization of the forms they assume in Latin America.

2

━ ━ ━ ━ ━

Agrarian Crisis in Latin America:
The Facts

━ ━ ━ ━ ━

Before presenting an interpretation of the agrarian crisis in Latin America (Chapter 4) and analyzing the reformist role of the state in dealing with some aspects of this crisis (Chapters 5–7), we must start with facts. In this chapter we will first look to history for an understanding of the patterns of integration of Latin American agriculture into specific economies and the world economic system as a whole. We will then provide a detailed empirical description of the two principal dimensions of the agrarian crisis: stagnation tendencies and sharply uneven development in production; and rapid differentiation and massive rural poverty among peasants. In Chapter 3 we will characterize the agrarian structure in terms of social classes and types of farm enterprises and use this characterization to identify the patterns of transformation of the peasantry under the forces of the development of capitalism.

INTEGRATION OF LATIN AMERICAN AGRICULTURE
INTO THE NATIONAL AND WORLD ECONOMIES

The Latin American countries were integrated into the world economic system at a time when mercantilism was the dominant form of international economic relation. Feudal production relations were still the rule in Western Europe, and industrial capitalism was as yet unknown. However, colonization of the New World by the Spanish and Portuguese was to provide a strong stimulus to the birth of capitalism in Europe.[1] The precious-metal reserves of Peru, Bolivia, Brazil, and Mexico were plundered by the Iberian colonizers and channeled through trade into the coffers of British and Dutch merchants. The massive inflow of bullion created strong inflationary pressures that depressed real rents and wages and stimulated capitalist investment in industry.

In Latin America, the two distinct patterns of settlement that occurred during the colonial period depended upon labor availability and natural production conditions in relation to international demand.[2] Agricultural colonies were established in temperate regions such as the River Plate, southern Brazil, and Chile, where production conditions were ecologically similar to those of Europe and where indigenous labor availability was minimal. The colonizers in these areas were independent settlers seeking to escape the social and economic conditions of Europe. This pattern of settlement was, however, relatively insignificant in Latin America, where the predominant motivation of colonization was exploitation of the tremendous natural wealth of the region for repatriation to the metropolis. Colonies established for these purposes were located either in areas with large mineral deposits or in the tropics, where exotic agricultural goods such as sugar, cotton, or cacao could be produced and exported to Europe. Their creation required the availability of extensive masses of cheap labor.

Direct enslavement of the indigenous population, which would have been the most direct method of obtaining cheap labor, was forbidden by the Spanish crown as early as 1528. However, the *encomienda* system, which gave full control over the indigenous population to an elite group of settlers, provided a substitute mechanism.[3] Under this system, the natives were legally obliged to pay tribute in labor services or in kind to the elite settlers. Although the *encomienda* was supposed to protect the Indians from slavery, in reality the native laborers were brutally exploited in mines and plantations and were decimated in many areas.[4] African slaves had to be imported in large numbers in the Caribbean, Guyana, and northeastern Brazil, where Indian labor was rapidly being exterminated.

The plantation system was established in those areas with potential for intensive large-scale monoculture of a high-value tropical product for export. Sugarcane was the most important such crop for the first three centuries of colonization. Its cultivation spread quickly throughout the West Indies, northeastern Brazil, the Veracruz coast in Mexico, and Peruvian coast. The motivation for plantation production was profit, and the operations were quite efficient and commercially oriented. However, since the importation of African slaves was necessary to provide the basis for cheap labor and since plantation management relied on paternalistic relations characteristic of feudalism, the plantations certainly could not be characterized as capitalist enterprises.[5]

The hacienda system appeared in those areas that were not appropriate for intensive production of export crops. Whereas the *encomienda* had only granted settlers the right of levying tribute on the indigenous population, the hacienda system permitted more direct forms of labor control. Precapitalist relations of bondage known as *yanaconaje* in Peru, *inquilinaje* in Chile, and *huasipungaje* in Ecuador were established to entrap on the land of the hacienda a scarce labor force often composed of mestizos and dispossessed migrants.[6] Productive activities of the hacienda were oriented toward a self-sufficient supply of food, fiber, and other agricultural goods, along with some commercial production for export to the colonial mining and administrative settlements and to the foreign market. The relative isolation of the hacienda from the forces of capitalist competition allowed it to survive for centuries, despite low levels of investment and inefficient production methods.

Thus, in the first three centuries of domination of Latin America, the European colonizers established monopolistic control over the most productive agricultural lands. Outside the agricultural colonies located in temperate areas, land settlement implied the quest for cheap labor, a quest that was satisfied either through the importation of slaves or the establishment of feudal bonds over native and free labor. Cheap labor in Latin American agriculture was an additional factor that increased the mercantile profits circulating in the world economic system during the colonial period.

The pattern of domination of the Latin American colonies started to change at the beginning of the nineteenth century. The old mercantile colonial powers Spain and Portugal began to decline, and their weakening resulted in the political independence of Latin American countries and in the formation of liberal republics. At the same time, industrial capitalism, evolving primarily in Great Britain, was increasingly the center of power in the world economic system. The extraordinary productivity of the new manufacturing enterprises afforded Britain comparative advantage in the trade of many products and provided the logic for its support of a regime of international free trade. The period of free trade under British hegemony lasted more than a century and resulted in the division of the world into the industrialized center and the primary-product-exporting countries of the periphery. This division was reinforced by the structural changes that occurred in the industrialized centers, particularly the tendency toward concentration and centralization of capital, which resulted in the appearance of imperialist attempts to capture high rates of profit through direct investments in the periphery.[7]

External domination of the Latin American countries developed in the context of competition between the United States and Britain for control of the region. In 1825 the U.S. government promulgated the Monroe Doctrine, warning nonhemispheric nations to stay out of the American continent. The measure ostensibly protected the new liberal regimes in Latin America from intervention. However, as it was implemented, it served more to advance U.S. economic interests than to dissuade the powerful Europeans. As Gerassi notes:

In 1833, for example, England invaded the Falkland Islands, belonging to Argentina, and instead of invoking the Monroe Doctrine, the United States supported England.... Two years later, the United States allowed England to occupy the northern coast of Honduras, which is still British Honduras. England then invaded Guatemala, tripled its Honduras territory, and in 1839 took over the island of Roatan. Instead of reacting against England, the United States moved against Mexico. Within a few years, Mexico lost half of its territory—the richest half—to the United States.[8]

At the end of the nineteenth century, the United States continued to intervene frequently in the internal affairs of other South American countries and in 1898 annexed Puerto Rico.

With regard to agriculture, the new international division of labor between industrial center and primary-commodity-exporting periphery gave a strong stimulus to the growth of some exports in Latin America. Those countries producing temperate agricultural products (primarily Argentina; to a lesser extent, Uruguay and Brazil) were able to greatly expand production of cereals and animal products for trade with the food deficit countries in Europe. Heavy investment from the center, particularly from Britain, financed the large-scale transport, storage, and shipment facilities necessary for this type of extensive agricultural production.

But for most Latin American countries engaged in the intensive production of tropical export products, the period of British hegemony was not one of uninterrupted trade expansion. They did not receive British protection unless they were in the Commonwealth, and they were forced to compete with Asian and African colonies more organically linked to the British umbrella of protection. Highly dependent on the export of a few commodities, they were seriously affected by the booms and busts of prices on the world market. The cases of rubber and cacao are instructive. Brazil held a virtual monopoly on natural rubber when demand soared in the late nineteenth century with the discovery of vulcanization. The rubber boom brought instant prosperity to the Amazon region, but the rubber market collapsed in 1913, and rubber prices fell to a quarter of their previous levels. The crisis was brought on by new supplies from rubber plantations in Malaysia and Ceylon that had been planted with seeds smuggled out of Brazil in 1875. By 1919, Brazil was supplying only one-eighth of the rubber consumed world-wide.[9] Similarly, the production of cacao was long identified with Ecuador and Venezuela, where it had been produced since colonial days. In the late nineteenth century, its production spread to the Brazilian northeast, a former world center of sugar production that had fallen into decline in the late seventeenth century because of competition from sugar plantations in the Dutch West Indies. Brazil became the largest exporter of cacao; but by 1920 it had again lost its leading position owing to competition from plantations developed by the British in their African colonies—especially Ghana.

In Central America the production of tropical exports was less volatile because it developed through the direct penetration of North American capital. Until 1850, the Central American economies had been integrated into the world system mainly as suppliers of natural dyes. At midcentury, however, these markets were destroyed by the introduction of synthetic substitutes.

First, a rush of European and American investors bought interest in lands to grow coffee; but the real transformation in the area's agricultural economy came with the introduction of the modern refrigerated steamship in the early 1900s. As bananas became a common wage food in the center, U.S. concerns—particularly United Fruit—began large-scale production in Honduras, Guatemala, and Costa Rica. Railroads were built, and communications systems were installed by the foreign investors; and the U.S. government continued to intervene with force in the Central American countries to secure U.S. investments. Panama and Honduras were invaded militarily six times each between 1901 and 1925, while Nicaragua was twice invaded and was occupied continuously for thirteen years.[10]

In summary, during the era of economic liberalism, 1820–1930, Latin America was integrated into the global process of accumulation as agroexporter to the central capitalist countries. Exchange of its products was, however, subject to the forces of free trade under British hegemony and to both European and American imperialism. European capital investments in Latin American agriculture were focused principally on the processing, marketing, and transportation of temperate products for export. The penetration of capital into the production of tropical goods came largely from the United States. Its capital investments were concentrated in sugar plantations in the Caribbean and in banana enclaves in Central America. As for the other producers of tropical exports—those not so directly controlled by American or British interests—they were left prey to the boom-and-bust cycles of international free trade.

The expansion of industrial capitalism in Latin America never proceeded at an even pace. Cycles of expansion and stagnation brought on periodic crises and necessitated restructuring of the productive forces. None of these crises had as far-reaching an impact on the global economy as did the one of the 1930s, however. Not only did the apparatus of free trade collapse in that crisis, but the position of Britain as the dominant imperial power also came into question. For the world as a whole, the value of trade in 1931–35 was only 41 percent of the 1921–29 average. In 1931, Britain's financial position was so strained that it was forced to adopt radical changes in financial and commercial policy, including abandonment of the gold standard. The other central economies adopted protective trade policies to insulate their domestic economies as much as possible.

The collapse of the international market was particularly detrimental to the primary-product-exporting countries of the periphery. These countries depended on their trade relationships to obtain manufactured goods. Furthermore, when outflows of financial capital from the center, which also were important in sustaining the peripheral economies, ceased, financial crisis befell the dependent states. This crisis was so severe in Latin America that all countries except Argentina were forced to suspend payments on the external public debt at some time during the 1930s.[11]

In response to the crisis, the center economies adopted a number of internal policies that were to result in a basic restructuring of the world economy. Policies such as those of the New Deal in the United States provided for more government regulation of the functions of private enterprise. Labor and the petty bourgeoisie were co-opted into social democracies that temporarily relieved some of the contradictions of capitalism and firmly established the pattern of articulated accumulation in the center. These measures also included extensive policies designed to develop national agriculture and reduce dependence on agricultural imports. In the periphery—especially Latin America—response to the crisis required the development of an independent industrial base to produce those manufactured commodities that had formerly been imported.

The impact of the crisis on Latin American agriculture—especially the agroexport sector—was severe. By 1933, prices of wheat in Buenos Aires had fallen to 29 percent of their 1927 levels, international sugar prices to 33 percent of their 1927 levels, coffee prices to 27 percent, and cacao prices to 23 percent.[12] In Argentina, the government reacted with attempts to diversify the agricultural base and foster industrialization. Wheat production was restricted, and incentives for increasing the production of cotton, oilseeds, fruit, rice, and maté were enacted. Currency was devalued, and bilateral trade agreements with the United Kingdom, Brazil, the Netherlands, and Belgium were signed. Import-substitution policies succeeded in reducing the share of imports in internal consumption from 40 percent in 1928 to 26 percent in 1938. In Brazil, nearly a million tons of coffee had been burned by 1933 as the government attempted to support prices. Currency devaluation and exchange restrictions reduced the value of imports by 76 percent between 1928 and 1932; the value of exports fell somewhat less—by 62 percent—in the same period. The pattern of government intervention to diversify the export base and introduce import-substitution industrial production was similar elsewhere in the region. A brief period of autonomous growth resulted and was bolstered by the recovery in prices and levels of foreign trade (based on bilateral trade and commodity treaties) that occurred in the rearmament period before World War II.

The transition of the United States to the central position of global power after World War II made the threats of the Monroe Doctrine no longer necessary. During the New Deal, that doctrine had formally been replaced by the "good neighbor policy," which purported to end American imperialism. In place of the Monroe Doctrine, a new form of economic dependency emerged in Latin America, a dependency associated with the new structure of global accumulation. Whereas the advanced industrial countries had adopted the policies necessary to perpetuate articulated accumulation in their economies, the secular balance-of-payment difficulties and low investment capacity of the peripheral countries prevented them from sustaining such developments after World War II. If they were to maintain accumulation in their industrial sectors, sources of cheap labor and external capital had to be found. Thus, accumulation in Latin America industry increasingly assumed the character of disarticulation, which had long been typical of export-enclave capitalism.

Latin America's new economic dependency was rooted in policies enacted before World War II. It was in this period that the Organization of American States was founded, and bilateral agricultural aid and other types of development loans were initiated. According to Furtado, the new dependency was characterized more by an increasing importance of technology transfers and public investment than by a growing dependence on net foreign private investment. Between 1950–54 and 1960–63, the annual amount of international public investment in Latin America increased almost sixfold from $177 million to $1,022 million, whereas net direct investment declined from an annual average of $309 million to $282 million. Vigorous expansion of U.S. manufacturing subsidiaries did occur during the period, but the growth was financed mainly by undistributed profits and loan funds obtained in local capital markets. These subsidiaries were able to compete for local capital because of their superior access to foreign technology. The new dependency was further reinforced by the growing importance of intermediation by international credit agencies such as the World Bank and the Inter-American Development Bank between Latin American governments and world capital markets.[13]

Since the early 1960s, the trend toward multinational control of key sectors of the Latin American economies has continued, with the bulk of investment still financed by profit retention and domestic savings. However, as the Latin American countries have, as a whole, joined the ranks of the international middle-income countries, lending from official agencies has decreased relative to lending from private banks and bank consortia. Neither the rapid growth of industry and an increased ability to withstand external shocks nor the demands for a new international economic order aimed at improved terms of trade, access to the markets of center economies, control over multinational corporations, and availability of inexpensive financial capital have eliminated the fundamental structural characteristics of disarticulation and dependency.[14]

The new world structure and disarticulated accumulation brought with them continuing setbacks to Latin American agricultural development. On a per capita basis, the levels of agricultural production in the region had not regained their 1934–38 levels by the 1968–72 period. In 1968–72, the FAO index for per capita agricultural production was four points lower than the prewar level, and the per capita food production index was two points below the prewar level.[15] This stagnation led to a growing gap between supply and effective demand, particularly for those crops that were competing with US surpluses disposed of on the world market. Many countries that had been exporters or self-sufficient producers of grains became increasingly dependent on imports. A second consequence of the new world structure and of disarticulated accumulation for Latin American agriculture was a change in the traditional land tenure patterns that led both to the transformation of semifeudal estates into large-scale capitalist commercial farms and to the creation of a labor force of rural semiproletarians. The new tenure pattern was what we have described as functional dualism, and it provided the basis for the cheap labor needed under disarticulated accumulation. The extent and nature of the agricultural stagnation and functional dualism that developed will be considered in the remainder of this chapter.

PATTERNS OF GROWTH AND STAGNATION

At first glance, the growth of Latin American agriculture in the last twenty years appears to have been quite satisfactory. The growth rate of total agricultural production was 2.9 percent per annum from 1955 to 1974. This was higher than both the U.S. and Canadian growth rates, which for the same period were 1.9 percent and 2.1 percent respectively (Table 2.1, col. 1). The production of food expanded in Latin America at the even higher rate of 3.3 percent between 1960 and 1974; this, too, exceeded North America's performance. And the dollar value of agricultural exports tripled during this same period. Yet these growth figures hide a serious economic and social crisis in Latin American agriculture.

The growth of agricultural production actually declined between 1950 and 1973 from a yearly rate of 3.8 percent in 1950-60 to that of 2.7 percent in 1965-1973.[16] This contrasts sharply with the performance of industry, where growth rates were much higher and increased continuously over the same period from 5.5 percent to 7.8 percent. As a result, the agricultural sector's percentage of the domestic product fell in every nation but one, Uruguay.[17] Moreover, Latin America's share of world agricultural trade declined steadily from 20.9 percent in 1950 to 14.3 percent in 1960 and 12.6 percent in 1975.

Because Latin America's demographic growth rate was still the same in 1973 as it had been in 1950—2.8 percent—agricultural production only kept pace with population growth during much of the period and fell below it in 1965-73. On a per capita basis, the growth rate of agricultural production for all of Latin America was exactly zero between 1960 and 1974. It was below population growth in Mexico, the Dominican Republic, El Salvador, Colombia, Peru, and Paraguay (Table 2.1, col. 6). And the growth in food production was inferior to that in domestic demand in eleven of the eighteen major Latin American countries (Table 2.1, col. 7). This deficit is expected to worsen in the years to come: for the period 1970-85, the FAO projects a 2.9 percent annual growth rate in food production, but a 3.6 percent increase in domestic demand.[18]

The balance of agricultural trade was consistently negative in Chile, Venezuela, and Bolivia from 1955-59 to 1970-74. In that same period, it worsened in Chile, Venezuela, Peru, and Mexico. And on a per capita basis, it was positive but declining in Colombia, Ecuador, Peru, the Dominican Republic,

Percent

Countries	Total agriculture		Growth rate			Per capita growth rate, total agriculture (6)	Difference between growth production and domestic demand (7)	Grain dependency ratio (8)	Per capita agricultural trade balance (1957 U.S. $)	
	1955–74 (1)	1960–74 (2)	Total food (3)	Subsistence crops (4)	Export crops (5)				1955–59 (9)	1970–74 (10)
United States	1.9	1.9	2.3	—ᵃ	—	0.7	0.4	-25	—	—
Canada	2.1	2.0	2.1	—	—	0.5	-0.3	-37	—	—
Mexico	3.8	3.2	3.8	2.5	1.5	-0.1	1.0	12	11	6
Dominican Republic	2.2	2.2	2.3	4.0	1.5	-1.0	-1.4	200	57	43
Costa Rica	4.3	4.1	4.5	2.4	4.6	0.8	0.6	92	65	78
El Salvador	3.7	3.0	3.7	5.4	5.0	-0.4	-0.5	16	46	39
Guatemala	6.1	4.8	5.2	3.4	5.0	2.3	-0.1	15	53ᵇ	28
Honduras	3.7	4.4	3.2	1.5	4.4	0.2	-0.2	18	36	34
Nicaragua	5.4	4.3	4.2	4.0	4.3	1.3	1.0	19	42	59
Panama	4.3	4.3	4.5	1.5	3.4	1.5	-0.5	43	9	21
Venezuela	5.5	4.4	4.3	2.4	4.0	1.3	2.1	186	-13	-17
Bolivia	2.6	2.3	1.6	2.0	13.4	0.0	2.3	45	-5	-2
Chile	1.8	2.0	—	0.2	6.1	0.2	-1.1	67	-7	-22
Colombia	3.1	3.0	3.4	2.2	2.8	-0.2	-0.8	16	27	20
Ecuador	3.9	3.6	3.7	4.2	2.6	0.3	1.4	35	27	25
Peru	1.7	0.7	1.7	2.7	-1.1	-2.2	-1.0	75	11	3
Brazil	3.5	3.2	4.2	3.1	2.9	0.4	0.4	9	16	21
Argentina	1.5	1.7	2.0	—	2.3	0.0	-0.2	-45	43	57
Paraguay	1.9	1.9	1.2	0.7	10.2	-0.6	-0.8	25	9	21
Uruguay	0.1	-0.6	0.1	—	4.0	1.7	-0.4	-10	35	44
Latin America (22 countries)	2.9	2.8	3.3	2.8	2.7	0.0	—	1	—	—

Sources: (Col. 1, for 1955–74) U.S. Department of Agriculture, *Agriculture in the Americas: Statistical Data*, FDCD Working Paper (Washington, D.C., 1976), p. 26. (Cols. 2–6, for 1960–74) ibid., pp. 1, 3, 5, 7, and 2, respectively.
(Col. 7, for 1952–72) Food and Agriculture Organization of the United Nations, *Monthly Bulletin of Agricultural Economics and Statistics* 23, no. 9 (September 1974).
(Col. 8, for 1970–75) U.S. Economic Research Service, *Agriculture in the Americas*, p. 76.
(Cols. 9 and 10, for 1955–59 and 1970–74) Food and Agriculture Organization of the United Nations, *Trade Yearbook* (Rome), 1958, 1959, 1961, 1971, and 1975.
ᵃ— = data not available.
ᵇFor 1963–64.

Guatemala, El Salvador, Honduras, and Mexico (Table 2.1, col. 9). As seen in the following figures, food imports to Latin America as a whole accelerated rapidly after the 1950s, but the growth rate of agricultural exports declined:[19]

Latin America: Annual Rate of Growth
of Agricultural Exports and Imports

	1951-61	1961-71	1971-74
Exports	3.2	2.6	1.0
Imports	3.1	6.2	12.3

Dependency on grain imports has increased dramatically. While Latin America as a whole is almost self-sufficient, all countries except Argentina and Uruguay are dependent on grain imports. In 1970-75, grain dependency (as measured by the ratio of net imports to production) was as high as 45 percent in Bolivia, 67 percent in Chile, and 75 percent in Peru; before the 1930s, these countries had been traditional grain exporters (Table 2.1, col. 8). During the same period, the dependency ratio for wheat reached 179 percent in Ecuador, 240 percent in Bolivia, 536 percent in Peru, and 675 percent in Colombia. In the most recent period, the rapid rise in grain prices on the international market has led to substantial strains on the balance of trade, inflationary pressures, and hardship for low-income consumers. For 1985-86, the International Food Policy Research Institute predicts that the grain dependency ratio will rise to 96 percent for Central America (excluding Mexico) and the Caribbean, 160 percent for Ecuador, 217 percent for Venezuela, and 65 percent for the other South American countries (excluding Argentina and Brazil).[20] Argentina's surplus would remain at about 50 percent, while Mexico and Brazil would become grain-exporting countries with a surplus ratio of 6 percent. Already the latter predictions appear highly optimistic.

In recent years, faced with the dilemma of feeding itself and in response to a more favorable domestic price structure, Latin America has dramatically shifted its agricultural production toward grains, but it has failed to measurably curb its growing grain dependency. While only 27 percent of Latin America's arable land was planted in grain in 1948-52, by 1976, 47.4 percent of the arable land was in grains according to the FAO—up from 40 percent in 1970 and 33 percent in 1957-58.[21] This poor production performance occurred in spite of a high degree of underuse of available natural resources—particularly land and water. This observation eliminates the scarcity of natural resources as a potential explanation of stagnation. Thus, the U.S. Department of Agriculture estimated in 1974 that while the ratio of cultivated land to potential cropland area was 80 percent in the United States, it was 63 percent in Mexico, 39 percent in Argentina, 22 percent in Central America, 14 percent in Uruguay and Paraguay, 13 percent in the five Andean countries, 11 percent in Venezuela, and only 10 percent in Brazil.[22]

Water, a key production factor in semiarid areas, is dramatically underused and misused as well. In Peru and Mexico, respectively, only 63 percent and 50 percent of the irrigable land was actually irrigated in 1970. In the other Latin American countries, this percentage was smaller. Considerable production increases could also be obtained through a more rational system of distributing water and a more efficient use of it.[23]

Horizontal expansion remains an important source of output growth, even though it slowed down considerably in most countries after the 1930s. Thus, while agricultural land increased at a rate of 7.4 percent per year between 1900 and 1932 in Argentina, this growth fell to 0.4 percent in the period 1932-64.[24] Similarly, land expansion in Chile fell from a yearly rate of 4.9 percent between 1910 and 1935 to 0.1 percent between 1935 and 1955.[25] Yet for Latin America as a whole, the area in grains production increased by 27 percent between 1950-54 and 1962-64 and again by 24 percent between 1960-64 and 1970-74.[26] Horizontal expansion was still a more important source of output growth than yield increases, for it explained 57 percent and 59 percent of the growth in total grain output in each of these periods. It has been particularly significant in the countries bordering the Amazon basin, where large-scale programs of infrastructure investment have been implemented. In Brazil and Venezuela, respectively, horizontal expansion explained 89 percent and 83 percent of the growth in grain production between 1950-54 and 1970-74. Elsewhere, however, area expansion has been a secondary source of output growth relative to yield increments, particularly in the nations of the Andean and River Plate regions. In these countries the important sources of growth must be land-saving technological changes such as the "Green Revolution" and the development of a land-saving infrastructure, particularly irrigation projects.

While Latin American technological levels are low relative to those of North America or Europe,[27] there has been a rapid increase in the use of modern inputs since 1960. Between 1960 and 1974, for instance, the number of tractors used in agriculture increased at a yearly rate of 8.4 percent. Fertilizer use, possibly the technological input of major consequence for the level of yields,[28] increased at a yearly rate of 14.3 percent between 1962-64 and 1972-73.[29] Yet technological change has been severely biased in three ways: it has benefited principally the medium- and large-scale capitalist producers; it has been applied principally to the production of industrial, export, and luxury crops; and in many countries it has been oriented toward labor-saving techniques (machinery in Colombia, Brazil, and Argentina) rather than land-saving programs and hence yield increases. The result has been a highly *uneven* pattern of growth among crops, farms, and regions.

While the mean growth rate of the production of all agricultural products has been low relative to population and especially to effective demand, there have been substantial differences in the rates of growth of particular crops on particular types of farm and in particular regions (Table 2.2). Consequently, a

Table 2.2. Rate of Growth of Production by Commodity and Country, 1948–52 to 1968–72

Country						Percent					
	Wheat	Rice	Corn	Beans	Manioc	Sugarcane	Coffee	Bananas	Cotton	Meat	Population
Costa Rica	—[a]	4.8	-2.1	3.8	2.2[b]	4.8	6.4	3.4	—	5.4	3.9
Dominican Republic	—	5.4	0.3	1.3	1.1	3.6	2.2	1.4	—	2.9	3.6
El Salvador	—	3.8	2.3	0.3	7.6[b]	4.6	3.1	-2.8	20.9[b]	2.0	2.7
Guatemala	2.3	4.0	2.3	3.9	4.0[b]	8.3	4.1	1.5	19.6[b]	3.1	3.1
Honduras	—	-4.6	2.5	4.4	—	4.4	5.4	2.6	—	1.6	3.0
Mexico	6.9	4.2	4.2	6.6	—	6.2	5.6	5.0	3.0	7.3	3.2
Nicaragua	—	5.4	3.5	3.3	6.4[b]	5.6	3.2	10.9	12.4[b]	6.0	2.9
Panama	—	2.6	0.5	-3.0	-3.0	6.9	3.0	5.3	—	4.7	2.9
Argentina	1.0	4.4	5.1	1.7	-1.4	2.1	—	15.9[b]	-0.2	-0.9	1.5
Bolivia	2.4	6.7	2.8	—	5.4	8.3	6.9[b]	7.5	—	2.2	2.4
Brazil	5.3	4.5	4.4	3.4	4.5	5.0	0.9	5.7	2.4	2.9	3.0
Chile	1.5	-0.2	6.7	-0.2	—	—	—	—	—	0.0	2.4
Colombia	-2.7	6.1	1.0	0.5	2.5	2.3	2.5	4.0	14.8[b]	2.8	3.3
Ecuador	6.0[b]	2.0	5.5	3.1	16.7[b]	7.9	5.8	10.7	5.6[b]	5.1	3.0
Paraguay	19.3[b]	4.8[b]	3.5	2.5	3.1	5.7	—	3.0	-0.8	1.8	2.2
Peru	-0.8	4.7	3.8	4.1	2.3	3.6	13.0[b]	—	1.0	2.9	2.1
Uruguay	-1.5	5.8	-0.5	0.0	3.6	10.0[b]	—	—	—	0.4	1.5
Venezuela	-7.7	8.2	4.2	-1.9	3.6	8.2	1.7	-8.5	6.5[b]	5.4	3.7

Sources: For wheat, rice, corn, beans, manioc, sugarcane, coffee, bananas, and cotton (1948–52), see Food and Agriculture Organization of the United Nations, *Production Yearbook* (Rome), 1971; for meat (1948–52), ibid., 1970.

For wheat, rice, and corn (1968–72), ibid., 1972; for beans and manioc (1968–72), ibid., 1973; for coffee, cotton, and bananas (1968–72), ibid., 1971 and 1972; for sugarcane (1968–72), ibid., 1971 and 1973; and for meat (1968–72), ibid., 1973.

For population (1950–60), see World Bank, *World Bank Tables, 1976* (Baltimore: The Johns Hopkins University Press, 1976).

[a] — = data not available or zero production in either period.
[b] Indicates small-scale production in the base period.

description of agricultural development in Latin America must go beyond a global characterization of stagnation and also account for the existence of these highly uneven performances.

We can observe in Table 2.2 the frequency with which the production growth rates of various commodities equaled or exceeded the population growth rates of Latin American countries during the 1948-52 to 1968-72 period. Accordingly, the commodities can be ranked as follows:[30]

	Frequency with Which Growth Rates in Production Equaled or Exceeded Population Growth Rates
Commodity	*(percentages)*
Sugarcane	94
Rice	78
Coffee	71
Bananas	60
Manioc	60
Cotton	55
Corn	55
Beans	53
Meat	44
Wheat	42

The rate of growth of sugarcane production was systematically high in almost every country. This was also the case for rice. Cotton production grew extremely rapidly in several Central American countries (El Salvador, Guatemala, and Nicaragua) and in Colombia. In contrast, manioc, corn, and beans generally incurred lower growth rates. The poorest performance was clearly that of wheat; while production in Mexico and Brazil increased rapidly, production in Venezuela, Colombia, Uruguay, and Peru actually declined. As for coffee and bananas, production was good, if unstable, during this period.

As seen in Table 2.3, price tendencies were generally exactly the opposite of production tendencies for all crops produced and consumed internally. The real prices of those crops whose rate of production increased fastest (e.g., rice) declined, while the prices of crops whose production rates were most stagnant (e.g., manioc) nearly doubled between 1950 and 1975.

Dynamic crops also tend to be produced on larger farms. This is the case for irrigated rice, cotton, and sugarcane. In Brazil, farms above 20 hectares grow more than half of the bananas, cacao, coffee, rice, sugarcane, corn, soybeans, and wheat produced, while farms under 20 hectares grow more than half of the manioc and bean crops.[31] The contrast in wheat production between Brazil and Colombia is illustrative of the role of large farms. In Brazil, owing to

Table 2.3. Real Price Tendencies (Rate of Change per Year), 1950–70

	Percent							
Crop	Costa Rica[a] (1)	Dominican Republic[b] (2)	El Salvador[c] (3)	Guatemala[d] (4)	Panama[e] (5)	Venezuela[f] (6)	Colombia[g] (7)	Mexico[h] (8)
Rice	−0.5	−0.8	−0.6	−0.9	−0.8	0.1	−1.5	0.0
Corn	0.3	0.2	−2.6	−0.9	1.5	0.2	−0.7	0.9
Beans	0.3	1.6	1.5	1.1	1.0	1.0	−0.5	0.2
Manioc	0.9	2.2	—[i]	1.8	2.6	2.6	2.0	—

Sources: (Col. 1) Dirección General de Estadística y Censo, "Indices de Precios al por Menor," nos. 139–50 (1964); nos. 205–16 (1972).

(Col. 2) Banco Central de la Republica Dominican, Producción y Precios Agrícolas (1975).

(Col. 3) Dirección General de Estadística y Censo, "Boletin Estadístico," no. 60 (1963) and no. 88 (1970).

(Col. 4) Dirección General de Estadística, "Trimestre Estadístico," *Anuario Estadístico, 1970* (1974).

(Col. 5) Dirección de Estadística y Censo, *Panamá en Cifras,* 1970; idem, *Panamá en Cifras,* 1965.

(Col. 6) Ministerio de Agricultura y Cría, Dirección de Economia y Estadística Agropecuario, División de Estadística, *Anuario Estadístico Agropecuario, 1969* (1970); idem, *Anuario Estadístico Agropecuario, 1970* (1971).

(Col. 7) Salomon Kalamanovitz, *Desarrollo de la Agricultura en Colombia* (Bogotá: Editorial la Carreta, 1978); all nominal price tendencies are deflated using the consumer price indices in United Nations, *Statistical Yearbook,* various issues.

(Col. 8) Secretaría de Industria y Comercio, *Anuario Estadístico Compendiado de los Estados Unidos Mexicanos,* 1964; idem, *Anuario Estadístico de los Estados Unidos Mexicanos,* 1970–71.

[a] Consumer prices, 1972/1952.
[b] Farmer prices, 1970–71/1950–51.
[c] Wholesale prices, 1969–70/1953.
[d] Consumer prices, 1970–71/1950–51.
[e] Farmer prices, 1968–69/1960–61.
[f] Wholesale prices, 1969–70/1956–57.
[g] Producer prices, 1970–71/1950–51.
[h] Wholesale prices, 1969–70/1956–57.
[i] — = data not available.

strong protectionism and public subsidies, wheat has been a fast-growing capitalist crop: in 1962–66, 71 percent of the wheat was grown on medium-size and large farms, 72 percent was cultivated mechanically, and fertilizers were used on 70–80 percent of the area planted.[32] In Colombia, wheat has faced highly unfavorable price conditions, largely permitted by Public Law 480 imports, with the result that wheat production has stagnated and been largely relegated to peasant agriculture: only 34 percent of the area planted was cultivated mechanically in 1960; improved varieties and fertilizers were rarely used,[33] and in Cundinamarca—the main wheat-producing state—40 percent of the wheat was grown on farms of less than 10 hectares.[34]

The role of large farms in the production of dynamic crops is generally increasing, and more so where production is increasing fastest. In Colombia, farms over 50 hectares accounted for 39 percent of rice production in 1960 and 50 percent in 1970.[35] In Venezuela the share of farms above 100 hectares

Table 2.4.　Share of Large Farms in Total Production,
and Mean Area Harvested per Farm, 1950–71

Country	Rice	Corn	Beans	Manioc	Coffee	Sugar	Cotton	Bananas	Wheat
Costa Rica									
Share farms > 70 hectares, 1950 (percent)	51	40	37	46	58	48[a]	—[b]	—	—
Share farms > 100 hectares, 1970 (percent)	67	21	13	10	26	57[t]	—	—	—
Mean area, 1950 (hectares)	5.9	5.9	4.8	2.0	6.6	3.6	—	—	—
Mean area, 1970 (hectares)	4.3	1.7	1.4	0.7	2.6	4.1	—	—	—
El Salvador									
Share farms > 100 hectares, 1961 (percent)	17	27	12	—	46[t]	46	69	—	—
Share farms > 100 hectares, 1971 (percent)	28	21	16	—	40[t]	33	73	—	—
Mean area, 1961 (hectares)	0.5	1.7	0.7	—	3.8	26.8	1.4	—	—
Mean area, 1971 (hectares)	0.7	1.7	0.6	—	3.6	21.4	2.1	—	—
Dominican Republic									
Mean area, 1950 (hectares)	1.1	0.5	—	0.3	—	—	—	—	—
Mean area, 1970 (hectares)	2.7	0.8	—	0.6	—	—	—	—	—
Honduras									
Mean area, 1952 (hectares)	0.7	1.6	0.8	—	1.7	—	—	9.1	—
Mean area, 1965 (hectares)	0.7	2.2	1.2	—	3.1	—	—	1.8	—
Panama									
Mean area, 1950 (hectares)	0.9	0.8	0.4	0.3	—	0.7	—	—	—
Mean area, 1960 (hectares)	1.3	1.1	0.5	0.1	—	0.8	—	—	—
Guatemala									
Share farms > 90 hectares, 1950 (percent)	20	18	13	—	94	75[t]	—	—	—
Share farms > 90 hectares, 1964 (percent)	30	15	13	—	87	75[t]	—	—	—
Mean area, 1950 (hectares)	0.7	2.1	1.2	—	—	2.8	—	—	—
Mean area, 1964 (hectares)	1.2	0.9	1.3	—	—	2.2	—	—	—
Venezuela									
Share farms > 100 hectares, 1950 (percent)	50	22	—	—	46[t]	46	69	—	—
Share farms > 100 hectares, 1960 (percent)	55	19	13	14	—	—	—	—	—
Share farms > 100 hectares, 1970 (percent)	70	37	12	11	50[t]	53	73	—	—
Mean area, 1950 (hectares)	2.5	2.3	1.2	1.1	5.4	1.4	26.8	—	—
Mean area, 1970 (hectares)	15.3	4.2	1.7	1.0	5.0	2.1	21.4	—	—
Colombia									
Share farms > 100 hectares, 1959 (percent)	53	21	18	15	9	32	—	8	10

(*continued*)

Table 2.4—*Continued*

Country	Rice	Corn	Beans	Manioc	Coffee	Sugar	Cotton	Bananas	Wheat
Mexico									
Share private farms > 5 hectares, 1960 (percent)	35	43	47	—	62	49	65	—	65
Share private farms > 5 hectares, 1970 (percent)	29	30	33	—	27	—	53	—	67
Share *ejido* sector, 1960 (percent)	63	47	49	—	27	48	35	—	33
Share *ejido* sector, 1960 (percent)	70	64	64	—	72	—	47	—	32

Sources: For Costa Rica, see Dirección General de Estadística y Censos, *Censo Agropecuario de 1950* (San José, 1953); idem, *Censos Nacionales de 1973*, Agropecuario (San José, 1974).

For the Dominican Republic, see Dirección General de Estadística, Oficina Nacional del Censo, *IV. Censo National Agropecuario, 1950*; Secretariado Tecnico de la Presidencia, Oficina Nacional de Estadísitica, *VI. Censo National Agropecuario, 1971*, vol. 1.

For El Salvador, see Dirección General de Estadística y Censos, *Segundo Censo Agropecuario 1961* (San Salvador, 1967); idem, *Tercer Censo Nacional Agropecuario, 1971* (San Salvador, 1975), vol. 2.

For Honduras, see Dirección General de Estadística y Censos, *Primer Censo Agropecuario, 1952* (Tegucigalpa, 1954). idem, *Segundo Censo Nacional Agropecuario, 1965* (Tegucigalpa, 1966).

For Mexico, see Secretaría de Industria y Comercio, Dirección General de Estadística, *IV. Censo Agricola-Ganadero y Ejidal* (Mexico City, 1975); idem, *V. Censos Agricola-Ganadero y Ejidal, 1970* (Mexico City, 1975).

For Panama, see Dirección General de Estadística y Censo, *Censos Nacionales de 1950*, Primer Censo Agropecuario (Panama City, 1957), vol. 1; idem, *Censos Nacionales de 1960*, "Segundo Censo Agropecuario" (Panama City, 1963), vol. 1.

For Colombia, see Departamento Administrativo Nacional de Estadística, *Directorio de Explotaciones, Agropecuarias (Censo Agropecuario), 1960*, "Resumen Nacional," pt. 2.

For Venezuela, see Ministerio de Fomento, Dirección General de Estadística y Censos Nacionales, *Censo Nacional de 1950, II. Censo Agropecuario*, vol. 1; idem, *III. Censo Agropecuario 1961*, "Resumen General de la República," pt. B; idem, *IV. Censo Agropecuario 1971*, "Total Nacional."

[a] Share of total area rather than total production.

[b] — = data not available.

in total rice production increased from 50 percent in 1950 to 70 percent in 1970 (Table 2.4). In the case of relatively stagnant crops like manioc, the role of large farms is unimportant compared to their role in the production of the dynamic crops; however, the role of *small* farms in the production of such crops is increasing. In Venezuela the share of farms above 100 hectares in total manioc production declined from 14 percent to 11 percent between 1960 and 1970. The same pattern was repeated in Mexico. There, between 1960 and 1970 the share of private farms above 5 hectares in total wheat production increased, while the share in corn and beans declined.

Even though the statistics are incomplete, it is evident that capitalist social relations dominate in the production of the dynamic crops. Sugarcane, rice, and bananas tend to be produced on the basis of hired labor, whereas crops like beans and corn, but especially manioc, tend to be produced to a much larger extent by family labor. Thus, in the Dominican Republic, hired labor accounts for 100 percent of the labor used to produce sugarcane, while for rice, corn, and manioc the figures are 80 percent, 44 percent, and 30 percent respectively (Table 2.5, col. 4).

We would note that of the crops that were important for local consumption by urban consumers, those that were not available through P.L. 480, or that were available only at a price that was not much lower than local prices, performed best. Wheat imports competed with national wheat in almost every country except Mexico (until the late 1960s) and Brazil, where producer prices were supported favorably, but this was not so much the case with rice imports, because P.L. 480 rice prices were high. Since P.L. 480 imports were available on much softer terms than were commercial imports, the fact that P.L. 480 rice was relatively expensive protected rice production in Latin America. Balance-of-trade constraints created a preference for wheat and corn rather than rice imports (Table 2.6). For Latin America as a whole, from 1948–52 to 1968–72 the share of wheat imports in total consumption increased from 22 percent to 36 percent, that of corn climbed from 0 percent to 3 percent, while that of rice declined from 8 percent to 4 percent.

Dynamic and stagnant crops can also be characterized from the demand side. Consumer expenditures on specific food items show that wheat and rice tend to be the major staple foods for urban workers, while corn, beans, and manioc are of secondary importance (Table 2.7). Corn, beans, and manioc are, to a significant extent, produced for home consumption. As Table 2.5 shows, for example, in the Dominican Republic only 58 percent of the manioc produced and 72 percent of the corn and bean crops are sold on the market,

Table 2.5. Share of Production Sold and Share of Labor Hired, by Crop

	Percent			
	Share of production sold on the market			Share of labor hired
Crop	Dominican Republic (1)	Costa Rica (2)	Panama (3)	Dominican Republic (4)
Rice	84	95	12	80
Corn	72	67	8	44
Beans	72	59	8	54
Manioc	58	91	—[a]	30
Sugar	100	100	29	100
Coffee	97	100	58	60
Bananas	—	95	56	—

Sources: (Cols. 1 and 4) USAID, Bureau for Latin America, Office of Development Resources, Sector Analysis Division, *Statistical Working Documents*, no. 1 (Santo Domingo, November 1977); ibid., no. 2 (Santo Domingo, 1978).

(Col. 2) Costa Rica, national agricultural census, 1971.

(Col. 3) Panama, national agricultural census, 1950.

[a] — = data not available.

Table 2.6.   Grain Dependency: Share of Imports in Total Consumption, 1948–52 and 1968–72

	Percent					
	Wheat		Corn		Rice	
Country	1948–52	1968–72	1948–52	1968–72	1948–52	1968–72
Costa Rica	100	100	—[a]	29	20	1
Dominican Republic	100	100	0	18	7	0
El Salvador	100	100	5	4	4	0
Guatemala	67	68	0	2	18	0
Honduras	100	100	0	0	31	0
Mexico	40	7	1	2	0	0
Nicaragua	100	100	0	3	0	0
Panama	100	100	—	10	7	2
Argentina	0	0	0	0	0	0
Bolivia	65	74	0	0	31	0
Brazil	70	60	0	0	0	0
Chile	8	25	0	52	0	35
Colombia	28	82	0	0	0	0
Ecuador	64	53	0	—	0	0
Paraguay	100	69	0	0	6	—
Peru	59	85	0	6	7	3
Uruguay	0	12	3	0	0	0
Venezuela	97	100	3	15	7	8

Sources: For trade data, see Food and Agriculture Organization of the United Nations, *Trade Yearbook*, 1959 and 1972. For production data, see Table 2.2 above.

[a] — = data not available.

while the delivery rate rises to 84 percent for rice, 97 percent for coffee, and 100 percent for sugar. The share of foods in the urban wage basket and the share of crops retained for home consumption permit us to establish a contrast between wage foods (rice and wheat) and peasant foods (manioc, beans, and corn), although, of course, the two categories overlap.

Crops can finally be characterized in terms of domestic disappearance versus exports. Thus, we see from Table 2.8 that by 1968–72, coffee, cotton, and bananas had become important export crops and that meat was also being produced increasingly for export. By contrast, wheat, corn, and rice continued to be produced principally for domestic consumption.

Using the above characterizations of the main crops produced in a given area, we can construct a typology of crops in specific countries on the basis of the conditions of supply and demand. Supply is insured through both imports and domestic production. Domestic production originates in capitalist and peasant enterprises, where the differentiating variables are jointly the scale of production and the use of hired labor. This permits us to establish three types of crops on the supply side: crops that are imported, crops that are produced under capitalist conditions, and crops that are produced under peasant conditions. The conditions of demand are set by the geographical locus of disap-

Table 2.7. Share of Selected Foods in the Urban Wage Basket, Selected Years and Countries

Percent

Crop	Costa Rica[a] 1949 (1)	Dominican Republic[b] 1969 (2)	El Salvador[c] 1954 (3)	Guatemala[d] 1946 (4)	Honduras[e] 1950 (5)	Nicaragua[f] 1956 (6)	Panama[g] 1954 (7)	Venezuela[h] 1962 (8)	Colombia[i] 1955 (9)
Wheat	5.4	3.1–1.8	7.7	19.3	12.2	4.6	3.1	5.0	6.9
Rice	3.7	8.4–4.2	3.3	3.6	8.4	4.4	3.6	1.4	3.3
Corn	1.6	2.5–1.1	9.5	9.7	8.4	4.6	0.3	1.1	1.6
Beans	2.4	3.1–1.8	3.5	5.7	4.0	3.2	0.5	1.1	0.5
Manioc	0.4	0.5–0.3	—[j]	—	0.7	—	0.3	0.2	—

Sources: (Col. 1) Direccion General Estadistica y Censos, *Ingresos y Gastos de las Familias la la Ciudad de San José*, encuesta de 1949.
(Col. 2) Banco Central de la Republica Dominicana, *Estudio Sobre Presupuestos Familiares*, 1969, vol. 2.
(Col. 3) Direccion General de Estadistica y Censos, *Costo y Condiciones de Vida en San Salvador*, 1954.
(Col. 4, 5, 6, and 9) Inter-American Statistical Institute, *Metodologia*, 1964.
(Col. 7) *Estudio de los Ingresos, Gastos, y Costo de Vida, Ciudad de Panama, 1952–53*, 2nd ed. rev.
(Col. 8) Oficina Central de Planificacion, *Primera Encuesta Nacional de Ingresos y Gastos Familiares en Venezuela*, doc. 7, vol. 1.

[a] All families in the city of San José; total budget.
[b] Family income levels under $50 and between $200 and $300; total budget.
[c] Workers' families in the city of San Salvador; total budget.
[d] All consumers in Guatemala City; total consumption.
[e] Moderate income; total consumption.
[f] Workers' families; total budget.
[g] All families in Panama City; weights in the Consumer Price Index.
[h] All families in Caracas; total consumption.
[i] Workers' families; total consumption.
[j] — = data not available.

79

Table 2.8. Share of Exports in Total Production, 1948–52 and 1968–72

Percent

Country	Wheat 1948–52	Wheat 1968–72	Corn 1948–52	Corn 1968–72	Rice 1948–52	Rice 1968–72	Coffee 1948–52	Coffee 1968–72	Bananas 1948–52	Bananas 1968–72	Sugarcane[a] 1948–52	Sugarcane[a] 1968–72	Cotton 1948–52	Cotton 1968–72	Meat 1948–52	Meat 1968–72
Costa Rica	—[b]	—	0	2	0	1	83	89	58	78	6	33	—	80	—	35
Dominican Republic	—	—	48	0	0	0	59	58	18	3	96	88	0	0	9	13
El Salvador	—	0	0	5	4	15	89	79	—	11	8	43	45	81	—	0
Guatemala	—	—	0	0	0	5	93	78	88	57	0	22	0	86	3	20
Haiti	—	—	1	—	0	0	77	65	10	0	6	6	70	—	—	3
Honduras	0	4	0	6	0	0	48	73	46	70	0	6	—	68	—	33
Mexico	—	—	8	5	12	3	73	51	19	0	6	17	67	64	2	4
Nicaragua	—	—	—	3	20	9	75	83	100	22	10	34	50	100	0	31
Panama	—	—	38	—	0	0	0	20	57	62	5	33	0	—	—	5
Argentina	36	32	0	55	3	21	—	—	0	—	0	10	16	0	12	25
Bolivia	0	0	2	0	0	0	—	3	0	0	0	5	0	22	—	0
Brazil	0	0	0	7	4	1	94	83	8	3	3	14	35	48	1	5
Chile	0	0	0	0	5	0	—	—	—	—	—	—	0	0	—	0
Colombia	0	0	0	1	1	1	87	68	38	37	2	11	0	43	—	2
Ecuador	—	0	0	0	33	0	82	74	60	48	0	9	0	—	1	—
Paraguay	—	—	0	4	0	0	0	40	1	0	59	3	62	64	—	8
Peru	0	0	0	0	0	0	17	69	—	0	—	47	80	71	0	—
Uruguay	25	9	1	—	24	40	—	—	—	—	0	—	0	—	18	30
Venezuela	—	0	0	—	0	0	57	28	2	2	0	12	0	—	0	0

Sources: For production data, see Food and Agriculture Organization of the United Nations, *Production Yearbook*, 1970–73. For trade data, see idem. *Trade Yearbook*, 1959 and 1972.

[a] Assuming that sugarcane yields sugar at a 10 percent conversion rate.

[b] — = data not available.

pearance (domestic use versus exports); the weight of the crop in the consumer price index (high for wage foods; low for industrial crops, luxury foods, peasant foods, and exports); and the share of the crop marketed (low for peasant foods). This permits us to establish four major categories of crops on the demand side—peasant foods, wage foods, industrial and luxury crops, and exports.

Crossing the conditions of supply and demand thus permits us to identify situations in which the evolution of production and price are markedly different. Clearly, there is tremendous unevenness among countries, and each crop would need to be classified specifically for each country. Yet some general patterns do emerge from the data we have reviewed here. Imported wage foods have generally offset stagnant domestic production and have been low priced (wheat, excluding Mexico and Brazil); wage foods (rice and sugar) and industrial inputs and luxuries (cotton and beef) produced under capitalist conditions have been dynamic, with decreasing prices; peasant-produced wage foods (corn and beans) and peasant foods (manioc and sweet potatoes) have generally stagnated and evidenced increasing domestic prices; export crops produced both on capitalist farms (cotton, bananas, sugar, and beef) and on peasant farms (coffee, cocoa, and tobacco) have generally undergone favorable, although unstable, growth and pricing.

Latin American agriculture has thus been characterized by a sharp unevenness in the growth of production among crops, farms, and regions and by global stagnation relative to industrial growth and to effective demand. A number of competing explanations of these phenomena have been provided. We will discuss them and provide an alternative interpretation in Chapter 4. In the meantime, we turn to the social aspects of the agrarian crisis in Latin America.

THE RISE AND LOGIC OF FUNCTIONAL DUALISM

As mentioned earlier, the hacienda system of production became the basic agrarian tenure institution during the colonial period in Latin America in response to the demographic catastrophe caused by colonization. Slavery, an alternative social relation, was successfully used to overcome the constraint of scarce labor in plantation areas. However, the spread of the ideology of economic liberalism in the second half of the nineteenth century, combined with the increasing economic disfunctionality of slavery, brought pressures to legally prohibit this form of coercive exploitation. For example, slavery was formally abolished in Brazil in 1888. In the twentieth century the hacienda system also began to crumble under the combined forces of the development of capitalism, revolutionary peasant upheavals, and reformist state policies. The decay of these social relations of agricultural production in Latin America coincided with the appearance of a large sector of smallholding peasant producers.

Smallholder settlements first developed in many areas from the fragmentation-by-inheritance of the smaller farms and haciendas. Internal migration and colonization by smallholding agricultural producers also occurred in response to domestic demand for food products. But it was when commercial penetration of rural areas became more widespread and the basic infrastructure for capitalist production (e.g., transport) became more readily available that the peasant sector increased significantly as the haciendas expropriated internal peasants and established capitalist social relations.[36] However, it was not until labor scarcity fully disappeared that the coercive forms of labor bondage were eliminated. As Pearce observed, "In most countries [of Latin America] a crucial moment was reached in the third or fourth decade of this century when the supply of free available labor caught up with and overtook the demand and the market replaced coercion and the squeeze on subsistence lands."[37] Thus, a profound process of transformation of Latin America's agrarian structure was initiated. Feudal social relations were rapidly eliminated; internal peasants were expelled from the haciendas and hired as wage workers; semiproletarianization and functional dualism between capitalist and peasant agriculture became the dominant pattern of social relations; and a landless rural proletariat began to emerge in the areas most closely integrated with multinational agribusiness.

The changes in the class structure and types of farm enterprises that occurred in Latin America, as well as the role of the state in this process of transformation, are described in detail in the following chapters. What we analyze here are the logic of functional dualism as a type of social relation and the associated contradictions that characterize it and, at the same time, in our opinion, negate its sustained reproduction over time.

As mentioned before, the social relations in Latin American agriculture have been directed at assuring cheap labor to satisfy the exigencies of disarticulated accumulation. These relations have included, over time, slavery, servile labor, and semiproletarian and proletarian labor. Each of these types of social relations has a logic that corresponds to particular economic and ideological conditions.

When a slave is a scarce good, the minimum cost of his reproduction is a fixed quantity independent of his work. He cannot be overexploited, because the possibilities of replacing him are limited. Conditions that will allow for recovery from the wear of his work efforts must be provided, and he must be supported during periods of idleness and sickness. Only when the supply of slaves is highly elastic and their price is low is overexploitation possible, and it results in early exhaustion through death or incapacitation. But this condition never evolved in Latin America, where slavery consequently assumed relatively paternalistic forms.

With the elimination of slavery and the *encomienda*, servile social relations became an alternative effective means of capturing labor at low cost. This system was established through a variety of processes, including free sharecroppers falling into debt and consequently having to provide labor services to landlords (Chile)[38] and Indian communities being trapped within haciendas on a land basis that prevented them from subsisting on their own (Bolivia).[39] Under this system, the laborer receives in payment for his work the usufruct of a patch of land, some consumption goods, and a small amount of cash. For the employer, the cost of servile labor power is less than the price of labor power, even for mere subsistence, because the opportunity cost of the land given in usufruct to the worker is less than the value of production the laborer can generate on it through use of family labor. Thus, the cost incurred is less than the price of labor power by an amount equal to the net between the value of production on the land plot and the opportunity of this plot for the landlord.[40] This difference can be very large: on the one hand, the land of the *latifundio* is used extensively and consequently its opportunity cost is low; on the other hand, the value of production per hectare on the serf's plot can be extremely high since, as a captive of the *latifundio,* family labor power has an opportunity cost of nearly zero. The fact that the price of labor power can be maintained at the cost of subsistence—even when the worker's opportunity cost is higher in the rest of the economy—results from a set of legal and traditional measures that are an integral part of the effectiveness of precapitalist relations of production in gaining individual control over laborers and in tying them to the land. Relative to slavery, servitude already permits a better relating of labor costs to work effort. While the land plot is a fixed component of labor cost, the payments in kind and cash are directly related to the work effort. In periods of sickness, reproduction, or reduced labor needs, these costs need not be incurred.

The salaried labor of "free semiproletarians" settled on subsistence plots outside the *latifundio*—the *minifundistas*—constitutes a source of labor power that can be still cheaper for the landlord than servile labor. In this case two advantages are secured: the possibility of exploiting family labor on subsistence plots that cost the employer nothing and the possibility of paying the worker for his effective labor only when it is needed. On the average the price of labor power will be the difference between the cost of subsistence for the worker and his family and the production of use values or petty commodities that can be obtained from the land plot. Use of labor is now fully flexible, for it will be paid only for work that is strictly necessary in conditions of needs that fluctuate between seasons and between years according to the climate and the market. Labor costs are thus transformed from fixed to variable.

Clearly, free semiproletarian labor can be used at this cost only when the whole economy enters into conditions of surplus labor and when the state is able to exercise disciplinary control over the labor force on behalf of the landlords.[41] Servile relations of production, with labor tied to the land—what Engels called "the second slavery"—are an effective means of reducing the price of labor power as long as there is labor scarcity in the economy and as long as labor-force discipline must be exercised by individual landlords. Once marginality is rampant and once the state assumes its disciplinary functions, servitude loses economic and political rationality; then free semiproletarian workers gradually dominate.

Proletarianization of free labor thus came to characterize the social relations of production in agriculture as capitalism developed in both center and periphery. For the center, however, full proletarianization of the labor force implies that the level of wages (direct wage payments plus indirect payments through social security and public transfers that constitute a social wage) must be sufficient to at least cover the subsistence needs of the worker and his family in order to insure maintenance and reproduction of the labor force, even though wages are paid by employers only for time actually worked. In the periphery, by contrast, semiproletarianization permits the wages paid to be far below the price of labor power. The peasant economy and the informal urban sectors are thus important sources of subsidies for the modern capitalist sector.

With the peasantry thus established under capitalism as a readily available source of semiproletarian labor, the agricultural sector of Latin America is characterized by a *functional dualism* that emerged between the capitalist sector, which produces commodities (on capitalist *latifundio* and commercial farms) on the basis of hired semiproletarian labor, and the peasant sector, which produces use values and petty commodities on the basis of family labor and delivers cheap wage labor to the capitalist sector. As we saw, the creation of this dualism can be explained by the peculiar contradictions of disarticulated accumulation.

In the central economies—characterized by social articulation—the freeing of labor serves the double purpose of providing the basis of relative surplus value and its transformation into profit through realization in an expanding market for wage goods. In the periphery, proletarianization also provides the basis for profits, but due to social disarticulation, realization of the value of commodities does not depend appreciably on the level of workers' wages. Hence, whenever possible, as in agriculture and the informal urban sector, subsistence economies will be maintained as long as they allow the further lowering of labor costs. Whereas the fully proletarianized worker loses both control of the production process and ownership of the means of production, the semiproletarianized worker maintains these two forms of control. Because semiproletarians seek to protect this control, they compete fiercely on the labor market and accept wages below the price of subsistence. In the product market, they compete against commercial farmers, who employ their own semiproletarian labor. Thus, in the periphery, the freeing of labor power in an agrarian structure characterized by functional dualism provides the cheap labor and cheap food that increase the level of exploitation of labor in the modern sector to heights that eventually exceed those in the center. The capitalist agriculture-peasant sector binomial is the structural reflection of the rationality of peripheral accumulation. It temporarily constitutes a functional system that symptomizes and embodies the contradictions of peripheral capitalism. Yet as we will see, these contradictions are at the very basis of the negation of its reproduction over time.

THE CONTRADICTIONS OF FUNCTIONAL DUALISM

Functional dualism between peasant and commercial sectors in Latin American agriculture implies the increasing proletarianization and impoverishment of the rural masses. As the domination of capital over the peasantry increases, the struggle for survival induces not only a fierce competition for wages and product sales among peasants but also an intense search by peasants for additional productive resources (land and labor power) in order to increase the productivity of labor. And as we will see, this search is largely contradictory, for the very instruments of survival available to peasants turn out to be factors of destruction of the peasantry in the longer run.

In absolute terms the dimensions of rural poverty are staggering. According to a 1966 ECLA study, at least 60 percent of the rural households earned less than $300 per annum.[42] This implied an annual per capita of less than $60 for some 60–70 million people, an income level that ECLA considered to be at the margin of survival. Similarly, in 1975 the World Bank found that 50 million rural inhabitants—representing 42 percent of the total rural population—had per capita incomes under $75 per year.[43] In 1978, ECLA again estimated that 62 percent of the rural households in Latin America could not satisfy minimum basic needs.[44] And there is evidence that in most countries the absolute income levels of poor peasants have remained virtually unchanged or have worsened in the last two decades.[45] In El Salvador, for example, the real income of 75 percent of the rural population (who control less than 1 hectare of land per family) decreased by 25 percent between 1961 and 1975, while the rest of the rural population registered positive increases in real income.[46] For Guatemala and Ecuador, Griffin observes that the income level and consumption of the rural poor deteriorated during the 1960s.[47] Webb estimates that 15–25 percent of the poorest in Peru (principally small peasants) have seen no absolute improvement in their living standards.[48] And for Colombia, Berry and Urrutia calculate that in the rural areas, "real daily wage rates appear to have been about the same in the latter part of the 1960's as they were in the mid-1930's."[49] Griffin thus concludes his survey of poverty in Latin America by stating that "significant groups of the rural population, notably small farmers and landless workers, either have experienced no increase in their material well-being or have suffered some decline."[50] As for the distribution of income in Latin American agriculture, it is clear that it is extremely unequal, more unequal than that in the urban sector (except in Brazil), and becoming more regressive over time.[51]

The magnitude of rural poverty is best perceived by putting together its multiple symptoms in particular areas. Consider, for example, northeastern Brazil and Honduras—two areas where peasants constitute a majority of the population. A 1974 World Bank study of northeastern Brazil showed that (1) 90 percent of rural households earned less than the legal minimum salary of $50 per month; (2) more than 20 percent of the labor force was openly unemployed; (3) average life expectancy was only twenty-seven years; (4) among rural families, 50 percent of the children died before the age of five (and nearly 70 percent of these deaths were related to malnutrition), 95 percent of the heads of family had never been to school, 30 percent spent more than half of their cash incomes on medicines, and 80 percent were hopelessly indebted; and (5) absolute rural poverty had increased between 1960 and 1970.[52] In the rural sector of Honduras, in the early 1970s, 80 percent of the population was illiterate; 70 percent of the dwellings were below minimum acceptable standards; and annual per capita income was $100, although 65 percent of the agricultural population earned an average of $40 per year. In the country as a whole, 90 percent of the children under the age of five were undernourished—45 percent were at the first-degree level of malnutrition.[53]

The determinants of such extreme poverty as that described above reside in the contradictions of disarticulated accumulation and functional dualism. Although the semiproletarianization of an independent peasantry is functional in sustaining peripheral accumulation, it is accompanied by a collapse of the resource base controlled by peasants and by ecological and demographic contradictions that cumulatively deepen the development of underdevelopment in peasant agriculture. It is these objective contradictions that negate the perpetuation of primitive accumulation on the basis of cheap labor and cheap food delivered by peasants.

To address the ecological contradiction of functional dualism, it should first be recalled that the peasant sector has always been established on a very precarious productive base. Grabbing of the land by commercial and plantation agriculture has relegated peasant agriculture to the least-fertile and most easily destroyed lands. In addition, technological innovations have not been available for this type of agriculture: research has concentrated on cash crops or on food crops produced under commercial conditions. Virtually no research has been done on the production conditions that characterize peasant agriculture—e.g., on intercropping instead of sequential crop rotations, manual instead of mechanical cultivation, organic and biological fertilization and pest control instead of chemical, production systems that allow for high-risk aversion and balanced nutritional needs, and use of plant residues as animal feed or fuel. Furthermore, marginalization from the institutions that distribute credit, information, and education limits the diffusion of techniques that might improve the productive base of peasants. Poor land and backward technology thus result in low yields and low productivity.

The most immediately obvious contradiction into which poverty forces peasant agriculture is the destruction of the few productive resources at the peasants' disposal. As poverty increases, the subjective rate of discount for time also increases, and more intensive use of available resources is immediately necessary. The land is mined; its fertility declines. Lower yields imply growing poverty, which in turn forces more mining of the land. The search for land and energy implies rapid deforestation, and erosion increases. The resource base is gradually destroyed, and poverty progresses. In many areas of Latin America, destruction of the land and deforestation are already irreversibly advanced.[54] In Mexico, for example, it is estimated that 15 percent of the agricultural land has been totally lost to erosion, 26 percent is highly advanced in this process of destruction, and another 24 percent is in the initial stages of deterioration.

A more insidious but equally dramatic contradiction into which peasant agriculture is pushed relates to population growth. Clearly, the population explosion in the Third World has been identified as one of the most antagonistically contradictory aspects of development. Recent estimates show that population in Latin America grows at a yearly rate of about 2.5 percent, which implies a doubling of the population every twenty-eight years.[55] The population growth rates of thirteen Latin American countries are among the highest in the world.[56] Demographic growth is highest in those countries with high shares of population in rural areas. Of those countries with growth rates below 2 percent, only Cuba has more than 25 percent of its population in rural areas. In some countries with large rural populations, growth rates are below 3 percent only because the poverty levels are so pronounced that death rates are relatively higher there than in other countries. This applies to Haiti, Guatemala, Paraguay, and Bolivia.

While numerous family-planning programs have been implemented in the last two decades, their impact has been remarkably insignificant. In large part this is due to the failure to tailor these programs to the specific logic of the division of labor by sex and to the individual rationality of couples in the peasant sector of a disarticulated economy. Failure to conceptualize these conditions underlies severe misunderstandings of the population question and failure of population programs.

The explanation of the population explosion must be traced first to the survival strategies of peasant households and, in particular, to the division of labor by sex and age, which is markedly different in socially articulated and disarticulated economies. In the central economy, an important number of women participate in the labor market. In the United States, for example, about two fifths of the labor force is composed of women; and the wages women receive average only three fifths of male workers' earnings.[57] Exploitation of women as production agents thus exists in the central economy, but the principal aspect of their subordination to the needs of advanced capitalism lies not in this context. It is found in the role of women as consumption agents. Continued accumulation in the center is conditioned by sustained expansion of demand for industrial goods by the working classes. With men confined to the production of commodities for a major part of the day, the responsibility for managing consumption accrues largely to women. The alienation of women under advanced capitalism originates principally in their forced function as transformers of commodities into use values.

In the central economy, children are essentially consumption items for their parents.[58] For this reason, the Chicago School's theory of fertility argues that the process of decision making regarding family size is essentially the same as consumer rationality in the purchase of durable goods.[59] However, it is generally observed that family size is smaller in the more affluent countries and families—a relation which tends to contradict standard theory unless one makes the unpalatable assumption that children are inferior goods. A decline in fertility as income increases can, however, be explained by the fact that as income rises, (1) increasing substitution is made of children by other consumption goods and services and of quantity of children by quality of children, and (2) the increasing opportunity cost of time for parents takes them away from bearing and rearing children. As a result, factors such as the rise in education of women, urbanization, improvements in women's rights, the decline of the extended family system, increases in socioeconomic and geographical mobility, and the introduction of superior chemical and mechanical contraceptives are repeatedly found to be strong determinants of the fall in fertility in developed economies. In the United States, completed family size has decreased steadily with economic progress to a level that is now compatible with zero population growth.

In the peasant sector of the peripheral economy, the division of labor by sex is between production of commodities and production of use values, in contrast to the center, where it is primarily between production and consumption functions. Thus, by contrast, rural women's subordination in the periphery originates in their role as production agents of use values and petty commodities to cheapen semiproletarian male labor—not in their role as consumption agents. Exploitation of women in the periphery often manifests itself in brutal forms, for women assume an enormous number of physically demanding tasks to be carried out under highly primitive conditions—caring for the animals, preparing food, rearing and feeding children, tending the dwelling, going to the market, and in many cases also cultivating the subsistence plot. As CIDA observes, "Intense work wears her out to the point of exhaustion. At an early age, she appears old and weary."[60] Children are needed to assist her with the work, which is highly labor intensive and which can be performed only by family labor, for only family labor can be overexploited to the necessary degree. In coincidence with the role of women, children are thus raised as production and protection agents and are incorporated into the labor process of the *minifundio* at an early age.[61] As a result, Mamdani correctly observed in contrast to conventional wisdom, "People are not poor because they have large families. Quite the contrary: they have large families because they are poor."[62]

The fact that fertility rates in rural areas of Latin America are high is incontrovertible. Indeed, rural populations in Latin America tend to demonstrate patterns of maximum biological reproduction throughout the reproductive years.[63] Marriages occur at an early age (the median age of the first union in rural areas is 17.4 years in Costa Rica and 16.5 years in Mexico) and large families are achieved (the average is 8.6 children by the age of thirty-four in Costa Rica and 8 children by the age of thirty-five in Mexico). There is also a marked difference in patterns of fertility between rural and urban Latin America. For example, in Chile the fertility rate in rural areas of the central valley (Colima) is 97 percent higher than the national average.[64] In Colombia it is 61 percent higher in rural areas than in urban areas.[65] And demographic explosion in the rural areas specifically originates among peasants: in Mexico the number of live births per woman legally married or in consensual union is 3.5 for white-collar workers, 4.6 for blue-collar workers in the capital city, and 4.5 in commerical agriculture as compared with 8.0 in peasant agriculture in the rural area of Pabellón.[66] The pattern is also robust over time. In Colombia, for example, while urban fertility declined 24 percent between 1960–64 and 1967–68, rural fertility declined only 6 percent during the same period.[67]

The point of departure toward an explanation of this fertility behavior among peasants is the well-evidenced observation that most couples, however primitive the conditions under which they live, are individually rational in adjusting the number of children they have to the economic, political, juridical, and ideological conditions of their lives.[68] Among these conditions, the economic structure ultimately tends to be the major determinant of behavior, especially at low-income levels. The degree of efficiency in applying this rationality to family size is conditioned by the use-effectiveness of the means of contraception available to individual couples. Family-planning programs often succeed merely in inducing those couples already practicing birth control to switch to more efficient modern methods, and thus have only a minor overall effect on family size.

Individual economic rationality does not exist in the abstract—it is conditioned by the social position of the household relative to productive resources and to the social division of labor. It is also conditioned by the absolute income level relative to the consumption and security needs of the couple. In peasant agriculture, poverty implies pressure to seek control over additional productive resources. Since producing children is often the only means whereby peasants can secure access to additional resources, more children are raised in order to increase the labor applied to a fixed piece of land so that it will not fall below subsistence level. As the impoverished peasants of the Sierra in the Dominican Republic put it, "Every child is born to the world with a loaf of bread under his arm." It is thus the farmers with the least land who need the most children.[69] Even limited improvements, such as raising a goat or a pig (animals are the savings accounts of peasants), imply the need for additional child labor. And the valuation of child labor is most often determined by the substitution that takes place between adult and child labor, the resulting freeing of parental time, and the opportunity cost of this time on the farm plot or the labor market. As for tenants, the more hands a family can muster, the more land it can contract from the landlords. In this process, all but the very young and the very old make some productive contribution to the economy of the household.

Children also provide a protective function by defending scarce productive resources in a highly competitive environment and by providing parents with security against health hazards, disability, and old age needs; against unemployment; and against structural and economic changes to which the work process has to be adjusted when parents may not have the needed flexibility to do so.

Clearly, the organization of production varies with farm size, and for this reason so do the productive and protective functions of children. On larger farms the productive role of children is reduced because nonfamily labor is employed, labor-saving machinery is used, the nature of the tasks performed is more complex and physically demanding, etc. Greater access to credit, information, and protective institutions in general, which is invariably associated with farm size, reduces the social security function of children. Better standards of living for children and school attendance increase maintenance costs. As a result, *ceteris paribus*, larger farms tend to be associated with smaller family size.

Even with widespread surplus labor in peasant agriculture, the return from additional children as production agents is positive, although it decreases with family size. This is due to the fact that family labor can be overexploited to a far greater degree than labor hired from outside the family unit to meet the peasant household's labor needs. Since increasing poverty leads to the dual need of generating more productive resources and increasing the degree of overexploitation of labor, both inexorably imply having more children. But what are the conditions that permit greater overexploitation of family labor than of hired labor? One such situation is that where labor available for hire is fully proletarianized. In this case the wage paid has to compensate the worker for production and reproduction of labor power; that is, it must cover both his and his family's subsistence needs. Clearly, in this case, family labor is cheaper since only the survival cost of the laborer himself needs to be covered. But this is not the characteristic situation in rural Latin America, where labor is largely semiproletarian. In this case, then, why is family labor cheaper than labor that is available for hire and that also has part of its production and reproduction covered in the subsistence economy? Anthropological information on the subsistence sector in Latin America is largely unavailable at the present time, but existing knowledge suggests that the total claim of the family on the lives of its children until adulthood severely limits the existence of a labor market for rural children and hence alienates children from capturing their own potential opportunity costs outside the family enterprise.

As poverty increases, however, children are induced earlier to capture their opportunity costs by migrating away from the family. And as the migration age decreases, procreation of children is needed to maintain a constant stock of working children—a stock which itself needs to increase with poverty. Even though children cease to perform a production function when they migrate, they continue to insure protection by supplying material support to their parents when possible. Thus, while the private cost of a migrated child is zero, the return is by no means negligible. Through migration, optimum family size in the peasant sector is brought yet closer to biological maximum.

It is clear, as we saw in Chapter 1, that massive migrations toward the urban sector have occurred since the 1950s in spite of mounting urban unemployment. CIDA estimated that between 1950 and 1960, net rural-urban migration was, as a percentage of total rural population in 1950, 3.6 percent in Guatemala, 13.6 percent in Peru, 16.6 percent in Colombia, 17.0 percent in Ecuador, 19.0 percent in Brazil, 24.9 percent in Argentina, and 29.0 percent in Chile.[70] However, employment opportunities have not increased at nearly the rate that migrations have occurred. For example, in the Latin American industrial sector, the increase in production was three times greater than the increase in employment opportunities in the period 1950-65.[71] In fact, the estimated rate of unemployment increased steadily from 7 percent in 1955 to 11 percent in 1965 and 13 percent in 1975.[72] Most of the rural migrants therefore fell into extremely precarious service-sector employment and subsistence activities in the informal sector.

The demographic contradiction that propels population growth, the collapse of peasant agriculture, and migration also has a qualitative dimension relative to society's ability to provide for the adequate development of the bodies and minds of children raised in the peasant sector. We have seen that more poverty implies the private need for more children, but it is also true that more children imply the social cost of more poverty. Under disarticulated accumulation, where provision of basic necessities is not an objective requirement for uninterrupted accumulation of capital, rapid demographic growth is accompanied by continually precarious levels of living. This is particularly visible in the levels of health and education of the rural poor. Together, insufficient sanitation and malnutrition in rural areas undermine prospects for health; and even where free education is available, the cost of education is high to the peasant households in terms of forgone revenue.

At the level of society, supplies of food are adequate; the average availability of calories per person is about 2,570 per day in Latin America as a whole. However, extreme inequality in the distribution of income implies that 32 percent of the population in the highest income group has the luxury of being wasteful (with an estimated consumption of over 3,500 calories per person per day), while the 23 percent having the lowest incomes suffer from serious malnutrition (probably consuming fewer than 1,600 calories per day).[73]

Malnutrition is particularly devastating for children because of its irreversible consequences on them. According to Monckeberg's 1966 studies of infant malnutrition in villages of the central valley of Chile, 20 percent of the infants and preschool children under six years of age were affected by serious malnutrition.[74] Furthermore, a longitudinal study of severely malnourished Chilean infants indicated that although these children recovered from the physical retardation by age six, mental retardation due to nutrition-related brain damage was permanent.[75] In the rural areas of Mexico, only one of every five children is of normal weight and height.[76]

The joint consequences of poor nutrition and sanitation show up particularly in data on causes of death. In ten Latin American countries surveyed by the United Nations, enteritis and other diarrheal diseases were among the top three causes of death—a phenomenon which does not occur in situations where sanitation and water systems are adequate. The relatively high levels of death by infectious and parasitic diseases can also be attributed to the synergism of malnutrition and poor sanitation. In 1971, Mexico, with around one fourth the population of the United States, had a little over six times the number of deaths attributable to these causes; Colombia, whose population was approximately one tenth that of the United States, had double the number of these deaths; and Peru, with about one fifteenth the U.S. population, had two thirds again the number of deaths from these causes.[77]

As one might expect, children are the principal victims of these deplorable living conditions. In every Latin American country the death rate of children under five years of age is at least double that in the United States, and in eight Latin American countries it is more than four times as great. While in the United States the typical childhood diseases account for 52.2 percent of the deaths of children under five, in Latin America substantially more of the deaths are attributed to gastrointestinal disease, influenza, and pneumonia—all of which may be traced directly to food and environmental deficiencies.

Because the labor processes in which semiproletarian peasants are involved—both on the home plot and on the labor market—tend to be highly routinized, the returns from formal education are extremely low and quickly fall below opportunity cost. Even when education is compulsory, large numbers of children in the peasant sector do not attend school and thus remain illiterate—this in response to the strictly rational individual economic behavior of parents. As these children later migrate, their absorption into the urban labor force will place them among the ranks of the least qualified. At still higher levels of poverty health and nutrition interfere with the ability of children to benefit from what education they receive and thereby impair the qualitative reproduction of labor power.

The data indicate that Latin America is plagued by high rates of illiteracy and an inadequate and ineffective rural educational system. For a large percentage of the countries of Latin America, rural illiteracy runs from 30 percent to 50 percent of the population and is occasionally even worse.[78] School attendance declines radically after the first or second year of studies, reflecting the inability of the school system to retain students in the face of economic rationality that draws them into the work force at an early age.

In summary, it has been shown that under functional dualism, sheer individual economic rationality in reacting to the pressures of poverty leads to quantitative and qualitative demographic contradictions that reinforce ecological contradictions and reproduce conditions of impoverishment and misery in rural areas. These demographic contradictions characterize the social costs of the massive exploitation and gradual elimination of peasant producers in Latin America.

3

━━━━━

Transformation
of the Agrarian Structure
and the Peasantry

━━━━━

To analyze the agrarian structure and its transformation in the postwar period through the combined forces of the development of capitalism and public reforms, we must develop a typology of farm enterprises based on the concepts of mode of production, articulation of modes of production within a specific historical social formation, and social classes within modes of production.[1] Doing this inevitably draws us into the thorny controversy over the empirical use of the concepts of modes and classes. It also implies taking sides in the active debate on the appropriate characterization of peasants: who they are, how they behave economically and politically, and whether they will disappear or remain as a social category. Answers to these questions are directly conditioned by whether or not peasants are considered to constitute a specific mode of production. The debate on the empirical use of the concept of mode is therefore more than semantic. It is only after we localize peasants in particular modes of production that we can appropriately characterize their class position, derive their economic and political rationality, and make inferences about their permanence or transformation as capitalism develops.

In the previous chapter the development of capitalism in agriculture was analyzed with respect to the changing nature of the social relations of production in agriculture. We argued that these changes were fundamentally guided by the continuous quest for cheap labor under disarticulated accumulation as economic, demographic, and political conditions were evolving. With this in mind, we raise here the question of whether or not peasants can be conceptualized as pertaining to a specific peasant mode of production, and we follow the implications of alternative answers to this question. From there, the nature of the development of capitalism in agriculture can be established and the corresponding social classes identified. A typology of farms is thus obtained which is translated into empirical categories. Some examples of changing land tenure patterns and other indicators of the development of capitalism are then given. The central thesis of this chapter is that Latin American agriculture today is no longer feudal and that the present class structure, including the social position of peasants, must be understood in terms of both the capitalist mode of production and the particular historical forms of the development of capitalism in the periphery.

THE NATURE AND FUTURE OF THE PEASANTRY

In spite of massive rural-urban migrations during the last thirty years, large numbers of peasants still exist in most countries of both the center and the periphery. In recent years, recognition of the significant role of peasants in political struggles since World War II and of their contributions to the production of low-cost wage foods and to the reproduction of the labor force has led to the rediscovery of their political and economic importance. The consequence has been the reopening of an active debate on peasants which has been of very much the same nature as the debate between Russian Narodniks and Bolsheviks and that within the German Social Democratic party in the late nineteenth and early twentieth centuries. The debate centers on the nature and future of the peasantry: Who are the peasants? What is their economic logic? What political attitudes do they assume? What is their role in food production, and how do they respond to programs of modernization? Are they disappearing as a social group or, as capitalism develops, are they remaining by assuming a logical function within the new economic system? Resolution of this debate is important for the purpose of our study because it will permit us to (1) classify peasants in Latin American society according to mode of production and social class location and thus to construct the proposed typology of farm enterprises; (2) specify the mechanisms of preservation and elimination of peasants and, hence, the dynamics of their existence as a social category; and (3) anticipate both the expected response of peasants to reformist programs such as land reform and integrated rural development and the likely impact of these programs on the peasantry.

Two sharply contrasted positions have been assumed in the debate over peasants, each of which has definite implications regarding the nature and future of peasants. On the one hand, there are those who claim that peasants constitute a specific mode of production that is articulated to and dominated by other modes but that has inherent rules of reproduction and, consequently, a certain degree of stability. From this interpretation derives the position that peasants have a place in the social division of labor that becomes established in the process of the development of capitalism and that, consequently, they will remain in existence as a social category under that economic system. On the other hand, there are those who argue that there is no specific peasant mode of production and that peasants are merely a class or a fraction of a class within different types of modes. In some modes, such as feudalism, the peasant class (serfs) is an *essential* class; thus, peasants assume the stability of the mode. As a class, they will disappear only if the whole mode of production disappears. In other modes, such as capitalism, they are only a *transitory* fraction of a class that is differentiating as it is being absorbed by the essential classes, bourgeoisie and proletariat. As capitalism establishes itself as a dominant mode, both precapitalist modes and transitory capitalist fractions of class disintegrate. Peasants are here seen as an unstable and eventually disappearing social category.

The Marxist Classics

In this debate, the Marxist classics—Marx, Lenin, Kautsky, and Preobrazhensky—analyzed peasant problems without postulating a specifically peasant mode of production. Marx, however, did frequently use the term "peasant mode of production"; later Marxists, who sought truth in the word of Marx, relied upon this terminology to postulate the existence of a peasant mode of production in an Althusserian sense. The transposition is, however, misleading. It is well known that Marx did not give a definition to the concept of mode in any of his work. Instead, he used "mode" to refer to different things according to need—sometimes it refers to the manner (i.e., mode) of material production and sometimes to the broad organization of society; sometimes it is a concrete historical object and at other times an abstract model. It is only the Althusserians who attempted to fully specify the category of mode by defining it as an abstract model composed as a set of dialectically related structures (infrastructure characterized by productive forces and social relations and superstructure) that are meant to give a holistic description of society. In using the concept to refer specifically to peasants, Marx, however, did not apply it in that broad sense but used it merely to characterize the technological and social organization of the labor process.

Three aspects of Marx's characterization of peasants can be usefully retained here. First, peasants are a class and yet not a class. They form a class insofar as their form of life makes them distinct from other classes; but insofar as their form of living and producing separates them from one another, they are not a class.[2] It is precisely "their mode of production which isolates them from one another instead of bringing them into mutual intercourse."[3] Hence, the peasantry *is* not a mode; it *has* a mode of producing which isolates each peasant from the others and thus negates the existence of specific peasant social relations. Here, consequently, mode of production plays the role that the organization of the forces of production takes in the Althusserian notion of mode. Second, peasants in a capitalist society hold a contradictory location within class relations in that they are simultaneously both and neither bourgeois and/or proletarian.[4] This helps explain the class-nonclass contradiction: some peasants are more bourgeois; others, more proletarian; but all are partly both and neither one. This contradictory class location is characteristic of social formations in which the capitalist mode of production is dominant but in which not all social relations are yet characteristic of the dominant mode in its pure form. Third, Marx saw the peasantry under capitalism as an outcome of the dissolution of feudalism and as a transitory form whose downfall originates in the development of large-scale capitalist agriculture. The backward nature of peasant farming dooms peasants to misery and disappearance.[5]

It is thus clear that those who propose the existence of a peasant mode of production based on Marx's use of the term are taking it out of context and distorting the essence of his thought. Another source of confusion derives from Marx's use of the concept of a simple commodity (or petty commodity) mode of production which he himself identified with peasants and artisans and which has lately been used extensively to characterize peasantries under domination of the capitalist mode of production. As defined by Marx, the simple commodity mode has been explained by Morishima and Catephores as the situation where there is

... production of goods not for own-use but for the market under a spontaneously developed regime of division of labour among independent producers, independent in a triple sense: first, in that there is no *ex-ante* co-ordination of their activities under any social production plan, secondly, in that each of them has individual ownership over his means of production, so as not to be subject to a capitalist or other master and, thirdly, in that the mobility of labour among jobs is not limited by any reasons— sociological and geographical—so that income per man-hour is equalised throughout society.[6]

This simple commodity mode of production has been used by Marx to develop the labor theory of value under conditions where an average rate of profit among branches of production is not being formed and where commodities consequently are exchanged (as in Ricardo) at their value.[7] The question, however, is whether this mode of production has a historical reality or whether it is useful only for the theoretical purpose of developing the labor theory of value—first under simplified conditions—before later enriching the concept of value-price relations by extending it to the capitalist mode of production, an intellectual process characteristic of Hegelian dialectics. For Engels, and later for Meek and Nell,[8] simple commodity production did indeed characterize society

from the beginning of exchange, which transforms products into commodities, down to the 15th century of the present era. But the exchange of commodities dates from a time before all written history, which in Egypt goes back to at least 2,500 B.C. and in Babylon to 4,000 B.C., perhaps 6,000 B.C.; thus the law of value has prevailed during a period of from five to seven thousand years.[9]

This, as Morishima and Catephores argue convincingly, is a serious theoretical error because the labor theory of value requires the concepts of abstract labor and value that can hold only under a fully capitalist economy. The historical possibility of a petty commodity mode of production that antedates capitalism is thus inconsistent with Marx's categories of analysis. Use of this mode by Marx himself could only be a purely logical tool in the exercise of dialectical logic.

In *The Agrarian Question,* Kautsky analyzes the situation in which the capitalist mode of production is dominant but vestiges of other modes remain.[10] Nowhere is there mention of a peasant mode of production or of a peasant-based petty commodity mode, even though peasants are acknowledged to be petty commodity producers. Sometimes the peasant appears as a serf,[11] sometimes as a commodity producer,[12] and sometimes as an "American farmer";[13] but he is never the exclusive constituent of a "subordinated mode" that is "articulated" to a "dominant mode." He is always a member of a class that is dominated by another class in either the dominant mode of the social formation or in outgoing dominated modes; and in no case is there a stable social division of labor between modes.

There can exist, however, a functional interrelation between commercial and peasant farmers within the capitalist mode of production:

Precisely this tendency shows how absurd it is to suppose that if small holdings continue to survive, then it must be because they are more productive. The real basis of their survival is the fact that they cease to compete with the large capitalist farms which develop by their side. Far from selling the same commodities as the larger farms, these small holdings are often buyers of these commodities. The one commodity which they do possess in abundance, and which the bigger holdings need, is their labor power. . . . Under this state of things, both types of farms do not exclude each other but, on the contrary, coexist like capitalist and proletarian, even though the small peasant becomes increasingly proletarianized.[14]

This functional dualism is, however, unstable; and the peasant is ultimately bound to disappear as a social category under capitalism. The state may intervene through reform programs to shore up functional dualism for some additional period of time and thus attempt to prolong the existence of peasants. As Lenin mentions in reviewing Kautsky's book:

It would not even be advantageous for the big landowners to force out the small proprietors completely: the latter provide them with hands! For this reason the landowners and the capitalists frequently pass laws that artificially maintain the small peasantry. Petty-farming becomes stable when it ceases to compete with large-scale farming, when it is turned into a supplier of labour-power for the latter.[15]

As we shall see in Chapter 7, some types of rural development projects and "basic needs" programs promoted in Latin America in the 1970s served exactly this purpose.

Similarly, Lenin does not use the concept of peasant mode of production in his analysis of the development of capitalism in agriculture. The categories that he uses are those of the feudal and capitalist modes of production, taking petty commodity production as a purely transitory form between the two and not as a mode of production in its own right. Peasants as such do not constitute a barrier to the development of capitalism in agriculture; on the contrary, they are "its deepest and most durable foundation."[16] Thus, argues Lenin, "the system of economic relations in the 'community' village does not at all constitute a special economic form ('people's production,' etc.) but is an ordinary petty-bourgeois one."

Lenin bases his argument on the process of differentiation among the peasantry that arises with the development of capitalism in agriculture. The result of this process of dissolution or "depeasantization" is the disappearance of the old patriarchal peasantry and the emergence of two new social classes—the rural bourgeoisie and the rural proletariat.

The old peasantry is not only "differentiating," it is being completely dissolved, it is ceasing to exist, it is being ousted by absolutely new types of rural inhabitants—types that are the basis of a society in which commodity economy and capitalist production prevail. These types are the rural bourgeoisie (chiefly petty bourgeoisie) and the rural proletariat—a class of commodity producers in agriculture and a class of agricultural wage-workers.[17]

With the development of capitalism in agriculture, some members of the peasantry form a portion of the rural bourgeoisie while the vast majority join the ranks of the rural proletariat. Lenin points out, however, that the rural proletariat is not composed solely of propertyless wage laborers but is mainly comprised of allotment-holding farm laborers who are thus "the most typical representatives of the Russian rural proletariat." Their distinguishing features are "insignificant farming on a patch of land, with the farm in a state of utter ruin, inability to exist without the sale of labour-power, an extremely low standard of living (probably lower than that of the worker without an allotment)."[18] Thus, the rural proletariat very often has the appearance of a peasant, owing to his control over a small plot of land, even though the social relations that characterize it are more those of a worker.

It is the existence of this allotment-holding rural laborer which accounts in part for the Narodniks' insistence on the permanence of the peasantry, even under capitalism. To the same extent, Lenin warns, the Bolsheviks themselves were often guilty of a too theoretical characterization of the development of capitalism in agriculture and thus ignored the proletarian nature of the allotment-holding rural worker. Thus, argues Lenin:

Our literature frequently contains too stereotyped an understanding of the theoretical proposition that capitalism requires the free, landless worker. This proposition is quite correct as indicating the main trend, but capitalism penetrates into agriculture particularly slowly and in extremely varied forms. The allotment of land to the rural worker is very often to the interests of the rural employers themselves, and that is why the allotment-holding rural worker is a type to be found in all capitalist countries.[19]

The semiproletarian thus takes on the appearance of a peasant, even though the social relations that characterize him are more those of a worker.

Like the other Marxist classics, Preobrazhensky is rather informal and flexible in his use of the concept of mode of production. Peasants are not a mode of production, but under capitalism are a subset of the petty bourgeois economy and are engaged in petty commodity production.[20] Again, consequently, peasants are seen as a differentiating and hence transitory social category.

Peasantry as a Specific Type of Economy

By contrast to the Marxist classics, there exists a broad spectrum of positions among those who consider the peasantry to constitute a specific type of economy. The spectrum ranges from those who conceive of the peasantry in terms of the organization of the household in relation to the production process to those who conceptualize the peasantry as a mode of production in the full Althusserian sense. This current of thought presumably started with the Russian populists at the end of the nineteenth century, and it was principally Chayanov and members of the Organization and Production School who between 1912 and 1925 laid explicit theoretical bases for the analysis of the peasant household. It is, however, incorrect to claim—as Harrison, for example, has done—that Chayanov attempted to develop a theory of the peasant mode of production.[21] His analysis was much more limited and simply aimed at "understanding what the peasant farm is from an organizational viewpoint."[22] Beyond this, he claimed that peasant units could indeed be the building blocks of feudal, "natural," or capitalist modes of production. Similar positions were later assumed by Thorner and Stavenhagen.[23]

Many modern Marxist authors—frequently relying on Chayanov's study of peasants and on Marx's simple commodity mode of production—have, however, claimed that modern peasantries do constitute a specific mode of production. Some say that peasants are representatives of the simple commodity mode of production; others, taking the most extreme stand on this issue, argue for a specific peasant mode of production.

Servolin's position is that today's peasants were "born from the dissolution of the feudal mode of production" and are now representatives of the simple commodity mode of production, which he defines according to two presuppositions:[24] (1) the direct producer owns the means of production and organizes the process of production; and (2) the purpose of production—peasants' objective function—is not profit but simple reproduction—that is, survival year after year under the same material conditions as before. This petty production develops in coexistence with capitalism and under its domination. Coexistence among modes "takes the aspect of a division of labor between them."[25] A rigorous study of the articulation of modes of production, like P. P. Rey's study of the articulation between feudalism and capitalism, for example, would, however, require a previous specification of the social relations of each mode.[26] Servolin does not do this for the simple commodity mode; he merely discusses the impact of the individual peasant's objective function on the performance and on the functionality (articulation) that the peasant mode thus acquires for the capitalist mode.

Vergopoulos similarly conceives of peasants as members of a simple commodity mode by relying both on the organization of the peasant household, where only family labor is used, and on the objective of production for subsistence and not for profit.[27] His thesis is that "agrarian capitalists are progressively removed," leaving the countryside to the "peasant production network." According to him, "peasant agriculture does not constitute a precapitalist residual, but a form recreated by modern capitalism that is articulated to it in an exemplary manner." However, this form is not capitalist, but is a "capitalism without capitalists." The peasant entrepreneur is not interested in "profits or accumulation, contenting himself with the equivalent of a salary." He is a "salaried worker working on piece-rate." For this reason, it is cheaper to produce food under peasant production than under capitalist production since the latter requires the average rate of profit whereas peasants do not. As a result, a set of conditions is created by the state, in particular through terms of trade, that is adverse to the penetration of capitalism into agriculture. As Mouzelis explains in his discussion of Vergopoulos's thesis:

> Private capital tends to shun the countryside, preferring to exploit the direct producer in the sphere of circulation through the impersonal market mechanism—the state becoming the main provider of capital to the rural economy. Thus a situation is created in which the agricultural producer, under the strict control of merchant/industrial capital and the state, is constantly forced to modernize his exploitation and to increase his productivity, not in order to maximize his profits but in order to cover his expenses and to meet his debts.[28]

Increasingly often, a specific peasant mode of production has been proposed in contemporary Marxist literature—in particular, by Diaz-Polanco in Mexico, Gutelman in France, and Rojas and Moncayo in Colombia.[29] For them, the peasant mode appears every time other precapitalist modes dissolve. It is articulated to and dominated by the capitalist mode of production to which it surrenders a surplus. Like the simple commodity mode, it is characterized by family labor and its objective is simple reproduction. It, however, differs from the simple commodity mode in that production is fundamentally for home consumption and not for sale on the market.[30] In order to make peasants a mode and not merely a form of organization of the household, as in Marx and Chayanov, Gutelman attempts to specify the social relations of this mode in terms of inheritance by emphasizing the fact that those who keep control of the land must buy the land again from the other family members in each successive generation. The basic social relation in the peasant mode of production would thus be a relation among generations of kin.

In summary, conceptualizing peasants as belonging to a specific mode (simple commodity or peasant) leads to a particular understanding of the nature and future of peasants: because they are motivated not by profit but by survival, they are functional to the dominant capitalist mode of production in ensuring a supply of cheap food and, as such, acquire a stable existence in capitalist society.

An Alternative Conceptualization of Peasants

There really is no debate on the correct social location of peasants in precapitalist modes of production (feudal, Asiatic, or communal). In these cases they constitute a class within each particular mode, and they are expelled from the mode as it decomposes under increasing domination by another mode. But when capitalism dominates, should peasants who are external to precapitalist modes be conceptualized as part of a peasant (or simple commodity) mode or as a transitory class or fraction of a class within the capitalist mode?[31] To take a position in this debate, we need to analyze the plausibility of each of the four defining characteristics of a peasant mode. They are:

1. Nonseparation of the producer from the means of production. Peasants are engaged in a production process based on family labor and the household consequently constitutes simultaneously a unit of production, consumption, and reproduction. As we have seen above, this defining characteristic is accepted by both schools of thought and thus is not part of the debate.[32]

2. The production of commodities (simple commodity mode) or of use values (peasant mode) or of a combination of both (the most likely case) is not for profit-making but for simple reproduction.

3. The peasant mode of production has specific social relations.

4. This uniclass mode never exists in isolation but always exists under the domination of another mode—in particular, the capitalist one.

In this section we will discuss each of the last three propositions and, by rejecting them, suggest that the classical Marxist position of conceptualizing peasants as a transitory fraction of a class within capitalism is the most appropriate.

Before discussing the proposition that peasants do not seek to maximize profit, we must first explain why this proposition is a necessary component of the argument in favor of a peasant mode of production. This can be done by looking at the features of a hypothetical peasant mode of production and at the conditions for its reproduction. By definition, a peasant mode can have only a single class—that of peasant producers. Consequently, relations of exploitation, if they exist, must be external to the mode: a surplus is extracted from the peasant mode through a variety of mechanisms and is captured by external social classes. For this reason, when a surplus is created by peasants and appropriated by others, the peasant mode is always postulated to exist not in isolation, nor in a dominant position in a social formation, but in an articulated and dominated position with other modes.[33] Reproduction of this uniclass mode thus requires that internal class differentiation be prevented or at least held to a minimum; otherwise the mode does not have stable rules of reproduction, and this contradicts the legitimacy of the very notion of mode.

There are three possible means of holding internal differentiation within the peasantry in check. The first is for relations of external exploitation to be so thorough that peasant surplus is fully extracted. Lack of surplus retention would presumably negate the possibility of differentiation. Yet the extractive mechanisms to which the peasant mode is subjected are market, and not individually, imposed and thus apply with equal intensity to all peasants. As a result, even if the community's surplus were fully extracted, positive surpluses would still be appropriated by the more favored and successful peasants while others would be driven below simple reproduction; and differentiation would occur. Intense market exploitation of the peasantry is thus insufficient to prevent internal differentiation.

The second possible means of blocking internal differentiation lies in the existence of redistributive mechanisms within the peasant community that equalize individual appropriation of the surplus retained by the community. In this case, accumulation would be possible without differentiation, and differentiation itself would occur among communities instead of within each. There may be some instances left in Latin America of socially organized redistribution like that practiced through ceremonies by the Zapotecs in Oaxaca.[34] This is, however, a most exceptional situation among Latin American peasants today; and it cannot serve as a justification for the concept of peasant mode of production on a significant scale.

The last and most plausible possible means of maintaining a uniclass structure is to ensure that peasants be motivated not by profit but only by the quest for simple reproduction. If this definition of peasant motivation were true, surplus would not, for behavioral reasons, be generated beyond what is appropriated externally; and internal differentiation would be made impossible. Thus, it is necessary to assume that peasants do not produce for profit in order to show that the peasant mode of production, with its single class, has internal laws of reproduction.

Moreover, the postulate that peasants do not produce for profit is used to explain the functionality and hence the stability of peasants under capitalism. Peasant farms will keep on producing without profit and rent and under implicit wage conditions eventually below the going wage on rural labor markets. By contrast, capitalist farms must include in their production costs a normal profit rate (interest paid and equilibrium user cost on their own capital), a normal rent for the land, and market wages. The result is that if the productivity of labor is equal on capitalist and peasant farms, peasants will outcompete capitalists.[35] More generally, peasants will have lower production costs if their lower productivity is more than compensated for by the sacrifice of profit, rent, and equilibrium wage. As a result, peasants are seen to be functional to capitalism since they deliver cheaper food to the rest of the system. Vergopoulos thus argues that the ultimate capitalist reform, implemented through the control of food prices, is to turn agriculture to the peasants—that is, to create in agriculture a capitalism without capitalists.[36] The peasant farm retains the formal appearance of autonomy but is, in fact, fully controlled by agribusiness and merchant capital as well as by industrial capital through the policies of the state, particularly cheap food policies. And since peasants are allowed a global return on resources no greater than a worker's wage, they are, in fact, reduced to the status of workers working at home for capital.[37] However, this real submission to capital is seen not to be antagonistic, for it leads to an organic division of labor on a commodity basis between capitalist and peasant farms. Servolin uses this rationale to explain the presumed absence of class struggle in the countryside.[38]

The next question, then, is to determine whether there is justification for the presupposition that peasants do not seek profit. Marx's opinion on this is that the small producer does not produce without seeking profit. On the contrary, the absence of profit is the "absolute limit" to which he can be exploited.[39] The absence of profit is thus clearly not the result of a behavioral tendency on the part of peasants as Servolin presupposed. Furthermore, according to Marx, this type of enterprise (i.e., one that will, if forced to, produce for no profit) is found essentially in societies where the marketed production is only a minor part of total production and where capitalism is weakly developed.[40] Amin and Vergopoulos call on Chayanov to justify the nonprofit presupposition.[41] For Chayanov, however, the validity of using the concept of profit as a category of analysis depends upon the existence of a labor market. Chayanov does not use the category "profit" to analyze the peasant economy, simply because there is no, or only an incipient, labor market.[42] As a result, the return to individual factors of production cannot be singled out. Thus, in the works of Marx and Chayanov on peasants, the nonexistence of a profit category is recognized not as a behavioral "presupposition" but as a fact derived from objective reality.

The small producer may indeed appear economically irrational if he does not sell out and become a proletarian, even when his income is below the wage income. In modern capitalist social formations, there are even large numbers of petty bourgeois who live no better than workers in unionized industry but who do not become workers. Many of these conform with what O'Connor has called the "competitive sector."[43] If, however, the peasant does not sell out and become a capitalist in another sector, it is usually because the mass of his capital would not allow him to capture a large enough mass of surplus value to survive. And if he does resist proletarianization, it is because the uncertainty of employment opportunities implies lower expected incomes, besides loss of direct control of his labor process.

In conclusion, we see that what those who argue for the peasant mode posit as a defining behavioral characteristic of the peasant (i.e., continued engagement in production without profits) is, in fact, the *result* of a class relation where the peasant's surplus labor is extracted through a variety of channels.

Surplus extraction from peasants is indeed so prevalent that it has been used by Eric Wolf and Theodor Shanin as the defining characteristic of peasants.[44] Advocates of the peasant mode incorrectly use simple reproduction—an observed fact—as a defining behavioral characteristic of peasants because they confuse the inability of peasants to capture profits with their presumed nondesire for profits. And if there is no class struggle in the countryside, it is merely an ideological characteristic of all peasants who, as petty bourgeois, tend to identify ideologically, through ownership of a plot of land, with the farmer, in spite of advanced levels of proletarianization. In other words, if there is no class struggle, it is because peasants are a "class and not a class." Given this, the other two debatable characteristics of a peasant mode fall on their own.

One is the issue of the existence of social relations specific to peasants. Clearly, for a peasant mode to exist, not only must a specific type of production process be identified but the social relations that correspond to this process must be characterized.[45] Most of those who propose a specific peasant mode of production either leave the social relations unspecified or describe social relations that are not specific to it at all. Rojas and Moncayo, however, describe the social relations that are characteristic of the peasant mode in terms of the lack of separation of the direct producer from the conditions of real appropriation of nature[46]—what Balibar calls "relations of possession."[47] But this is inadequate for two reasons: (1) because relations of possession characterize productive forces and not social relations; and (2) because there are many other modes in which laborers hold relations of possession, which makes these relations insufficient to characterize the peasant mode. It is Gutelman who presented the most elaborate specification of what could be social relations for the peasant mode. According to him, as we saw before, the basic social relations are those between generations and between kin. The peasant must buy the land anew every generation once the peasant mode has been established for some time. This need results from the smallness of the available plot of land, which prevents subdivision. The family member who receives the land thus must buy it over time from his relatives. The price paid is the capitalized surplus labor of the peasant. The social relations are thus "those that tie the working peasant . . . to the owner-sellers of the land."[48] Gutelman also specifies juridical-political and ideological instances. They are the private property rights and the "freedom" of the artisan who is his own boss. These social and superstructural characterizations are, however, terribly similar to those of the petty bourgeoisie—particularly once the lack of accumulation motivation has been demystified. Indeed, the social relations that are relevant to an understanding of peasants are external to the family: they are the relations of domination and surplus extraction to the benefit of other social groups.

The last defining characteristic of the peasant mode is its condition of articulation with and domination by other modes. But here again, once behavior is demystified, all we are left with are class relations through which peasants surrender a surplus according to the rules of the prevailing mode: rent under feudalism; surplus value through the labor market or surplus labor through the terms of trade under capitalism. The perceived relations of dominance that are posited as an articulation of modes of production are merely the social relations of production in the dominant mode of production. And because articulation is taken as a substitute for these social relations, it becomes impossible to define social relations for a specifically peasant mode.

Use of the concept of peasant (or simple commodity) mode is therefore an attempt to transform what are essentially exploitative class relations into an "articulation" between two modes where the producers in one "mode" are content without a rate of profit and where the buying and selling of labor power is blatantly ignored. Whenever the unequal nature of this articulation is admitted, it is seen as a conflict between peasant and capitalist farming or between agriculture and industry rather than between classes. Consequently, the approach has been ideologically useful for those who, for political reasons, have attempted to minimize awareness of the development of classes in the countryside. This, of course, was the exact purpose of the Russian Narodniks and is today the goal of neopopulists like Servolin, Mamalakis, and Lipton.[49]

We conclude this discussion by rejecting the concept of a peasant (or simple commodity) mode of production articulated to capitalism. Peasants are to be seen instead as a class or fraction of a class within different modes of production—a class that is essential in modes like feudalism and transitory (and hence only a fraction of a class) in others, like capitalism. Because different modes of production tend to coexist in a social formation— particularly feudal, communal, and capitalist in Latin American agriculture—different peasant classes correspond to each of these articulated modes. We will use this fact as a basis on which to construct a typology of farm enterprises in Latin America.

ROADS TO THE DEVELOPMENT OF CAPITALISM
IN AGRICULTURE

Capitalism can penetrate agriculture and transform existing social relations in a variety of ways that result in different class and land tenure configurations. In their classical studies on the development of capitalism, Lenin and Marx identified three different roads.

In analyzing rent, Marx described the emergence of a rural bourgeoisie in England through the expropriation of peasants from the large landholdings and their replacement by capitalist tenant farmers. This led to the formation of a class structure composed of a gentry that leased out its estates for a cash rent; a class of capitalist farmers who gained access to the land through rental but also increasingly through direct ownership; and a class of rural workers that originated in the dispossessed peasantry. Under this "trinity formula," the landlords earned rent, the farmers a profit, and the laborers a wage. This road, which is theoretically important for the study of rent, is of limited historical importance. As Marx pointed out, "This form can become the general rule only in those countries which dominated the world market in the period of transition from the feudal to the capitalist mode of production."[50]

Lenin, in his study of the development of capitalism in prerevolutionary Russia, identified two others roads through which capitalism could develop in agriculture—one based on the slow transformation of the large feudal estates into capitalist enterprises, patterned after the junker road of the Prussian landlords; and the other based on a multiplicity of small farms, such as the farmer road in the United States.[51]

Based on the historical development of capitalist agriculture in East Prussia, on the first road the feudal estate is converted into a large capitalist enterprise, and the feudal landlord becomes a capitalist entrepreneur. The peasants, who were previously internal to the estates and were paying rent in either labor services or in kind, are expropriated and dispossessed. The social relations on the estates are transformed into those between capitalists and free workers hired for a wage. Politically, the junker road leaves the landowning elites in a dominant position at the level of the state and hence tends to perpetuate the existence of absolute rent in agricultural production. The massive dispossession of the peasants implies the need for strong political control over the rural inhabitants since the development of capitalism along this road leads to the transformation of a majority of peasants into semiproletarian or landless workers and the forcible maintenance of the peasants and rural proletariat at a pauper standard of living. The development of capitalism among peasants is blocked by the superiority of the large farms, where scale allows greater division of labor, use of indivisible farm machinery, and lower average fixed costs.[52] It is a road which consequently tends to be highly regressive for the distribution of income, blocks the development of a domestic market for wage goods in agriculture, and is associated with nondemocratic forms of government.

The other road of capitalist development in agriculture which Lenin identified is the "farmer" or "American" road.[53] This road originates from a proliferation of small farmers who constitute a petty bourgeoisie. These small farmers or free peasants are created either by the violent elimination of the feudal landowning class through revolution or land reform or through the colonialization and homesteading of new lands. Thus, on the farmer road, "the peasant predominates, becomes the exclusive agent of agriculture and evolves into the capitalist farmers."[54] The development of capitalism along the farmer road requires the elimination not only of the feudal landlords and their estates but also of the peasant allotments that evolved under the domination of the feudal land tenure system, for agricultural production must be free from all feudal constraints. Thus, according to Lenin:

In order to establish really free farming in Russia, it is necessary to "disenclose" all the lands, those of the landlords as well as the allotments. The whole system of medieval landownership must be broken up and all lands must be made equal for the free farmers upon a free soil. The greatest possible facilities must be created for the exchange of holdings, for the free choice of settlements, for rounding off holdings, for the creation of free, new associations, instead of the musty, tax-extorting commune. The whole land must be cleared of all medieval lumber.[55]

The development of capitalism in agriculture via the farmer road results in a far-reaching social differentiation among rural producers as the most enterprising and fortunate peasants as well as those who emerged from feudalism with more favorable endowments accumulate land and capital and hire labor power, while the majority suffer losses and are eventually converted into proletarians. The end point of this process of differentiation is that "an insignificant minority of small producers wax rich, 'get on in the world,' turn into bourgeois, while the overwhelming majority are either utterly ruined and become wage workers or paupers, or eternally eke out an almost proletarian existence."[56]

For Lenin, the farmer road is economically and politically superior to the junker road because the development of capitalism based on a multiplicity of small farms would have the result of enlarging the domestic market as well as freeing the creative initiative of the masses:

If capitalist development proceeds along this course it should develop infinitely more broadly, more freely and more rapidly as the result of the tremendous growth of the home market and of the rise in the standard of living, the energy, initiative and culture of the whole of the population.[57]

Since the emerging rural bourgeoisie cannot gain hegemonic control of the state, this road of development prevents the existence of absolute rent and thus cheapens food prices. By fomenting the emergence of a national bourgeoisie, it favors, but in no way ensures, articulated patterns of accumulation and democratic forms of government.

The applicability of the junker road to the development of capitalism in Latin American agriculture is obvious in those areas with a strong legacy of *latifundia* domination in the agrarian structure and a relatively weak peasantry.[58] This road can be found, for example, in Peru before the land reform of 1969, where large landowners had largely expropriated peasants from within their estates and shifted to a semiproletarian labor force of free peasants. It is also found as a dominant path of development in Colombia, Ecuador, Bolivia, and Venezuela.[59] There are other regions in Latin America, such as Mexico after 1934, where a variant of the farmer road of capitalist development emerged as a direct result of peasant revolution and government-sponsored land reform. Other countries dominated by the farmer road as a result of land reforms that eradicated the large estates include the Dominican Republic, Peru after 1969, and Chile between 1967 and 1973.

There are, of course, a number of other roads along which capitalism is developing in Latin American agriculture—roads which correspond to the specificity of Latin American social formations and to the current international division of labor. One of these roads, which is found specifically in Colombia but also in other parts of Latin America, results from the investment of local capital, generated in mercantile or other urban activities (in particular, among the new petty bourgeoisie of professionals, military, and technocrats), in the purchase of agricultural land. In this fashion, urban control is established over rural enterprises. Agricultural production on this road is generally modernized, on medium-sized farms, and is characterized by absentee management. Accordingly, there is a high degree of reliance on wage workers; and social relations of production are fully proletarianized. We have used the term "merchant road" to denote this type of control over agricultural production, although it must be emphasized that not only merchant capital but also financial and industrial capital are involved.

Another road of capitalist development which is found increasingly in Latin American agriculture is that of the contract farmer or other types of lease arrangements in which multinational agribusiness firms establish contracts with local landowners who in turn are responsible for the actual production process.[60] Often contracts are drawn up which specify the type of crop to be grown, the type of technology to be used (usually supplied by the multinational firm itself), and the final price of the commodity. Production along this road is therefore highly modernized and takes place on medium- and large-scale units. In Mexico, for example, this road of capitalist development tends to encourage the production of seasonal crops for export, such as winter vegetables, and relies predominantly on seasonal migratory labor. Contract farming is one of the increasingly important means by which international capital penetrates Latin American agriculture, particularly in countries where landownership by foreign nationals is prohibited—for example, Mexico.

MODES OF PRODUCTION, SOCIAL CLASSES, AND TYPES OF FARM ENTERPRISES

A Typology of Farm Enterprises

The typology of farm enterprises given in Figure 3.1 is based on the modes of production and the social classes that have existed in Latin American agriculture since World War II. The agrarian structure, composed at each point in time on the basis of particular subsets of these modes and classes, has changed markedly with the development of capitalism and with the reforms implemented by the state. While the typology is presented as a fixed set of modes and classes, it is not meant to offer a static picture of the agrarian structure. On the contrary, it permits the construction of a changing mix of

Modes of production	Social classes	Types of farm enterprises	Control of the state	Status on labor market	Forms of labor payment	Dynamic status as capitalism develops
Primitive community	Cacique					Disappearing
	Incorporated peasants	Incorporated subsistence farms				
Semifeudal	Traditional landed elite	Precapitalist estates (LMF)	Hegemonic as landed elite	Users of bonded labor	Paid in land usufruct, kind, and cash	Disappearing
	Internal peasants and sharecroppers	Internal subsistence farms (SF)	No	Bonded semiproletarians	Paid in land usufruct, kind, and cash	
Capitalist	Capitalist landed elite	Capitalist estates (LMF)	Hegemonic as landed elite	Employers	Paid in cash	Emerging in junker road
	Farmers: rural bourgeoisie	Commercial farms (MMF)	Shared with nonagricultural bourgeoisie	Employers	Paid in cash	Emerging in peasant and merchant roads
	Upper peasants: rural petty bourgeoisie	Family farms (F)	No	Small employers or self-sufficient	Paid in cash and labor exchange	Emerging and differentiating
	Lower peasants: semi-proletarians	External sub-family farms	No	Semiproletarians	Paid in cash	Emerging rapidly
	Rural proletariat	Landless workers	No	Proletarians	Paid in cash	Emerging slowly

Figure 3.1.   Social Classes and Types of Farm Enterprises in Latin America

modes, classes, and enterprises that will allow us to map the structural implications of economic development and reformism.

Each type of farm enterprise is identified with a corresponding class position. In turn, social classes are defined by (1) the mode of production to which they belong (primitive community, semifeudal, or capitalist) and, in particular, by the social relations within that mode which define the forms of payment to labor (in usufruct of productive resources, in kind, or in cash); (2) their respective statuses in the labor market and, in particular, whether access to means of production results in their being buyers or sellers of labor power; and (3) the degree of control they exercise over the state. Control of the state implies control of the definition, generation, and appropriation of public services (credit, technology, information, infrastructure, etc.) and policies (terms of trade). Both control of the means of production (private productive resources) and control of public services (public productive resources) are key determinants of surplus appropriation by specific social classes.[61]

Since the typology of farm enterprises presented here is based on the underlying mode and class structure, it permits us to directly relate farm enterprises to the dynamics of the development process. Indeed, accumulation and distribution are determined by surplus generation and appropriation, which in turn originate in a particular mode and social class structure. The components of this typology are the following:

PRECAPITALIST ESTATES.   Market oriented from the outset and for this reason not strictly a feudal enterprise, the precapitalist estate maintains feudal internal relations of production that are characterized, in particular, by the presence of internal peasants paying rents in labor services and commonly bonded to the landlord by debts (debt peonage) and extraeconomic coercion. By controlling the state on a political basis—essentially because they dominate large masses of peasants—the traditional landed elites are able to define the nature of public services for agriculture and to appropriate the lion's share of them. As a result, this institutional rent, together with intense exploitation of internal peasants, permits the maintenance of high land rents in spite of eventually deteriorating food prices, and thus insures the economic viability of the estate. With the development of capitalism in agriculture, the traditional landed elites are either transformed into capitalists along the junker road or are expropriated by land reform programs that open the way for the farmer road.

SUBSISTENCE FARMS INTERNAL TO THE PRECAPITALIST ESTATE.   Within the precapitalist estate, peasants, with family labor, work captive plots of land for which they pay rent in labor services and/or in kind. Severely controlled by landlords—in terms of access to land, labor, product, and capital markets, as well as through extraeconomic coercion—a slow process of differentiation takes place along an "internal farmer road." A minority group—usually closely related to the landlord as administrators or specialized workers—controls enough productive resources to hire seasonal or permanent workers as a complement to family labor. The large mass of internal peasants is, however, incapable of accumulating, and on the contrary slowly loses its access to land as the estate becomes more capitalist in nature under the inducement of market forces and the pressure of public reforms. It is thus a class in transition toward increasing proletarianization and relocation in external subsistence farms.

CAPITALIST ESTATES.   Development of capitalism along the junker road transforms precapitalist estates into large-scale capitalist enterprises. The (now capitalist) landed elite remains in a powerful position at the level of the state through the economic power it derives from its role in the generation of foreign exchange and the production of wage goods. Public services and policies thus remain oriented toward the appropriation of an institutional rent by this elite. The labor force is composed of workers paid in cash, many of whom maintain their families in subsistence farms adjacent to (but sometimes very distant from) the capitalist estates. This type of farm thus pertains to the capitalist mode of production and is functionally related to the peasant subsistence sector through labor relationships. It has emerged as the most prevalent type of capitalist enterprise in Latin American agriculture.

COMMERCIAL FARMS. These enterprises constitute the economic basis of the high and medium rural bourgeoisie—the farmers—which stems in part from the farmer road but also, and in fact principally, from the penetration of capital of merchant and urban origin into agriculture along what we called the merchant road. In the case of plantations, which we include here somewhat artificially among commercial farms, ownership is often in the form of corporate capital and is frequently associated with foreign interests. The labor force is fully proletarianized but generally remains tied to the subsistence sector owing to insufficient wages to maintain workers and families. Extraeconomic relations do not exist, and the bourgeoisie derives its power from its economic basis. This power is shared with the nonagricultural bourgeoisie in controlling the state and results in public services oriented toward the development of capitalism in agriculture through land-saving technology (Green Revolution) and infrastructure investments (irrigation). Farm sizes are generally smaller than capitalist estates, management is more direct, and portfolios are less diversified with nonagricultural assets (except perhaps for farms originating on the merchant road rather than on the farmer road). Stimulated by land reform programs and fostered by functional dualism, but confined in their dynamism by unfavorable terms of trade and by less access to institutional rents than that enjoyed by the capitalist landed elite, commercial farmers are an emerging group in rural society.

FAMILY FARMS. A rural petty bourgeoisie—usually created by the sale of marginal lands from large estates or by land reform, settlement, and rural-development programs—is largely absent from the Latin American agrarian class structure. Blocked by unfavorable prices, unable to translate cheap food into cheap semiproletarian labor because it is at most only a small employer, and excluded from control of the state, this fraction of a class is incapable of insuring the going rate of profit to its capital or a normal rent to its land. To face up to competition from the landed elite and the bourgeoisie, the household on the family farm is forced to overexploit its own labor to a great degree. This group is thus highly unstable and quickly differentiates into farmers and semiproletarian peasants, with the largest mass being drawn to the latter. Rapidly rising semiproletarianization in colonization projects in Argentina (Santa Fe and Entre Rios) and Venezuela and in the *ejido* sector of the Mexican land subjected to reform demonstrates the difficulties of viability of a petty agrarian bourgeoisie. Exceptions are households whose farms are best located relative to markets for labor-intensive and delivery-intensive products—especially those around the urban metropolis. However, their number and economic prosperity are severely limited by lack of effective demand for wage foods on the urban markets and by competition from the capitalist sector.

EXTERNAL SUBFAMILY FARMS. With the development of capitalism in agriculture, the peasantry is increasingly confined to independent subsistence farms. These farms are created by both the junker and farmer roads. In the first case, peasants expelled from the estates resettle on external subsistence farms. In the second case, peasant family farms are increasingly pulverized under the pressure of demographic growth and insufficient employment opportunities, which reduce off-farm migration. These farms cannot insure the needs for maintenance and reproduction of the whole family. And neither can wage levels permit full proletarianization. As a result, peasant households on these farms must rely on both farm production and external sources of income (wage labor, trade, crafts, etc.), a dependence that gives them the status of semiproletarians. These external subsistence peasants constitute the reserve of cheap labor for capitalist enterprises.

SUBSISTENCE FARMS IN CORPORATE COMMUNITIES. As remnants of precolonial modes of production and sometimes established through officially conferred property rights by the colonial regime, Indian communities are today highly divided into individual farms and are not essentially different from atomized external subfamily farms. In these communities—observed mainly in the Andean highlands and in Meso-America—access to the land is strictly reserved for community members. However, land is almost always farmed by individual families, as on external subsistence farms. The only significant distinguishing feature is the permanence of communal institutions, which can be used to mobilize labor for public works and as a basis for political organization, however limited its impact. These institutions can nevertheless prove effective in the context of land reform or rural-development projects.

LANDLESS WORKERS. Due to the intense competition of peasants from subfamily farms on the labor market, rural wages tend to be below the needs for maintenance and reproduction of labor power. As a consequence, a fully landless proletariat emerges only slowly. Full-fledged proletarians tend to be individuals in age groups that do not support families. Census observations in some countries show relatively large groups of rural proletarians. However, these statistics tend to be misleading because they dissociate wage workers from the households (i.e., the consumption units through the life cycle) to which they are related and thus fail to reveal the permanence of linkages to subsistence agriculture. As a result, many wage workers who are members of households partially supported by subsistence agricultural production falsely appear as proletarians. However, the rapid growth of export-oriented and mechanized agribusiness is producing a growing landless proletariat in specific areas like northwestern Mexico and São Paulo and Paraná in Brazil (the *boias frias*).

Empirical Characterization of the Rural Class Structure

It is possible to characterize quantitatively the agrarian social classes that have been identified above by using the information on land tenure obtained by the Inter-American Committee for Agricultural Development (CIDA) in Latin America in 1950 and 1960 for seven Latin American countries.[62] In this monumental work, farms are classified into four groups (large multifamily, medium multifamily, family, and subfamily farms) according to their employment capacity relative to the size of a typical rural family. Since the hiring and sale of labor is one of the elements we have used to characterize social classes, a partial correspondence can be established between CIDA's farm groups and the modes and classes in agriculture in our typology. This correspondence is as follows:

LARGE MULTIFAMILY FARMS (LMF).   Since these farms employ more than twelve workers, they correspond to the precapitalist and capitalist estates. They display a range of social relations of production, from semifeudal to capitalist, with a slow evolution over time from the former to the latter.

MEDIUM MULTIFAMILY FARMS (MMF).   These farms provide employment for from four to twelve active workers on a permanent basis and thus correspond to the commerical farms. They display fully capitalist relations of production.

FAMILY FARMS (F).   These farms provide employment for from two to four persons, which is approximately the average number of workers in a rural family; these farms correspond to our definition of family farms. Only a minimum hiring of labor is possible. The class position of these farmers is in the petty rural bourgeoisie and they are therefore enmeshed in capitalist social relations but are subject to exploitation and domination by more-powerful capitalist groups.

SUBFAMILY FARMS (SF).   These farms "have insufficient land to satisfy the minimum needs of a family or to allow the utilization of their work throughout the year."[63] They correspond to both the internal and external subsistence farms in our typology.

These four categories were used throughout the CIDA study. In Table 3.1 the CIDA data have been rearranged according to the social class positions of our typology. The data show the distribution of households among social classes and the land area that they control for six countries in the study. These

Table 3.1. Rural Social Classes in Latin America: Distribution of Households and Land

Percent

Social Class	Argentina (1960) Families	Argentina (1960) Area[a]	Brazil (1950) Families	Brazil (1950) Area	Chile (1955) Families	Chile (1955) Area	Colombia (1960) Families	Colombia (1960) Area	Ecuador (1960) Families	Ecuador (1960) Area	Guatemala (1950) Families	Guatemala (1950) Area
Landed elites (LMF)												
Traditional and Capitalist	0.4	36.9	1.8	59.5	3.0	81.3	1.1	49.5	0.3	45.1	0.1	40.8
Rural bourgeoisie (MMF)	4.8	15.0	12.8	34.0	6.5	11.4	3.9	23.3	2.1	19.3	1.5	31.5
Rural petty bourgeoisie (F)												
Total	32.6	44.7	14.9	6.0	17.7	7.1	23.3	22.3	9.5	19.0	7.8	13.4
Owner-operators	16.4	—[b]	12.0	—	14.8	—	17.9	—	8.0	—	6.6	—
Tenants	16.2	—	2.9	—	2.9	—	5.4	—	1.5	—	1.2	—
Internal peasants												
Total	3.8	0	20.0	0	30.8	0	16.1	0	7.4	0	12.5	0
Administrators	1.3	0	2.1	0	2.1	0	1.5	0	—	0	2.2	0
Specialized workers	0.6	0	3.1	0	8.5	0	2.6	0	—	0	—	0
Peasant workers	1.9	0	14.8	0	20.2	0	12.0	0	7.4	0	10.3	0
Semiproletarians (SF)												
Total	40.4	29.6	58.0	0.5	30.5	0.2	55.6	4.9	80.7	16.6	78.1	14.3
Subsistence peasants[c]	25.9	—	50.6	—	6.5	—	55.6	—	74.1	—	78.1	—
Communities	0	—	0	—	16.6	—	0	—	1.3	—	0	—
Seasonal workers	14.5	—	7.4	—	7.4	—	0	—	5.3	—	0	—
Proletarians												
Landless workers	18.0	0	0	0	11.5	0	0	0	10.9	0	7.2	0
Total No. of Households (1,000)	786.6		5,404.2		344.9		1,368.8		440.0		417.4	

Source: Solon Barraclough, ed., *Agrarian Structure in Latin America* (Lexington, Mass.: Heath, Lexington Books, 1973), pp. 326, 327, 331, and 332.

Note: Data on Peru not available.

[a] Agricultural land owned.

[b] — = data not available.

[c] "Unidentified" rural households were included in this category.

data typify the structure of traditional Latin American agrarian society, for all the observations were made prior to any significant land reform in these countries and prior to the massive development of capitalism that occurred in the 1960s and 1970s. The social breakdown reveals the relative importance of six of the social classes identified: landed elites, rural bourgeoisie, petty bourgeoisie, internal peasants, semiproletarians, and proletarians. The precapitalist landed elite is aggregated with the capitalist landed elite since the CIDA data did not distinguish among modes of productions.

Extreme social polarization is clearly evident. Among the seven countries, the landed elites (LMF and MMF) constituted 10.5 percent of the rural families and monopolized 76.8 percent of agricultural land. These figures range, respectively, from 14.6 percent and 93.5 percent in Brazil to 1.6 percent and 72.3 percent in Guatemala.[64]

Due to the more intensive use of the land on the smaller farms, the distribution of income is somewhat less unequal than that of land, but it is still extremely skewed. In Chile, for example, the CIDA study found the family income of the landed elite class to be 5 times higher than that of the rural bourgeoisie, 26 times higher than that of the internal peasants, 35 times higher than that of the full-time proletarian workers, and 137 times higher than that derived by the external semiproletarians from their activities as agricultural producers.[65]

The data clearly show the nonexistence of a significant rural petty bourgeoisie among peasants except in Argentina (32.6 percent of the rural households) and, to some extent, Colombia (23.3 percent). This reflects the weakness of the farmer road under conditions of disarticulated accumulation and institutional control by the traditional agrarian elites.

The importance of external semiproletarianization in the process of peripheral capitalist development is shown by the data. But here the CIDA studies are not precise, for the committee's objective did not include the full characterization of social relations of production in agriculture; rather, in the context of the CIDA's interest in land reform, it was primarily confined to generating information on the distribution and use of land. Nevertheless, in spite of imprecisions in the data, it is apparent that the external semiproletarians were already of extraordinary numerical importance in the late 1950s. They accounted for some 30 percent of the total number of families in Chile, 40 percent of the families in Argentina, 56 percent of the families in Colombia, 58 percent of the families in Brazil, 78 percent of the families in Guatemala, and 81 percent of the families in Ecuador (Table 3.1). Although it can be noted that in Brazil and Chile at the time of the 1950 censuses, internal peasants still accounted for sizable fractions of the rural population (30.8 and 20 percent respectively), and that semifeudal relations were still present, the process of substitution of internal peasants for external semiproletarians was already advancing rapidly, as is repeatedly evidenced in the CIDA studies.[66] As we will see in the following section, it progressed even further through the 1960s and 1970s.

Dynamics of Class Differentiation

The process of class differentiation following the junker and farmer roads described above can now be interpreted in terms of the categories of social classes given in Figure 3.1 and represented graphically in Figure 3.2. This will permit us to visualize the possible trajectories followed by each social class or fraction of a class as capitalism develops.

The nature of the relations that each social group maintains with the means of production and the net income positions of these groups are important factors in locating social classes and following the processes of differentiation. Operationally, the two dimensions to be used are the level of income derived from control of means of production (production income) and the level of income derived from the sale of labor power (wage income). They define the two axes in Figure 3.2. The parallel lines represent isoincome levels, while the tangent of angle Θ (the ratio of wage to production income) measures the degree of proletarianization of each social group, ranging from zero on the horizontal axis (full-time producers) to infinite on the vertical axis (full-time proletarians). The arrows represent the two dominant patterns of social class differentiation within agriculture: the junker and farmer roads. Figure 3.2 thus reflects the double impact—social and economic—of the development of capitalism in agriculture. On the one hand, there is a process of *social differentiation* through which some groups gain increasing control of the means of production while others lose it and become increasingly proletarianized; on the other hand, there is an *economic welfare* effect whereby some groups enrich themselves more than others (increasing relative poverty),

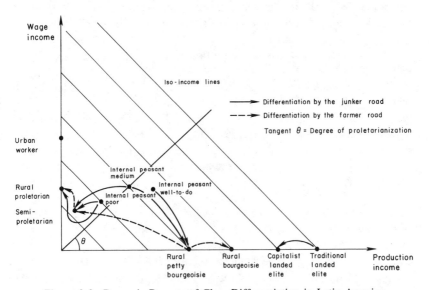

Figure 3.2. Dynamic Process of Class Differentiation in Latin America

and some are eventually absolutely impoverished (increasing absolute poverty).

Following the junker road, the traditional elite is gradually transformed into a capitalist landed elite as social relations in the *latifundio* evolve from internal peasants to wage labor. The internal well-to-do peasants, who control some means of production, join the petty bourgeoisie, while the internal peasant workers are expelled and relocate as external semiproletarian peasants, join the rural landless, or migrate to the cities. The medium internal peasants oscillate between the other two groups and differentiate toward petty bourgeoisie or semiproletarians and proletarians according to capability and destiny.

Similarly, the petty bourgeoisie differentiates along the farmer road into those who accumulate means of production and join the rural bourgeoisie, thus escaping the peasant status, and those who, on the contrary, gradually lose control of the means of production and become semiproletarian peasants or rural proletarians, or migrate to the city. The rural bourgeoisie is also reinforced by farmers on the merchant road who capture lands from either landed elites or peasants.

Empirical Characterization of Class Differentiation: Global Data

It is evidently much more difficult to make empirical statements on the dynamics of change in the Latin American agrarian structure than to characterize it at one point in time as we did above with the CIDA data. Dynamic statements require comparable global data over successive periods of time when such data are often not available; moreover, a straightforward interpretation of the global data in terms of roads of development is generally prevented by the simultaneous occurrence of several patterns of development (e.g., the junker, farmer, and merchant).

What is clear from census data on forms of land tenure is that precapitalist social relations are disappearing rapidly and today characterize only a small fraction of the total number of farms. In Table 3.2, forms of tenure are characterized as either capitalist (owners and rents in cash) or noncapitalist (rents in labor services and kind; and communal and *ejidal* lands). These data show that rent in labor services is declining rapidly in every country where it still exists and represents only a small fraction of farms. In Chile, where 21 percent of the farms were still under rental in labor services in 1964, this form of tenure was essentially eliminated by the land reforms of Frei and Allende.[67] In Ecuador as well, rent in labor services went down from 13 percent of the farms in 1954 (Table 3.2) to 7 percent in 1960 (Table 3.1) and was eradicated by the land reform law in 1964. In El Salvador, rent in labor services (*colonato*) started to disappear rapidly with the introduction of minimum-wage laws in 1950. By 1971, the land in *colonato* had declined by 77 percent relative to 1961, and 70 percent of the farms under this form of tenure in 1961 had disappeared.[68]

Table 3.2. Dynamics of Land Tenure Systems: Initial and Terminal Percentages

Initial and terminal year, by country	Land tenure	Percentage of farms and land				
		Capitalist mode		Noncapitalist mode		
		Owner	Rent in cash	Rent in kind	Rent in labor	Communal
United States						
1940–69	Farms	51–72	35.0–15.0		—[a]	—
	Land	36–35	29.0–13.0		—	—
Mexico						
1950–60	Farms	49–45	0.3– 0.7	0.2–0.4	—	50–53
	Land	62–57	3.9– 3.8	0.2–0.6	—	27.26
Dominican Republic						
1950–71	Farms	60–53	1.7– 1.6	4.5–4.5	1.6– 1.9 (1960)	—
	Land	58–71	0.9– 1.3	1.5–1.4	0.6– 1.7 (1960)	—
Costa Rica						
1950–73	Farms	81–85	2.1– 1.8	1.5–0.4	—	
	Land	90–91	0.7– 0.8	0.2–0.1	—	
El Salvador						
1950–71	Farms	62–39	19.0–13.0		19.0–25.0 (1961)	—
	Land	92 76	5.8– 7.4		2.1– 2.8 (1961)	—
Guatemala						
1950–64	Farms	56–58	17.0–11.0		12.0–12.0	4.9 (1964)
	Land	80–77	2.8– 3.1		1.6– 2.6	1.7 (1964)
Honduras						
1952–66	Farms	21–22	13.0–23.0		4.1 (1952)	34–25
	Land	46–46	3.6– 5.1		0.5 (1952)	25.15
Panama						
1950–71	Farms	13–12	9.1– 8.2		—	—
	Land	18–26	12.09– 3.7		—	—
Venezuela						
1950–61	Farms	42–39	15.0– 8.1	6.2–4.8	—	—
	Land	81–82	3.1– 1.9	1.9–0.5	—	—
Chile						
1955–64	Farms	82–47	7.7– 4.9	7.0 (1964)	21.0 (1964)	—
	Land	70–74	21.0–12.0	1.4–0.8	0.5–0.3	—
Colombia						
1960–70	Farms	62–69	11.0– 5.8	12.0–8.3	—	—
	Land	72–75	3.8– 2.7	3.5–2.6	—	—
Ecuador						
1954–68	Farms	68–76	5–13	3.9–4.2	13 (1954)	1.7–0.3
	Land	82–83	7–9	1.1–1.1	4 (1954)	0.4 (1954)
Brazil						
1940–70	Farms	72–63	12.0–13.0	N.A.[b]	—	—
	Land	64–86	9.7– 4.8	N.A.	—	—
Argentina						
1937–60	Farms	38–40 (1952)	44–22 (1954)			
	Land	38 (1952)–59	16 (1952)–14			
Paraguay						
1943–61	Farms	16–37	6.5– 6.0	1.9 (1956)–1.4	—	—
	Land	74 (1956)–81	5.7 (1956)–4.0	0.3 (1956)–0.1	—	—

(*continued*)

Table 3.2—*Continued*

Initial and terminal year, by country	Land tenure	Percentage of farms and land				
		Capitalist mode		Noncapitalist mode		
		Owner	Rent in cash	Rent in kind	Rent in labor	Communal
Uruguay						
1937–71	Farms	49–59	38–20	8.4–3.0	—	—
	Land	44–53	39–18	2.7–0.9	—	—
Nicaragua						
1963	Farms	39	4.7	2.8	7.4	8.0
	Land	67	1.4	0.4	2.5	8.1
Bolivia						
1950	Farms	75	16.0	3.5	N.A.	4.5
	Land	68	6.1	1.2	N.A.	23.0
Peru						
1961	Farms	67	9.4	6.3	N.A.	4.9
	Land	69	11.0	1.0	N.A.	10.0

Sources: U.S. Department of Agriculture, *Agriculture in the Americas: Statistical Data,* FDCD Working Paper (Washington, D.C., 1976), pp. 35 and 36; James Wilkie, ed., *Statistical Abstract of Latin America,* vol. 18 (Los Angeles: UCLA Latin American Center, 1977), pp. 65–68.

[a]— = form of tenure nonexistent or not recorded.

[b]N.A. = not available.

Similarly, communal or *ejidal* holdings are disappearing in every country except Mexico and represent significant numbers of farms only in Mexico and Honduras. A product of the land reform of 1934, however, the Mexican *ejido* can hardly be considered noncapitalist, and this for the very reasons we brought out in rejecting the concept of a peasant mode of production. We will return to this problem in the next section.

Finally, rent in kind is disappearing in every country (where it is recorded as a separate category) except Mexico and Ecuador. Even in these two countries, however, it characterizes only an insignificant fraction of farms.

We can thus conclude that precapitalist social relations (semifeudal and communal) have virtually disappeared from Latin America. Today, Latin American agriculture is essentially capitalist throughout. Its social relations and the development of its forces of production must be analyzed in terms of the particular logic of peripheral capitalism that constitutes a historically specific phase in the development of capital in the periphery of the world system.

As precapitalist forms of tenure disappear, the land becomes increasingly incorporated into capitalist farming. Table 3.2 shows that this has occurred in all countries except Mexico, where the share of the land in privately owned capitalist farms has decreased relative to the *ejido*. In the United States, Guatemala, and El Salvador, the increasing share of the capitalist mode of production has occurred through a rise of mixed forms of tenure between ownership and cash rental that are not reported in Table 3.2.

This is accompanied by a process of concentration of production among a small number of capitalist producers, either landed elites following the junker road or a rural bourgeoisie following the farmer road. In Costa Rica, for example, in 1973, farms greater than 20 hectares generated more than 60 percent of the production of the eight most important products, and this share has increased since 1963. In El Salvador, the concentration in medium and large capitalist farms of the production of six of the eight most important products increased between 1960 and 1970. And in Mexico, in spite of the extensive programs of rural development aimed at peasant agriculture, the share of farms of less than 5 hectares in the production of ten of the eleven most important crops decreased between 1960 and 1970.[69]

The census data on the transformations of peasant agriculture reported in Table 3.3 indicate that between 1950 and 1970 the number of peasant farms increased in all countries except Mexico and Panama. In Mexico, the peasantry did expand, but this occurred in the *ejido*. In Panama, the decline in the number of peasant farms was due to the modernization of sugarcane and rice production, which led to the rapid absorption of peasants into a proletarianized labor force. In the majority of countries, the growing number of peasant farms led to an increase in both the percentage of farm holdings and the percentage of total agricultural land controlled by peasants, even though here there are more exceptions. The reinforcement of peasant numbers occurred equally in countries that followed the junker road, such as Brazil, Ecuador, Colombia, and Chile (before 1964), and in countries that followed the farmer road, such as Mexico and the Dominican Republic. This was due not to the specific features of the roads but to the general lack of opportunities for full proletarianization under peripheral capitalist development.

Even though there has been rapid migration toward the cities and wage employment has been created in the rural areas, these have not been sufficient to absorb a peasant population that has increased rapidly as a result of demographic growth, the modernization of precapitalist estates along the junker road, and land concentration along the farmer road. Thus, between 1950 and 1960, 5.3 million peasants migrated to the cities; another 4.5 million migrated between 1960 and 1970.[70] Agricultural wage employment increased by only 0.5 percent per year, accounting for 24 percent of the growth of the total agricultural labor force between 1950 and 1970.[71] As a result, peasant agriculture became an important refuge for a majority of the growing rural population, absorbing 76 percent of the growth in the agricultural labor force between 1950 and 1970. This growing pressure on the land led to a decline in the size of peasant farms. The data in Table 3.3 show that this change characterized seven of the eleven countries for which information exists.

What the census data evidence, consequently, is a process whereby the peasantry grows in size but simultaneously loses its status as commodity producer.[72] It is forced onto more and more minute and eroded land plots, where it is of necessity increasingly semiproletarianized. And lack of em-

Table 3.3.   Size of Farms Less Than 5 Hectares in Area for Eleven
Central and South American Countries, 1950–70

			I Average size of small farms (hecares)		II Annual percentage change of I	Annual percentage change in number of small farms	Small farms as percentage of total number of farms	
Country	Year A	Year B	Year A	Year B			Year A	Year B
Brazil[a]	1950	1970	4.25	3.61	−0.8	6.2	34	51
Chile	1955	1965	1.40	1.67	1.6	7.5	37	49
Colombia	1954	1960	1.84	1.64	−1.6	6.0	55	63
Costa Rica[b]	1955	1963	1.69	2.24	3.2	6.1	29	36
Ecuador	1954	1968	1.72	1.50	−0.9	3.7	73	69
El Salvador	1950	1970	1.35	1.21	−0.5	2.5	81	87
Guatemala[c]	1950	1960	1.73	1.76	0.2	1.5	88	87
Mexico	1950	1960	1.36	1.48	8.8	−1.0	72	66
Nicaragua[c]	1950	1960	3.00	2.56	−1.4	10.1	35	51
Panama[d]	1950	1971	2.16	1.82	−0.8	−0.3	52	45
Peru	1961	1972	1.48	1.44	−0.2	3.4	83	78

Source: Peter Peek, "Agrarian Change and Rural Emigration in Latin America," ILO Working Paper, World Employment Programme Research (Geneva: ILO, 1978).

[a] Includes farms of 0–10 hectares.
[b] Includes farms of 0–4.89 hectares.
[c] Includes farms of 0–7 hectares.
[d] Excludes farms of less than 0.5 hectares.

ployment opportunities blocks sufficient outmigration and perpetuates rural misery. Thus, while the number of peasants increases, the social relations that characterize these peasants are increasingly those of a labor reserve with erratic and low-paying employment opportunities.

The nature of the agricultural labor market also has been changing, from permanent to seasonal employment, particularly in the areas where agriculture is highly modernized and integrated with multinational agribusiness. This increased seasonality in labor requirements results from the partial mechanization of the labor process whereby some tasks remain manual and hence highly demanding of labor power for short periods of time. In São Paulo, for example, Graziano da Silva shows that mechanization of soil preparation, planting, and cultural practices and use of herbicides reduce labor needs throughout the year, while harvesting remains a manual operation and increased yields augment labor needs at that time of the year.[73] This leads to emergence of a mass of seasonal workers, the *boias frias,* who are hired on a daily basis through the intermediation of labor contractors. In 1975, the *boias frias* constituted about 25–30 percent of the agricultural labor force in São Paulo.[74] On farms of more than 500 hectares in the region, Lopes estimates that while total employment declined by 45 percent between 1940 and 1970, the number of temporary workers increased rapidly to 40 percent of the labor force.[75] In turn, the seasonal availability of labor is made possible by the integration of labor markets with both the subsistence peasant economy and the urban informal sector, sometimes through long-distance migrations. Thus, while the bulk of seasonal workers are still tied to peasant farms, an important fraction come from the urban sector.[76] In São Paulo, 27 percent of the population that is economically active in agriculture is urban. In Mexico, city-dwelling farm workers in major metropolitan fringe areas represent between 3 percent and 9 percent of the agricultural labor force in the surrounding areas.[77] And women and children count importantly in this seasonal work force.[78]

These patterns of class differentiation and transformation of the agrarian structure are, however, highly complex and must be characterized specifically at the level of each country. To do this, we consider now in some detail the cases of Mexico, Colombia, and Peru.[79]

Empirical Characterization of Class Differentiation: Country Studies

MEXICO.   In the years following the peasant uprising that culminated in the revolution of 1910, capitalism in Mexican agriculture has developed at a rapid pace, fostered in large part by the intervention of the state in agricultural production through a variety of programs. Mexican agricultural policies have followed two successive directions since the revolution: one, under the leadership of General Cárdenas, emphasized the growth of the *ejidal,* or nonprivate, sector and, in particular, the collectivized *ejido,* which was seen as an alternative to the large-scale capitalist enterprise; the other, which was begun under Camacho and continued by his successors, emphasized the growth of large capitalist farms, particularly in the northern regions of the country, which specialize in the production of commercial crops for domestic use and the world market. While apparently contradictory, these two policy thrusts were to create, until the late 1960s, a remarkably productive and politically stable agrarian structure.

The growth of capitalism in Mexican agriculture is based on a small minority of producers who operate efficient, large-scale modern farms and contribute the largest percentage of total agricultural production, and a majority of producers, using rudimentary techniques on minute plots of land, who contribute but a small proportion and serve as a reservoir of cheap labor. Four main categories of agricultural producers are found within Mexico: (1) the capitalist farmers, who dominate production; (2) the *ejidos,* which control a large percentage of agricultural land but contribute a much smaller amount of total product; (3) the smallholding peasants, who control only small parcels of land and depend on wage labor as their primary source of support; and (4) the landless wage laborers, who comprise nearly 63 percent of the agricultural labor force. The *ejidatarios* and smallholding peasants together constitute the Mexican peasantry.

Capitalist farmers.   During the period of massive land redistribution under Cárdenas, precapitalist relations of production were definitively liquidated in

Mexican agriculture and the large haciendas were broken up. The *ejidal* share of total cultivated land increased from 13 percent to 47 percent. However, in spite of this extensive redistribution of land to the peasantry, large capitalist farms were to emerge in the 1940s as the dominant element in Mexican agriculture. Since the farms created were under the legal maximum size limit of 100–200 hectares, the development of capitalism in this private sector followed the farmer road, on which differentiation took place in part through the accumulation of large areas of land far in excess of the legal limit.[80]

The dominance of the large capitalist farms in Mexican agriculture is attributable in part to the state policies that were initiated to stimulate import-substitution industrialization. The increased imports of capital and intermediate goods necessitated by import substitution would have created a large deficit in the Mexican balance of payments if exports had not been increased. State policy makers, in response to the need for export promotion, turned to large-scale capitalist agriculture, particularly in the north and northwest, as a source of exports. Thus, while agricultural exports in 1940 contributed only 16 percent of the value of total exports, by 1950 this share had increased to 47 percent. Throughout the 1950s and 1960s, agricultural products were the primary source of foreign exchange for the Mexican industrialization program.[81]

One major policy through which the state subsidized the growth of agricultural exports was the increase of public investment in rural infrastructure, primarily irrigation. Between 1941 and 1952, 18 percent of the federal budget and 90 percent of all public expenditures in agriculture were devoted to irrigation projects. The major proportion of these newly irrigated farmlands were then sold as private farms, many of which greatly exceeded the legal size limit.[82] The irrigation projects benefited principally the northwestern states, where irrigated croplands expanded from 4 percent to 53 percent of the cultivated area between 1940 and 1960. The next-largest beneficiaries were the northern states, while the states of the central, gulf, and southwestern regions, where the largest percentage of the peasant population is concentrated, showed minimal increases (Table 3.4).

In addition, state policies favored the expansion of production on large-scale capitalist farms through research and diffusion of the high-yield seeds and inputs of the Green Revolution. Because of the specific requirements of these seeds, the use of which necessitates large amounts of fertilizer and other inputs, it is largely the well-capitalized, irrigated farms of the north and northwest that have been able to use this new technology successfully.[83] The introduction of the Green Revolution in Mexico, as in many developing nations, has contributed to a worsening of income distribution within the agricultural sector; the large private farmers have reaped much higher profits through increased yields, while freeholding peasants and *ejidatarios* have experienced no such increase.[84]

Public and private credit also has been concentrated in the hands of the

Table 3.4. Mexico: Hectares of Land Benefited
by Major Federal Irrigation Projects as a Percentage of
Total Hectares Cultivated, 1940–60

States	Percent		
	1940	1950	1960
North	4.0	12.0	15.0
North Pacific	4.0	39.0	53.0
Gulf	0.0	0.3	3.0
South Pacific	0.0	1.4	1.2
Center	3.0	6.0	9.0
Mexico as a whole	3.0	9.0	14.0

Source: Clark W. Reynolds, *The Mexican Economy: Twentieth-Century Structure and Growth* (New Haven: Yale University Press, 1970), p. 156.

large private farmers, particularly those in the north and northwest, while the *ejidos* and freeholding peasants in all states have received a much smaller per capita amount. Because the large private farmers control infrastructure and credit, production on their farms is in general much more capital intensive than production in peasant agriculture. In 1960, nearly 80 percent of all the tractors used in agricultural production were owned by large private farms, while the peasant sector, which controlled nearly as much land, had only 20 percent.[85] These capitalist farms evidently rely on a much higher percentage of hired laborers than do peasant producers. In 1970, close to 53 percent of the workers on farms of over 5 hectares were hired laborers, compared with 27 percent for the peasant sector.[86]

The large capitalist farms are the principal producers of exports, raw materials for industry, and luxury foods for the domestic market such as coffee, fresh fruits, vegetables, cotton, and wheat. In addition, all but a small fraction of the rapidly growing cattle production is controlled by capitalist farmers. The peasants, by contrast, are primarily producers of the basic wage foods—corn, beans, and rice (Table 3.5). These last three crops are the staples of the Mexican diet, but they are unattractive to capitalist farmers because of the low profitability of their production, which results from state controls on the prices of wage foods.[87] Because of these controls and because of the increasing lure of export markets, land devoted to the production of staple commodities within Mexico has stagnated or declined since 1960. As a result, the production of rice and beans (as well as wheat) barely kept pace with the increases in population between 1960 and 1977,[88] and corn production declined on a per capita basis. Imports of this last commodity have increased dramatically, growing from 8 percent of domestic consumption between 1970 and 1974 to 24 percent in 1975 and 26 percent in 1977. These massive imports have had the effect of discouraging production not only on the capitalist farms but also on peasant plots.

Table 3.5.   Mexico: Value Share of Agricultural Production, 1950 and 1960

Value share	Rice	Corn	Beans	Coffee	Sugar	Cotton	Wheat	Cattle
	\multicolumn{8}{c}{Percent}
1950								
More than 5 hectares	39	45	52	67	48	59	57	—[a]
Less than 5 hectares	0	15	6	0	4	1	5	—
Ejidos	61	40	42	33	48	40	38	—
1960								
More than 5 hectares	35	43	46	62	49	66	68	88
Less than 5 hectares	3	10	3	11	3	0	2	2
Ejidos	62	47	51	27	48	34	30	10

Source: *Censo Agrícola-Ganadero y Ejidal* (Mexico City, 1950 and 1960).
[a] — = data not available.

As the import of basic food products has increased, so has the export of agricultural products such as cattle and meat products, coffee, and fresh winter vegetables and fruits—the majority of which is sold on the U.S. market. Thus, as Mexico lost self-sufficiency in basic foodstuffs, which were primarily produced by peasant producers, production on capitalist farms continued to expand, as evidenced by the growth in exports.

Of increasing importance in Mexican agricultural production are the large multinational corporations—almost exclusively North American—which control a growing share of total production—the majority of which is for export. Because the ownership of land by foreigners is prohibited by the Mexican Constitution, these corporations are not direct landowners but rather control production through the establishment of contracts with Mexican producers, predominantly the large capitalist farmers in the north and northwest, who are thus reduced to the status of local managers with only minimal decision-making authority. To date, no global analysis of the extent of foreign investment in Mexican agriculture has been made. However, recent studies have noted the dominance of foreign investment in the production of fruits, vegetables, tobacco, cotton, cattle, milk products, alcohol, and some corn products.[89]

The increased integration of Mexican agriculture into the world market and the growing participation of international capital in the production of commercial crops within Mexico have thus led to the growth of export production and the relative decline in the production of staple crops. As a recent NACLA study of the Bajio Valley noted:

The growers who survive the pressures of capitalist agriculture are driven to produce for the national and international markets instead of raising staples for local consumption. The three largest crops that Del Monte contracts for [in the Bajio Valley] are sweet corn (1,000 acres), peas (1,500 acres), and asparagus (2,250 acres). . . . None of these crops figure predominantly in the diet of the Mexican people. Canned peas and sweet corn are marketed as delicacies and purchased exclusively by the middle and upper classes. Del Monte's asparagus production is even more marginal to the Mexican diet: over 90% of it is shipped abroad to markets in the industrialized countries.[90]

Barkin similarly concludes his study of the internationalization of Mexican agriculture by observing that "this clearly stimulates the production of fruits and vegetables, industrial grains, and livestock, and leads farmers to abandon basic food production or induces them to work as laborers in commercial operations and leave their own farms idle."[91] This deep crisis of staple foods reflects the victory of the doctrine of comparative advantages, after the mid-1960s, over the philosophy of self-sufficiency, implemented in the 1950s and early 1960s, through the achievements of the Green Revolution. And the crisis of staple foods is, of course, also the crisis of Mexican peasants.

Peasants. The dynamic growth of capitalist agriculture within Mexico during the 1950s and 1960s was the main contributor to the high rates of growth of agricultural production that occurred during that period. The increase in agricultural production was 7.4 percent between 1944 and 1953, and 4.3 percent between 1956 and 1966. Hidden by these impressive figures, however, are large regional differences in production and productivity as well as huge inequalities between peasant and capitalist agriculture. The declining rate of growth of agricultural production, which reached 0.8 percent between 1966 and 1976, reflects the crisis of peasant agriculture in both the *ejido* and freeholding peasant sectors.

Ejidatarios. The *ejido,* the most noted aspect of Mexican agrarian reform, in fact flourished during only one brief period—that of the Cárdenas administration between 1934 and 1940. With the emergence of the large capitalist farms as the dominant element in Mexican agriculture in the postwar period, the *ejido* declined markedly in importance. Between 1940 and 1950, the *ejidal* share of cultivated land declined from 47 percent to 44 percent; and the *ejidal* value share of total agricultural production dropped even more dramatically—from 51 percent to 37 percent (Table 3.6). Between 1960 and 1970, however, there was a large increase in the amount of *ejidal* lands as

Table 3.6. Mexico: Distribution of Cultivated Area and Value Share of Production[a] by Farm Size, 1940–70

	Percent					
	Cultivated land			Value share of agricultural production		
Year	More than 5 hectares	Less than 5 hectares	Ejido	More than 5 hectares	Less than 5 hectares	Ejido
1940	46	7	47	40	9	51
1950	50	6	44	54	9	37
1960	52	5	43	54	6	40
1970	42	3	55	45	4	51

Sources: *Censo Agrícola-Ganadero y Ejidal* (Mexico City, 1950, 1960, and 1970).
[a] Agricultural production includes crops but not cattle.

well as in the contribution of the *ejido* to total agricultural production. The *ejidal* share of cultivated lands increased to 55 percent, and the *ejidal* contribution to total agricultural production increased to 51 percent. During this same period, the proportion of the total agricultural labor force employed on the *ejido*, both as *ejidatarios* and as outside laborers, increased from 45 percent to 65 percent of all agricultural workers.

Although these figures seem impressive on the surface, in actual fact the land distributed to the *ejidos* during this period was often of extremely low quality. Thus, while there was an increase in the total area per household, there was actually a slight decline in the area cultivated (Table 3.7). The *ejidatario*, while controlling in general 2.6 more hectares of cultivated land than the freeholding peasant, had nowhere near the 13.4 hectares of cultivated land controlled by the "average" large farmer. (This average, of course, conceals a large proportion of farmers who controlled more than 100 hectares.) In addition, while the cultivated land area controlled by the *ejidatarios* declined, that controlled by the large farmers actually increased by 9 percent.

The data on value share of agricultural production can be quite misleading because they do not include the value of cattle production, animal products, and forest products. When these are added, the value share of agricultural production of the *ejido* is only 37 percent of the total, with the private farms of more than 5 hectares contributing 51.2 percent and those with less than 5 hectares contributing 11.8 percent.[92] Given this calculation, the *ejido*, with 51 percent of all cultivated lands and 55 percent of irrigated lands, contributed a much smaller proportion of Mexico's total agricultural production than did the capitalist farms.

The reemergence of the *ejido* as an important element in the national agrarian structure has prompted some observers to proclaim a "refunctionalization" of peasant agriculture through state intervention.[93] Although the retention of population in the rural areas, which is perhaps the main contribution of the *ejido* to the Mexican political economy, has been effective in stemming the flood of rural migrants to the urban areas and in ensuring a stable clientele to the ruling Institutionalized Revolutionary Party, it is not at all clear that peasant agriculture is actually being re-created on the

Table 3.7.   Mexico: Average Area per Landholding, 1960 and 1970

Landholding	Total area (hectares)		Cultivated area (hectares)	
	1960	1970	1960	1970
More than 5 hectares	123.9	95.8	12.3	13.4
Less than 5 hectares	0.6	1.0	0.6	0.8
Ejidos	15.5	18.8	3.6	3.4

Source: *Censo Agrícola-Ganadero y Ejidal* (Mexico City, 1960 and 1970).

ejidos. Given the extremely heterogeneous mixture of modern and traditional production methods used on the *ejidos,* it is difficult to analyze this sector in the aggregate at all. Nonetheless, in spite of the aggregate nature of the data, a great deal of evidence indicates that the *ejidatarios* are becoming increasingly dependent on outside wage labor as their principal source of income.

According to 1960 census data, only 66 percent of the *ejidatarios* were able to obtain even half of their income from *ejidal* production. To supplement this income, the vast majority of these *ejidatarios* worked as wage laborers in agricultural production outside their own *ejido.* In addition, 34 percent of the *ejidatarios* could not cover even half of their expenses with income from production on the *ejido.* These persons thus received the major proportion of their income from wage labor outside the *ejido.*[94] A recent survey of migratory agricultural workers carried out by the Secretariat of Agrarian Reform found that more than half of the migratory workers were *ejidatarios,* many of whom had abandoned their plots entirely in favor of wage labor outside the *ejido.*[95]

Closely tied with the increased reliance on wage labor outside the *ejido* is the rising frequency of the rental of *ejidal* lands. Although by law the alienation and rental of *ejidal* lands is prohibited and therefore is not recorded in any national statistics, field researchers have noted a high incidence of rental transactions between *ejidatarios* and capitalist farmers. Usually it is the best portion of the *ejidal* lands which is rented; and the *ejidatario* is often employed as a wage laborer to work on his own land.[96] When the land is marginal, it is simply abandoned for more-profitable wage earnings. Thus, recent estimates suggest that as much as one half of all the rain-fed land in Mexico that had previously been opened to cultivation is now left idle.[97]

In conclusion, even though the *ejido* has increased both its share of the land and its share of the rural population, the social relations of *ejidal* production have been rapidly changing toward proletarianization. The increase in the number of peasants on the *ejido* dissimulates their qualitative disappearance as peasants.

Smallholding peasants.   Peasant agriculture in the private sector is rapidly collapsing. The absolute number of these farms declined 39 percent between 1950 and 1970, and the peasants' share of the total number of private-sector farms fell from 74 percent to 61 percent. In spite of their continued numerical importance, smallholding peasants controlled only 3 percent of cultivated land and contributed a mere 4 percent of agricultural production in 1970 (Table 3.6). Because of the rapid decrease in the number of peasant plots, the average area increased from 0.6 hectare to 1.0 hectare, which is, however, still insufficient to meet the subsistence needs of the peasant family. Since 1940, freeholding peasants have consistently had the largest number of farms in the private sector but have controlled scarcely 1 percent of the land in private agriculture. Capitalist agriculture, on the other hand, has consistently controlled almost 99 percent of the land in private agriculture (Table 3.8).

Table 3.8.   Mexico: Number of Farms, Percentage of Farms,
and Total Land Area in the Private Sector Controlled by Farms,
by Farm Size, 1940–70

Farm size	Hectares			
	1940	1950	1960	1970
Number of farms:				
More than 5 hectares	290	361	447	388
Less than 5 hectares	929	1,005	889	609
Percentage of farms:				
More than 5 hectares	24.0	26.0	33.0	39.0
Less than 5 hectares	76.0	74.0	67.0	61.0
Percentage of land:				
More than 5 hectares	98.8	98.7	98.9	98.7
Less than 5 hectares	1.2	1.1	1.1	1.3

Source: *Censo Agrícola-Ganadero y Ejidal* (Mexico City, 1940, 1950, 1960, and 1970).

The present food crisis in Mexico is, to a large extent, a crisis of peasant agriculture and particularly of the smallholder in the private sector. These peasants have continued to specialize in the production of corn, devoting over 78 percent of their land in 1960 to the cultivation of this crop.[98] However, the capitalist farmers and, to a certain extent, the *ejidatarios* have turned to the production of other, more remunerative crops, and the area planted in corn has declined since 1966, necessitating the importation of increasingly large amounts of this cereal from foreign producers—principally the United States. The fact that these large imports depress the domestic price of corn is a disincentive to domestic producers and, in particular, leads to the ruin of the smallholders.

The basic explanation for the decline in the production of corn in Mexico can be found in the evolution of domestic corn prices during the last two and a half decades. Since the mid-1950s, state policies have imposed a ceiling on both rural and urban prices of the basic food commodities—corn, rice, and beans. Although nominal prices of all these foods have continued to increase, in real terms there has been a decline in their prices and particularly in that of corn, which fell 33 percent between 1963 and 1972.[99] Because peasant producers need to produce principally for their own consumption, they have not been able to switch to the production of other crops. The artificially low price of corn has meant a devaluation of home production and an increased need for income from other sources—mainly wage labor.

Landless laborers.   Complementing the fast pace of proletarianization within peasant agriculture, the landless agricultural labor force also has increased rapidly. In 1930, preceding the period of large-scale agrarian reform under Cárdenas, landless laborers represented two thirds of the agricultural labor force and numbered 2.5 million persons. In 1970, out of a labor force of approximately 5 million persons, 3 million were not property owners, renters, sharecroppers, or *ejidatarios*. Thus, while 35 percent of the agricultural labor force is composed of property owners and *ejidatarios* and another 2 percent consists of tenants and sharecroppers, the remaining 63 percent has no direct access to land and thus derives its subsistence primarily from wage labor.[100] The number of agricultural workers without any land whatsoever is presently larger than the number of such workers in 1930 prior to the large-scale land redistribution under Cárdenas. Thus, despite some fifty years of agrarian reform, the largest percentage of the Mexican agricultural labor force is comprised of landless workers who are dependent on wage labor.

According to the findings of the extensive study of Mexican agriculture conducted by CIDA, the average length of employment for wage laborers in agriculture declined from 190 days in 1950 to 100 days in 1960.[101] The average real income of these workers declined 18 percent in this period.[102] The high rate of population increase and the continuing process of mechanization on the large capitalist farms contributed to a further decline in the average length of employment and real income of the landless workers between 1960 and 1970. Although the rural minimum wage rose during this period, the average length of employment continued to decline; and the average real income fell an additional 29 percent—a decline of 41 percent between 1950 and 1970.[103]

The majority of landless laborers are concentrated in the states of central and southern Mexico, which are also the states where smallholdings and *ejidal* agriculture predominate. From these regions, the landless laborers migrate in large numbers in search of employment. Only a small proportion of the agricultural laborers are employed full time on the modern capitalist farms of northern and northwestern states. The majority are employed only a small proportion of the time, if at all, in capitalist agriculture and find employment, although under much worse conditions, in peasant agriculture. The single largest source of employment for these laborers is perhaps the market for undocumented workers that exists in the United States. In recent surveys of returned migrants, more than a third reported that they were landless agricultural laborers while in Mexico, although in the United States they had often found employment in nonagricultural activities.[104] In addition, the largest percentage of these workers reported that they were unemployed in Mexico before their migration to the United States. Due to the low levels of employment within Mexican agriculture for the landless laborers and the high rates of unemployment in urban Mexico, the United States offers the only source of income and survival for a large percentage of these three million persons. Massive migrations to Mexican cities and to the United States are thus the symptoms of the breakdown of the Mexican peasantry.

COLOMBIA. Capitalism in Colombian agriculture, while less developed than that in Mexico, has greatly expanded in the period since World War II and dominates agricultural production almost exclusively. Agrarian capitalism in Colombia follows principally the "junker" and "merchant" roads of development. Newly important commercial crops such as cotton, rice, sugar, soybeans, and sorghum are produced predominantly on the larger farms, which employ highly capital-intensive methods of production and are oriented strictly toward production for the market. Coffee is somewhat of an exception because several of the areas where it is produced (Antioquia, Caldas) were settled on the basis of family farms that are today differentiating rapidly along a "farmer" road under the combined impacts of demographic explosions, new coffee varieties, and higher international prices.[105] The bulk of Colombia's coffee, however, was produced from the very beginning in large precapitalist haciendas that later, under the combined pressures of peasant rebellions, economic opportunities, and land reform laws, modernized following the junker road.[106] Precapitalist relations of production are rapidly disappearing from the Colombian countryside as a growing body of semi-proletarian peasants and proletarians provides a ready source of labor.

The history of agricultural development in Colombia is dominated by the rapid and sometimes savage expansion of large-scale commercial agriculture at the expense of peasant agriculture. The first land reform law in 1936 led to massive displacement of sharecroppers and tenants because it declared that these forms of tenancy did not fulfill the social responsibilities of ownership. The 1936 law was repealed in 1944, but rural violence in the 1950s led to the further displacement of peasants in a manner reminiscent of the enclosure movement in seventeenth-century England and created the labor basis for the junker road. A new land reform law following the Punta del Este conference in 1961 again threatened to expropriate sharecroppers and tenants as well as lands deemed inadequately exploited. A massive influx of credit and technology supported the transformation of semifeudal estates into modern, large-scale commercial farms. The Currie Plan in 1971 recommended that agriculture be "rationalized" through the elimination of the peasantry, the strengthening of commercial farms, and the absorption of the rural poor into the urban labor force. Concentration of the land increased, urban migration avalanched, and the precarious position of the peasantry created serious political tensions. At the same time, unfavorable wage-food prices associated with industrialization policies induced commercial farms to turn to the production of exportables, industrial inputs, and luxury foods, thus precipitating a serious food crisis in spite of spectacular growth in agricultural production. With successful modernization of the large estates but mounting peasant militance and urban migration, the land reform program was essentially cancelled in 1973 (pact of Chicoral between liberals and conservatives), and integrated rural-development projects became a key policy in the López Michelsen administration's plan "to close the gap."[107]

The value share of capitalist crops (cotton, rice, sugar, sorghum, and soybeans) in total agricultural production grew an impressive 191 percent in the

Table 3.9.   Colombia: Value Share of Total Production
by Type of Crop, 1950–55 and 1971–76

Type of crop[a]	Percent		
	1950–55	1971–76	Change
Capitalist	10.6	30.8	191
Peasant	23.8	24.2	2
Mixed	25.5	17.8	−30 .
Coffee	40.1	27.2	−32

Source: Salomon Kalmanovitz, *Desarrollo de la Agricultura en Colombia*
(Bogotá: Editorial la Carreta, 1978).
[a] For the definition of types of crops, see Table 3.10.

period between 1950–55 and 1971–76 (Table 3.9). However, only 10–15
percent of these crops were grown on farms of under 5 hectares; the major
proportion was grown on farms of over 100 hectares, thus indicating the
relative concentration of production on larger units. The peasant crops (beans,
plantain, manioc, and sugarcane [for unrefined sugar called panela]), which
rely on predominantly labor-intensive methods of production and 40 percent
of which are produced on farms of under 5 hectares, showed an increase in
value share of total production of only 2 percent. On the other hand, mixed
crops (corn, potatoes, and wheat) and coffee, which are produced by both
capitalists and peasants, declined 30 percent and 32 percent, respectively, in
terms of value share of production.

The increased volume of production of capitalist crops is due both to the
widespread adoption of modern inputs, such as high levels of use of machinery and fertilizers, and to the large expansion of land area devoted to the
cultivation of these crops. Since 1950 the land area used for cotton has
expanded 337 percent and that for rice has grown 105 percent (Table 3.10).
Land area used for the cultivation of all other crops has grown very slowly,
and production of many of these crops is virtually stagnant. In addition, the
land area used for the production of wheat has declined 66 percent since
1950—a direct result of the large-scale importation of P.L. 480 wheat into
Colombia and the consequent depressed domestic price levels.

The increased land area used for the cultivation of capitalist crops reflects
the tremendous expansion in the number and total area of the large farms that
occurred between 1960 and 1970. While the farms of over 50 hectares expanded in both absolute and relative numbers, those of under 10 hectares
declined.[108] The decline in the number and area of small farms is due in large
measure to the liquidation of sharecropping and rental agreements on small
parcels traditionally used as a means of tying labor to the land in precapitalist
estates. While sharecroppers and renters remain a source of labor on some of
the large estates, their importance has been steadily undermined by the growth

Table 3.10.   Colombia: Land Area Cultivated, by Type of Crop,
1950–55 and 1971–76

Type of crop	Thousand hectares		Change (percent)
	1950–55	1971–76	
Capitalist			
Cotton	60.8	265.8	337.0
Rice	157.3	323.2	105.0
Sugar	50.5	113.0	124.0
Sorghum[a]	25.2	131.7	442.0
Soybeans[a]	19.2	56.3	193.0
Peasant			
Panela	217.3	303.0	39.4
Beans	102.8	116.0	12.8
Plantain	259.7	315.7	21.6
Manioc	122.7	158.3	29.0
Mixed	790.0	831.6	10.5
Corn	790.0	831.6	10.5
Potatoes	101.8	130.8	28.5
Wheat	177.8	59.8	−66.0
Coffee	752.8	882.3	17.2

Source: Salomon Kalmanovitz, *Desarrollo de la Agricultura en Colombia*
(Bogotá: Editorial la Carreta, 1978).
[a] Estimated from 1960–65 to 1971–76.

of a body of proletarianized and semiproletarianized agricultural laborers and
by passage of a set of land reform laws restricting these forms of social
relations.

During the 1960s, the number of rented farms of under 10 hectares declined
54 percent; and the number of farms of that size that were worked on a
sharecropping basis declined 35 percent. On the other hand, the number of
farms of 50–200 hectares that were worked by sharecroppers increased 22
percent, while those of over 200 hectares increased 24 percent. This signifies
both the widespread dissolution of precapitalist relations of production in
Colombian agriculture as well as the growing penetration of merchant and
industrial capital into agricultural production through the use of capitalist
sharecropping agreements.[109]

Therefore, the development of capitalism in Colombian agriculture has
taken place on the basis of rapid growth in the cultivation of capitalist crops;
the concentration of production and land into large units, many of which are
rented; and the decreased importance of crops produced by peasant producers.
Peasant farms—those under 10 hectares—have decreased both in total number
and in area, while all other farm sizes have expanded absolutely (Table 3.11).
The combination of a bias in the development of capitalist agriculture toward
exports and industrial crops and the crisis of peasant agriculture has precipitated a food crisis in Colombia that is leading to the rapid increase in food
prices and food imports.

Table 3.11.   Colombia: Land Distribution by Number and Size of Farm
and by Total Area, 1960 and 1970

Farm category	Farm size (hectares)	Number of farms (thousands)		Distribution of farms (percent)			Distribution of area (percent)		
		1960	1970	1960	1970	Change	1960	1970	Change
Subfamily	0–5	757	700	62.6	59.5	−7.5	4.5	3.7	−7.5
Family	5–10	169	160	13.9	13.6	−5.6	4.3	3.5	−6.6
Commercial									
Medium	10–50	201	218	16.6	18.5	8.4	15.4	15.0	10.5
Large	50–200	63	74	5.2	6.3	19.3	20.8	21.8	18.9
Latifundio	> 200	21	25	1.7	2.1	20.1	55.0	56.0	15.3
Total		1,210	1,177	100.0	100.0		100.0	100.0	

Source: DANE, *La Agricultura en Colombia, 1950–1972* (Bogotá: DANE, 1977).

The changes in crop production and land tenure provide us with a relatively clear picture of the evolution of capitalism in Colombian agriculture. Equally important but unfortunately more difficult to obtain are data on the impact of the development of capitalism on the peasant producers and the consequent differentiation and semiproletarianization that occurred within the rural population.

The most evident impact of capitalism, both rural and urban, has been the high rate of farm-to-city migration that has taken place in Colombia since the 1950s. Pushed out by worsening conditions in the rural economy and attracted by the possibility of high-wage industrial jobs in the urban centers, rural migrants contributed to urban growth rates that were on the order of 6 percent per year during the 1960s. Notwithstanding these high rates of migration, the density of the rural population increased from 80 persons per square kilometer in 1960 to 98 persons in 1970.[110] Undoubtedly, this concentration is higher on the farms of under 10 hectares, which continue to predominate in terms of numbers.

Rural workers who obtain their entire income from wage labor in agriculture accounted for 40 percent of the agricultural labor force in both 1951 and 1964. In 1973 this category apparently declined in numbers but increased its participation relative to other categories.[111]

While it would appear that the percentage of the agricultural labor force that is fully proletarianized has remained stable, the rapid increase in commercial crop cultivation has created a large and growing demand for seasonal wage workers. A portion of this demand is filled by the fully proletarianized labor force, while another important portion is met by part-time wage workers drawn from the peasantry. It has been estimated that one third of the peasants earned the major portion of their income from wage labor in 1960 and that two thirds of the agricultural labor force earned at least a portion of its income working for wages in agriculture.[112] Since that date, as noted above, the demand for seasonal labor has continued to increase at the same time that the concentration of population on the *minifundios* has grown more acute, which in turn increases the percentage of peasant producers relying on wage labor as their main source of income.

PERU. The analysis of agriculture in Peru, beginning with that of José Mariátegui in the 1920s, has generally emphasized the coexistence of large capitalist enterprises in the coastal regions engaged in the cultivation of export crops with the feudal haciendas of the Sierra oriented toward food production.[113] This conceptualization of the feudal character of Sierran *latifundio* and its effect in retarding the development of agrarian capitalism was the professed motivation for the Peruvian land reform program of 1964. As Fernando Belaúnde, president of the republic during the period of this reform, stated:

We understand by agrarian reform the elimination of the feudal structure, which is the greatest obstacle to the overall development of the country. With this in mind, we will encourage the redistribution of rural property which presupposes the abolition of the feudal *latifundio* and serfdom.[114]

In actual fact, this 1964 land reform program accomplished very little redistribution—its main achievement being the legal recognition of land invasions that had taken place in areas such as La Convención and Lares. It had, however, a definite impact on large landowners in the Sierra and elsewhere, who were thus given notice of the intentions of the government to expropriate the large precapitalist estates. This advance warning not only discouraged investment in agricultural production but also provoked the decapitalization of many estates as landlords sold off some assets and did not replace others. Additionally, it encouraged the sale of small plots of land to tenants, continuing a process of expansion of the peasant economy which began in the 1950s.[115]

The so-called feudal nature of agricultural production in the Sierra had actually been radically altered during the 1950s by the growth of transportation and communication facilities, which provided a strong impetus toward the expansion of commercial agricultural production following the junker road. Many landowners attempted to convert their land to commercial production through the eviction of the traditional tenants and the introduction of hired agricultural laborers. Others continued the process of parcelization by selling off all but the most productive of their lands in small plots to tenants.[116]

To a large degree, the attempt to convert tenant farmers into wage laborers was effectively combated by peasant communities, which responded by means of massive and well-organized land invasions. The success of these efforts was recognized by the introduction of land reform legislation in 1964 which in effect legalized the occupation of "privately owned" land by peasant organizations in several regions. Agrarian reform measures in these regions tended to favor the relatively well-off tenants at the expense of small subtenants and landless laborers—a process which has been continued by recent agrarian reform legislation.

Although agrarian reform was not the foremost priority of the military government that took power in 1968, it has become widely recognized as the leading "achievement" of that regime.[117] It differed from its predecessor, as well as from other land reform programs in Latin America, in its proposed rapid expropriation of commercial estates—primarily in the nation's coastal areas. Through the expropriation of these enterprises, the new government was able to destroy the power of the landed oligarchy, long dominant in Peruvian politics, as well as a large base of support for APRA, which was strongly represented by organized workers on these estates. In addition, the regime sought to build a base of support and political legitimation among the beneficiaries of the reform.

Aside from rapid and extensive expropriation of commercial estates in the coastal areas, the other major innovation of land reform in Peru has been the creation of rural cooperatives and precooperatives. Agrarian production cooperatives, the CAPs, defined legally as indivisible production units in which the ownership of all assets is collective, have been established on the expropriated commercial estates on the coast. Within these cooperatives, which are composed of the permanent wage labor force from the preform period, individual production is not allowed; and profits are distributed equally to the members, or in proportion to the number of days worked. Sugar cooperatives have been the most successful segment of the reform sector; their members were skilled workers, and they benefited from the large capital investment left over from the previous period. The members of these cooperatives have become among the highest income earners of the Peruvian working class as profit sharing within the cooperatives has contributed to a substantial increase in incomes.[118]

The precooperative units, the SAISs, were formed predominantly in the highland areas, where large livestock estates were threatened with land invasions by the surrounding communities. The formation of the SAISs was an attempt on the part of the government to preserve intact the administration and assets of the expropriated estates while at the same time defusing and controlling peasant demands for land. In the SAISs, the most productive lands of the ex-haciendas are controlled by a hired administrator and representatives of the state. On the less-productive marginal lands, members of the community are allowed to engage in individual cultivation and/or to graze their own small herds. There have been continuous conflicts between the administration, which is devoted to maximization of profit, and the *comuneros*, who wish to use the improved pastureland and cropland for their own production.[119] Beneficiaries of the reform on the SAISs have gained very little improvement in their material status, for wages have remained roughly similar to those of the prereform period.

Outside the reform sector, which has been localized to the large coastal estates and some of the livestock estates of the Sierra, landlords have responded by initiating their own land reform program, which consists primarily of the sale of small plots of land to tenants. While some well-established tenants have benefited, thus promoting further the development of a rural bourgeoisie in Peruvian agriculture, most permanent and temporary laborers have either gained access to minute plots of land or been completely displaced. One study estimates that in the Cañete Valley, for example, 2,000 permanent laborers (approximately 40 percent of the total labor force) were deprived of their jobs because of the reduced labor requirements of the new parcels of land.[120]

Land reform in Peru has not directly affected all sectors of agricultural production. To date, only one fourth of total cropland and one third of the pastureland is managed by groups established under the land reform program. Roughly one quarter of the rural population belongs to these reform enterprises. However, agrarian reform has succeeded in restructuring rural social classes and, in particular, in accelerating the process of social differentiation among rural producers. The most obvious beneficiaries of land reform have been the wage workers on the collectivized coastal estates—particularly the workers on the sugar cooperatives—who represent only 2 percent of the agricultural labor force but who have received one third of the resources available for redistribution in the countryside.[121] Agrarian reform has had the effect of redistributing income progressively within the reform enterprises but not between reform enterprises nor between the reform enterprises and the private sector.

Along with the permanent labor force on the commercial cooperatives, well-off tenants have generally benefited from the reform through the expanded opportunities to purchase land from private landlords. However, temporary or seasonal wage earners, as well as small subtenants, have seen their status substantially deteriorate as opportunities for employment have diminished both in the reform enterprises and on the private farms that have been parceled out. This group of landless laborers, which in 1970 was estimated at three million people, or one fourth the total population of Peru, has been ignored by the reform process.[122] In addition, the restricted access to employment in large enterprises and the high level of indebtedness among many small landholders indicate that a substantial number of small proprietors will be unable to retain their land and will be forced into the wage labor force.

The progress of the development of capitalism and of the initial stages of agrarian reform in Peru can be measured by a comparison of the data from the agricultural censuses of 1960 and 1970 (Table 3.12). From this information it can be seen that the largest group of farms—farms with less than 5 hectares of land—comprised 83 percent of all farms in 1960 but controlled only 5.7 percent of total land. By 1970, this category of subfamily farms had di-

Table 3.12. Peru: Distribution of Farms and Agricultural Land by Farm Size, 1960–70

Farm size	1960			1970			Rate of change, 1960–70	
	All farms (percent)	Total farmland (percent)	Area per farm (hectares)	All farms (percent)	Total farmland (percent)	Area per farm (hectares)	Number of farms (percent)	Land area (percent)
< 1 hectare	35	0.7	0.44	35	0.5	0.23	65	−16
1–5 hectares	48	5.0	2.20	43	6.0	2.30	4.7	52
5–20 hectares	13	5.0	8.20	16	9.0	9.10	106	129
20–100 hectares	3	5.0	38.10	5	9.0	36.40	140	129
> 100 hectares	1	84.0	1,350.00	1	76.0	1,184.00	36	20

Source: Peru, national agricultural census, 1961 and 1972.

minished somewhat to 78 percent of all farms but continued to control only 6.5 percent of all land.

The largest increase in the number of farms and in the percentage of land area took place in commercial farms of 20–100 hectares, which have been formed from haciendas in which the least productive lands have been sold off. The large increase in the number of these farms, as well as in the number of farms with 5–20 hectares of land, indicates the formation of a capitalist class in agriculture which develops along the farmer road. Simultaneously, it is notable that the increase in the number of plots of less than 1 hectare was on the order of 65 percent, while the land controlled by these farms declined 16 percent. The average land area of these parcels declined to one fifth of a hectare. The increasing number and decreasing size of these plots indicate the qualitative nature of the transformation of the peasantry; in spite of their rising numbers, Peruvian peasants are increasingly semiproletarianized and transformed into a labor reserve.[123]

In summary, the development of capitalism in Peruvian agriculture, which was established before 1969 on the junker road, accelerated rapidly in the 1970s through large-scale state intervention in agricultural production. The process of land reform not only destroyed the power of the landed elites on the coastal plantations, but it also provoked the appearance of a large number of middle-size commercial farms that were formed by subdivision of the haciendas. Thus, agrarian reform had the effect of promoting the development of capitalism along a farmer road under strong dependency of the state, while the vast majority of agricultural producers are concentrated on plots of less than 5 hectares of land and are becoming increasingly proletarianized.

The land reform and the new military leaders' efforts at boosting agricultural production after 1975 resolved neither the food crisis nor the country's massive rural poverty. The serious crisis in Peru's balance of payments (where servicing of the debt accounts for 35–50 percent of export earnings) led to fiscal measures to stimulate exports while domestic food prices were kept low in response to massive popular pressures. Reallocation of land in the reformed and capitalist sectors to the production of agroexports was induced, dependence on food imports increased, and a massive crisis in peasant production was created.[124]

As Caballero evidences, the land reform accelerated social differentiation within the peasantry and the process of proletarianization. The diminution of employment opportunities on reform enterprises and on the parceled-out estates has meant that the status of the roughly 700,000 families without land and the vast majority of poor peasants has deteriorated. In 1978, the International Labor Office estimated that as much as 54 percent of the rural population did not satisfy its minimum basic needs. Of these families, 80 percent were peasants with farms under 5 hectares, 12 percent were landless rural workers, and 8 percent were nonagricultural workers with a rural residence.[125]

4

━━━━━

Disarticulated Accumulation
and Agrarian Crisis

━━━━━

Equipped with a theoretical outline of the underlying global forces identified from the laws of accumulation in the center-periphery structure (Chapter
1), with factual information on the food and poverty crises (Chapter 2), and
with a characterization of the different types of rural social classes and farm
enterprises and of their position in the social division of labor (Chapter 3), we
can now seek an explanation of the dual problem we set out to understand—
the stagnation and unevenness in food production and the dynamics of rural
poverty.

PREVALENT THESES ON THE FOOD AND HUNGER CRISIS

In reviewing the voluminous and controversial literature on the problem of
food and hunger, six dominant lines of thought can be identified, none of
which goes beyond at best a partial explanation of the facts involved. With
some arbitrariness and all the bluntness of name-calling, they can be labeled
Neo-Malthusianism, technological determinism, monetarism, structuralism,
overconsumption, and poverty. Three of these theses consider the supply side
of food (technological determinism, monetarism, and structuralism) while the
others focus on the demand side (Neo-Malthusianism, overconsumption, and
poverty).

A review of the arguments introduced by each of these theses reveals the
many interrelated facets that this complex crisis assumes as well as the
ideological underpinnings of alternative interpretations. By analyzing the in-
adequacies of these arguments in capturing the essence of the phenomenon,
we can identify the dimensions that a superior thesis would need to embody.

141

Thus, in this section, we review the six prevalent theses and develop a critique of each one. In the next section, we develop an alternative interpretation that goes to the essence of the problem by identifying the material determinants of the food and hunger crisis in Latin America and accounts for the arguments introduced in the critiques of the prevalent lines of thought.

Neo-Malthusianism

According to this school of thought, which derives from the "magnificent dynamics" of Malthus and the classical economists, population growth is permanently outstripping growth in food supplies. For most modern advocates, the birth rate is taken as an exogenous variable that remains at ancestral high levels despite a collapse in death rates brought about by international transfers of health technology. Others, like Garrett Hardin, are more Malthusian than Malthus himself in claiming that "more food means more babies."[1] Faithful to the logic of arithmetical ratios, the implication is that population growth is the prime cause of poverty because it decreases income and food per capita.[2] As Borgstrom says: "It is neither capitalism, as Marx believed, nor communism, as many Westerners maintain, that foster poverty and misery. It is the tragic imbalance between population and resources."[3] In addition, a fast-growing population means that a high percentage of the population is young, and thus not in the labor force, and is imposing high rearing, feeding, and educational costs on society, which is thus drained of its investable surplus.[4] The dominant policy implication is the need for drastic, eventually coercive, population-control programs to "put on the demographic brakes."[5]

The validity of the Neo-Malthusian thesis is seriously questionable. As we have seen in analyzing the contradictions of functional dualism, the causal relation seems more logically to run from poverty to overpopulation than the other way around.[6] This opposite relation is particularly strong in subsistence agriculture, where the conjunction of poverty *and* control of some productive resources makes children both essential and possible means of production and protection. The rural poor thus have large families because it is economically rational for them to do so. Improvement in the material conditions of life diminishes these functions and gradually transforms children into only "consumer goods," which leads to a decline in birth rates and to a demographic transition.

Clearly, the optimum rate of population growth and optimum population size are determined in relation to the nature of social systems. A population surplus does not exist absolutely. Yet if the social valuation is that population growth is excessive, the crux of the solution lies in reconciling individual rationality (according to which poverty and subsistence production induce large families) with social rationality. Only when this reconciliation obtains can population programs be effective. Historically, this has been achieved in two ways: (1) through increased income levels that ensure the meeting of subsistence needs and of social security for the bulk of the population (this has been the basis of the demographic transition in the center nations);[7] and (2) through social mobilization, whereby social rationality supersedes individual rationality in decision making on family size. As China has shown, this is possible and effective even at low levels of income.

Technological Determinism

Agriculture has gone through several major revolutionary epochs, each of which corresponded to a new technological and institutional basis. In the Neolithic Age, some 9,000 years ago, agriculture and the domestication of animals replaced hunting and gathering. A second agricultural revolution started in the Low Countries and England in 1700, spread during the eighteenth century to France and the United States, and during the first half of the nineteenth century reached the rest of Europe, including Russia. With new crops and new rotations as its basis, the revolution spread only to the temperate zones, for which the crops were fit, and thus helped establish the current north-south geography of center and periphery. While these agricultural revolutions created a proletariat through the expropriation of peasants and thus the necessary (if not sufficient) conditions for industrial revolutions, which lagged behind some thirty to fifty years,[8] industrialization in turn permitted the modernization of agriculture. A third great agricultural leap forward thus began in 1850, in the center countries, with the industrialization of agriculture based on new sources of energy, machinery, and chemicals.

In the periphery, the second agricultural revolution failed to spread, for ecological reasons;[9] and the third revolution, which came during the period of intense colonial expansion, was confined to plantation crops. Food crops continued to be produced by means of ancestral farming methods. Only in the 1960s, with the externally induced development of Green Revolution technology, did the third agricultural revolution spread to food crops. The Green Revolution thus marked the industrialization of food production in the periphery, but it lacked a national industry or was based on an incomplete industrial structure. It thus reinforced dependency on imported industrial means of production for agriculture or on imported capital goods and the technology to manufacture them locally. In both instances, the industrialization of agriculture did not produce backward linkage effects on a capital-goods-producing sector in the periphery the way it did in the center.

Concentrating on the supply side, technological determinists look to the development of superior technologies to resolve agricultural stagnation.[10] Needed along with research are extension and credit programs that will ensure the diffusion of new technologies,[11] but it is usually claimed that such institutional innovations are induced by the economic attractiveness of the new technological options. Thus, for Hayami and Ruttan, technological innovations—induced by changing relative factor prices that reflect changing relative factor scarcities—in turn induce institutional innovations that will "enable both individuals and society to take fuller advantage of new technical opportunities."[12] According to this linear reasoning, which is also common among orthodox Marxists, the development of the forces of production leads to changes in the social relations of production—a causal sequence that is clearly insufficient to explain the relation between technological and institutional change since there are at least as many examples of the opposite causality.[13]

While the development of improved technology is certainly necessary,[14] it is commonly accepted that humanity could easily be fed if available resources were put into production using existing technology.[15] The food crisis is thus a social problem rather than a technological or ecological one. The limits of the thesis of technological determinism are further revealed when we consider the restricted and uneven diffusion of the Green Revolution by crops, farm types, and regions.[16] Why, for example, is Mexico the only Latin American country that has had a significant Green Revolution in wheat? The logical answer is found in such variables as the social class structure and control of the state, the terms of trade for agriculture, and the land tenure system, not in the physical absence of new technologies, which are themselves a social product determined by these same variables.

Monetarist Thesis of Stagnation

Advocated principally by neoclassical economists and conservatives, the monetarist thesis finds its most lucid and vocal advocates in the Chicago School of Economics, particularly in T. W. Schultz and H. Johnson.[17] In their view, public interventions distort the free operation of market forces and thus reduce the profitability of agricultural investments and increase their risk, thereby leading to stagnation of production and rural poverty.

After 1930, stagnation originated with government promotion of policies with an urban-industrial bias detrimental to agriculture.[18] Specifically, economic policies have been aimed at inducing industrialization by import substitution through the maintenance of overvalued exchange rates to cheapen needed imports of capital goods and through the imposition of protective tariffs on nationally produced industrial goods. With exchange rates overvalued, not only are the proceeds from agricultural exports reduced but prices of import substitutables also are depressed, because imports are in this fashion heavily subsidized, and the competitive advantage of foreign food producers is artificially fostered. Simultaneously, "cheap food policies" aimed at checking inflationary pressures and the rise of wages lead to the imposition of price controls on food, export quotas, and export taxes. As a result, market prices for both products and factors differ markedly from efficiency prices, and the terms of trade are highly unfavorable to agriculture.

Schultz attributes these market distortions and the resulting discrepancies between market and efficiency prices to "policy mistakes." He does not give them a rationality in terms of specific contradictions of the political economy within which they occur.

Simultaneously, policy mistakes are compounded by "neglect" of investment in institutions that generate the two most important sources of agricultural growth—agricultural research and extension for the release and spread of new technological opportunities and rural schools for the formation of human capital. Not only would managerial ability be enhanced by the availability of quality education in the rural sector, but management absenteeism would be reduced inasmuch as a major cause of landlords' migration to cities is the desire to provide their children with a good education, which heretofore has been obtainable only in the urban sector.

Given both unfavorable terms of trade and limited investment opportunities in new technologies and in education, the marginal rate of return to investment in agriculture is below opportunity cost. Since farmers are economically rational, resources are diverted to other sectors of the economy. Technology remains traditional and agriculture stagnates.

The policy implications of this interpretation of stagnation follow straightforwardly. First and foremost, efficiency prices for farm products and agricultural inputs must be restored. To this end, markets must be rid of distortions and the role of the state must be minimized:

The obstacles to agricultural growth can be removed by the restoration of the rules of the competitive game: minimum government intervention in the pricing process for inputs and outputs; a framework of equitable fiscal and legal institutions, neutral monetary policy, and an as-extensive-as-necessary government intervention to remove bottlenecks, including the redistribution of land; and the undertaking of investments which yield low private profits, such as social overhead capital formation.[19]

Second, effective public agricultural research and extension institutions must be developed and the quality and availability of rural schools must be improved. Public investment in technology and in farm people would in turn provide opportunities for profitable private investment in the most important sources of agricultural growth.[20]

In this context, land reform is "fundamentally a political reform." Its economic rationality as a means of attacking agricultural stagnation is explicitly rejected: within the framework of the given price structure and the given availability of overhead capital investment and technological opportunities, farmers, who are economically rational enterpreneurs, are making efficient use of resources. Efficiency levels, which are the ultimate economic test for this school of thought, would not be affected by changes in land tenure or in the distribution of land. But land reform may be justified to hedge against political instability or on humanitarian grounds. As Schultz says, land reform is "basically political in the sense that it would attempt to bring the rank and file of farm people into the mainstream of the political process."[21]

Empirical support for the monetarist thesis is based on the convincing demonstration that (1) there is economically rational behavior in agriculture, so higher and more stable terms of trade would indeed lead to increased supplies;[22] and (2) the terms of trade have been badly distorted and thus have imposed high negative tariffs on agriculture.[23]

However appealing it may be in terms of identification of the facts, the monetarist thesis has a major shortcoming. Systematic market distortions and lack of investment in technology and education cannot be attributed to "mistakes" and "neglect." Both have an objective rationality which is to be uncovered in the laws of accumulation of capital within a particular social formation and in the social class structure and role of the state. By failing to uncover this rationality in terms of political economy, the policy recommendations arrived at by monetarists are bound to be utopian propositions or ideological statements.

Structuralist Thesis of Stagnation

For the structuralists, agricultural stagnation and rural poverty result from the land tenure system. In Latin America, this system is characterized by the *latifundio-minifundio* dualism, whereby the former produces commodities for the national and international markets and the latter supplies labor to the former. The main advocates of the thesis were the urban-based liberal political forces (populists and Christian Democrats) and the international consensus of the 1960s under the aegis of the Kennedy administration (Punta del Este conference of the OAS). Its major analysts in Latin America have been the members of the Inter-American Committee for Agricultural Development.[24]

Structuralists claim that agricultural prices have not been particularly unfavorable in the last forty years and that stagnation results from producer behavior under archaic land tenure systems. Survival of precapitalist relations of production imply rigidities in supply response: bonded labor is a fixed cost that cannot be tailored to fluctuating labor needs; absentee management and autocratic, hierarchical labor relations impede the spread of innovations. The high degree of monopoly of productive resources and of institutional services (credit, information, etc.) permits the landlords to derive enormous economic rents and social advantages even while using the land highly extensively. As a result, behavior of the landed elite is oriented more toward maintenance of the economic and social status quo than toward profit maximization and capital accumulation. Strong integration of landed, commercial, financial, and industrial interests within the same familial groups implies that land is often held for portfolio diversification purposes. It is then a low return–low risk store of wealth that counterweights the high return–high risk urban investments to which managerial skills are dedicated.

The need for land reform programs is the primary policy implication of the thesis. Land reforms are seen to permit an increase in production by expropriating precapitalist estates and creating a tenure structure that is oriented toward intensive use of natural resources, land-saving technology, and labor power. The new land tenure system is not clearly defined—family farms and labor cooperatives are proposed for their specific advantages.[25] However, the policies proposed reflect a clearly *agrarian* philosophy, for their advocates seek solutions to stagnation and poverty within the agricultural sector without recognizing the need for structural changes in the rest of the economic system.

The structuralist thesis finds empirical support in the existence of an inverse relation between farm size and intensity of land use. However, the pattern of resource use on peasant farms is really not comparable to that on capitalist and semifeudal farms, for the two belong to different economic systems. Higher land productivity on peasant farms reflects higher degrees of self-exploitation and lower rewards to resources and labor. When peasant farms are omitted, the relationship between size and intensity of land use turns out to be relatively weak.[26] The larger farms, in spite of management absenteeism and labor-extensive activities, often make greater use of modern technology because of their privileged (if not exclusive) access to credit, information, and infrastructure.

Given the existence of a land market and cases of small-scale capitalist farming development (urban fringes and land settlement programs), the structuralists are unable to explain why these capitalist developments also eventually stagnate and why the large estates are not eliminated through competition in the land market. They thus appear to confuse a symptom of stagnation—the permanence of archaic land tenure systems—with the essence of stagnation. Indeed, farm management studies tend to indicate that, given unfavorable price conditions, large-scale, absenteeist, traditional farms are an optimal means whereby Latin American landlords can maximize rates of return on assets, an observation that is consistent with the monetarist thesis.[27] Changing the land tenure system per se, then, is only a secondary factor in affecting the stagnation of agriculture, for such change is unable to modify the logic of cheap food.

A further criticism of the structuralist thesis is that while it is still used extensively today to explain the agrarian crisis in Latin America,[28] the *latifundio-minifundio* complex on which it rests has been drastically transformed since the early 1960s, when the thesis was first developed in the context of the controversy over land reform. Where once the complex was the embodiment of servile relations, today it takes on very capitalistic overtones: as we saw in Chapter 3, the *latifundists* are increasingly capitalists and the *minifundists* are semiproletarianized. The theoretical mistake was that the structuralist description of the *latifundio-minifundio* complex was a quantitative one centering on farm size rather than a qualitative one based on modes of production and social relations. The quantitative relation does not necessarily change as the qualitative one does, as the landlords become large-scale capitalist entrepreneurs. Yet in the process, economic behavior and social relations have been fully transformed.

Overconsumption: Austerity and Aid

Turning to the demand side, several analysts of the world food situation denounce the excessive absorption of available food by the center countries. This is due, in particular, to the fact that the diffusion of meat-based diets is widespread, while the transformation of vegetal protein into animal protein is highly inefficient: an acre of cereals can produce five times more protein than an acre devoted to meat production.[29] In addition, it takes as many as 21 pounds of protein fed to livestock to produce 1 pound of protein for human consumption. The result is that 78 percent of the grain produced in the United States is fed to livestock, and U.S. livestock eats as much grain per year as all the people in China and India. As Lester Brown observes: "In a world of scarcity, if some of us consume more, others of necessity consume less. The moral issue is raised by the fact that those who are consuming less are not so much the overweight affluent but the already undernourished poor."[30]

This leads to the advocacy of reducing excessive consumption in the center and shifting consumption habits to lower and hence more efficient levels in the food chain.[31] Simplified diets would free food resources for aid to the periphery. More "realistic" proposals invoke use of the "triage" principle to allocate scarce food aid to those (friendly) nations that are thus likely to survive a food crisis, while leaving to die the hopelessly hungry.[32] Those who are more politically expedient identify the power of food aid as an explicit political instrument in foreign policy.[33] In 1974, 80 percent of U.S. food aid went to such domino countries as South Vietnam, Cambodia, South Korea, and Egypt.

Emergency aid for relief from catastrophic events and for stabilization of world food prices is clearly needed and justifies implementing a world food-stocks program. Limiting wasteful and harmful overconsumption in the center is also a must in order to promote conservation of exhaustible resources, reduce pollution, and protect consumers. But increased food aid to the periphery on a sustained basis is a proposition that could not significantly reduce world hunger, for the amount of food released in the center would be too small relative to the quantities needed by the poor, principally because a decline in consumption in the center, associated with simpler diets, would lead to a fall in production.[34] Furthermore, this proposition reinforces one of the very mechanisms that has contributed to stagnation in the production of a number of staple foods in the periphery, most particularly wheat.

Stagnation of food production in the periphery began in the 1930s with the United States' rise to world hegemony. Because of the political strength of the "farm bloc," the overproduction crisis in agriculture in the 1930s was never resolved. Instead, it has been translated into government protectionism and absorption of the surpluses produced. This intervention took the form of the 1933 Agricultural Adjustment Act, which created the Commodity Credit Corporation—an agency responsible for purchase of surplus farm commodities, establishment of price supports, and production control through direct contracts with farmers. This legislation was modified in 1938, primarily with respect to the farm-program financing mechanism, but served as the basic enabling legislation in the postwar years.

These policies, in conjunction with wartime demand, succeeded in stabilizing farm incomes and prices and thus fueled the "Mill-Marshallian technological treadmill,"[35] which led to rapid yield increases and further growth in production. As a result, surplus commodity stocks became an expensive and embarrassing side effect of these policies. The agricultural overproduction crisis that ensued was resolved not by price deflation but by export. The sizable surpluses of wheat in particular, but also those of corn, rice, cotton, and tobacco, were distributed below cost on the world market, primarily through the P.L. 480 program authorized by the Agricultural Trade Development and Assistance Act of 1954. A complex set of import barriers and export subsidies also was instituted to protect domestic markets from overseas competition. With chronically overvalued exchange rates in the periphery, imported food became so dramatically cheap that it outcompeted national farm goods. On the domestic scene, the promotion of new consumption habits stimulated effective demand, in particular through the shift to higher levels in the food chain. "Being the least efficient of ruminants as a converter of plant to animal protein, yet able to put high-demand food on the table, the steer was ideally suited to our needs."[36] Clearly, austerity and increased aid are inconsistent with both the economics of the farm problem at home and the resolution of the food crisis in the periphery.

This inconsistency has become increasingly evident in recent years. Although the farm bloc lost its power to oppose urban interests' demands for cheap food in the 1960s, the food crisis of the early 1970s temporarily restored high food prices. Promotion of commercial exports, in particular through devaluations of the dollar, has become the key to shoring up the U.S. balance of payments and to strengthening the dollar. The explicit policy is "food for cash."[37] And shipments under Food for Peace dropped from 14 million tons of grains in 1965 to 1 million tons in 1974 (P.L. 480, Title I), precisely when major famines struck in the Sahel and in Bangladesh.

Poverty: Employment and Nutrition Programs

An increasing number of analysts in the liberal-reformist tradition are identifying poverty and the consequent lack of effective demand as the core issues of both the food and hunger crises. Lack of effective demand not only implies hunger and malnutrition but also discourages production due to lack of buyers and low prices. "It is inequality and inequality alone that can be blamed for hunger today."[38] As we saw in Chapter 1, the data do show that inequality has increased over time, both between center and periphery and within the periphery. In the periphery, higher rates of industrial growth have almost invariably been accompanied by more-regressive patterns in the distribution of income,[39] and absolute poverty has often increased.[40]

Poverty is blamed on subsistence peasants' lack of access to productive resources and on unemployment or low-productivity employment (petty services, etc.).

The policy implication is that the productivity of the poor should be increased. "Development policies need to be aimed at upgrading the well-being of the poor, not through charity, but by increasing opportunities for them to participate in productive activities."[41] For the rural poor, this implies the promotion of land reform and rural-development programs. Modernization of smallholder, labor-intensive agriculture must be enhanced through the development of intermediate technologies and their diffusion via extension and credit programs. Health, education, and rural public works also must be promoted in the rural sector in an effort to decrease outmigration. For the urban poor, employment creation must be fostered by policies that induce industrialization while decreasing the capital-intensive bias in the choice of techniques.

Here again, facts and essence are being confused. Low productivity in the traditional sector, unemployment, and regressive income distribution patterns are identified as causes of poverty, but the objective logic of those facts in terms of the laws of capital accumulation and the social class structure is not uncovered. Poverty is understood not in terms of its functionality in the economic system but as a separate phenomenon; as in Schultz's traditional agriculture[42] and in Vekemans's theory of marginality,[43] the poor are those who stayed behind, who were by-passed by progress, and who remained at the margin of society. As a consequence, policy recommendations regarding poverty assume a reality separate from the functioning of the economic system and are directed by idealistic and humanitarian concerns.

Thus, in summary, this review of the most prevalent explanations of food and hunger problems in peripheral countries shows that in their present formulations, none of these explanations is adequate. Neo-Malthusians observe the impact of population explosion on poverty and hunger but fail to identify it as an endogenous force brought about by the laws of motion of capital under social disarticulation. Technological determinists witness the permanence of ancestral production methods, which they relate to a deficient supply of new techniques and not to the lack of demand for them as a reflection of the rational economic behavior of farmers under unfavorable price conditions. Monetarists correctly identify distorted terms of trade and the unprofitability of modernization but fail to explain the logic for such distortions in the political economy where they occur. Structuralists confuse causality relations in attributing to the permanence of archaic land tenure systems the blockage of the development of capitalism in agriculture and of the rise of an agrarian bourgeoisie. In advocating austerity and aid, overconsumptionists propose actions that are admirable per se but that tend to reinforce both the realization crisis in the center and the food crisis in the periphery. And meliorists fail to capture the origin of the symptoms they single out to explain poverty—lack of employment creation in the modern sectors, limited resources and low productivity in the peasant sector, and increasingly regressive income distribution patterns.

MATERIAL DETERMINANTS OF THE AGRARIAN CRISIS

The basic thesis that underlies our explanation of the agrarian crisis, which has been described in Chapter 2, is that it is the correlate of the development of capitalist relations under the specific conditions that characterize Latin American countries today. Why and how peripheral capitalist development in these countries results in these contradictions is the substance of our explanation.

Before proceeding further, it is convenient to restate three departing points that we derived from the analysis of the laws of motion of capital in Chapter 1 and from our characterization of the development of the agrarian structure in Chapter 3.

The first of these points is that under the dominance of the socially disarticulated class alliance in the periphery, there is a powerful logic to sustain the development of capitalism on the basis of cheap labor. While this is partially obtained by sheer repression of workers' demands, *cheap food* also is essential for this purpose since at the subsistence level the price of labor power is principally the price of food. As a result, systematic downward political pressures on the price of wage foods, a fact observed and exposed by the monetarists, tend to develop.

The second point is that import-substitution industrialization under sectoral disarticulation implies the increased need for foreign exchange to permit importation of capital goods. This requires the development of the capacity to *export,* which still remains principally ensured by agriculture and mining. Social disarticulation also places high demands on foreign exchange: the call on foreign capital implies the need to ensure hard currency for the repatriation of profits and the servicing of debts; and the internationalization of consumption patterns requires the capacity to pay royalties for the importation of advanced technology and to import luxury goods from the center.

The third point is that even though the transition to capitalism is only a recent phenomenon and is by no means fully completed, the social relations in agriculture are essentially *nonfeudal:* land and labor are increasingly commodified and their appropriation is more and more established on a competitive basis. The majority of the product is the result of either capitalist or peasant (petty bourgeois) production. The only difference between a capitalist producer and a peasant one is the capacity to generate and expropriate a surplus via the use of hired labor: the closer this surplus is to the average rate of profit, the closer our producer is to capitalist production. It is not that peasants do not aim for a profit (a surplus); it is that they will remain in production *even* in the face of their inability to earn a profit. A capitalist will not. We observed, furthermore, that in an agrarian sector composed of capitalist and peasant producers, the state will be preferentially responsive to the demands of the former. And the power of agrarian capitalists over the state will be particularly great if the development of capitalism follows the "junker" road.

The Contradiction Between Rent and Profit in the Transition to Capitalism

Before looking at the mechanisms through which the cheap-food and foreign-exchange requirements of disarticulated accumulation have been ensured, it is useful to analyze the specific conditions of the transition to capitalism along the junker road in order especially to understand the role of the state both in promoting this type of development and in attempting to reconcile it with the exigencies of industrialization.

Private property in the hands of a landlord class plays an essential function in the transition to capitalism, but the cost of this type of private property— absolute land rent—tends later to become a fetter on the development of capitalism. The role of rent is thus central to classical economics. In Ricardo's model of the steady state, economic growth comes to a halt due to the rising share of rent going to landlords who squander it on luxury consumption. Similarly, Marx clearly identified how absolute rent constitutes an appropriation of surplus value and hence collapses the average rate of profit in the economy and slows down the pace of accumulation. Recently, Neo-Marxists such as Rey, Amin, Vergopoulos, and Moncayo reestablished the importance of land rent in understanding the role of the state in both transition and post-transition periods.[44]

Due to the contrasting roles of private appropriation of land in the transition and posttransition periods, agricultural policy aimed at fomenting the development of capitalism in agriculture will have a markedly different content during these two periods. During the first period, the legal property rights of the landed elite are reaffirmed (preservation), while precapitalist forms of land use are eliminated (adequation). During the second period, the existence of an absolute rent among producers of wage foods is opposed. According to the nature of class alliances, different mechanisms are used to reach these ends in each period.

To establish itself, capitalism needs a labor market where labor power can be transformed into a commodity. Two conditions must prevail if such a transformation is to occur: labor power must be liberated from semifeudal bonds and be free to dispose of its energies, and simultaneously, it must be dispossessed from control over the means of production. Free and dispossessed, labor power can ensure its survival only by offering itself for a wage on the labor market. Essential for this purpose is the private appropriation of the land by a landlord class and the elimination of precapitalist forms of land use where labor is bound to the land and is in the possession (if not the ownership) of the means of production. In England this process of preservation-adequation of landownership was ensured by the landlord class itself through enclosures of their estates, which resulted in the massive expropriation of peasants and migration to the cities and their factories. In Colombia, peasant militancy in the 1920s and 1930s, oriented toward the abolition of precapitalist forms of rent obligations and toward extraeconomic forms of coercion by landlords, induced initiation of this same process.[45] While the objective means of industrial development were still a weak driving force, the subjective nature of class conflict, reflected in peasant struggles, forced initiation of a process of transformation in the old patriarchal forms of tenure. By militating against feudalism—thus inducing the development of capitalist social relations in agriculture under the aegis of the landed elites— peasants were, of course, digging their own graves. Inevitably, the adjustment of tenure relations to capitalism without change in the hegemonic dominance of the landed elites implied dispossessing and freeing large segments of the peasantry. During this transition period—between 1938 and 1951—the rural population declined from 71 percent to 61 percent of the total population, the proportion of salaried workers in agriculture increased from 27 percent to 40 percent of the rural population, and precapitalist forms of tenure decreased as the proportion of independent peasants went down from 34 percent to 24 percent.[46]

In this process of preservation-adequation, absolute rent is retained as the power of the landed elite remains unabated; absolute rent thus exists under capitalism as a precapitalist category for purely historical reasons and not as an essential theoretical category of the capitalist mode of production. Its level is determined like any monopoly price—by the strength of the landlord class in relation to both the emergent urban bourgeoisie (particularly with respect to the determination of the terms of trade for agriculture) and the rural proletariat (with respect to the determination of wages).

Once capitalism has established itself, permanence of an absolute rent implies higher food prices and hence higher wage costs; lower profits for capitalists in the whole economy and hence a reduced rate of capital accumulation; and a tendency for agriculture to stagnate because competitive pressures for the junkers to modernize are weak and a large fraction of the rent tends to be spent on luxury consumption (as in Ricardo's growth model). Development of capitalism in agriculture along the junker road presents a high cost to the development of capitalism at large. Thus there exists a logic for capital, acting through the class actions of capitalists, to seek to cancel absolute rent. Yet this is possible only if the alliance between urban capitalists and landlords can be broken by the former without threatening their hegemonic position—that is, only if the urban capitalists are sufficiently powerful to simultaneously control the proletariat and oppose landlords.

For this very reason, Ricardo and John Stuart Mill, as representatives of the liberal industrial bourgeoisie, endorsed the abolition of private ownership of land. Similarly, on a theoretical basis, Lenin projected that nationalization of the land to wipe out absolute rent would constitute the ultimate radical bourgeois reform.[47] The *ejido,* product of Mexico's land reform of 1915 and an important source of peasant foods and wage foods, is one of the few examples of the implementation of this solution on a massive scale. However, less-dramatic measures have also proved effective. The land reforms in Guatemala (1952–54), the Dominican Republic (1963), Chile (1967–73), and Peru (1969) weakened or cancelled the power of the landed elites and hence reduced the level of absolute rent. In England, repeal of the Corn Laws in 1846 and implementation of the Manchester Doctrine opened up internal markets to free trade. With the import of cheap American wheat, absolute rent was wiped out. Politically, this was made possible by the advanced integration of the English gentry's economic interests into industry and the rise of a social-democratic alliance with the working class. In other countries and, in fact, in most Latin American countries, absolute rent was selectively struck down by state manipulation of the terms of trade against certain segments of agriculture, the phenomenon we have called "cheap-food policies."

Price suppression via trade or state control can, of course, cancel not only absolute rent but also profit and even part of the residual implicit wage for owner-operators. In this case the landlord class (feeding on rent) and the capitalist farmer-manager class (feeding on profits) are thrown out of agriculture. As Chayanov and the neopopulists (Servolin and Vergopoulos) have construed it, agriculture would then be left to the peasants, who would be reduced to the status of workers working at home for an implicit wage. There would thus exist a logic for industrial capital to introduce and foment the development of peasant agriculture. We will return to this controversial proposition in a later section.

In most Latin American countries, weakness of the industrial bourgeoisie keeps it locked in an alliance with the junker landed elites. This is due to the following two reasons. On the one hand, accumulation under conditions of social disarticulation limits the role of wage increases in creating the modern sector's capacity to consume and hence dissociates wage levels from labor productivity. As argued in Chapter 1, the objective basis for a social-democratic alliance that could offer the capitalist class an alternative to alliance with the landed elites is consequently absent. On the other hand, due to the importance of agricultural exports in generating foreign exchange for industry, the close integration between landed elites and dependent bourgeoisie compromises capital's opposition to rent. As a result, the land-owning class has maintained its traditional domination of the state directly through the holding of high public office and indirectly through powerful agricultural pressure groups. Payment of rent to this class has thus remained the heavy cost of this development model.

Industrializing countries of the periphery, however, had to submit to the exigencies of international capital and to the pressures of organized labor. The average rate of profit had to be ensured and even surpassed. Workers' pressures for higher real wages also had to be at least partially accommodated in certain segments of the labor force. As a result, a fundamental contradiction developed between the exigencies of international capital (profit) and preservation of junker capitalism in agriculture (rent). At issue was the price of wage foods. To resolve this contradiction, rent was *selectively eliminated* in the production of most wage foods but was preserved in specific lines of production (exportables, industrial inputs, and luxury foods) on the basis of discriminatorily allocated "institutional rents." Price suppression of wage foods came about through free trade, concessional imports, overvalued exchange rates, and direct state control of price levels. As a result, the production of wage foods was either displaced to the peasant margins of agriculture or had to be subsidized in capitalist agriculture via technological change, institutional rents, and functional dualism with peasant agriculture to capture cheap semiproletarian labor. The cost of the junker way has been uneven development, a growing food crisis, and increasing dependency on food imports. Overcoming the contradiction between profits and rents has reposited the barrier to accumulation at another level—that reflected by the food crisis and high fiscal costs.

Colombia is a good example of the nature and magnitude of insitutional rents under junker capitalist development.

The major avenues of institutional rent include tax advantages, public-works projects, technological progress, selective price support programs, and credit and exchange-rate policies. The tax structure for rural property promotes and protects the accumulation of land. In the early 1960s, the rate of taxation of farmland in Colombia was 0.4 percent of the assessed value. The average assessed value per hectare of holdings between 1,000 and 2,500 hectares was $30; for holdings between 2,500 and 5,000 hectares, $15.50; and for holdings in excess of 5,000 hectares, $2.00.[48] Thus, for instance, the average tax paid on estates of 2,500 hectares was $300. Because the assessed value was based on actual, as opposed to potential, utilization, the incidence of the tax was highly regressive. Obviously, the rural tax structure favored extensive patterns of land use (e.g., cattle ranching) and horizontal, as against vertical, expansion.

In addition, the services provided by these and other tax revenues are highly biased in favor of the Colombian landowning class. According to CIDA, "the investments made in services and infrastructure in the rural zones . . . tend to reflect the arrangements made by local political leaders with their friends and clients [the *latifundists*] rather than the basic needs of society.''[49] In the only two public irrigation projects that existed in the early 1960s ''large properties monopolized practically all the irrigated and potentially irrigable lands.''[50] According to Berry and Urrutia, ''the location of new roads tends more often to reflect the interests of large owners than small ones.''[51] Elsewhere, they note that ''[agricultural] research has been directed primarily toward the crops and the variety types that could be used by the large farmers and . . . the extension [service] has traditionally given commercial farmers much more attention than the small farmer.''[52]

In 1962, the only crops in Colombia receiving price supports that yielded prices above the general price index were cotton, barley, and sesame. The prices of all subsistence crops were below the general price index.[53] By the 1970s, price supports had been extended to a variety of commodities produced primarily by large landowners, while the subsistence foods produced mainly by the peasant sector (wheat, corn, and food grains)[54] remained without price supports or were subject to price controls. Thus, a clear dichotomy exists between exportables, luxury foods, and industrial inputs produced by junker agriculture under favorable price (and rent) conditions, while price suppression of wage foods marginalizes them in peasant agriculture. Several products of commercial and plantation agriculture enjoy integral packages of services (credit, research, and extension) provided by autonomous Colombian government agencies (e.g., the Institute for the Development of Cotton Production).

With respect to credit, the landed elite receives the lion's share at highly subsidized rates. In the words of Berry and Urrutia, ''Agricultural credit has normally been made available at the most attractive interest rates used for any sector of the economy, often at about a zero real rate of interest and sometimes even negative.''[55] In the early 1960s, for instance, interest rates on agricultural credit for large borrowers varied from 6 percent (short-term) to 9 percent (long-term),[56] while the rate of inflation in 1963 equaled 33 percent. Ten years later, with a rate of inflation of 25 percent and interest rates substantially unchanged, the policy of subsidized credit continued.[57]

In terms of the distribution of credit, only 4.2 percent of the value of Colombian government agricultural credit went to individuals with assets under the mean (10,000 pesos) in 1970. On the other hand, individuals or corporations in agriculture with assets in excess of 500,000 pesos (equal to 1 percent of all producers) monopolized 50 percent of government agricultural credit.[58] Also, between 1940–44 and 1965–67, the ratio of outstanding loans to value of agricultural output rose from 5.6 percent to 20.1 percent.[59]

Discrimination between activities in the growth of credit provided by the Colombian Agricultural Financial Fund also is symptomatic of the systematic support of junker agriculture as against the peasant sector. Between 1966–67 and 1969-70, the increase in credit was 933 percent for African palm, 821 percent for soybeans, 607 percent for cotton, 371 percent for tobacco, and 304 percent for cocoa—crops that are typical of large-scale capitalist agriculture. By contrast, the increase in credit for traditional food crops was 33 percent for plantain, 69 percent for potatoes, 72 percent for vegetables, 83 percent for fruits, and 96 percent for cassava. The cattle sector is the one that has received the greatest share of credit, holding 19 percent of the total outstanding loans made by the banking sector, as against 18 percent for industry and 15 percent for all crops. As Kalmanovitz observes, there is, however, no notable relationship between volume of credit and increase in production, which tends to indicate that the cattle sector has received an oversupply of credit that has been used in large part to finance other kinds of investments (e.g., real estate and private loans).[60]

Colombia exemplifies the importance of institutional rents throughout Latin American agriculture and particularly in those countries dominated by the junker road. Thus, the proportion of rural households receiving institutional credit is only 27 percent in Colombia (1968), 22 percent in Venezuela (1972), 20 percent in Honduras (1971), 16 percent in Mexico (1970), 6 percent in Peru (1970), and 5 percent in Ecuador (1973), even though institutional credit amounts to as much as a third of the gross value of agricultural production in Latin America.[61] Similarly, the proportion of rural households benefiting from extension services is only 19 percent in Venezuela (1972), 13 percent in Honduras (1971), 13 percent in Mexico (1970), 12 percent in Peru (1970), 7 percent in Guatemala (1977), 9 percent in Colombia (1971), 4 percent in Costa Rica (1970), and 3 percent in Bolivia (1971).[62] In terms of both credit and extension services, those benefited are systematically the largest and wealthiest farmers.

To recapitulate, the contradiction between rent and profit that originated in the transition period and materialized in the posttransition period was both overcome and re-created. It was overcome by selectively eliminating absolute rent in the production of wage foods through imports and cheap-food policies while maintaining that rent in the production of exportables, industrial inputs, and luxuries and subsidizing production in junker agriculture through institutional rents. The contradiction between rent and profit was thus re-created at the level of the food crisis. And by compensating for cheap food through institutional rents on the junker road, this contradiction was also operational at the level of the fiscal crisis of the state.

Cheap Food and Foreign Exchange: The Contradictions

Under disarticulated accumulation, the need for an inexpensive supply of foodstuffs has historically been met in three different ways: (1) through development of capitalist production in agriculture under the active encouragement of the state via the forced elimination of remnants of semifeudal social relations, and through protectionism, public subsidies, technological innovations, and the use of cheap labor supplied by semiproletarianized peasants; (2) with cheap imports obtained under soft credit terms (P.L. 480 exports) and further cheapened on internal markets through overvalued exchange rates that favor industrial imports; and (3) by direct state intervention in internal pricing via price ceilings, taxes and quotas on exports, consumer rationing, and state marketing monopolies, and by eventual direct state intervention in production.

Similarly, the need for foreign-exchange earnings from increased agricultural exports has been met through incentives to the development of capitalism in the production of exportables via public subsidies, technological innovations, and functional dualism. It has also generally required integration with multinational agribusiness, especially through contract farming, in order to secure access to world markets and international technology.[63]

Each of these mechanisms for insuring cheap food and foreign exchange is, in turn, contradictory. In particular, there are four major contradictions that we want to discuss here. They are the contradictions between (1) food self-sufficiency and comparative advantages, (2) cheap-food policies and the development of capitalism in agriculture, (3) land-saving versus labor-saving technological change in the development of the forces of production, and (4) the use and reproduction of the peasantry as a source of cheap food. These contradictions have led the state to implement a set of agrarian reforms in an attempt to counteract them; in turn, these interventions have re-created other contradictions. The political economy of these reforms, and in particular, that of land reform, rural development, and basic-needs projects, will be analyzed in Chapters 6 and 7.

FOOD SELF-SUFFICIENCY VERSUS COMPARATIVE ADVANTAGES. The existence of both limited natural resources and a limited public budget implies that there is competition between the production of food for domestic consumption and that of agricultural products for exports. In Brazil, for example, the development of soybean production for exports led to the massive displacement of black beans, a staple in the Brazilian diet, to the point that production of black beans fell at the rate of 2 percent a year between 1967 and 1976; and by 1976, black beans had to be imported to meet domestic demand.[64] Lappé and Collins observe that "in Central America and in the Caribbean, where as much as 70 percent of the children are undernourished, at least half of the agricultural land, and the best land at that, grows crops for exports, not food for the local people."[65]

In this competition, exports are usually given priority over food for two reasons. On the one hand, cheap-food policies tend to induce the diversion of land use away from the production of wage goods toward that of exportables, industrial inputs, and luxury foods. On the other hand, the pressure of meeting the needs of the nation's balance of payments and, in particular, of servicing the foreign debt—which has reached extraordinary proportions in countries like Brazil, Mexico, and Peru—imposes an immediacy on the production of exportables that is far greater than the provision of cheap food, which can be partially met through concessional imports, and the demand for which can be partially reduced via repression and lower real wages. The role of international lending agencies—especially the International Monetary Fund—has been determinant in establishing this priority.[66]

Attempts at simultaneously achieving cheap food and increased exports through trade policies have, however, often limited the production of exportables. Overvalued exchange rates (to subsidize imported capital goods for industry and to cheapen both imported and exportable food) and export controls and taxes (to provide government revenues) have implied a generalized negative pressure on the profitability of the external sector. A few data serve to illustrate this effect, which was particularly strong during the 1950s and 1960s.

Little et al. estimated the rate of overvaluation of the national currency to be 100 percent in Argentina (1958), 50 percent in Brazil (1966), and 15 percent in Mexico (1960).[67] In Chile, too, the rate of overvaluation was high, fluctuating between 30 percent and 52 percent in the 1960s. With this overvaluation, the nominal protective tariffs valued at the shadow exchange rate are highly negative. For the period 1964-69, these nominal tariffs averaged −23 percent for wheat, −10 percent for corn, −38 percent for rice, −52 percent for potatoes, and −17 percent for beef. Simultaneously, tariffs on the import of agricultural inputs raised the costs of production. In 1969 the nominal protective tariffs were 20 percent for machinery, 60 percent for nitrogen, 80 percent for fuels, and 140 percent for pesticides. The combination of overvalued exchange rates, negative nominal protective tariffs on agricultural products, and positive protective tariffs on means of production implies net effective protective tariffs that are highly negative.[68] Valdés thus calculates that the average net effective tariffs in Chile during the period 1947-65 were −38 percent for wheat, −35 percent for beef, and −30 percent for lamb.[69]

Balassa estimates that net effective protection for the whole agricultural sector in Chile (1961) was −6 percent, while it was 54 percent for the manufacturing sector. Similarly, in Brazil (1966) it was 15 percent for agriculture against 79 percent for manufacturing and in Mexico (1960), the respective figures were −3 percent and 21 percent. Balassa concludes that "there is a strong tendency to discriminate in favor of manufacturing and against primary activities in the countries under study. . . . The existence of such discrimination is already apparent in the observed differences in nominal rates of protection that are substantially higher on manufactured goods than on primary products."[70]

The performance of the external sector is also affected by highly unstable commodity prices on the world market when there are relatively limited substitution possibilities in production, for exports are concentrated in just a few crops, which are mainly perennial in nature. While weather-induced to a certain extent, the booms and busts in commodity prices are largely the result of international speculation on commodity markets and the transmission and amplification, through the multiplier-accelerator effect, of business cycles in the center economies.

During the 1970s, growing balance-of-payments crises and increasing integration with international capital led many countries to shift to more-orthodox monetary and trade policies, which thus maintained the exchange rate closer to equilibrium and let international prices determine domestic price levels for exportables, inputs for industry, and luxury foods while maintaining price controls on wage foods and peasant crops. The result was an increasingly serious bias in prices that led to the rapid expansion and modernization of the first set of activities while inducing stagnation in the latter. Thus, in Brazil, the terms of trade between food products for the domestic market (potatoes, manioc, rice, beans, onions, eggs, pork, and milk) and industry increased by 30 percent between 1965–67 and 1974–76, while the terms of trade between agricultural products for the external markets and for processing (cotton, soybeans, peanuts, castor oil, tea, coffee, sugarcane, oranges, and bananas) and industry increased by 83 percent.[71] As a result, between 1968 and 1973 the area planted in traditional food crops in the state of São Paulo (rice, beans, and manioc) fell by 28 percent, while the area planted in export and industrial crops (cotton, sugar, oranges, soybeans, etc.) expanded by 53 percent.[72] In Chile, the price of traditional food crops (wheat, potatoes, beans, and corn) fell by 34 percent between 1965 and 1977, while that of export crops (grapes, apples, pears, and apricots) increased by 35 percent. This led to a 21 percent decline in the production of traditional food crops and a 743 percent increase (between 1970 and 1977 only) in the production of export crops.[73]

The price bias is reinforced by an allocation of agricultural credit that also systematically favors export crops. In Guatemala, 87 percent of government credit between 1964 and 1973 financed exports crops, while rice, corn, and beans received only 3 percent.[74] Export agriculture has also absorbed the lion's share of modern inputs. Thus, 62 percent of Brazil's fertilizers are used in sugarcane, cotton, and soybean production; in Ecuador, the production of sugarcane, coffee, and bananas accounts for 64 percent of fertilizer consumption.[75]

The contradiction between cheap food and agricultural exports is at the heart of the controversy between national self-reliance and comparative advantages. Advocates of self-reliance in food expose the following facts:

1. Relying on food imports by exporting agricultural products is highly risky owing to the instability of world commodity prices.[76] Basic foods must be purchased in markets that are monopolistically controlled and where price fluctuations can be engineered as a source of profits for the trading companies. In addition, political and economic vulnerability is increased, since exporting countries can unilaterally impose embargoes on exports in attempts

to use food as a diplomatic weapon. The political behavior of the United States during the world grain crisis in 1974 clearly demonstrated this possibility.

2. On the world markets there is a tendency toward deterioration of the terms of trade against tropical products. Thus, while it cost Latin American countries 160 bags of coffee to purchase one tractor in 1960, the same tractor cost about 400 bags in 1977, in spite of the massive increase in coffee prices.[77]

3. Because exporting agricultural commodities requires dependence on marketing channels controlled by multinational agribusiness, most revenues from the sale of these commodities in the center do not accrue to the periphery. UNCTAD thus estimates that in the sale of bananas, only 11 cents of every dollar remains in the producing country.[78]

4. Agricultural exports and food dependency, while good for the balance of payments and capital accumulation, have a regressive effect on the distribution of consumption, for food imports are biased toward high-income consumers and hardly reach the more remote areas. They also have a regressive effect on the distribution of production, since the peasants, who produce food (90 percent of Mexico's corn), are bankrupted by low prices and are deprived of credit, physical infrastructure, and technical assistance, while the large-scale commercial sector, oriented toward the production of agroexports, receives favorable prices and public support.

5. The doctrine of comparative advantages, when these advantages are not natural but are historically acquired through relative advances in productivity, is oriented toward preserving the status quo in the international division of labor by keeping the low-productivity activities in the periphery.[79] As Ricardo correctly showed, trade according to comparative advantages is a source of gains in the short run, but it can also be a factor of underdevelopment in the longer run.

Lappé and Collins thus summarize the food self-reliance position by saying that "the devastating impact of export agriculture on the majority of the people will become more and more undesirable, and food dependency will continue to translate into food shortages and rising prices for the politically volatile urban centers." By contrast, "Food self-reliance is the cornerstone of genuine self-determination and it is possible for every country in the world."[80]

Advocates of comparative advantages derive their propositions from the static Ricardian and neoclassical theories of trade, according to which global welfare is increased by specialization and exchange. They seek support for their arguments by exposing the inefficiencies and social failures of import-substitution industrialization, which runs counter to free trade because it originates in import restrictions and direct public subsidies to industry. They also observe the "failure of planning in the developing countries"[81] and the ineffectiveness of Common Market agreements in Latin America. As a result, the International Monetary Fund has denounced rising protectionism and advocates a return to free markets: "Determined and broadly conceived efforts at the national and international level will be required to arrest the drift toward protectionism, with the determining impulse for directing policies towards renewed liberalization coming from national governments."[82] Similarly, the International Labour Office's study of the failure of public policies to obviate growing unemployment concludes that "in the long run, it is clear that both industrial and developing countries would benefit from greater specialization along the lines of comparative advantages."[83] For agriculture in the periphery, this means increasing exports of tropical, labor-intensive (fruits, vegetables, and specialty crops), and land-intensive (beef-breeding) products while relying on grain imports from the United States—a division of labor increasingly advocated by the World Bank and consistent with the hegemonic reproduction of the disarticulated class alliance. However, the building of world buffer stocks of grains to stabilize international prices also is recommended.[84]

The controversy between food self-reliance and comparative advantages is, in our opinion, incorrectly formulated because it dissociates the issue from the key structural concepts of social articulation and disarticulation and from the corresponding social class structure. The real issue is to identify the social and economic aspects of peripheral nations that need to be changed in order to transform a disarticulated structure into an articulated one. In particular, the optimum degree of external dependency can be judged only in terms of the normative criterion of articulation. Clearly, the answer will vary widely from country to country and period to period. We defer this normative discussion to the last chapter of this book.

CHEAP-FOOD POLICIES VERSUS DEVELOPMENT OF CAPITALISM IN AGRICULTURE.   Cheap food can be obtained through either extractivist or developmental policies. The former imply the imposition of cheap-food policies, while the latter consist in fomenting the development of the forces of production in capitalist agriculture by unleashing a "technological treadmill" and extracting the surplus thus created via deterioration in the terms of trade or tax schemes.[85] And the balance between extractivist and developmental measures has always been a key aspect of agricultural policy. Indeed, the debate on the terms of trade between agriculture and industry is a central theme in political economy.[86] What these debates reveal is that the determination of the terms of trade cannot be understood in abstraction from the underlying class structure.

This is clear, for example, in the famous Soviet debate on the New Economic Policy (1921–28). Agricultural stagnation during the period of war had by 1923 resulted in high agricultural prices and favorable terms of trade for peasant producers. Within the Communist party, the left opposition, led by Trotsky and Preobrazhensky, regarded the peasants, especially the kulaks, as a potential danger to the Soviet state. They argued that the goals of socialism could be more rapidly advanced by taxing the petty bourgeois elements through enforced unfavorable terms of trade and thereby promoting both the stagnation of the kulaks and accumulation in the socialized industrial sector. Bukharin held the opposite position, that a policy of economic repression of the peasants would interrupt the even flow of agricultural commodities to industry and the urban population. The industrialization process would be disrupted. He advocated instead more-moderate measures, such as voluntary collectivization, to preserve the alliance of the peasantry with the proletariat.

As we saw before, the debate between monetarists and structuralists on the causes of stagnation in Latin American agriculture is also a class-based argument on the terms of trade. The monetarists defend the interests of the landlord class in showing that landlords are price responsive but that the terms of trade have been highly uncertain and unfavorable to agriculture. For the landlords, better prices would allow higher profits and rents and hence higher levels of investment. The structuralists, by contrast, side with the urban bourgeoisie in arguing that the terms of trade have not been unfavorable and that any further improvement in the terms of trade would lead to income transfers to the landlord class without a resulting increase in production.

The fact that cheap-food policies have badly suppressed the price of wage foods is fairly evident, even though it appears on first inspection that the terms of trade for agriculture have remained relatively constant since the 1930s. Observing, for example, the evolution of prices in Chile from 1947 to 1964, the CIDA concluded: "It can thus be said that, in general, changes in agricultural prices relative to other prices during the post-war period cannot be considered as one of the factors that have limited agricultural development."[87] The same fact is observed in Mexico, where the index of relative prices received and paid by farmers changed from 100 in 1939 to 103 in 1960-61.[88] In Brazil the index of real prices for agricultural products remained constant between 1948 and 1967.[89] There has also been no significant long-run tendency in Argentina.[90] It can therefore be concluded that agricultural prices have generally maintained their position since the 1930s relative to prices in other sectors of the economy.

This observation is the key to the structuralists' rejection of the monetarists' thesis. It is nevertheless misleading, since what matters is not the *trend* in terms of trade during the stagnation period but the comparison of their *level* with that of pre-1930 expansion or, better yet, with the equilibrium level they would reach if existing market distortions were eliminated.

Such a comparison clearly reveals a post-1930 deterioration in the terms of trade against agriculture. In Argentina, for example, the terms of trade collapsed from 100 in 1926-29 to an average of 61 in the 1930-64 period.[91] But this comparison of pre- and post-1930 price levels cannot be made systematically, for data are generally unavailable for the first period. Calculations of net effective protective tariffs are thus more revealing of the net disequilibrium in the value added by production resulting from the difference between prices that would prevail under a free market economy and existing prices.

Distortions in the internal terms of trade for agriculture result from market interventions both to cheapen agricultural products and to protect industry. In addition, incentives for import-substitution industrialization through systematic overvaluation of the exchange rate in order to cheapen the cost of necessary imports of capital goods are detrimental to the prices of agricultural products. A tax on exports is implied, and since food products usually do not receive tariff protection, a deterioration in internal prices is implied as well.

Market interventions to cheapen food products consist principally in producer and consumer price controls, consumer rationing (e.g., meatless days), export quotas, and export taxes.[92] To this is added the promotion of industry through tariff protection, restrictive import quotas, and foreign-exchange rationing. As a result, the price level of most nationally produced industrial goods is well above that on the world market, and the price level of food is below it. Little, Scitovsky, and Scott thus observe that "although subsidies are sometimes provided for agriculture, in the form of protection against agricultural imports, extension services, irrigation, and the provision of fertilizers, such subsidies are certainly a very low proportion of value added in agriculture and do not significantly affect the bias against agriculture created by the protection of industry, and its concomitant, an overvalued exchange rate."[93]

A good indicator of the degree of negative protection of agriculture and of the consequent disincentive to modernization is obtained from international comparisons of the price of nitrogen relative to those of corn or wheat at the producer level. In Table 4.1, the relative prices calculated indicate the number of kilos of corn or wheat that farmers need to sell in different countries in order to cover the cost of one kilo of nitrogen derived from the cheapest local source. U.S. data show that technological change in the production of ammonium nitrate brought about a 50 percent reduction in price between 1958 and 1969. In the center economies the price of nitrogen relative to that of wheat is on the order of 2.5. In Latin America, with the exception of Mexico, relative prices are sharply more unfavorable; they are 5 in Chile, 8 in Argentina and Brazil, 9 in Ecuador, and 10 in Uruguay. Except on very exhausted lands, or in production under irrigation, relative prices above 4 or 5 virtually prohibit the use of fertilizers in cereal production under present technological conditions.[94] The obvious consequence is that only in Mexico have the terms of trade allowed for massive use of Green Revolution technology.

In a recent study, Peterson calculated an index of the terms of trade (product prices measured in wheat equivalent relative to nitrogen price) received by farmers in the center and periphery (Table 4.2).[95] The index shows the dramatic impact of cheap-food policies. On the average, for the countries listed, the terms of trade were more than twice as favorable in the center than in the

Table 4.1. Price of Nitrogen Relative to That of Wheat and Corn
at the Producer Level in Latin America and Elsewhere

Country and year	Corn price, P_c (U.S. $ per quintal)	Wheat price, P_w (U.S. $ per quintal)	Nitrogen price, P_N (U.S. $ per kg nitrogen)	$\dfrac{P_N}{P_c} \times 100$	$\dfrac{P_N}{P_w} \times 100$
CENTER ECONOMIES					
United States					
1957–59	4.4	—[a]	0.18	4.1	—
1967	4.8	5.8	0.14	2.9	2.4
1968	4.4	—	0.11	2.5	—
1969	4.5	—	0.09	2.0	—
Western Germany					
1965–66	—	10.4	0.28	—	2.7
Belgium					
1965–66	—	9.6	0.26	—	2.7
Holland					
1965–66	—	10.0	0.26	—	2.6
England					
1965–66	—	6.8	0.17	—	2.5
Japan					
1965–66	—	13.0	0.26	—	2.0
Canada					
1967	—	5.4	0.14	—	2.6
France					
1966	—	—	—	—	2.9
LATIN AMERICA					
Mexico					
1967	—	6.8	0.19	—	2.8
Argentina					
1969	3.2	3.5	0.26	8.1	7.5
Chile					
1943–47	7.4	8.5	0.33	4.5	3.9
1948–52	8.5	8.7	0.33	3.9	3.8
1953–57	7.8	7.3	0.40	5.1	5.5
1958–62	6.6	7.0	0.36	5.5	5.1
1963–66	7.1	7.1	0.36	5.1	5.1
Brazil					
1961–64	—	—	—	8.2	—
Ecuador					
1966	—	—	—	—	9.0
Uruguay					
1966	—	—	—	—	10.0

Sources: For United States and Argentina, see Alain de Janvry and R. Koenig, "Economia de la Fertiliza-
ción del Maiz y Trigo en Argentina," mimeographed (Castelar, Argentina: INTA, Department of Economics,
1972).

For Mexico, see H. Borlaug, *El Programa Coordinado de Investigación y Producción de Trigo del INTA,*
INTA Technical Bulletin no. 104 (Buenos Aires: INTA, 1968).

For Chile, see A. Valdés and C. del Campo, "Fertilizantes en Trigo y Maiz," mimeographed (Santiago de
Chile: Catholic University of Chile, Faculty of Agronomy, 1970).

For Brazil, see G. E. Schuh, *The Agricultural Development of Brazil* (New York: Frederick A. Praeger,
1970), p. 343.

For Ecuador and Uruguay, see R. H. Brannon, *The Agricultural Development of Uruguay* (New York:
Frederick A. Praeger, 1967), p. 12.

For all other areas, see Food and Agriculture Organization of the United Nations, *Prices of Agricultural
Products and Fertilizers in Europe* (Rome, 1966).

[a] — = data not available.

Table 4.2.   Wheat Yields and Relative Prices
Received by Farmers, 1968–70

Country	Wheat yield (quintals per hectare)	Price of wheat divided by price of nitrogen
CENTER ECONOMIES		
Japan	23.5	52.5
United States	20.8	44.0
France	35.1	41.2
West Germany	39.1	38.0
Belgium	38.3	37.6
United Kingdom	40.9	36.7
Netherlands	44.5	29.4
Italy	23.0	29.2
Canada	18.2	27.8
Average	31.5	37.4
LATIN AMERICA		
Mexico	29.4	25.8
Chile	18.3	25.4
Colombia	11.0	25.4
Panama	0[a]	19.9
Guatemala	7.5	18.2
Peru	9.0	15.8
Uruguay	11.8	15.5
Argentina	13.2	13.4
Paraguay	12.5	8.4
Average	14.1	18.6

Sources: (Col. 1) Willis Peterson, "International Farm Prices and the Social Cost of Cheap Food Policies," *American Journal of Agricultural Economics* 61, no. 1 (February 1979): 12–21.

(Col. 2) U.S. Department of Agriculture, *Agricultural Statistics* (Washington, D.C., 1970, 1971, and 1972); Food and Agriculture Organization of the United Nations, *Production Yearbook*, 1972.

[a] No wheat production.

Latin American countries. Wheat yields were similarly more than twice as high in the center than in Latin American countries. Among Latin American countries, Mexico's favorable price policy and higher levels of wheat yields are again outstanding.

As we saw before, price distortions have been more severe for wage foods than for exportables, industrial inputs, and luxury foods. The result has been a bias in the development of capitalism in Latin American agriculture away from the production of wage foods and peasant crops.

Neoclassical economists have attempted to assess the impact of cheap-food policies on agricultural production and on the balance of agricultural trade by simulating the effect that elimination of these policies would have on output levels, using for this purpose product supply functions and derived demand functions for factors of production. Valdés[96] thus calculated that in Chile, production increases that would have resulted from elimination of negative protection would have virtually cancelled the trade deficit in wheat and meat. Using fertilizer-response functions for wheat, he also calculated that during 1969-71 free imports of urea would have increased nitrogen consumption by 40-60 percent, which in turn would have increased production by 5-8 percent. Such a result implies that at the 1973 international price, each dollar spent on fertilizer imports would allow a net saving of from \$4.50 to \$6.50 on wheat imports during the same year.[97] Similarly, Schuh estimated that the yearly Brazilian exports of corn would have increased by more than 500 percent during 1960-66 had the overvaluation of the *cruzeiro* and export quotas been eliminated.[98] And Peterson found that if the terms of trade in the periphery had been at the average level of those in the center, output in the periphery would have been 63 percent above the actual level, in which case "the evidence is quite strong that there would be no such thing as a world food problem."[99] Even though these results certainly overestimate the potential output effect of removing market distortions (because they use behavioral models that are static and use them with strict capitalist rationality), they nevertheless provide one of the most objective defenses of the monetarist thesis.

Having empirically established the existence of serious price distortions against agriculture, and particularly against wage foods, we now need to identify the conditions under which successful development of capitalism has occurred in the production of certain wage foods in certain countries. There are three such conditions.

The first is the availability of a technology that allows capitalists to outcompete peasants. As we saw in Chapter 3, the rule of elimination between capitalists and peasants is given by the relative magnitude of the gap in productivities and the gap in costs between the two production systems. The cost gap originates in the fact that peasants will remain in production even if rents and profits are driven to zero and implicit wages are pushed below those in the labor market. Clearly, not all crops can be produced on a capitalist basis with equal ease, because the productivity gap is to a certain extent crop specific. The productivity gap will tend to be larger and to favor capitalists where the most efficient production requires relatively large amounts of market-purchased inputs and where the production time can be reduced to increase the turnover rate of capital.[100] Similarly, some crops can be produced efficiently only after massive investments in irrigation. Only the state or capitalists are able to make such investments. Therefore, it is generally capitalists who appropriate these lands and use them to grow those crops for which irrigation increases productivity to the point where they can compete with peasant producers, who do not have irrigated lands. By contrast, where efficient rates of production can be reached with little investment and where the share of labor in total cost is high, those producers who use their own labor will be able to reach levels of efficiency close to those of capitalists and to outcompete them, since they tolerate zero profits and implicit wages below market levels. Capitalist production also develops where the unit cost of production is lowered by increasing the scale of operation beyond that accessible to peasant producers and where, at the same time, the share of labor in total costs declines. This is obtained in particular via mechanization. Rice responds extremely well to irrigation, and especially when irrigation is combined with market-purchased inputs requiring large cash outlays, inputs such as modern seeds, fertilizers, and insecticides. It is consequently a crop that has brought the rapid development of capitalism to Colombia and the Dominican Republic.[101] Manioc responds to none of these inputs; efforts to develop a technology that will lower per-unit production costs have failed, at least until recently.[102]

While there is no exogenous technological determination of which crops are produced by capitalist farming versus peasant farming, for the reason that technology is a social product and thus is ultimately controlled by the capitalist class, it is, however, the case that for both historical and biological reasons, capitalism tends to monopolize at a differential rate different crops in relation to the technological nature of their production.

The second condition under which capitalist relations develop in the production of a certain crop is the direct intervention of the state to ensure some degree of protection from foreign competition. Indeed, there is competition from imports in many of the crops that are technologically amenable to domestic capitalist development. In Colombia, FEDEARROZ (the national association of rice producers) was able to obtain protectionist price policies until 1973, when massive technological change finally made rice production competitive on the world market.[103] In Brazil, FECOTRIGO (the federation of wheat growers) has effectively lobbied for higher producer prices. By importing cheap P.L. 480 wheat, reselling it at a higher price to local mills, and using the revenues to establish a minimum producer price above the price to the mills, the state has thus acted as the sole purchaser of both domestic and imported wheat and subsidized domestic products.[104]

In agriculture, as in industry, modern technology is of such a nature that assistance from the state is often a third necessary condition before the production and marketing of a certain crop can develop on a large, capitalist scale. This public support is necessary in establishing marketing channels capable of handling massive production, credit facilities that can meet the need for large cash outlays, technical extension agents, etc. Solon Barraclough thus observes that it is often the lack of such assistance that perpetuates reliance on imported foods.[105] Furthermore, these services often must be subsidized—at least for a period—to encourage development. But the capacity of a group of producers to elicit these services from the state depends on their previous control of surplus; and since these services embody a transfer of surplus, a lobby to fight for the permanent extension of the surpluses is likely to form. For this reason, we have called this state-provided subsidy an "institutional rent." Indeed, instances of spectacular development of capitalism in the production of food crops generally correspond to the existence of powerful commodity-based agricultural lobbies capable of obtaining protectionism and institutional rents from the state: this is the case for rice in Colombia (FEDEARROZ) and the Dominican Republic (National Association of Rice Producers) and for wheat in Brazil (FECOTRIGO).

Thus, we can expect capitalist production in each country to develop in those crops that are most amenable to economies of scale and to a high productivity of labor because of technological or natural reasons and because of state protection through tariffs and institutional rents.

Capitalist production is synonymous with accumulation and growth; it is those who *can* accumulate who end up investing in the "capitalist" crops. The production of these crops expands; production costs fall and prices drop. Those crops which continue to be produced on a peasant basis show relatively stagnant production trends and increasing prices within the margin allowed by cheap-food policies.

TECHNOLOGICAL BIAS TOWARD LABORSAVING.   As capitalism progresses in agriculture, the development of the forces of production assumes markedly different patterns according to whether the state is controlled by the (junker) landed elite or by the bourgeoisie at large. In the latter case agrarian interests have only a secondary influence over the state. The former pattern characterizes countries like Colombia, Ecuador, Bolivia, Venezuela, Argentina, and Brazil, while the latter characterizes Mexico (after the land reform of 1934), the Dominican Republic, and Costa Rica. Under domination of the state by the landed elite, there is a strong tendency for technological change to be biased in a direction that saves on labor but does not necessarily increase yields (i.e., does not save on land). This technological bias, which is important in understanding the tendency for food production to stagnate, can be explained as follows.

The institutional rent derived and monopolized by the landed elite through political control of the state is an element that helps counteract, for this class, the otherwise disastrous effects of cheap-food policies and the general bias against agriculture on the rate of profit in agriculture. Capitalized into land values, institutional rents raise the real price of land despite the low rates of return implied by price distortions against agriculture. This explains the oft-cited paradox of stagnant food production, cheap food prices, and positive increases in the real price of land.

However, a more complete understanding of the poor performance of food production under junker capitalist development requires an understanding of the process through which the landed elite ensures the reproduction of the conditions under which it controls the state and consequently the conditions under which the derivation of an institutional rent is perpetuated.

The premise on which the argument presented below is established is the following: if political control of the state makes it possible to derive an institutional rent that helps to make capitalist agriculture profitable despite low food prices, the guarantee of profitability in the future requires the exercise of institutional control toward the generation of institutional services that do not jeopardize the reproduction of control of the state.

How can the institutional process be managed so as to generate selective rents without undermining the social status quo upon which the political domination of the state is based?

The answer requires, first, the identification of the basis upon which political control of the state by the landed elite rests and, second, the identification of possible threats to this basis. Clearly, political control is based on the social control over large segments of the population which the landed elites enjoy through monopolization of the land. As CIDA observed, "Land tenure relationships tend to coincide with power relationships."[106]

One of the most subtle, yet most powerful, aspects of the control of institutional processes is the management of technological developments. Technology is a component of the means of production that can substitute for or complement other factors according to the biases that determine the pattern of its generation and application. Social control of technology implies a significant degree of control over the rate of economic growth and over the distribution of income.[107]

Given these factors, control over the generation and application of technology is a key source of institutional rents—a source that, we repeat, must be managed in such a fashion that it does not threaten the basis upon which its appropriation is made possible. The choice of technology is thus crucial.

Technology in agriculture can be divided into two types—mechanical and biochemical. Mechanization is labor-saving, promotes economies of scale, and reduces management needs; however, it generally does not increase yields. Biochemical technology—best exemplified by the Green Revolution—is land-saving (yield-increasing) and increases both management and labor needs.[108]

In terms of the rationality of the individual producer, it is immaterial which type of technology is adopted, provided that the type chosen increases profits. But this does not hold for the generation of technological innovations in agriculture. Agricultural technology is principally generated in public research institutions, and its diffusion is regulated by public credit and information institutions and by price and trade policies. And it is at the level of the generation and diffusion of technology that the impact of policies reflecting the objective needs of the landowning class is evident.

In total contrast to biochemical technology, the consequences of the application of mechanical technology to agriculture are perfectly tailored to the reproduction of the social status quo and consequently to the perpetuation of state control by the landed elite. By saving labor and not land, mechanization not only reduces labor costs for the individual producer but contributes to a reduction in labor costs throughout the economy. Biochemical technology, on the other hand, reduces unit costs for the individual producer but, by increasing the demand for labor, contributes to an increase in labor costs throughout the economy. Furthermore, once the frontier is closed, mechanization protects the land monopoly of the landed elite, whereas biochemical technology, by being land-saving, threatens it. Finally, mechanization allows individual control of the generated surplus in the form of rising differential rents, whereas with biochemical technology the surplus is extracted through market prices and therefore cannot be monopolized.

This last contrast can be explained as follows. Mechanical innovations fundamentally reduce costs without increasing output. As a result, with a fixed land base, the surplus generated by mechanization is captured by landlords independently of the elasticity of demand and is capitalized into land values. By contrast, given an inelastic demand for food, the surplus from the application of biochemical technology is automatically extracted from the agricultural sector through a decline in the price of food.[109] In the first instance, the surplus can be extracted from agriculture only by means of tax schemes or forced deliveries at low prices. In the second, surplus extraction is automatically ensured by the market mechanism that imposes a dynamic "squeeze on agriculture." Owen has characterized this mechanism as the Mill-Marshallian model.[110]

Finally, mechanization displays several other features that are attractive to the landed elite, including a reduction of management needs (which favors absenteeism) and the hierarchization of the labor process (which favors divisiveness within the labor force and thus facilitates control by the landlord).

In summary, mechanization is consistent with the rationality of landowners at an individual and class level as it increases the surplus produced on the junker estates while reinforcing the social status quo. In contrast, biochemical technology introduces a contradiction between the rationality of landowners as individuals and as a class, erodes the basis upon which the superstructure of elite control rests, and proscribes individual control of the surplus. Indeed, the massive adoption of Green Revolution technology would not only require the previous elimination of the landed elite but a transition to a competitive capitalist economy in which absolute land rent disappeared and profits were based upon entrepreneurial behavior and were therefore always ephemeral and dependent on management's dedication. As the experiences of Mexico (wheat), the Dominican Republic (rice), and Colombia (rice) with the farmer or merchant road have shown, land-saving technology (Green Revolution and irrigation networks) could then become a powerful source of output growth.[111]

Thus, political control of the state by the landed elite and use of this control to derive institutional rents that compensate for unfavorable prices are determinants of the stagnation and unevenness in agricultural output that are observable in those Latin American countries in which the landed elite controls the institutional process.

The technological bias in favor of mechanization results from the lack of allocation of state funds to research in land-saving technologies and infrastructure investments, unfavorable prices for fertilizers, and heavily subsidized mechanization via negative real rates of interest[112] and overvalued exchange rates. The cost of machinery has consequently been highly distorted downward. On the other hand, as we have seen before, the extent to which the prices of fertilizers are unfavorable is equally impressive. And biochemical technology has not been as extensively available, since it requires additional research to adapt it to local conditions, while mechanical technology can be directly transplanted without intervention of the state.

The result has been a fast pace for mechanization, while the use of fertilizers for food production (and consequently yield levels) has lagged behind. Between 1949 and 1974, the average annual percentage change in the use of tractors was 45 percent in Brazil, 24 percent in Argentina, 21 percent in Bolivia, 18 percent in Peru, 15 percent in Colombia, and 13 percent in Mexico.[113] By contrast, the annual rate of increase in fertilizer use in the 1963–64 to 1972–73 period was 14 percent.[114] In Chile, CIDA observed "a more rapid increase in the use of tractors, harvesters, etc., than of fertilizers, of more intensive planting techniques, and of improved management of crops and livestock."[115] And fertilizer has been used principally on export crops instead of on food crops. For example, in Brazil, 62 percent of fertilizers are used in sugarcane, cotton, and soybean production, while in Ecuador, sugarcane, coffee, and banana production account for about 64 percent of fertilizer consumption.[116] The result of this technological bias is that for Latin American agriculture as a whole, labor productivity (mechanization) increased 60 percent faster than land productivity (biochemicals and irrigation) between 1960 and 1973, as the following data demonstrate:[117]

Latin American Agriculture, 1960–73

Annual percentage increase

Total production	3.3
Land cultivated	1.8
Land productivity	1.5
Labor productivity	2.4

USE VERSUS REPRODUCTION OF THE PEASANTRY AS A SOURCE OF CHEAP FOOD.   Under the impact of cheap-food policies, a number of wage foods are marginalized out of capitalist production and into peasant farming. Under these economic conditions and given their position in the political economy, peasants are unable to accumulate as their surpluses are drained. In particular, the middle peasantry disappears as a set of *producers* of commodities relative to the ever-increasing weight of capitalists in total production. As the peasants' resource base deteriorates and they are forced onto less-fertile lands, their meager production becomes relatively scarcer, and its price tends to increase. The destruction of the peasantry contributes to the crisis in wage foods and peasant crops.

The peasantry is ousted from the production of agricultural crops when it cannot compete with large-scale capitalist production of those crops or with the undervalued imports of foodstuffs via overvalued exchange rates and price subsidies. But there are further processes at work in the struggle between capitalists and peasants. The need to cheapen wage foods leads to the provision of subsidized agricultural inputs to the capitalist sector of agriculture, chief among which are credit with negative or very low interest rates, extension services, research, infrastructure, and marketing facilities. Since these inputs are provided below market cost, non-price-rationing devices appear. The main such device is political power, which depends essentially on the prior ability to control a surplus. Thus, it is capitalist agriculture which will capture these institutional rents. Even in the case where there are downward pressures on product prices, these subsidies translate into high land prices. Therefore, peasants are driven out of production through the factor market when inputs are discriminatorily subsidized.

A class of producers thus emerges which meets the need for cheap food and massive exports on an increasingly efficient basis, even though it does so insufficiently relative to effective demand and foreign-exchange needs. These producers squeeze the peasantry on the product side by lowering the price of foods, as in the case of rice, and on the input side, by driving up either the prices of inputs or the price of land if the inputs are subsidized. As they lose control over resources, peasants increasingly remain in production only to feed themselves—to complement the wage they receive for the labor they are now forced to sell to those who control the resources. Capitalist producers benefit from this semiproletarianization by paying a wage which is below the cost of maintenance and reproduction of the labor force, since the function of the peasant sector is to add the necessary complement.

This dual agricultural development, which we have called "functional dualism," together with technological innovations and institutional rents, sustains capitalist development in agriculture in spite of unfavorable price policies. The foods produced by capitalists tend to become wage foods because of increasing production and technological improvement, which render supply response increasingly reliable and elastic. Peasant foods cease to be produced as the upper peasantry is destroyed; to the extent that they are still produced, the semiproletarians and the remaining middle peasantry produce them. But even the semiproletarians increasingly consume the wage foods they themselves produce on the capitalist farms. It is this process of destruction of peasants as commodity producers that becomes manifest in the increasing inequality of income distribution and the frequent decreases in absolute income at the bottom level of the distribution. This process, then, is the root of rural poverty and is the social embodiment of the contradictions of capitalist development in the periphery today.

The increase in the price of peasant foods, while still insufficient to allow capitalist development in the production of these crops (manioc, for example), has nevertheless stimulated research into the production and storage of peasant crops. If manioc could be efficiently produced, processed and/or stored, and transported, all on a large, or at least a small but industrial, scale, then it could become an important wage food or animal feedstuff or source of fuel. The fact that it is today a peasant food apparently orients research toward the "smallholder." But it is clear that to the extent that such research is successful, it cannot help but increase the process of social differentiation, for it will extend the list of crops that can be produced most efficiently only with relatively large cash outlays and with little labor. Indeed, this is why the Green Revolution sharpened the process of social differentiation.[118]

While the *tendency* of peasants to disappear as commodity producers seems unavoidable, their total disappearance as producers of *use values* today lacks economic rationality at the level of the system as a whole in terms of labor supply and product-market creation. Also, the process is one which creates enormous social tension and thus calls into question the legitimacy of the state. As we have shown, a full-time proletariat in peripheral agriculture is as yet unnecessary except in a few areas of export agriculture: there is already a tremendous reserve army of labor, and the market in the disarticulated accumulation process has historically been outside the national economy and in consumption by the upper classes. But there is a tendency for the system to proletarianize the peasantry anyway through competition with capitalist agriculture. It is the purpose of strategies such as those of rural development and the "basic-needs" policies to deal with this contradiction. We will consider them in detail in Chapter 6.

The Global Crisis

We started by observing the existence of both uneven development among crops, farms, and countries and a global food crisis. This crisis manifests itself in increasing prices of foods (which put upward pressure on wages) and in the increasing need to import food (which therefore limits a country's ability to import capital goods) and thus results in a tendency for overall growth to slow down or for indebtedness to increase.

This global crisis is due to the breakdown of production of three sets of crops: (1) wage foods importable via cheap credit or payment in local currency and sold on domestic markets at overvalued exchange rates; (2) peasant foods; and (3) those wage foods whose prices are held low by government intervention and for which institutional rents do not offer sufficient compensation. In all these cases production is excluded from capitalist agriculture and stagnates as the peasantry loses its role as supplier of a marketable surplus. The global crisis is thus characterized by uneven development: on the one hand, the development of an efficient, large-scale production structure that benefits from subsidies and protection of the state and where the productive forces develop rapidly but with a general bias toward exportables (in association with multinational agribusiness) and industrial inputs and a bias toward labor instead of land-saving technology under junker capitalism; on the other hand, the breakdown of peasant agriculture, the stagnation of importable grains and of a number of important wage foods, and massive rural poverty. Under the constraint of cheap food and unstable external markets, the global tendency is, however, one of stagnation of food production relative to effective demand and secularly declining per capita agricultural exports.

In light of the laws of capital accumulation on a world scale, the determinants of the food and hunger crisis become quite clear. And so do the errors and partiality of the prevailing explanatory theses we reviewed above.

In the center, accumulation under social articulation and the consequent contradiction between capitalists and capital creates a tendency toward underconsumption. Due to political pressures of farm interests and state intervention, the overproduction crisis in agriculture is resolved not by deflation but by exporting it on the world market. The international price of certain wage foods thus becomes extremely low and blocks the modernization of peripheral agriculture in some branches of production. However, it provides an external possibility of sustaining cheap labor in the periphery.

In the periphery, accumulation under dependent disarticulation creates the objective need for cheap labor and hence cheap food. And the *cheap labor–cheap food* logic creates the food and hunger crises. On the production side, the pressure for cheap food is met more systematically by expedient extractivist policies (unfavorable terms of trade, taxation, forced deliveries) than by the induction of developmental sequences (technological change, infrastructure investment). The result is uneven development and global stagnation. Cheap food is partially compensated for by institutional rents and is passed along in the form of miserable wages to semiproletarian peasants, who thus contribute, through destructive functional dualism, to primitive accumulation in the capitalist sector. On the consumption side, malnutrition and hunger result from cheap labor (unemployment, low wages, and low productivity in the informal sector) enforced by repressive regimes. In peasant agriculture the mass of rural population is relegated to poverty, which induces both demographic explosion and ecological destruction as individually rational components for survival strategies. And poverty, in canceling the effective demand for wage goods, reinforces both uneven development and the global food crisis.

THE NEW WORLD ORDER: A NEW INTERNATIONAL DIVISION OF LABOR FOR AGRICULTURE?

In order to identify what effects the crisis of the 1970s and the emerging new international economic order are having on the global division of labor in agriculture, we will first examine the role of food and agriculture in the crisis in both the center and the periphery, with particular emphasis on the United States and Latin America.

With respect to the United States, there are those who claim that food was one of the essential weapons used by the American government to counteract the crisis. Boddy and Crotty, for example, argue that the 1973 world food crisis was "the inevitable and foreseen result of an economic strategy planned by the ruling class and implemented by the Nixon administration for the purpose of protecting U.S. international economic and political hegemony against serious challenges."[119] They attribute the tight grain markets of 1973 not to adverse weather but to the conscious intervention of representatives of multinational corporations in the formation of government policies designed to expand agricultural exports. While it is clear that the increase in agricultural exports since 1972 has proven beneficial to the U.S. balance-of-trade position, Boddy and Crotty's instrumentalist assessment of the role of food in the general economic crisis is insufficient. Although it is true that world grain trade is highly concentrated in the hands of six transnational companies capable of influencing U.S. policies and monopolizing world trade,[120] definite structural transformations in the global agricultural economy are more important in explaining the present situation. These structural changes must be understood in relation to the evolution of U.S. agricultural production and policy.

In the years 1938–52, U.S. farmers enjoyed an especially favorable investment climate maintained by government price-support policies that had become an integral part of the pattern of articulated accumulation. The rapid adoption of yield-increasing innovations that ensued resulted not only in rapid productivity increases but also in a reduction in the real price of farm commodities, which in the 1950s and 1960s was sufficient to offset the rising costs of food processing and marketing and to keep food-price inflation below the general rate (Table 4.3). Despite the side effects of large carry-over surpluses and high fiscal costs, on balance, federal management of the agricultural sector made a positive contribution to accumulation and growth.

However, as early as 1965 the New Deal policies came under increasing scrutiny. The 1965 farm bill addressed some of the irrationalities of prior food-supply management schemes by reducing the "loan rate" (support price) to world price levels, making deficiency payments to compensate for higher U.S. costs, and offering large incentive payments for voluntary land diversion. The logic of the 1965 bill was that steady productivity increases would be forthcoming and would continuously lower costs and eventually obviate the need for deficiency payments as U.S. farm products became competitive on world markets. This system was successful in making U.S. agricultural products more competitive and in reducing surplus stocks. Food prices were temporarily kept low, but direct treasury outlays for farm programs increased drastically. Not only did fiscal costs become more visible, but the direct payment system also made the unequal distribution of farm program benefits more obvious to begrudging urban groups. Dissatisfaction with these policies among farmers emerged in 1968 when farm income returned to a historical low comparable to that of the Depression years and food-price inflation began to accelerate.

The structural changes that were occurring in U.S. agricultural production became more obvious after 1968. As reflected in Table 4.3, after 1968, agricultural prices and retail food prices increased at annual rates that were greater than the general rate of increase of consumer prices. However, the rates of increases of farm input prices were even higher. At the same time, the expected rates of growth of land and labor productivity failed to materialize; these growth rates fell below pre-1968 levels.[121]

Table 4.3.   Comparison of Annual Rates of Change
in Selected Economic Indicators in the
United States, 1950–68 and 1968–77

Economic indicator	Average annual rate of change (percent)	
	1950–68	1968–77
Consumer prices (all items)	2.0	6.4
Retail food prices	1.9	7.1
Farm commodity prices (all)	−0.2	7.2
Crops	−0.2	7.6
Livestock	0.1	6.0
Farm input prices (all inputs)	0.8	8.0
Agricultural land prices (United States, all land)	5.6	11.4
Farm machinery prices	3.2	9.6
Fertilizer prices	−0.6	8.3
Agricultural chemical prices	0.0[a]	10.0
Agricultural land productivity (output per acre)	2.5	0.9
Agricultural labor productivity (output per man-hour)	6.8	4.3
Value of farm production assets per farm (United States)	6.6	14.8[b]
Value of agricultural exports (United States)	4.5	13.8
Value of agricultural imports (United States)	2.8	11.6
Net real farm income		
Total	−3.2	−0.7
Per farm	1.2	0.6

Sources: National economic indicators were calculated from data in President's Council of Economic Advisers, *Economic Report of the President* (Washington, D.C., 1978), appendix tables; agricultural data were calculated from U.S. Department of Agriculture, *Agricultural Statistics,* various issues.

[a] Refers to period 1965–68.
[b] Refers to period 1968–76.

Hoping for an improvement in the farm situation, the Nixon administration at first postponed consideration of agricultural legislation. In 1970 a bill that was practically identical to the "market-oriented" 1965 legislation was passed. However, it was Nixon's 1971 New Economic Policy, with its emphasis on agricultural export expansion, which succeeded in bringing agriculture out of the 1968 slump. A combination of devaluations, the Russian grain sales, and world-wide harvest shortfalls suddenly increased the demand for U.S. farm products so much that farm incomes almost doubled between 1971 and 1973. Loan rates and target prices were lowered below market prices in 1973, deficiency payments became unnecessary, and in 1974 all set-aside land diversions were stopped, allowing farmers to return 50 million acres of land to production. Food exports increased by 77 percent between 1969 and 1973; and the dollar value of these exports increased by 126 percent, accounting for 25 percent of total U.S. export earnings in 1973. These massive food exports increased farm incomes dramatically and reduced the deficit in the balance of payments. Yet they also contributed to the creation of serious inflationary pressures at home. As James Grant, president of the Overseas Development Council, observed, "Just four years ago [1973–74], rising food prices added as much to U.S. and global inflation, according to a Federal Reserve study, as did rising oil costs."[122]

Thus, in 1975, for the first time since the Korean War, the U.S. government no longer regulated important agricultural markets. According to all indications at that time, the requirements of articulated accumulation in the United States appeared to no longer entail federal protection of agricultural income and profits.

However, events since 1975 suggest that the U.S. farm problem has not been solved and that what happened in the 1973 boom was a rupture in the class alliance between industrial and agrarian capitalists as a result of the secular disappearance of the family farm and the new demands on agriculture implied by the general economic crisis. Following the 1975 recession, farm income was squeezed by rapidly rising input prices and land values. Although urban groups had taken a new interest in farm policy with the intention of preventing food-price inflation, they were not able to prevent the traditional farm and agribusiness groups from demanding a fair return on assets committed to agricultural protection. The Food and Agriculture Act of 1977 reestablished the traditional commodity programs, including direct farm subsidies, acreage controls, and government-supported food stocks. This apparent reversal of U.S. agricultural policy in such a short time period attests the still-powerful position of agricultural interests in the nation. Nonetheless, in the past two years, the return of farmer activism, with its virulent displays of discontent, is proof that farmer control over federal policy is not solid enough to protect their economic position in the present crisis and that there has been a modification in the articulation of the agrarian capitalist with other classes of society.

Thus, in the past thirty years of experience in U.S. agriculture, we see that at first it appeared that the phenomenal growth in productivity would continue indefinitely, enabling the United States to become the breadbasket of the world. This pattern, which seemed secure as late as 1965, proved vulnerable to the national and international structural changes that occurred between 1968 and 1975. As a result of the general slowdown in both agricultural productivity and general economic growth after 1968, pressures on the alliance between agrarian and industrial capitalists intensified, and the future course of farm policies in the United States became increasingly contradictory in the face of three types of disjunction: that between increased food-exports earnings to maintain the balance of payments and domestic food-price inflation; that between the short-term export drive and the long-term perpetration of comparative advantages in grain exports; and that between the support of farm income through traditional commodity programs and high, inflationary fiscal costs in a post-Keynesian economy.

As mentioned earlier, the most obvious ramification of the global crisis in the periphery has been the rapid expansion of external debt. As a result of this process, the contradictions between foreign exchange (balance of payments) and cheap food have intensified critically. The Williams Report[123] (the same report that was cited by Boddy and Crotty as proof of a conscious strategy to engineer the food crisis) elaborated a plan for reorganization of Third World agriculture in the emerging new world structure.[124] The report explicitly recommended that peripheral countries apply their comparative advantage to the production of labor-intensive crops such as fruits, vegetables, and sugar for export and thus earn foreign exchange with which to finance their balance of payments and import cheaper U.S. grain.

Indeed, there is evidence that Latin American countries have responded to the crisis by encouraging agricultural exports. The cases of Brazil and Mexico are instructive. In the past sixteen years Brazil has shed the image of a stagnant agrarian state, so much so that by 1977 it was the world's second-largest agricultural exporter. In addition to the traditional exports, coffee and cacao, soybeans were a major source of the $12 billion in foreign exchange that Brazil's agricultural exports earned in 1977. These earnings not only paid for Brazil's substantial petroleum imports but also provided a positive balance of payments. State policies, particularly credit policies, have been instrumental in providing the incentives for this revival.[125] In Mexico a tremendous growth in fresh fruit and vegetable production for export has occurred. U.S. imports of vegetables from Mexico increased from $36 million in 1964 to over $100 million in 1969 and $176 million in 1973. In 1975, vegetable exports constituted 9 percent of total agricultural output in Mexico, and sales of vegetable exports made up 10 percent of all commercial transactions between Mexico and other countries.[126]

However, these examples treat only one side of the contradiction. As shown earlier in this chapter, the other side of the ''comparative advantage'' coin is dependency on food imports. Given the trend of the past twenty years,[127] Grant estimates that an increase of 550 million tons in world grain production will be required to meet global demand by 1990.[128] This increase is roughly more than double the current level of grain production in the United States. The cost increases and slowdown in productivity growth that occurred after 1968 imply that it will be increasingly difficult for the United States and other developed countries to play the dominant role in making up these deficits. If in their zeal to capitalize on comparative advantages, the peripheral countries ignore production for the domestic market—"food first"—they may face serious internal difficulties when external sources of cheap food are no longer forthcoming. Furthermore, although increased specialization in agroexports may have a positive expected payoff in terms of net balance-of-trade position, it also involves greater risks—especially since Third World efforts at stabilizing international commodity markets have not been successful. Thus, the move toward comparative advantage is no panacea for crisis in the periphery.

Another aspect of disarticulated accumulation that we developed above is the contradiction between cheap-food policies and the development of capitalism in agriculture. In the context of the global accumulation crisis, the costs of cheap-food policies are magnified; and at least in Latin America, the tendency seems to be for states to provide incentives in the form of institutional rents for the development of capitalism in agriculture, with particular emphasis on attracting foreign agribusiness capital. The tendency has led many writers and organizations (such as E. Feder, NACLA, G. Arroyo, and S. George)[129] to emphasize the increased domination of transnational corporations over the agricultural processes of peripheral countries. A NACLA survey shows rapid increases in agribusiness investment in Latin America, particularly in the food-processing industry, where the number of subsidiaries more than tripled between 1960 and 1975.[130] Increased investments by multinational companies have also been observed in the production of agricultural machinery, food distribution, and actual land purchases.

A final aspect of the global structural changes that have occurred since 1968 concerns the foreign relations between the central and peripheral countries. Beginning with the Green Revolution in the late 1960s, there has been a marked redirection in development assistance between center and periphery toward a new emphasis on creating the basis for a rapid penetration of capitalism in agriculture and the political control and reproduction of peasant sectors. The World Bank's recent concern with rural development and basic needs falls within this category. The contradiction between use and reproduction of the peasantry is thus taking on such global significance that the peripheral states are protecting surplus extraction via functional dualism through their rural-development policies. This will be discussed more thoroughly in Chapter 7.

In summary, no smooth transition to a new international division of labor in agriculture is emerging out of the present crisis. Although both central and peripheral countries are attempting to expand agricultural exports, the attempt reflects not so much a movement toward international specialization in food production as a fundamental restructuring of accumulation on a world scale. In the center the contradiction between agricultural protection and export expansion has become central. In the periphery we see an intensification of the cheap food–foreign exchange dialectic, which is being addressed by policies for expansion of agricultural exports, promotion of agribusiness and multinational investments in agriculture, and international aid for reproduction of the peasantry under functional dualism. Thus, the bipolar (articulated-disarticulated) accumulation process is being transformed with respect to the role of food and agriculture, but at the same time, its internal logic is being preserved.

5

The Political Economy
of Reformism

"Liberty, Equality, Fraternity," the slogan of the French Revolution of 1789, summarizes the liberal democratic ideology of early bourgeois society conceptualized by Adam Smith and John Locke. According to this ideology, perfect competition is to prevail in economic relations and egalitarian democracy is to hold in the political sphere, leading to both consumer and citizen sovereignty. This, in turn, implies the automatic resolution of intraclass conflicts (reconciliation of divergent interests within the capitalist class) and interclass conflicts (legitimacy of class positions and the state), as well as maximally efficient resource allocation (Pareto optimality).

The ideal liberal capitalist state is portrayed as noninterventionist in character and its activities are confined to the passive role of guaranteeing private property rights and preserving laissez faire to prevent possible deviations from Pareto optimality. Exceptions include the control of externalities—to force their due internalization—and the management of public goods and services—in particular, the provision of a monetary framework and the raising of armies. But beyond this, the concepts of state interventionism and reformism are absent from the ideal of liberal democratic capitalism, even though the liberal bourgeois state was itself actively subversive in the context of feudal society. And yet the history of capitalism is that of the growing role of the state through numerous reforms and direct interventions of both an economic and a political nature in order to sustain continued accumulation and reproduce the legitimacy of unequal class positions. In particular, agrarian reforms such as land reforms and rural-development projects are typical cases of state interventionism that need to be explained in terms of a theory of the evolving role of the capitalist state. To explain them, we need to address the question of the nature of the capitalist state, the evolution of its ideological foundations, and the scope and limits of reformism.

THE CAPITALIST STATE

Although long neglected in economic theory, the role of the state has been increasingly analyzed since the Keynesian revolution in the 1930s, and theories of the state have again become essential components of social theory, just as they were in the works of Marx and Weber. While the pluralist interpretation of the state dominated Western social science in the 1950s and 1960s and still remains the ideological foundation of state legitimacy, a recent flurry of research on the state from the standpoint of political economy has produced significant advances.[1]

The main questions that this research has addressed concern the form (bourgeois democracy, fascism, bureaucratic-authoritarianism, etc.) and functions (rationalizations via the definition and implementation of reforms) of the capitalist state. How does an increasingly interventionist state develop in response to the contradictions of capitalist society, and why does it assume changing forms? How is the state able to enhance and preserve the existing social relations on both their objective and subjective foundations? How are particular state policies and structures determined, and how do they result in eventually effective reforms? And how do the ensuing developments, conditioned partially by the prior role of the state, give rise to new contradictions?

Numerous approaches have been followed to answer these questions. Some writers have argued that these approaches can be roughly divided into "instrumentalist" and "structuralist."[2] The former presumably assumes that the state is an instrument of the ruling class and hence focuses on the power elite and on the strategies and mechanisms it manipulates to perpetuate its dominant class position; the latter identifies the state as the mechanism through which the economic[3] or political[4] structural constraints that contradict the process of accumulation are overcome.

Both of these approaches have also been criticized. The instrumentalist theory is deficient because there is no identifiable unified ruling class; the many subsectors of "the" ruling class are divided over short-run issues and are therefore unable to attend consistently to the long-run reproduction of the system. The structuralists are criticized for (1) not specifying sufficiently the precise mechanisms whereby systemic constraints impinge upon the operation of the state itself and/or (2) separating the economic from the political. Yet we believe there is no need to side with one school or the other. Rather, they should be viewed as perspectives that are differentially appropriate according to specific circumstances of purpose and that thus reinforce each other. This is done, for example, by O'Connor, who in his important book *The Fiscal Crisis of the State* does not develop a new theory of the state but instead eclectically and judiciously blends the different approaches according to specific purposes.[5]

A more fundamental contrast between approaches—and one which permits a thorough understanding of the methodology of political economy—is that between "class theoretic" and "capital logic" analyses.[6] We seek here only to identify the main thrusts of these analyses, show how they complement rather than exclude each other, and finally propose our approach to the study of reformism.

A class theoretic analysis of the bourgeois state begins with an analysis of social classes and views the state as a locus of class struggle and a mediator between classes.[7] In this sense the capitalist state is seen as having similarities to states in class societies belonging to other modes of production. The approach seeks to develop a general theory of the state and, in particular, a theory of the state in capitalist society.

The state is viewed as being relatively autonomous from the process of accumulation and from the relations of production. Hence, the political is largely separated from the economic and is subjected to an analysis with special categories and its own inherent tendencies. Such an analysis often focuses on the constitution and legitimation of state structures and policies; the perpetuation of political institutions; and the struggle of classes over and within these structures, policies, and institutions.

This approach facilitates an understanding of several crucial aspects of the capitalist state, among them (1) the use of ideology to legitimate class rule; (2) the instrumental use of state power (e.g., through the repressive apparatus of the police and intelligence agencies); (3) the resulting appearance of the state as a crucial object of class struggle and, consequently, the Leninist approach to revolution; and (4) the formation of class consciousness as a decisive subjective element in the historical development of class societies.

However, any analysis that hopes to elucidate the development of the capitalist state and starts by separating the political from the economic confronts serious problems as soon as it turns from statics to dynamics, from a description of the present to a grasp of the present as history. For if capitalism develops dialectically through the resolution and reposition of contradictions and crises, and if the state plays an increasingly decisive role in resolving such crises, then the changing forms and functions of the state must be systematically related to capitalist development. This does not imply that all elements of the superstructure can be blithely reduced to economic processes but rather suggests that political analysis needs to be grounded in materialist development.

In general, then, the class theoretic approach can be faulted for neglect of the economic. By assuming the "displacement" of crises from the economic to the political sphere under late capitalism, these theorists generally fail to relate state crises (legitimation and fiscal) to the contradictory process of capital accumulation and hence fail to bring out both the economic origin of crises and the limits imposed on the reformist capacity of the state.[8] This destroys the unity of the Marxist vision by tending to locate the state *between* classes and *outside* the economy rather than as one aspect of a social totality.

An alternative approach, often termed "capital logic," attempts to derive the state from the category of capital and the essential elements of the capitalist mode of production.[9] It thus includes the state in the totality of capitalist social relations and denies that analysis can proceed from the separation of the economic and the political.[10] The state is seen as a phenomenal form of social relations, and these theorists seek to discover why economics and politics *appear* to be distinct under capitalism. Rather than assume that the state is relatively autonomous, they ask why the state appears to be an autonomous institution, an impartial authority.[11]

Efforts have been made to derive the forms and functions of the capitalist state at this theoretical level from various starting points: the competition between capitals and the need for regulation;[12] the forms of exploitation of labor by capital;[13] and the forms of appearance of social relations on the surface of bourgeois society.[14] These attempts have, however, ended in an ahistorical sterility and in a failure to explain concrete examples of capitalist states as (1) the result of subjective as well as objective forces, (2) the outcome of class struggles arising from specific forms of crisis as much as from the inherent requirements of the accumulation process, and (3) the consequence of the presence of noncapitalist modes of production and the struggle for the development of capitalism on a world scale. As Jessop correctly notes: "The state is the principal institutional locus of political power in capitalist societies and cannot be derived from an abstract consideration of the pure capitalist mode of production. Indeed, it is one of the principal difficulties of the capital logic school of analysis of the capitalist state, that it neglects the more concrete problem of state power in a given social formation in favour of the ideal collective capitalist in the capitalist mode of production."[15]

Thus, the capital logic approach can be criticized for overstressing the economic basis of political forms and objective material forces while neglecting class consciousness and class action. State interventions and reforms are made to appear to be too automatic and functional. The capitalist state is not grasped as a system of structures of political domination—the result of specific historical struggles among classes and nations.

We believe, as do Holloway and Picciotto, that the capital logic and class theoretic starting points for a theory of the state have been mistakenly portrayed as dichotomous: "To counterpose these two approaches is to create a false polarity: the 'logic of capital' is nothing but the expression of the basic form of class struggle in capitalist society. It is wrong to think that social development can be understood by an analysis of class struggle which is indifferent to the form of class struggle: such an analysis cannot do justice to the nature of the constraints and the impetus arising from that form."[16]

These two approaches thus represent two sides of a dialectical vision of the contradictory development of capitalism. Such a vision grasps the totality of social relations, whether they are viewed through the class struggles of an exploitative society or through imperatives arising from the crisis-ridden process of accumulation. Each approach subsumes the other, but each is useful to better grasp the nature of the subject under study. Class struggle is the dynamic of development, but it is mediated by past struggles and the objective functioning of the system that grew out of them; the process of capital accumulation and the crises that arise from it delimit the field of class struggle, but they do so in historically specific ways. As Marx said, "Men make their own history, but they do not make it just as they please; they do not make it under circumstances chosen by themselves, but under circumstances directly encountered, given and transmitted from the past."[17] Consequently, we need not choose between two methods of analysis; rather, both approaches should be employed dialectically in the attempt to understand the capitalist state and the origins and limits of reformism.

Much of the writing by the capital logic school has concentrated on the question of the *form* of the capitalist state—the tendency for the state to take the form of bourgeois democracy. No definitive answer has emerged, but one interpretation suggests that this form stems from the nature of surplus extraction under capitalism, the "double equality" of the working class.[18] Because workers are freed from the means of production and are free to sell their labor power, and because this sale appears to be an equal exchange, since the appropriation of surplus value is hidden from view, the state becomes the guarantor of "freely" executed contracts and appears to assume a neutral form. The state retains a repressive apparatus—and thus the possibility of exercising systematic but legitimate violence—but mystifies its class nature.

However, as capitalism develops, it increasingly needs intervention by the state to resolve crises and ensure the reproduction of social relations. Such *functions* are often of a class nature (e.g., suppressing wages after a long period of expansion when rising wages create a squeeze on profits) and this makes the ideology of state neutrality problematic and leads toward crises of legitimacy. This contradiction between form and function limits the state's ability to resolve systemic crises.

From a class theoretic viewpoint, though, popular democracy is clearly a result of working-class struggles. Moreover, through electoral politics and agitation, the working class has forced the state to institute numerous reforms promoting social welfare. These functions tend to limit the capacity of the state to boost accumulation and hence also create a contradiction between form and function.

An adequate understanding of the state is thus grounded on an analysis of (1) the class structure and consequent balance of political forces in the social control over the state and (2) the objective and subjective contradictions of capitalism and the consequent crises of accumulation and legitimacy. In its crisis management role, however, the state runs into narrow limits that derive both from reproduction of the essential contradictions of capitalism and from the state's fiscal, legitimating, and administrative capabilities. Since both the class structure and the form of crises assume historical specificity, the reformist programs of the state have to be analyzed in the context of concrete social formations. This historical approach is particularly important, since the very form of crises reflect the nature of past reformist interventions by the state.

THE PETTY BOURGEOISIE AND LEGITIMATION

In the pluralist interpretation of democratic politics, the state acts in the interest of society as a whole by reconciling the demands of various interest groups. These groups compete on an egalitarian footing for access to and control over public institutions. And it is this political equality that gives meaning to majority rule. Implicit in this "citizen sovereignty" interpretation of the state is a Jeffersonian-style petty bourgeois society where economic and social power are fairly evenly distributed. The same vision underlies the Pareto optimality of liberal economic systems: economic power is sufficiently dispersed so that all agents are price takers, and the personal incomes of households are derived from the market sale of the factors of production they own—land, labor, and capital. All factors are presumed to be owned by all individuals and to bring just returns corresponding to their respective contributions to production. The existence of conflicting social classes is thus assumed away. Here again, the ideal Pareto-optimal social structure is that of a petty bourgeois society expressed in the bourgeois revolutionary slogan "Equality."[19]

The ideological basis of bourgeois social science, in both political science and economics, is thus grounded on the actual or presumed existence of a significant petty bourgeoisie. This brand of social science reflects and elaborates the hegemonic ideology of liberal democratic capitalism. Its teachings are translated into everyday consciousness via the family, the school, the media, the workplace, social groups, and the church. It serves as a cohesive and stabilizing force by winning consent for the social order without the need for force or coercion.[20] As Gramsci said, "[Ideologies] cement and unify the social bloc."[21]

The existence of a petty bourgeoisie that provides the material basis for the ideology of laissez-faire economics and democratic politics is, however, ephemeral and contradicted by economic growth itself. As capitalism develops, the petty bourgeoisie inevitably differentiates into bourgeoisie and proletariat. In the political sphere this class polarization tends to negate the objective basis of the ideology of pluralist democracy as political issues become increasingly aligned on class interests and hence difficult to reconcile. The state is thus called on to fulfill its role in social control and legitimation. In the economic sphere, monopoly power replaces atomistic competition and negates the ideology of Pareto efficiency and consumer sovereignty as firms manipulate price levels and consumer wants. The role of the state as an active economic agent increases to the point where state planning partially replaces the operation of the market. In the workplace itself, the authoritarian and hierarchical organization of the labor process that results from the separation of labor power and labor negates democratic relations.[22] And so does the organization of the household, which under both liberal and monopoly capitalism, also is structured on authoritarian lines.

Economic growth thus creates a loss of correspondence between material base (the new class and economic structure) and ideology (laissez-faire economics and pluralist democratic politics). This is particularly serious because control of the state becomes more precarious for the capitalist class precisely when state intervention becomes more crucial for both accumulation and legitimation purposes. This increasingly precarious situation results from social pressures, legitimized by the ideals of liberal democracy, which force the extension of political participation to the propertyless, women, and minorities. With universal suffrage, the working class gradually becomes a numerical majority.[23] The result is a tendency for the bourgeoisie to redefine and limit the scope of democracy.[24]

This historical slippage between infra- and superstructure leads to the development of new mechanisms of social control that can be regrouped into four categories: co-option within social democratic systems, segmentation within the working class, separation among classes, and repression.

Co-option permits the confinement of class struggle to demands that can be accommodated within the existing social relations. It requires the formation and acceptance of a hegemonic ideology that legitimizes the new functions of the state—the ideology of state planning and the welfare state in economics and that of corporate democracy in politics. Under social articulation, the necessary link between productivity of labor and real wages provides the objective basis for this solution. The state thus acquires a new legitimacy as a class mediator in ensuring the balance between return to capital and return to labor. This legitimacy remains contradictory, however, and hence especially precarious during economic downturns, since the source of exploitation of labor by capital at the level of the production process has evidently not been eliminated. It also requires a restructuring of the state which maintains the form of liberal parliamentary democracy but substantially alters its content: the effectiveness of the electoral process is limited by the declining power of the legislature relative to that of the bureaucracy and the executive; control of finance and the media ensures control of the parties; and in a country like the United States, the emergence of third parties is effectively blocked by the organization of the electoral process.[25] This redefinition of the content of democracy led C. Wright Mills to observe that "we live in a society that is democratic mainly in its legal forms and its formal expectations."[26] The result has often been growing disillusionment, apathy, and abstention from voting, which reflect the partial depoliticization of the proletariat.

It would be wrong to believe that this new hegemonic ideology is unilaterally defined and imposed by the ruling class. On the contrary, it is the evolutionary product of negotiated settlements between classes in the context of structural changes, economic crises, conflicts within the ruling groups, and challenges between opposition forces and ideas.[27] Yet this negotiated settlement is made possible by the existence of an articulated social class alliance. However, as such, it excludes a number of social groups—even when the alliance has hegemonic power. Control over these excluded groups needs to be ensured by other mechanisms.

One such mechanism is the *segmentation* of the working class into competing elements which has occurred as the economic structure has evolved from competitive to monopolistic. While, under competitive capitalism, the formation of a proletariat led to the progressive homogenization of working conditions and labor markets—following a historical tendency to reduce real labor to abstract labor—this tendency was reversed with the rise of monopoly capital.[28] As the industrial structure became increasingly dual with the juxtaposition of competitive and monopoly sectors, so did labor markets. And within the monopoly sector, jobs became more dissimilar, opposing, in particular, professional, managerial, and technical jobs to semiskilled jobs. In the firm itself, tasks were systematically stratified and subordinated to hierarchical control. These segmentations were in turn reinforced by and institutionalized into sexual, racial, ethnical, national, and educational differences.

Segmentation of the labor market thus divides the working class. It effectively excludes certain segments of the population from the articulated alliance and maintains a pool of cheap labor. It also reduces the logic and strength of economic and political demands for the entire working class. Edwards, Reich, and Gordon thus characterize the conscious manipulation of sexual, racial, ethnic, national, and educational differences as a "strategy designed to divide and conquer the work force."[29]

A third mechanism of social control that can be effective when co-option under the ideologies of state planning, the welfare state, and corporate democracy is not sufficient or feasible consists of blurring class boundaries and *separating* the bourgeoisie and the proletariat by re-creating, under the aegis of the state, a petty bourgeoisie. The formation of this petty bourgeoisie creates the expectation or realization of some vertical mobility among the proletariat and partially revalidates the ideology of liberal capitalism. But mainly it is the contradictory class location of the petty bourgeoisie as an oscillating group between the two essential classes of advanced capitalism— the bourgeoisie and the proletariat—that gives it a potentially effective role in social stabilization. Like the bourgeoisie, it is characterized by control over the physical means of production (relations of possession) and over investment and resource allocation in the process of accumulation (relations of ownership). Unlike the bourgeoisie and like the proletariat, it does not have control over the labor power of others, for its main source of labor is the family.[30] The economic interests of the petty bourgeoisie are tied to those of the bourgeoisie because its economic welfare depends upon the defense of private property, the maintenance of social order, and the global performance of the economy. Its attraction, its vision of upward mobility, is toward the bourgeoisie; its fear of failure is proletarianization.[31] Its ideological and social affiliation tends, however, to remain with the social groups from which it is extracted, and, indeed, it often becomes the political representative of these groups. Its position is, however, openly anticapitalist only in the populist sense of opposing the monopoly sector. And its vision of the state remains in the liberal democratic tradition, for "this class has a strong tendency to see the state as an inherently neutral force whose role is that of arbitrating between the various social classes."[32]

Re-creation of a petty bourgeoisie thus places a political buffer between bourgeoisie and proletariat. This approach to social control is particularly effective under hegemony of the disarticulated alliance, which rules out the possibility of co-option beyond a meager workers' aristocracy, and under social articulation, in dealing with those segments of the working class which are excluded from the articulated alliance through labor market segmentation. In those cases, as we have seen, co-option under the new hegemonic ideology of corporate democracy has no objective basis.

A good example of political control through class separation is the program of black enterprise initiated by the Nixon administration in 1969. With the black population largely excluded from the articulated alliance, law and order in the ghetto was sought via creation of a petty bourgeoisie within the ghetto itself. As Nixon said: "We have to get private enterprise into the ghetto. But at the same time, we have to get the people of the ghetto into private enterprise—as workers, as managers, as owners."[33] This was to occur through tax and credit incentives and technical assistance to small businessmen. Some vertical mobility did result from the program, but economic success remained highly precarious and limited to a handful of the privileged. Clearly, doing business in the ghetto is a highly risky venture, and small businesses can hardly compete with monopolistic corporations in the economy at large. Politically, however, the program effectively contributed to breaking up the political unity of blacks by co-opting a "black elite" into assuming the maintenance of law and order in the ghetto, isolating blacks from other disadvantaged people (in particular, by creating a backlash among poor whites excluded from the benefits of the program), and creating an image of the domestic racial problem as not political but economic.[34]

Re-creation of a petty bourgeoisie under the aegis of the state for the purpose of social pacification is, however, highly artificial and unstable once competitive capitalism has given way to monopoly capital. As we shall see, this interpretation of the role of a petty bourgeoisie and the contradictions that it entails are useful in understanding the political significance of redistributive land reforms and rural-development projects in Latin America.

The last method of social control—direct *repression* of working class demands—is used when the mechanisms of ideological control—co-option, segmentation, and separation—are ineffective. As Kellner explains: "When hegemonic groups are directly threatened by revolutionary challenge, they will forgo ideological persuasion and resort to force. Otherwise, they are willing to make ideological concessions. Thus the limits of ideological discourse expand and contract in response to pressures from people's struggles, conflicts within the ruling groups, and socioeconomic crisis and development."[35] These limits are particularly narrow under hegemony of the disarticulated alliance because, in this case, only subjective forces contradict the cheapening of labor power. Repression assumes political (elimination or drastic control of elections and labor unions), economic ("austerity" programs), physical (torture), and psychological (culture of fear) forms. In Latin America, repression has been institutionalized by authoritarian regimes assuming a variety of forms (autocratic authoritarianism under Trujillo in the Dominican Republic and under Stroessner in Paraguay; populist authoritarianism under Peron in Argentina and Torrijos in Panama; and party authoritarianism under the Institutionalized Revolutionary Party in Mexico) but converging increasingly toward what Cardoso, O'Donnell, Ianni, Schmitter, Collier, and other Latin Americanists have labeled bureaucratic authoritarianism (military regimes in Brazil since 1964, in Argentina in 1966 and since 1976, and in Uruguay and Chile since 1973).[36] Under bureaucratic authoritarianism, the military and the bureaucracy dominate the state, which is managed according to technocratic principles without concern for popular mobilization and with widespread use of repression to create social stability and a favorable investment climate for disarticulated accumulation. The military and technocratic fractions of the administrative bourgeoisie become the guardians of the interests of the disarticulated alliance.

THE PERIPHERAL STATE

Our analysis of the state and reformism in relation to the agrarian question concerns the periphery, while the above characterizations of the state were mainly formulated in the context of the center. We must therefore decide whether or not these characterizations are adequate or if it is necessary to develop a special theory of the peripheral state.

In recent years, several authors have suggested that a special theory of the *dependent* capitalist state may be necessary.[37] For example, Hein and Stenzel claim that "there is obviously a great need for a theory of the peripheral capitalist state."[38] Two reasons are given for this supposed necessity. The first is that the planning of development calls for a more interventionist state, possibly up to the point where "the state in the underdeveloped society may (initially at least) perform the historical role of the capitalist class in the accumulation of capital."[39] The second is that the peripheral state assumes more varied forms: "Unlike in advanced capitalist societies, the class nature of the [peripheral] state varies among countries and may also vary within a given country over a period of time."[40] Yet these reasons do not seem to be sufficiently powerful to justify a separate theory. In the first place, much of the modern writing on the state in advanced capitalist societies has been motivated by an awareness that the role of the state in the economy has been growing and that much of this growth is necessitated by the planning process, if not by explicit plans.[41] It is not clear, however, that the role of the state is growing faster in the periphery than in many of the advanced capitalist nations, even if the role of the peripheral state tends to be important from the very beginnings of industrialization. In the second place, the class nature of the state, as well as the form of state, has changed significantly in the history of the advanced capitalist nations; it is hard, however, to say *where* it has "changed more." While at present there seems to be less cross-sectional variability in form among the states under advanced capitalism than among those under peripheral capitalism, this, per se, does not justify the need for a distinct theory. In spite of its specific contradictions, the analysis of peripheral capitalism and the peripheral state requires the same fundamental categories as the analysis of advanced capitalism. If we treat the difference between advanced and peripheral social formations as *essentially a difference in social class and economic structure,* then there is no major reason why we cannot use the same approaches in analyzing the peripheral state.

There are, however, historical specificities that condition the nature of the peripheral state and these must be taken into account. First, some countries are still characterized either by the existence of precapitalist social relations in a period of transition to capitalism or by the permanence in the posttransition period of a social class structure that implies the extraction of absolute surplus value and monopoly rents. As a consequence, the basis of profits in the transition period is still partially the extraction of absolute surplus value, which tends to be a fetter on the development of productive forces. And in the posttransition, rents constitute a subtraction from profits that reduces the pace of capitalist accumulation. Important missions of the capitalist state in the periphery will thus be attempts to eliminate remnants of precapitalist social relations, which block the development of the forces of production, and to oppose absolute rents, which reduce the average rate of profit and increase the price of wage foods. As we will see in the next chapter, these missions have been the principal purpose of land reform programs in Latin America.

A second specificity of the peripheral state derives from the simultaneous presence within the same social formation of both disarticulated and articulated class alliances. As we saw in Chapter 1, each of these alliances corresponds to a markedly different pattern of accumulation and hence makes sharply contrasting demands on the state. The struggle between these alliances to gain access to the state results in a tendency toward considerable instability in public policies as the state falls under the domination of one alliance or the other. It also implies that the relative autonomy of the state is lessened in the periphery as the state becomes a more direct instrument of domination of the class alliance in power. This is the case even when the bureaucratic-authoritarian state becomes the agent of the disarticulated alliance. While this form of state can acquire a high degree of autonomy from popular support as repression reduces the need to legitimize the state with the masses, it still remains a rather direct instrument of class rule for one fraction of the bourgeoisie. This instability and lesser relative autonomy lead to the fragmentation—a real Balkanization—of the public sector and its services. As a result, specific branches of government tend to fall under the direct control of specific interest groups. This fragmentation of the public sector is what permits a class theoretic understanding of the unevenness of the development of capitalism in Latin American agriculture that we observed in Chapter 2 and that we explained fundamentally in terms of capital logic in Chapter 4. In some countries and time periods, specific commodities become heavily pro-tected and endowed with institutional support as commodity-based interest groups gain control of the instruments of the state that condition the develop-ment of capitalism in that commodity. This has been the case, for example, with Colombia's federation of coffee growers (FEDECAFE), federation of rice growers (FEDEARROZ), and national association of sugar cane producers (ASOCANA), and with Brazil's federation of wheat growers (FECOTRIGO). The result has been major spurts of technological change confined to the production of these commodities instead of a fairly even pattern of modernization across branches of production.

A third specificity of the peripheral state that we discussed above is the objective incapacitation that comes of relying on co-option when the disarticu-lated alliance dominates the state, and the consequent need to use repression, segmentation, and separation as alternative means of achieving political stabilization.

A fourth specificity derives from the role of functional dualism in the process of disarticulated accumulation whereby large semiproletarian seg-ments in the labor force cheapen the reproduction of labor power, wages, and the provision of wage foods to the modern sector. Since this process of accumulation both feeds on functional dualism and negates its reproduction, as peasants become increasingly dispossessed of the means of production because of the encroachment of capitalist agriculture, the peripheral state eventually engages in reforms that attempt to reproduce functional dualism for both political and economic purposes. As we will see in Chapter 7, this is an important aspect of the strategy of integrated rural development.

REFORMS AND THE MANAGEMENT OF CRISES

The two essential characteristics of capitalism on which we based our study of its "laws of motion" are its unplanned and class nature. From this we derived both (1) the ideology of liberty (the state as noninterventionist) and equality (petty bourgeois society) of early capitalism and (2) the essence of crises arising in the contradiction between production and circulation, as well as identification of the historical forms that crises can assume. During these crises, the process of accumulation slows down, unemployment increases, and real wages fall. If decentralized adjustments are not sufficient, state intervention is induced both to attempt to restore profits and to ease social tensions. Intervention can then take the form of either repression or reform. Reform is thus a nondecentralized, nonrepressive form of state intervention that aims at overcoming the historical objective (accumulation) and subjective (legitimacy) forms that capitalist crises assume.

The use of reformism, however, implies growing state intervention in the day-to-day management of the economy, since reforms are embodied in institutions and laws that must be administered (e.g., the Federal Reserve System, the Social Security Service, etc.). As old institutions become insufficient to deal with new forms of crises, further reforms cause the nonreformist interventions of the state to increase. The active role of the state thus tends to grow and to negate the noninterventionist ideology of liberal capitalism.

From these observations, reform can be defined as a state intervention that originates in crisis and (1) is evidently short of revolution (in which case the dominant mode of production is overthrown, as is the state, which secured its dominance), but at least requires the introduction of new forms of intervention, and (2) does not call on sheer repression. A reform may change the social relations in dominated modes, but it leaves intact the essential social relations of the dominant mode of production.

Three types of reforms can consequently be identified in relationship to the peripheral state:

1. Reforms associated with the transition to capitalism and the immediate posttransition period (transition reforms). In this context, as we discussed in Chapter 4, the fundamental contradiction is between rent and profit. In the transition period, monopolistic control of the land by a landlord class is essential for the development of a labor market. To induce the emergence of free labor, reforms, which can be triggered by either the emerging bourgeoisie or the peasantry, aim at eliminating precapitalist social relations and thus at transforming the creation of surplus value from an absolute to a relative basis. In the posttransition period, however, the preservation-adequacy of private landownership by means of a powerful capitalist landlord class leads to the perpetuation of absolute and monopoly rents, which become fetters on the development of capitalism as they reduce profits, raise food prices and wage costs, and block the development of the productive forces in agriculture. In this period, reforms aim at eliminating rents by eroding the political power of the capitalist landed elite and removing it from control of the state. This can be accomplished by means of a variety of measures, including the opening up of free trade with areas of lower production costs, the imposition of cheap-food policies, land reform, direct control of rents, and the penetration of

capital into agriculture, which reduces the importance of land in the production process.[42]

2. Reforms associated with crises of accumulation (objective crises). These reforms are initiated by the bourgeoisie itself and are directed at the variables that affect the rate of profit—the price of labor power; the price of constant capital; and, since the rate of profit is a temporal concept, the turnover time of both constant and variable capital. These turnover times are a function of technology, but they are also, and more importantly, a function of the growth of aggregate demand. Maintaining the balance between production and consumption for social capital is consequently the main objective of reforms that attempt to counteract crises of accumulation.

3. Reforms associated with crises of legitimacy (subjective crises). Here, the main "variables" that create legitimacy are (a) the existence of a petty bourgeoisie, which, as we have seen, provides the material basis for the ideology of liberal capitalism (liberty, equality, and social harmony with maximum efficiency) and (b) the ability of certain segments of the working class to enter into social democratic arrangements for the improvement of wages and working conditions under the ideology of state planning and the welfare state. Of course, these improvements are not automatically granted as the productivity of labor increases, but are won through struggle. Nevertheless, the need to create legitimacy is one of the factors that make the success of such struggle possible.

THE LIMITS OF REFORMISM

Just as with reforms themselves, the limits of reforms need to be understood in relationship to crises. We distinguished between the essence and historical forms of crises. Similarly, reforms find limits in the essence of crises as well as in the historical forms crises assume.

The essence of crises derives from the basic feature of capitalism—its unplanned and class nature, which implies a periodic contradiction in the fundamental dialectic between production and circulation. By reproducing the essence of capitalism, reforms also reproduce this basic contradiction. Historical forms of crises can thus eventually be overcome by reforms, but in the process, reforms necessarily create new barriers to accumulation and/or social stability, which in turn become the source(s) of new forms of crises.

In mobilizing the countertendencies toward historical forms of crises and thus engaging in reformist programs, the state operates under three further constraints that can limit the scope and effectiveness of reformism: (1) a constraint determined by the degree of legitimacy of the state; (2) a constraint imposed by the fiscal capacity of the state; and (3) a constraint that derives from the administrative capability of the state. The state enters into legitimacy, fiscal, and administrative crises when the forms of crises and the required extent of reform are so severe that it runs into these limits.

Legitimacy Crisis of the State

To implement its reformist policies, the state needs to secure support from the different social classes and fractions of classes that compose its constituency. The bourgeoisie itself is composed of fractions that have conflicting interests—dependent, national, industrial, agrarian, financial, etc.[43] Competition among capitals thus threatens the unity of the bourgeois class and hence the effectiveness of its use of the state for crisis management. Simultaneously, crises tend to enhance class consciousness among workers and hence to reduce the legitimacy of the state by exposing its class nature precisely when its intervention is most needed.

To maintain cohesion of the bourgeoisie and to secure popular support, the state must appear to be a relatively autonomous institution that transcends parochial interests of fractions of the bourgeoisie and promotes the national interest. This requires the formation of a dominant ideology that establishes the state as an autonomous guardian of the values of "liberty," "justice," and "rights." Control of the dominant ideology thus becomes, indirectly, an important element of the control of the state. This, in turn, is ensured by the control of education and the circulation of information. Yet this control is far from perfect; and the legitimacy of the state imposes serious limits to its reformist capabilities. If the state attempts to go beyond the limits of its legitimacy in dealing with a form of crisis by imposing overtly authoritarian and repressive forms of control, the limits of reformism have then been exceeded.

Fiscal Crisis of the State

Faced with both objective and subjective crises, the reformist capacity of the state is also limited by its capacity to generate a public budget on the basis of tax revenues. Objective crises imply the need to increase social capital expenditures to counteract the fall in the rate of profit and sustain accumulation. These expenditures include public transfers to firms, tax breaks, subsidized credit, stimulation of aggregate demand, infrastructure construction, and subsidies to research and development. Similarly, subjective crises require increased social expenses to maintain the legitimacy of the existing social relations. Examples are medicare, social security, unemployment compensation, public education, conservation and recreation programs, police protection, international aid, and the provision of "basic needs." The objective limit to these reforms is the fiscal crisis of the state that occurs when government expenditures surpass fiscal revenues.[44]

The limit to these revenues is determined both objectively and subjectively. Objectively, the state depends upon revenues that originate in the sphere of production. Since the state is largely excluded from the direct organization of production and the allocation of private capital, these revenues are created outside its immediate control.[45] It is this contradictory position of exclusion and dependence that both limits the reformist capacity of the state and commits it, however autonomous it may appear for purposes of legitimation, to the promotion of the conditions necessary for accumulation.[46] Fiscal deficits can be temporarily postponed through deficit financing, inflation (printing money), and calling on foreign aid and loans. Yet these also have inescapable objective limits.[47] Subjectively, the state needs to legitimize its imposition on taxpayers while heeding the possibility of "tax revolts." Legitimacy and fiscal crises of the state are here closely interrelated.

Administrative Crisis of the State

Endowed with credibility and fiscal means, the state also needs to have an adequate administrative capacity to understand the nature of specific forms of crisis and to define and carry through the corresponding reforms. This implies the ability to develop a system of economic planning and to coordinate the administrative apparatus needed to ensure the implementation of such plans.

Here, too, the state operates within narrow limits. Effective planning is constrained by the opposition of fractions of the bourgeoisie when their private interests are threatened by such plans. And implementation eventually requires a prior major administrative reorganization. This is particularly true for "integrated" programs where the joint participation of several public agencies is required. Since these agencies were generally organized and staffed when they autonomously serviced their own clientele, new mechanisms of authority and coordination need to be instituted. This highly conflictive transformation implies an evolution toward the rise of powerful bureaucracies and the weakening of parliamentary institutions. Thus, the management of reform itself leads to the steady rise of state interventionism and to the deepening role of the state in crisis management.

AGRARIAN REFORMISM IN LATIN AMERICA

There has, of course, been a long history of agrarian reformism in Latin America, which we cannot review in detail here. The two great periods of capitalist reforms, in particular, antedate the period of central interest to us here, which is the one that began in the late 1950s when land reforms and rural-development projects acquired widespread importance. These reforms and projects will be analyzed in detail in Chapters 6 and 7.

The first great period was that of the liberal reforms, which started, in general, around the middle of the nineteenth century—for example, in Mexico under Juarez in 1857. The objective of these reforms was to batter down remnants of natural economy and induce the development of capitalism within the countries themselves. In particular, they involved the expropriation of the corporate property of the Catholic church and the communal property of the Indians in favor of private ownership and free trade in the world economy. The result of the reforms was the expansion and consolidation of agroexporter and commercial oligarchies in association with foreign capital and the massive concentration of landownership. It was also the massive ruin of the traditional handicrafts and manufacturers, which resulted in the formation of a free labor force. The most blatant expression of these reforms was the Porfiriato in Mexico.[48]

The second great period of reformism was that of populist reform, which generally took place between 1930 and 1955. It was spurred by the breakdown of oligarchic capitalism and occurred when the center countries were in the midst of economic crises and wars. The periphery thus benefited from a period of enhanced autonomy. Reforms were oriented toward promoting import-substitution industrialization: the loss of markets for export goods and the consequent scarcity of foreign exchange implied that the domestic demand for both wage goods and luxuries had to be met by domestic industry. Surplus was extracted massively from agriculture to sustain investment in industry, and free rural labor started to flow to the cities. Income was redistributed in favor of the urban working class. These reforms were the concerted effort of all the dominant classes—commercial bourgeoisie, agrarian oligarchy, and emerging national industrial bourgeoisie.[49] The articulated basis of accumulation created expectations that truly democratic forms of government would soon replace the corporatist nature of populist regimes.

The "failure" of articulated import-substitution industrialization—because the markets for wage goods were too narrow to begin with and the massive social adjustments that would have been required to expand them sufficiently could not be produced under the ruling class alliance—came in the form of rapid inflation and in balance-of-payments crises. The solution to these crises required either (1) a deepening of import-substitution industrialization through the creation of *sectoral articulation* with domestic capital-goods sectors or (2) *social disarticulation,* through the concentration of income distribution domestically and the promotion of outward growth. The developmentalist states of the 1960s attempted the first solution through comprehensive economic planning and fiscal reforms.[50] The evident insufficiency of this solution led the state to assume an increasingly technocratic and repressive role in the context of the rise of the disarticulated alliance to hegemony, increasing penetration of and submission to foreign capital, regressive concentration in the distribution of income, and strict control of popular demands and urban guerrillas. The model of disarticulated accumulation thus became established, bringing with it the emphasis on orthodox economic efficiency and order, but also its own economic and political contradictions and the consequent need for another set of compensatory reforms.

After the Cuban Revolution in 1959, agrarian reformism went through three successive phases as the broader political economy evolved from developmentalism to bureaucratic authoritarianism. Each phase was defined in relation to the world economic situation, food supply requirements, and levels of political tension.

In the early 1960s the Cuban example fueled peasant militancy and generated threats of agrarian rebellions in many countries. The agrarian leagues had large memberships, and strong claims were made for access to land in reaction to extremely unequal patterns of landownership that were still dominated by semifeudal social relations and massive rural poverty.[51] On the economic plane, huge grain surpluses had accumulated in the United States in spite of policies to remove land from production, and P.L. 480 shipments were at their peak. Cheap food imported through concessional sales thus sustained cheap industrial labor and the penetration of multinational capital. At the same time, cheap food negatively affected the production of grain crops in Latin America and sealed patterns of increasing dependency on food imports. Agrarian reformism in the early 1960s was thus centered not so much on the issue of food production as on the containment of peasant political pressures both through direct control of peasant organizations and through the legislation of mild land reform projects aimed at eradicating semifeudal estates from the agrarian structure. In 1961 the land reform charter of the Punta del Este conference of the OAS launched this strategy on a continental scale. The resulting threats of expropriation for insufficiently intensive use of land or for permanence of semifeudal labor relations effectively induced the transformation of traditional estates into large-scale commercial farms. Access to the land for some peasants on expropriated estates and through land settlement schemes created an incipient sector of capitalized family and cooperative farms, thus bridging, through the establishment of a politically stable rural petty bourgeoisie, the historical gap between *latifundio* and *minifundio*. The mix of repression and expectations of vertical mobility contributed to defuse political tensions in the peasantry. During this phase, the political dimension of agrarian reformism was thus dominant. It resulted in the consolidation of a structural pattern of functional dualism between capitalist and peasant agriculture that was molded on the experience of the Mexican land reform.

By the mid-1960s, the export of P.L. 480 foods to Latin America was on the decline. Stagnation of domestic food production did not permit the food deficit countries to compensate for decreasing concessional imports, and the industrialization strategy based on cheap food was compromised. The development of food production in commercial agriculture became the center of agrarian reformism. This was sought via the transfer of capital and technology to Latin America; a massive increase in research expenditures on food crops (the Green Revolution); the strengthening of extension programs; greater availability of agricultural credit; and the entry of multinational firms into agricultural production, the manufacturing of inputs, and the processing and distribution of products. Agricultural research expenditures doubled in real terms between 1962 and 1968, while expenditures in agricultural extension services more than doubled.[52] International agricultural research centers were created for wheat and corn (CIMMYT in 1966 in Mexico), tropical food crops and cattle (CIAT in 1968 in Colombia), and potatoes (CIP in 1972 in Peru).[53] World Bank loans for agricultural projects—principally large irrigation works—increased substantially to some 23 percent of total lendings. And in the land reforms of this period, the dominant objective became economic: to increase production, principally by inducing (through threats of expropriation) modernization of the nonreformed sector. The economic goal of promoting agricultural production in the commercial sector through the spread of Green Revolution technology, while relying on functional dualism with the peasant sector to obtain cheap labor, thus dominated agricultural reformism in the late 1960s and early 1970s.

But modernization of commercial agriculture led to massive rural impoverishment. Land became increasingly concentrated in the commercial sector at the expense of the peasantry. Mechanization severely limited employment creation in commercial agriculture, and high rates of urban unemployment reduced the possibilities of urban migration. The peasantry was increasingly marginalized in subsistence agriculture and semiproletarianized. Functional dualism between subsistence and commerical agriculture was thus reinforced, with the former providing a source of cheap labor for the latter. Simultaneously, P.L. 480 concessional sales became minimal: the world food crisis and devaluations of the dollar permitted the United States to restore its balance-of-payments position by exporting its grains on the commerical market. The strategy of modernizing commercial agriculture, however, bore only partial fruits as production increased at a faster rate after 1972 but without surpassing population growth or canceling a continental deficit in staple foods. This was due in large part to the diversion of land in commercial agriculture out of wage foods, where profitability was stifled by cheap-food policies, into the production of better-priced exportables, industrial inputs, and luxury foods. Agrarian reforms of this period thus concentrated on managing the political acceptability of the development of commercial agriculture in the social context of functional dualism and on capturing the capacity of the upper strata of the peasantry to produce food cheaply. Rural-development projects were initiated in many countries of Latin America following the model of Mexico's Plan Puebla. Their principal instrument was to promote the adoption of Green Revolution technology among that minority of rural poor who control enough productive resources to adopt it profitably and have the capacity to produce a marketable surplus. Consequently, these rural-development projects were based on improved access to agricultural credit (institutional change) and on research and extension (technological change). They were later extended into "integrated" rural-development projects through the addition of activities in infrastructure construction and the distribution of public goods and services. In 1973 the World Bank pledged to assist this strategy by lending U.S. $3.1 billion to smallholders during 1974–78, potentially reaching 100 million households and 700 million rural poor on a world scale.[54] Large-scale programs were initiated in Mexico (PIDER) and Colombia (DRI). Pilot projects were launched in Peru, Ecuador, Bolivia, Paraguay, and, in some form, in essentially every Latin American country.

In the next two chapters, we will analyze in detail these programs of land reform and rural development for the purpose of understanding their achievements and limits.

6

Types and Consequences
of Land Reform

All twentieth-century land reforms in Latin America except the Cuban and possibly the Nicaraguan ones have had the ultimate purpose of fomenting the development of capitalism in agriculture. In all cases, these land reforms were implemented to counteract some of the economic and social contradictions that at particular points in history characterized the development patterns of Latin American countries under the logic of social disarticulation. Yet the origins of land reforms and the particular purposes and forms they assumed have varied enormously over time periods and countries. It is thus impossible to understand the significance of land reforms without first identifying different types of reforms in relation to the underlying mode of production and social class structure in agriculture and the changes—or lack of change—the reforms were intended to bring about in them.

The social *origin* of land reforms changed dramatically in the late 1950s with the emergence of surplus labor. Prior to this date, the scarcity of labor that prevailed in most parts of Latin America conflicted sharply with the objective need for cheap labor in commercial agriculture. The resolution of this contradiction required that rural laborers be prevented from getting access to land as freeholders and from capturing their opportunity cost on labor markets. The precapitalist estate served this purpose ideally by monopolizing the bulk of the land and by bonding labor to the estates through debt peonage and extraeconomic coercion. As a result, the origins of land reform movements during this period were found primarily in the exercise of *subjective* forces by intellectual and peasant groups in reaction to the severe social contradictions associated with the expropriation of community lands and with labor exploitation through rent in labor services, usury, and forced labor.[1] All of these reforms were initiated outside the traditional institutional process, usually after violent revolutionary outbursts. This was true of the land reforms in Mexico (1917), Guatemala (1952), Bolivia (1952), and, to some extent, Venezuela (1959).

By the late 1950s, the emergence of a labor surplus in agriculture broke the logic of the internal subsistence economy in favor of functional dualism with free semiproletarian peasants and provided the *objective* basis for intervention by the state to eliminate remnants of precapitalist social relations through legal reforms. The economic purpose of unleashing the development of capitalism in agriculture was to increase food production and agricultural exports in order to meet the cheap-food and foreign-exchange requirements of industry. Reform was also spurred by subjective forces originating in peasant militancy (stimulated by the example of the Cuban Revolution, which generated threats and fears of agrarian revolutions in many countries); the extension of the social contradictions associated with surplus rural labor to the urban informal sector in the guise of rapid migration and extensive marginality; and the international pressures derived from the Punta del Este charter of the Organization of American States in 1961.

A TYPOLOGY OF LAND REFORMS

Corresponding to the contradictions of disarticulated accumulation, land reform has both a political and an economic *purpose*. The political purpose is fundamentally to further and stabilize the social relations of capitalism by changing the class structure in agriculture. According to this type of reform, this includes removing the landed elite from those groups controlling the state, eliminating semifeudal forms of labor exploitation, creating a petty bourgeoisie from among the peasantry, and reinforcing a class of capitalist farmers. The economic purpose is fundamentally to develop the forces of production in agriculture by putting idle lands into production, encouraging the reorganization of precapitalist estates on a capitalist basis, inducing their modernization, and in some cases transforming junker estates into medium-size commercial farms. A typology of land reforms must reflect these varied purposes and means of achieving them if it is to be useful in evaluating their achievements.

As a first step, it is important to distinguish between lands that are incorporated into the "reform" and "nonreform" sectors in the process of land reform. The reform sector is composed of lands appropriated (usually expropriated) from the former landlords and adjudicated on a variety of institutional bases (family farms, cooperatives, and state farms) to the beneficiaries of the reform. It is in the reform sector that peasants are given access to land and that a petty bourgeoisie is eventually created. The nonreform sector includes the unexpropriated lands retained or sold privately by their former owners, the lands that are subdivided by their owners to avoid expropriation through a restriction on maximum size (*hijuelas*), and the "reserves," which the former owners are allowed to retain or sell. The nonreform sector can thus include the lands of the precapitalist landed elite, the junker landed elite, or the capitalist farmers, depending on the type of reform.

Reform and nonreform sectors play different economic and political roles in the process of land reforms. Land reforms have usually been analyzed in terms of the creation of a reform sector (the more glamorous and visible aspect of reform), but we will show that this is only one, and generally a secondary, aspect of land reform, while the impact of the reform on the nonreform sector is another important, often principal, aspect of any reform.

To understand the economic impact of land reform, we must return to our identification of the determinants of stagnation and uneven development in agricultural production in Chapter 4. These determinants must be included among the variables chosen in constructing a typology of reforms if the typology itself is to help explain the impact of reforms on production. We identified three main causes of stagnation and uneven development under disarticulated accumulation: (1) the terms of trade, which are turned against food, in particular, and against agriculture, in general, in accordance with the laws of motion of capital under social disarticulation; (2) control of the state by the traditional or capitalist landed elites, who thereby obtain institutional rents biased toward reproduction of their hegemonic class position; and (3) the land tenure system, particularly if precapitalist estates are prevalent, but also if large-scale, absenteeist, junker estates are the principal type of enterprise. We also established a hierarchy in the relative importance of these determinants of the development of the productive forces—running from cheap food as the primary determinant, to control of the state by the landed elites as the secondary determinant, to the land tenure system as the least-decisive element.

The typology of land reforms outlined in Figure 6.1 is based on the impact of different reforms on the two determinants of stagnation that can be affected by a land reform: (1) the land tenure system, which is characterized by the dominant mode of production in agriculture (precapitalist or capitalist) and the type of farm enterprise (large estates or commercial farms); and (2) the social class that has hegemonic control over the state (landed elite or bourgeoisie). This gives three categories of agrarian systems before the initiation of land reform: those dominated by precapitalist estates, those dominated by capitalist estates, and those dominated by commercial farms. The precapitalist estates are, of course, found in precapitalist agriculture, while the capitalist estates and commercial farms both correspond to capitalist agriculture. On the other hand, control of the state by a landed elite occurs under a structure characterized by predominance of either the precapitalist estates or the capitalist estates. Under a structure in which the commercial farms predominate, the state is controlled by the bourgeoisie at large.[2]

Each of these three systems can be transformed through land reform into either of the other two. Consequently, in Figure 6.1, nine paths relate the

			Post-land reform		
		Control of the state	Landed elite controls the state		Bourgeoisie controls the state
		Mode of production	Precapitalist agriculture		Capitalist agriculture
		Land tenure	Precapitalist estates and reform sector	Capitalist estates and reform sector	Commercial farms and reform sector
		Pre-capitalist estates	*Pre-K Redistributive (PKR)* Mexico, 1917–34 Chile, 1962–67 Colombia, 1961–67	*Transition to Junker (TJ)* Colombia, 1968– Ecuador, 1964– Bolivia, 1952– Peru, 1964–69 Venezuela, 1959–	*Transition to Farmer (TF)* Mexico, 1934–40 Chile, 1967–73 Guatemala, 1952–54
		Capitalist estates	*Transition from Junker*	*Junker Resistributive (JR)* Costa Rica, 1963–	*Shift from Junker to Farmer (JF)* Peru, 1969–75
		Commercial farms	*Transition from Farmer* Guatemala, 1954–	*Shift from Farmer to Junker* Chile, 1973–	*Farmer Redistributive (FR)* Mexico, 1940– Dominican Republic, 1963–

Figure 6.1. Typology of Land Reforms in Latin America

agrarian systems before and after reform.[3] In all of these reforms, a reform sector is added to the dominant type of farm enterprise through land expropriation and redistribution in the form of family, collective, or state farms. While some reforms go so far as to change both the dominant farm type and control of the state, the major determinant of stagnation—cheap food—remains in all cases a given constant they cannot affect. This implies that functional dualism (the meeting of cheap food through cheap semiproletarian labor) also remains a derived constant. Land reforms are thus severely constrained in their impact on either production (by cheap food) or poverty (by functional dualism) owing to the permanence of the logic of accumulation under social disarticulation.

The typology of reforms contains three major types, all of which are undertaken with the capitalist mode of production dominant in the country at large: (1) reforms that imply some redistribution of land but that do not challenge the *precapitalist* estates' domination of agriculture; (2) reforms that promote the *transition* to capitalism in agriculture toward either the junker or the farmer road of development; and (3) reforms within *capitalist* agriculture, either to induce a shift from junker road to farmer road of capitalist development or to redistribute the land within either. To each type of reform that implies either a transition in mode or a shift of road there also corresponds the possibility of counterreform.

Undoubtedly, the classification of many of the reforms in Figure 6.1 will be questioned. Each is based on data and descriptions of modes of production, land tenure, and the distribution of public resources and services among different farm enterprises and social classes (to determine control of the state) from the pre- and postreform periods. Empirical information on each reform is given in Table 6.1. The specific allocation of one or more cases to each type of reform will be briefly discussed.

Table 6.1.   Statistical Information on Land Reforms
in Selected Latin American Countries, 1917–76

Country	Land reform Year (1)	Land reform Type (2)	Land in reform sector (percent)^a (3)	Peasantry in reform sector (percent)^a (4)	Size of reserve (hectares)^b (5)	Capital and water expropriated? (6)	Form of organization in reform sector (7)
Mexico	1917–34^c	PKR	6.3	11.3	100–200		Subfamily/family
	1934–40	TF	12.6	25.8	100–200^d	Yes	Subfamily/family; collective
	1940–76	FR	25.0	18.3	100–200		Subfamily/family
Total	1917–76		42.8	50.0			
Guatemala	1952–54	TF	33.6	33.0	90–200	Partially	Subfamily/family; cooperative
	1954–69	Counterreform	4.8	3.2			
Bolivia	1952–70	TJ	18.2	39.0	24–50,000	No	Subfamily/family
Venezuela	1959–70	TJ	15.7	14.7	No limit^e	No	Subfamily/family
Colombia	1961–68	PKR	^{f}		No limit	No	Subfamily/family
	1968–72	TJ			No limit	No	Subfamily/family
Total	1961–72		9.6	4.2			
Chile	1962–67	PKR	—^{g}	—	No limit	No	Subfamily/family
	1967–70^h ⎫	TF	9.0	6.0 ⎫	80 SBIH^i	Partially	Subfamily/family; cooperative
	1970–73 ⎭		31.0	14.0 ⎭			Cooperative; collective
Total	1962–73		40.0	20.0			
	1973–75	Counterreform	9.0	4.0			Subfamily/family
Peru	1963–69	TJ	3.0	7.1	845–12,675	No	Subfamily/family
	1969–76	JF	39.4	24.9	35–1,500	Yes	Cooperative; subfamily/family
Total	1963–76		42.4	32.0			
Ecuador	1964–69	TJ	1.1	3.5	No limit^e	No	Subfamily/family
Dominican Republic	1963–69	FR	2.0	2.0	No limit	No	Subfamily/family; cooperative

Sources: (Col. 1) Initial year corresponds to the year the land reform law was passed. Final year corresponds either to the end of the program or to the final year for which data are available (Mexico, Bolivia, Venezuela, Ecuador, the Dominican Republic, and Peru).

(Col. 2) Figure 6.1.

(Cols. 3 and 4) MEXICO: Various *Censo Agrícola-Ganadero y Ejidal* and government files in F. Barra Garcia, "Los Ataques a la Reforma Agraria," *Excelsior,* August 3, 1976, pp. 13 and 14. GUATEMALA: CIDA, *Tenecia de la Tierra y Desarrollo Socio-Económico del Sector Agrícola, Guatemala* (Washington, D.C.: Pan-American Union, 1965), p. 40; and James Wilkie, *Measuring Land Reform* (Los Angeles: UCLA Latin American Center, 1974), p. 5. BOLIVIA: Dwight

(*continued*)

Table 6.1—*Continued*

Heath, Charles Eramus, and Hans Buechler, eds., *Land Reform and Social Revolution in Bolivia* (New York: Frederick A. Praeger, 1969), p. 35; Angel Jemio Ergueta, "La Reforma Agraria en Bolivia" (Paper presented at the Seminar on Experiences and Evaluations of Land Reform in Latin America, United Nations Economic Commission on Latin America, San José, Costa Rica, March 1973), pp. 68, 69, and 71; and R. J. Clark, *Land Reform in Bolivia: Spring Review*, U.S. Agency for International Development (Washington, D.C., June 1970), p. 34. COLOMBIA: Departamento Administrativo Nacional de Estadística, "Censo Agropecuario, Resumen Nacional, 1960," mimeographed (Bogotá, 1962); and Instituto Colombiano de la Reforma Agraria, "Reforma Agraria Colombiana," mimeographed (Bogotá, 1972). CHILE: Dirección de Estadística y Censos, *IV Censo Nacional Agropecuario*, vol. 1 (Santiago de Chile: Dirección de Estadística y Censos, 1966); J. Petras and R. Laporte, Jr., *Cultivating Revolution: The United States and Agrarian Reform in Latin America* (New York: Random House, 1971), p. 205; and Solon Barraclough and J. A. Fernandez, *Diagnóstico de la Reforma Agraria Chilena* (Mexico City: Siglo XXI, 1974), p. 132. PERU: CIDA, *Tenencia de la Tierra y Desarrollo Socio-Económico del Sector Agrícola, Peru* (Washington, D.C.: Pan-American Union, 1966); J. Strasma, "Agrarian Reform," in *Peruvian Nationalism*, ed. David Chaplin (New Brunswick: Transaction Books, 1976), p. 299; and U.S. Department of Agriculture, *Western Hemisphere Agricultural Situation*, Foreign Agricultural Economic Report no. 136 (Washington, D.C., 1977), p. 22. ECUADOR: CIDA, *Tenencia de la Tierra y Desarrollo Socio-Económico del Sector Agrícola, Ecuador* (Washington, D.C.: Pan-American Union, 1965); and Charles Blankenstein and Clarence Zuvekas, *Agrarian Reform in Ecuador* (Madison: University of Wisconsin Land Tenure Center, 1974), p. 14. DOMINICAN REPUBLIC: James Wilkie, *Measuring Land Reform* (Los Angeles: UCLA Latin American Center, 1974), p. 5. VENEZUELA: Ministerio de Fomento, *III Censo Agropecuario 1961, Resumen General de la República* (Caracas, 1967); and O. D. Soto, *La Empresa y la Reforma Agraria* (Merida: Instituto Ibero Americano de Derecho Agrario y Reforma Agraria, 1973), p. 80.

[a] Percentages figured on the basis of land in farms and population economically active in agriculture (or, where possible, potential beneficiaries) for the following years: Mexico (percentage of land in reform sector), 1917–34 and 1934–40 (1923 base year for census data), and 1940–76 and total (1960 base year for census data); Guatemala, 1950; Bolivia, 1950; Venezuela, 1961; Colombia, 1961; Chile, 1965; Peru, 1961; Ecuador, 1954; and the Dominican Republic, 1960. When more than one period or reform is listed, the percentages are additive. For totals, percentages are cumulative, except for Mexico.

[b] Variability in size of reserve left to landowners affected by expropriation is due to differences between regions, irrigated and nonirrigated land, and crop and pasture land.

[c] Includes activities under a temporary 1915 agrarian law.

[d] In 1940, under Cardenas, the maximum reserve was reduced, but in 1942 that law was rescinded.

[e] In Venezuela, land may be expropriated only if land is inadequately utilized or for violations of the labor code. Thus, there is no specific ceiling on the size of holdings. In the event a landowner is affected by expropriation, he may retain between 150 hectares (irrigated land) and 26,000 hectares (unimproved pasturage). In Ecuador, similar stipulations apply. In the event of expropriation, the landowner may retain between 1,800 and 3,500 hectares, depending on the type of land.

[f] Blanks indicate separate data not provided.

[g] — = less than 1 percent.

[h] Includes expropriation and distributions carried out in 1965–66 under 1962 law.

[i] Standard basic irrigated hectares in central Chile; equivalent measure elsewhere.

Redistributive Reforms

The three types of reforms on the diagonal of Figure 6.1 leave both the dominant mode of production in agriculture and the classes in control of the state unchanged, affecting the land tenure system only quantitatively, by changing the distribution of land among different types of enterprises. These reforms are thus essentially redistributive. The reform itself does not relax any of the fundamental determinants of stagnation. Three types can be identified: redistributive reforms under the preserved dominance of (1) precapitalist estates (precapitalist redistributive [PKR]), (2) capitalist estates (junker redistributive [JR]), and (3) commercial farms (farmer redistributive [FR]). In every case a reform sector is created by expropriating either idle lands (PKR) or lands already under capitalist-junker (JR) or farmer (FR) use.

An example of precapitalist redistributive reform is the 1962-67 land reform in Chile. The state intended to acquire, in cash and at full market value, lands abandoned by landlords and to increase production by distributing these lands to peasants without otherwise altering the social relations of production in agriculture or affecting the privileged position of the landowning class. In fact, no land was expropriated under the 1962 law until Frei assumed office in 1965 (see Table 6.1).

In Colombia, application of the 1961 land reform law was used principally to settle peasants in colonization projects in outlying public lands and to subdivide into family farms unexploited lands and lands offered for sale to the state. By 1965, the Colombian Agrarian Reform Agency had been authorized to execute thirty-four projects, of which twenty-one were land settlements and the remainder were principally rationalizations of spontaneous land invasions.[4] Precapitalist estates were otherwise left unaffected.

In the decades since the expropriation of the precapitalist landed elites in the 1934-40 period, land reform in Mexico has redistributed land from commercial farms to the *ejidos* and is thus classified as a farmer redistributive reform. Similarly, in the Dominican Republic, the land reform of 1963 expropriated the rice lands held by the medium-to-large-scale commercial farms and reorganized them into labor cooperatives and family farms.[5]

Transition from Precapitalist Mode to Junker Road

These reforms induce a transition from precapitalist to capitalist agriculture either by threatening expropriation if land remains underutilized or by making semifeudal social relations illegal. The internal subsistence economy is eliminated, and the precapitalist estate is thus transformed into a large-scale capitalist ("junker") enterprise hiring wage laborers—mainly semiproletarian peasants. The landed elite retains control of the state, and hence, only the third determinant of stagnation, archaic land tenure, is eliminated. Both the 1968 land reform in Colombia and the 1964 reform in Ecuador provide clear examples of reforms that effect a transition from precapitalist to capitalist relations of production. Following the minimal 1961 redistributive reform, the 1968 legislation in Colombia prohibited *aparceria* (rents in kind paid by peasants in exchange for usufruct of land plots). Lands farmed under *aparceria* were expropriated in instances where landlords did not abide by the prohibition and were distributed to the occupants. The 1964 reform in Ecuador similarly proscribed *huasipungaje* (labor services in exchange for usufruct of land) and gave the occupants title to their minute plots.

The 1953 land reform in Bolivia is classified as a transition to the junker road (as opposed to the farmer road) because, with the important exception of the Cochabamba region, most landowners were able to retain part or all of their holdings. Of the 11,246 properties affected by expropriation proceedings through 1970, only 1,441 were classified as *latifundios* and suffered partial or total expropriation.[6] The remaining holdings were classified either as "medium properties," whose owners were entitled to retain 80-350 hectares in the Altiplano, 24-200 hectares in the Yungas (valleys), and 180-600 hectares in the Oriente, or as "agricultural enterprises," whose owners were entitled to retain 400-800 hectares in the Altiplano, 80-500 hectares in the Yungas, and 2,000 hectares in the Oriente.[7] Also, cattle ranchers were allowed an exemption of 50,000 hectares in the Oriente. At the same time, most observers agree that the *colonos* (peasants who provided rents and labor services to landlords in exchange for usufruct of land) received titles only to the plots they occupied at the time of the reform.[8] That is, although the *colonato* was abolished, the productive resources used by peasants were not generally increased by the land reform.

Also, many of the agricultural policies applied after the reform actually strengthened the economic position of the landed elites, particularly those in the Oriente. These included price supports, subsidized credits and machinery, and the construction of a sugar refinery in Santa Cruz.[9] Peasants, by contrast, received only minimal credit and access to public services.[10]

Transition from Precapitalist Mode to Farmer Road

This type of reform promotes a transition in both the agrarian mode of production and the classes in control of the state. Agriculture is transformed from precapitalist to capitalist, thus changing the basis of the social relations of production from internal to external semiproletarianization. Precapitalist estates are replaced by commercial farms as size limits are imposed on land-ownership, and a reform sector is created. The urban and rural bourgeoisie displace the landed elite from control of the state. With this transfer of class power, these reforms thus remove the second and third determinants of stagnation. Examples of this type of reform are Chile (1967-73), Mexico (1934-40), and Guatemala (1952-54). The 1967 legislation in Chile gave the state the power to expropriate the landed elite, a task completed under the same law by the Allende government. Precapitalist relations of production were prohibited, and a ceiling on landownership of 80 hectares of basic irrigated land was imposed.[11] Large capitalist commercial farms were thus created, while the reform sector was organized into labor cooperatives. The Mexican land reform of 1934 similarly imposed a ceiling on landownership of 100-200 irrigated hectares.[12]

Shift from Junker Road to Farmer Road

These reforms occur within the capitalist mode of production and bring about a shift from the junker road to the farmer road of development. Since they are aimed at transforming the basis of the agrarian structure from capitalist estates to commercial farms, a ceiling on landholdings is imposed. The landed elite is eliminated, and the bourgeoisie assumes control of the state. The second determinant of stagnation is thus relaxed. The military's land reform in Peru (1969) is the only example of this type of reform. Under the earlier 1964 land reform, precapitalist relations of production (*yanaconaje*) had been prohibited. The military effectively destroyed the landed elite class by imposing and enforcing a limit on the size of landholdings of 50 irrigated hectares on the coast and 30 hectares in the Sierra or their productive equivalent of rain-fed land.[13]

Transition from Junker Road to Precapitalist Mode

These counterreforms induce a transition from capitalist agriculture back to noncapitalist agriculture. There is clearly no objective basis for such a counterreform when surplus labor is prevalent, as is the case in most Latin American countries today. If labor were scarce, such a counterreform would be conceivable; indeed, isolated incidents of such reversals can be uncovered in the history of the Bolivian land reform.[14]

Transition from Farmer Road to Precapitalist Mode

Such counterreforms also induce a transition out of the capitalist mode of production as commercial farms are transformed into noncapitalist estates. A concrete example would be events in Guatemala after the overthrow of the Arbenz government and the reversal of the land reform in 1954. At the time of the counterreform, Guatemala was not yet characterized by surplus labor. As a result, not only did the counterreform return practically all expropriated lands but it also reinstituted the *colonato* system. The second and third determinants of stagnation were thereby restored.

Shift from Farmer Road to Junker Road

These counterreforms occur within the capitalist mode of production and create a shift between roads of development from farmer to junker. Commercial farms give way to capitalist estates. This type of counterreform occurred in Chile after the military junta seized power in 1973. While the reform sector included 39 percent of the total agricultural land area in 1973, it had been reduced to only 9 percent by 1975.[15] The return of expropriated lands to the former owners re-created large-scale capitalist farms beyond the size limit of 80 hectares of irrigated land that had been imposed by the land reforms of Frei and Allende.[16]

The typology presented here can be contrasted with alternative typologies of land reforms developed by Griffin, Frank, Barraclough, Warriner, Flores, and Feder.[17] None of these typologies uses the concepts of mode of production (transitions) or social class structure and control of the state (shifts among roads of development). Redistributive reforms within the capitalist mode (PKR) and reforms that induce a transition to junker agriculture (TJ) are usually characterized as "modernizing" or "technocratic," while reforms that induce a transition to the farmer road (TF), cause a shift from junker road to farmer road (JF), or redistribute land within the farmer road (FR) are classified as "reformist." According to these typologies, the Cuban experience is characterized as a "radical" reform. In our view, this is incorrect: the Cuban land reform was executed in the context of a transition to socialism, and as such, was not a reform, since it was not aimed at reproducing the dominant social relations in the national economy, those of peripheral capitalism. In addition, such typologies are insufficient to explain the expected consequences of reforms because the criteria on which they are based are specified ad hoc rather than derived from a theoretical framework. They also often erroneously consider together land reforms that occur in central and peripheral countries, although the contradictions of accumulation, and hence the purposes of reform, are markedly different in the two cases.

CONSEQUENCES OF LAND REFORMS

The major economic and political impacts of land reforms can be summarized in the following four observations.

Observation I: Market Expansion

The role of land reforms in expanding the domestic market for the modern industrial sector producing wage goods and thus contributing to social articulation via increased peasant consumption expenditures has been insignificant.

This observation is important because land reform has often been viewed by the national bourgeoisie and the political forces promoting a national bourgeois revolution as a means of transforming the national economy from socially disarticulated to articulated. For this to happen, however, the resulting employment and income effects would have to be sufficient to permit benefited peasants access to the consumption of modern-sector industrial goods.

Clearly, before land reforms, peasant incomes were far below the necessary levels to allow for any significant consumption of industrial goods. In Chile the average monthly per capita income (including the imputed value of wages in kind) of peasants and landless agricultural workers prior to the reform equaled $108 (or $65 cash per capita).[18] In Ecuador the per capita income for the same groups was $33.50,[19] and in Peru it ranged from $17 to $47.[20]

Land reform programs have had only a small net employment effect. On the one hand, few of those who actually received land were landless or external peasants, most having been laborers on the estates. On the other hand, during and after the process of land reform, some peasants were expelled from the estates; the number of permanent and seasonal workers was reduced.[21] And the labor force was often slashed when estates were privately subdivided to avoid expropriation by size limitations.[22]

The employment effect of the reform program in Ecuador on the internal peasants—the supposed beneficiaries of the reform—illustrates another negative social impact of land reform as well as the objective logic for destroying the internal subsistence economy when surplus labor exists. Because internal semiproletarian labor was nearly gratuitous, it was overemployed relative to actual labor requirements on the estates. For this reason, the internal peasants were fully employed and relatively better off than the external peasants. In commenting on the effects of the reform, CIDA stated: "The patron is no longer obligated to the workers. When they were [internal peasants] they enjoyed habitual work assignments; now, in contrast, they must compete in the labor market, which allows the patrons to tailor employment to their labor requirements."[23]

In other words, the expropriation of the internal subsistence economy transformed labor from a fixed cost to a variable one and thus made employment opportunities dependent on market conditions. While this may have had a favorable impact on production, CIDA found that it was not uncommon for the haciendas to reduce employment by as much as 50 percent after the reform.[24] In their study, the Costales cite cases in which employment of former internal peasants was reduced by 25–50 percent.[25]

The form in which the reform enterprises are organized also may create negative employment effects. The cooperatives established in Peru under the military's land reform (1969–75) and in Chile under Frei (1967–73) provided real incentives to reduce or limit employment. Indeed, in the cooperatives established on the former sugar plantations in Peru, members were extremely reluctant to incorporate new members, preferring instead to hire temporary laborers who would not share in the social benefits of the cooperative.[26] The same phenomenon was observable in Chile,[27] where, for the same reason, the substitution of machinery for labor power on the land reform cooperatives was particularly intense.[28]

Similarly, the organization of the reform sector into family and subfamily units creates little employment for nonbeneficiaries. In the case of the Venezuelan land reform settlements, only 2.1 percent of the total labor input was contracted for from outside.[29]

The income effect of land reform has been equally ambiguous. Ultimately, the net impact on the size of the market for industrial goods will depend on the general distribution of the income effect among those directly and indirectly benefited and those directly and indirectly harmed.

A survey of those directly benefited by the reform in Venezuela revealed that 37 percent had lower cash incomes after the reform than before, 28 percent remained unchanged, and 35 percent had higher incomes.[30] The per capita incomes of those benefited by the reform averaged $129, of which $105 was in cash. The sources of this income were: 19 percent, consumption of home production; 35 percent, sales of farm production; and 46 percent, outside employment. This high degree of semiproletarianization reflects the subsistence nature of the reform sector. Data on the prereform income levels of the beneficiaries of the reform were not supplied. In any event, it is clear that the absolute income levels attained were too low to permit a significant purchase of industrial goods. Indeed, according to Kirby, "[In Venezuela] the most serious criticism of the land reform so far is that the settlers (beneficiaries) have been able to increase their purchasing power to a very limited extent."[31]

A study of several of INCORA's land reform projects revealed similarly limited and often negative income effects on beneficiaries. Thus, in the Atlantico No. 3 project, production actually declined during the first three years; and 68 percent of Colombia's rural families suffered negative income effects during the project's first five years of operation.[32]

A 1966 study of consumption habits of land reform beneficiaries in the La Paz region of Bolivia showed that while nominal consumption expenditures had increased substantially—433 percent in fourteen years—the absolute level of family expenditures, $101 (or $17 per capita), was still far too low to include significant purchase of industrial goods.[33] And yet the group surveyed included recipients of some of the greatest benefits of the reform owing to their close proximity to the La Paz market.

The most privileged beneficiaries of the military's land reform in Peru—the permanent workers of the expropriated sugar plantations who became the members of cooperatives—saw their annual nominal wages (advanced against year-end profits) increase from $377 to $662 between 1968 and 1972, representing an increase of 33 percent.[34] Again, however, the absolute income levels of even these most privileged reform beneficiaries remained too low to permit significant participation in the market for industrial goods.

While expansion of the domestic market for final mass consumption goods has thus been insignificant, the acceleration in the development of capitalism induced by land reforms has increased the demand for means of production. This is true for reforms that establish the junker road—with its bias toward mechanization fomented by generous institutional rents derived from continued control of the state—as well as for those that establish the farmer road—with its consequent diffusion of land-saving technologies and infrastructure development. The labor-saving bias that came to exist on many labor cooperatives of the reform sector in Chile and Peru in an effort by the beneficiaries to ward off sharing revenues with additional members also created a significant market for capital goods. Since the delivery of agricultural inputs is largely controlled by transnational corporations, the backward linkage effects are, however, rarely captured by national capital. Sectoral disarticulation further implies that increased derived demand for capital goods is largely translated into increased imports. And as we saw in Chapter 1, increasing sectoral articulation does not lead per se to social articulation.

Observation II: Development of Capitalism in the Nonreform Sector

The production effect of land reform is sought through the development of capitalism principally in the *nonreform* sector, and this most particularly in the reforms that induce a transition to capitalism (TJ, TF) or a shift to the farmer road (JF). The objective is to increase the marketed surplus of both food and exportables in order to reduce wage costs and relieve the deficit in the balance of payments. Conversely, the impact of land reforms on marketable production through the reform sector is secondary. This observation follows from a study of the provisions of land reform laws as well as from the contrasted production performances of reform and nonreform sectors.

The development of capitalism in the nonreform sector is encouraged by land reform laws in a variety of ways:

1. Patterns of extensive land use are discouraged through threats of expropriation. This approach is typical of all land reforms and is the primary method applied under reforms that seek to induce the transition to junker agriculture. Indirect forms of farm management (absenteeism) are prohibited or restricted to corporate holdings. This encourages direct management and presumably promotes greater productivity. This provision is typical of most reforms except precapitalist redistributive reforms.

2. Through expropriation of internal peasant plots, prohibition of bonded labor, and the institution of minimum wages paid in cash, labor is transformed from a fixed cost to a variable cost; and the social relations of the noncapitalist estates are transformed into those of a capitalist enterprise. This is typical of the transition reforms.

3. Landlords affected by expropriation under the clause of farm size are allowed to retain a land "reserve" of maximum legal size on which fixed and variable working capital are concentrated. Consequently, the ratio of capital to land increases substantially on these farms. This is typical of the reforms that aim at establishing a farmer road in the nonreform sector. The size of the reserves may also vary with intensity of land use, thus encouraging the development of the productive forces.

4. To escape expropriation under the clauses restricting the size of holdings, landlords are encouraged, informally or officially, to subdivide their estates into smaller units with the objective of improving farm management and increasing the intensity of land use. This, too, is typical of the reforms that promote the farmer road.

These provisions of the law and the manner in which the law is applied thus aim at promoting the development of the productive forces in the nonreform sector while using the reform sector as an instrument for this purpose more than as a locus for production increase. This is confirmed by the following patterns of implementation of land reforms.

Exemptions from expropriations on the basis of size—the so-called reserves—have generally been quite liberal, as can be seen in Table 6.1, column 5, even under the Mexican, Chilean, and Peruvian reforms, which induced a transition or a shift to the farmer road. Since landowners were invariably allowed to choose the location of reserves, they established them on the best lands of the former estates. In most cases, since neither working capital (including livestock) nor water rights were affected by the reform (Table 6.1, column 6), the land incorporated into the reform sector had been decapitalized and lacked guaranteed access to water, while the capital/land ratio had increased substantially on the reserves.[35] There are also innumerable obstacles to expropriation in the land reform law; and the enforcement of the law was usually delayed, thus allowing time to decapitalize expropriated lands and capitalize reserves.

Intensively utilized land was entirely (transition to junker) or partially (transition and shift to farmer) exempt from expropriation. Generous delays were often given to allow for intensification of land use as well as to subdivide estates and escape expropriation on the basis of size.

The result was that the effective quantity of land under control of the landed elite was only marginally reduced under precapitalist redistributive and transition to junker reforms. As Table 6.1, column 3, shows, after the reform, the nonreform sector still included 99 percent of the land in Ecuador, 90 percent in Colombia, 84 percent in Venezuela, and 82 percent in Bolivia. Under reforms that create the farmer road, the nonreform sector is reduced to a smaller fraction of total land: 57 percent in Mexico, 58 percent in Peru, and 60 percent in Chile (1973). These lands, however, are usually the best in the country; they receive the bulk of public services in credit, infrastructure, extension, and research; and they produce most of the commodified agricultural product.

For instance, in Mexico, where the reform sector is proportionally larger in terms of land and labor force than that of any other country, the nonreform sector monopolizes the bulk of institutional services. During the 1956-69 period, although the private commercial farms sector encompassed 55 percent of total agricultural lands, it received 85 percent of public agricultural credit.[36] In Chile under Allende, where the reform sector was enlarged to the maximum allowed under the 1967 reform law, the nonreform sector still received 69 percent of state credit in 1971–72.[37] Also, while the 1967 land reform conferred upon the state control of all irrigation works, neither Frei nor Allende exercised that power, and as a result, the nonreform sector—and, in particular, the remaining large landholders—retained control of 77 percent of the capacity of the country's irrigation works.[38] In Bolivia, where 18.2 percent of agricultural land and 39 percent of the peasantry have been incorporated into the reform sector, all sources agree that the smallholders, both within and without the reform sector, have received virtually no production credit.[39]

The limited available production data do suggest that the production effect of land reform was obtained almost totally in the nonreform sector, not in the reform sector. Appropriate data exist only for Bolivia and Mexico, the two countries with the longest history of land reform in Latin America.

In Bolivia, the production of potatoes and cereals can be taken as a proxy for the performance of the reform sector and that of sugarcane and cottonseed for the performance of the nonreform sector.[40] Between 1952–53 and 1974, the average annual per capita increase in the production of potatoes and cereals was 2.3 percent and 0.5 percent, respectively. For sugarcane and cottonseed, the figures were 37.1 percent and 94.6 percent, respectively.[41]

In Mexico, there is a rough equivalence between the area contained in the reform (*ejido*) and nonreform sectors. The private commercial farms sector contains 55 percent of cultivable lands and 49 percent of irrigated lands and produces 51 percent of agricultural output.[42] It is clear, however, that these data overestimate the effective size and contribution to production of the nonreform sector, for an important fraction of the *ejido* land, which is not used for subsistence production, has been illegally rented out to large landowners. According to NACLA: "For most *ejidatarios,* whose incomes average less than $50 a month, the most viable solution today is to rent their plot to a large land-owner and then work full time as a day laborer in the tomato or cotton fields. In Sonora, about 70 percent of the *ejidos* are rented, especially in the irrigated areas of Navajoa and the Valle del Yaqui, while estimates for the percentage of rented *ejidos* in Sinaloa range between 40 and 80 percent."[43] Data on the relative production performances of the nonreform and reform sectors are consequently difficult to interpret and are still actively debated. It is clear, however, that the yields per harvested hectare are substantially higher on private capitalist farms than on *ejido* farms and that this gap has been increasing over time: it was 25 percent in 1960 and 35 percent in 1970.[44] It is only if labor inputs in the *ejido* sector are inputed at zero opportunity cost, while those used in the capitalist sector are valued at market price, that the *ejido* appears more efficient per unit of expenditure.

The production effect of a land reform consequently depends mainly on the nature of its impact on the nonrefrom sector. The greatest potential effect is obtained from reforms that promote the transition to a farmer road, followed, in decreasing order, by those that induce a shift from junker road to farmer road, a transition to the junker road, and by redistributive reforms. This theoretical ordering is derived from the effect of each type of reform on the hierarchy of determinants of stagnation: reforms that induce a transition to the farmer road remove the second (control of the state) and third (land tenure pattern) determinants; reforms that induce a shift from junker road to farmer road remove the second; reforms that create a transition to the junker road eliminate the third. Redistributive reforms do not affect any of the determinants of stagnation.

It is possible to verify that government policy aimed at increasing production has changed under those land reforms that induce either a transition to the farmer road or a shift from junker road to farmer road—both of which imply control of the state passing to the bourgeoisie.

After Mexico's landed elites were expropriated from their estates during the 1934-40 period, the Mexican government embarked on a massive program of agricultural development. The primary emphasis of this program was on extending the agricultural frontier through irrigation projects and on the diffusion of biochemical (land-saving) technologies.[45] Similarly, in Peru, after expropriation the government initiated the construction of massive irrigation works, one of which will irrigate 150,000 hectares.[46]

With respect to production performance, the contrasting experiences of Bolivia and Mexico—the only two Latin American countries that have undergone a long and uninterrupted process of land reform—do tend to confirm the hypothesis that potential production gains are greatest under reforms that create a transition to the farmer road. Thus, in Mexico between 1934-38 and 1950-51, total agricultural output increased 4.3 percent annually; between 1948 and 1963, 6.3 percent annually; and between 1960 and 1970, 5.8 percent annually. For Bolivia, which remained dominated by the junker road, the annual growth rates after the reform were only 1.2 percent (1951-64) and 1.7 percent (1960-70).[47]

Under precapitalist redistributive and transition-to-junker reforms, the bulk of the land incorporated into the reform sector is often found on the agricultural frontier and consequently is not only of low quality but is also hobbled by poor infrastructure and limited access to effective demand. For instance, in Colombia the World Bank found that "the land resources [acquired for the reform sector] are largely those which have been ceded by previous holders because it would be impossible for them to make the necessary investments to bring land into production. Consequently, much of the land held by INCORA [the land reform institute] is marginal whereas extensive good land resources continue to be underutilized."[48] The same problem characterizes much of the lands distributed to peasants in Venezuela, where the low quality of the land leads to poor economic conditions and a high rate of abandonment and reconsolidation of these lands into larger farms. Between 1967 and 1975, the reform sector's contribution to national crop production declined from 32 percent to 20 percent; between 1967 and 1972, its contribution to livestock production declined from 6 percent to 3.4 percent.[49] Growth in national production has been achieved by a small number of medium-size and large commercial farmers in the nonreform sector, the emergence of which has been stimulated by the threats and incentives of the agrarian reform.[50]

Under capitalist redistributive reforms, where the farmer road dominates, a shift of land resources out of commercial farms into a collective or family farms sector is likely to have a minimal or negative effect on production. In the Dominican Republic, the rice land expropriated by the ruling Reformist Party was part of highly efficient, large-scale farms before the reform. Available information seems to indicate that yields fell as a result of the shift to family farms, while intense public-sector assistance allowed yields to increase modestly in the cooperatives.[51] Similarly, in Mexico the lands distributed by Echeverría in the Sonora Valley in 1976 were part of highly modern, large-scale farms where land and technology were used intensively. Such reforms consequently have primarily a legitimating function, which is sought by creating a rural petty bourgeoisie among beneficiaries of land redistribution.

The organization of the reform sector into subfamily/family units (Table 6.1, column 7) proscribes access to cheap labor and thereby relegates the reform sector to stagnation because it is unable to compete with the nonreform sector. The small size of the units in the reform sector often requires that heads of families seek outside employment. In spite of legal constraints, reform sector land tends to gradually become appropriated by the nonreform sector.[52]

In reflecting the productive operations at which they labored prior to land reform, the social behavior of peasants also is an important determinant of the success or failure of production in the reform sector.[53]

When the pre–land reform tenure consists of decentralized productive operations characteristic of the large estates employing the *aparceria* form of labor exploitation, the subsequent organization of the reform sector into cooperative or collective farms is generally precluded in the absence of strong incentives, which are unlikely to come during domination by the capitalist mode of production. The consequent atomistic organization of the reform sector tends to imply little use of new technology, stagnant production, and a declining marketable surplus (e.g., in Bolivia and parts of the Peruvian highlands). Even when the bulk of productive operations is centralized prior to the reform, the strong desire for individual proprietorship tends to frustrate the formation of effective cooperatives or collectives (e.g., in Chile).

Experience shows that cooperative farms tend to be most effective when productive operations are completely centralized before the reform, as in plantations, centralized precapitalist estates, and junker estates. This has been the case for the production cooperatives created from the expropriated coastal plantations in Peru. Labor cooperatives are also most effective when their members share a common ideology or purpose usually derived from collective struggle for access to the land.[54]

Observation III: Political Stabilization Through the Reform Sector

With the production strategy of land reform centered in the nonreform sector, the primary role of the reform sector is political. By giving land to peasants, the reform sector creates a conservative agrarian petty bourgeoisie and thus reduces the threat of social instability in the countryside.

This observation is clearly illustrated in the philosophy of the INCORA, the Colombian Land Reform Institute. In an article it authored for USAID,

INCORA stated: "INCORA was founded and its funds and staff were systematically built up to levels which enabled it to invest substantially in land tenure modifications, land improvements, credit, and other services for a new class of campesino landowners. Politically, it [land reform] offers the hope of reducing the threat of instability in the countryside."[55]

The goal of political stabilization involves a dual strategy: co-option and patronage of reform beneficiaries,[56] and repression of the uprisings of peasants excluded from the reform. The most successful implementation of this strategy has occurred in Mexico, where political stability and democratic representation have been maintained since the refrom of Cárdenas in spite of growing rural poverty and highly unequal patterns of development. The strategy of political stabilization via land reform is, however, highly contradictory. Land reform can also open the door to increased instability, which has often been brought under control through counterrefrom and authoritarianism.

Reforms that attempt to establish the farmer road are potentially the most destabilizing because of the political reaction of expropriated landed elites and the frustrations of the large mass of peasants excluded from the reform. Preservation of the bulk of the land in the nonreform sector limits access to the land to a small fraction of the peasantry. The frustrations of those excluded can be a destabilizing force that pushes through strikes and land seizures for an acceleration, amplification, and radicalization of the land reform. This pressure is particularly acute in reforms that attempt to establish the farmer road, since the bourgeoisie requires political allies to successfully execute a land reform against the landed elite.

Thus, in an electoral context such as in Chile, the peasants had to be mobilized and peasant organization had to be reinforced. However, while over 100,000 Chilean peasants joined unions between 1965 and 1970, only 21,000 had gained access to the land by the end of this period.[57] Because of limited concrete benefits, workers' strikes on the land estates increased from 142 in 1965 to 1,580 in 1970, and land invasions multiplied from 7 to 456.[58] Meanwhile, the landed elite's strong opposition to the land reform and fear that it threatened their property in other sectors of the economy led to a rupture of the conservative-liberal alliance that had brought the Christian Democrats an electoral victory in 1964. In the 1970 presidential campaign, the combination of these two forces—division between liberals and conservatives and the increasing radicalization of the peasantry—brought the leftist Popular Unity to power. The political destabilization unleashed by the land reform under Frei intensified under Allende until the military intervened on the side of the propertied classes and canceled most of the redistributive effect of the reform.

In Guatemala as well, peasants were mobilized by the government to carry out the expropriation of the landed elite. However, with backing from the U.S. government, the expropriated landowners regained political control and the land reform was completely reversed after Arbenz was deposed in 1954.

Observation IV: Functional Dualism

With the need for cheap food maintained by the objective logic of cheap labor under social disarticulation, no land reform can eliminate functional dualism. Thus, irrespective of the type of land reform, the subsistence sector is maintained as the necessary source of cheap labor.

The proportion of the peasantry benefited by different land reforms is given in Table 6.1, column 4. Even after sixty years, the most extensive land reform in Latin American history, that of Mexico, has still not incorporated more than 50 percent of the peasantry into the reform sector. Similarly, in Peru, as of November 1976, 68 percent of the potential beneficiaries (the subsistence peasants and landless agricultural laborers existing in 1964) remained outside the reform sector; and according to government figures, the maximum percentage to be eventually incorporated into the reform sector is 39 percent.[59] In Chile, during the government of Popular Unity, the proportion of potential beneficiaries excluded from the reform sector was still 80 percent.

Thus, although the social relations of production are redefined under transition reforms, and the large estates are eliminated under the reforms that establish the farmer road, the *minifundio* always remains; this permits the continued transfer of the cost of cheap food and generally unfavorable agricultural prices to semiproletarian labor.

External subsistence peasants seldom gain access to additional land resources under any type of reform; and despite the popularity of the slogan *"consolidación de minifundios,"* no serious or even marginal attempt has ever been made to eliminate the *minifundio*. In fact, the reform sector is usually designed to extend, rather than curtail, functional dualism. This is achieved by tying beneficiaries to subfamily/family units in the reform sector, where they become purveyors of cheap labor to capitalist entrepreneurs (Table 6.1, column 7).

In Venezuela, reform beneficiaries average 107 days laboring in the reform sector and 106 days working outside the reform sector.[60] Kirby observes, "Far from being the foundation of an improving social welfare . . . in many cases the land reform has fixed families in a position where they can do little more than inflate the pool of cheap labor."[61] Elsewhere, he adds, "it is . . . clear that the reform has stabilized a pool of casual laborers to be called on at the convenience of the large landowners."[62]

The Mexican *ejido* is particularly illustrative of a contrived functional dualism. Under Cárdenas (1934–40), the *ejido* was viewed as a collectivist alternative to capitalist agriculture. Over time, however, under official or unofficial pressures, most *ejido* lands have been individually appropriated. Consequently, the vast majority of the *ejidatarios* differ from private peasants today only in that *ejido* plots may not legally be sold or transferred in any manner.

Although these stipulations are ostensibly designed to avoid the reconcentration of landholdings and to protect the reform beneficiaries, they effectively tie them to plots of land that are insufficient for family subsistence. Thus, while the *ejido* was initially "merely a response to the political pressures and land hunger of the peasants,"[63] it has become an integral part of agrarian policy since 1940 and serves as a purveyor of cheap labor to commercial agriculture in a regime of planned functional dualism. And the degree of semiproletarianization among *ejidatarios* has been increasing continuously. While in 1950 only 16 percent of *ejido* families earned over half of their income from sources other than their land, by 1960 this percentage had increased to 34 percent.[64] As Stavenhagen concludes:

On the one hand, the peasant economy (small *ejido* and private smallholders) provides a minimum subsistence income to its members at little cost to the national economy, and it helps to keep the process of rural to urban migration in check. On the other hand, it is unable to really increase levels of living substantially with the poor resources at its disposal, and thus necessarily forces peasants to seek complementary sources of income elsewhere. It constitutes, thus, a reserve of labour not only for the large agricultural farms but also for industry, construction, services and so forth. . . . As long as labour does not constitute a scarce or expensive element among the factors of production, it is in the interest of the system to maintain a numerous but unstable peasantry from which it can draw its inexpensive labour force for the process of capitalist accumulation.[65]

In summary, as long as social disarticulation remains unchallenged, no land reform can eliminate the primary determinant of stagnation—the low price of food. Consequently, no land reform can eliminate functional dualism. The subsistence sector remains the necessary source of cheap labor for both non-reform and reform sectors. And so, too, the fundamental economic and social contradictions of peripheral capitalism in agriculture remain a global tendency toward stagnation, sharply uneven development of the productive forces, and massive rural poverty.

THE END OF LAND REFORM

Today, precapitalist estates with rent in labor services have, for all practical purposes, disappeared in Latin America. Those with rent in kind remain important only in some Central American countries and in parts of Brazil, but even there they represent fundamentally capitalist social relations. In general, it can consequently be said that precapitalist social relations have been virtually eliminated.

This elimination resulted from the incentive of market forces, the subjective pressures exercised by internal peasants, and the coercion of reformist policies. Particularly effective were land reforms that threatened precapitalist estates with expropriation if they would not modernize (transition to the junker road) and took control of the state away from the landed elites to place it in the hands of the bourgeoisie (transition to the farmer road). Under these reforms, promoted against the remnants of feudalism, the conflict between production (accumulation) and distribution (legitimation) was presumed to be nonexistent. They consequently offered an attractive common rallying cause for the national and dependent bourgeoisies and their foreign allies. Such reforms also appealed to radical forces that saw land reform as a step toward the implementation of a national bourgeois revolution, which they deemed a necessary first stage in the transition to socialism. As a result of all this support, these transitional reforms were actively implemented beginning in the late 1950s. Today, they can be considered successfully terminated, for they fostered capitalist development, but the publicized goal of expropriation and redistribution toward formation of a reform sector has generally been held to a minimum.

With the noted exception of feudal remnants, future land reforms (redistributive under capitalism and shift to farmer road) must of necessity be directed at capitalist enterprises. Consequently, they are not likely to occur under the hegemonic domination of the capitalist mode of production except after the most severe social pressures, as in the case of Echeverría's 1977 land reform in the Sonora Valley in response to peasant invasions, or under the exceptionally favorable conditions of public budget endowments, as in the swap of urban properties on Trujillo's personal estate for rice land in the Dominican Republic.

Not only do redistributive reforms imply a questioning of the concept of private property by taking land away from some capitalists to distribute it to peasants and landless workers, but they enhance the conflict between production and distribution. Since large-scale farms in the commercial sector, with the full backing of state services, tend to be highly efficient (within the confines of cheap food and with the consequent product and technological biases we identified above), the family or cooperative farms created by expropriations of these lands will generally not be able to ensure delivery of an equivalent net surplus on the market, at least not in the short run or without a drastic redesign of agrarian policy toward servicing peasants.

Reforms that seek to shift the nonreform sector from the junker road to the farmer road also are unlikely to occur, even though some production gains could be expected from this change in tenure. The strongly entrenched position of the capitalist landed elites as part of the social class alliance that supports the model of disarticulated accumulation tends to eliminate the possibility of such reforms.

In addition, both the problem of deficient and uneven production performance in agriculture and the persistent problem of rural poverty increasingly arise from the first determinant of stagnation—cheap food—a constraint that derives directly from disarticulated accumulation and the associated logic of functional dualism. A resolution of these contradictions lies far beyond the scope of land reform. With the development of capitalism in agriculture, the agrarian question has become increasingly less agrarian.

For all these reasons, new land reforms are unlikely to occur in the near future in Latin America, even though land reform remains an active political issue for the elements of the national bourgeoisie and for radical forces that militate for reconstruction of the economic system toward a model of articulated accumulation.[66]

7

***

The Strategy of Integrated
Rural Development

***

While agrarian reformism via land reform has virtually reached its limits under the current geopolitical map of Latin America, dominated as it is by disarticulated alliances, the economic (food deficits) and political (poverty) aspects of the agrarian crisis still remain, although they are now situated in a transformed agrarian structure that has advanced farther along the road of capitalist development. In this new period, which began in the early 1970s, state interventions are oriented toward promoting simultaneously on three fronts the consistency between objective and subjective demands on agriculture of a strategy of managed agrarian dualism subject to the requirements of disarticulated accumulation: (1) the development of the forces of production in the medium- and large-scale commercial sector through agricultural development programs and an alliance with foreign capital; (2) the reinforcement of a minimal agrarian petty bourgeoisie through rural-development projects in order to ensure the subjective (political) conditions for the reproduction of functional dualism; and (3) the meeting of "basic needs" through the distribution of public amenities in integrated rural-development projects in order to provide the objective (economic) conditions for the reproduction of functional dualism. We now turn to the different components of this strategy and more specifically to rural-development projects.

A TYPOLOGY OF RURAL-DEVELOPMENT PROJECTS

Since there is no agreement on the meaning of the term "rural development," a necessary first step consists of defining the terminology we will use. For our purpose, it is sufficient to confine these definitions to the context of reforms.

224

Agrarian reformism in Latin America has been composed principally of three kinds of interventions—agricultural development programs, land reform, and different types of rural-development projects (Figure 7.1). Each of these reforms is defined by the clientele at which it is aimed, the economic and political goals it is supposed to accomplish, and the instruments of which it makes use.

The clientele of agricultural development programs is located in the commercial sector, which consists of capitalist enterprises—estates, plantations, and commercial farms—that are motivated by the quest for a full rate of profit. To different degrees, according to their respective positions in the political economy, the entrepreneurs of these enterprises have access to the public institutions that service agriculture (research, extension, credit, insurance, marketing, etc.) and can appropriate the services of these institutions without the assistance of comprehensive programs. They are "integrated" into the institutions of society.[1] Because they also participate in the political process through which these institutions and their services are defined (technological options, opening of specific lines of credit, price policies, infrastructure-development programs, etc.,), capitalist farmers also are "incorporated" into society.

Clearly, the primary goal of agricultural development programs is economic—to increase the delivery of an agricultural surplus on the market. As the terms of trade for wage goods are constrained by the global structure of accumulation, an escape from the profit squeeze in commercial agriculture is sought via technological change, marketing arrangements, institutional rents, and functional dualism. The principal instruments used in agricultural de-

Content of reform \ Types of reforms	Agricultural development projects	Land reform (PKR, TJ, TF)[a]		Rural development projects	
		Nonreform sector	Reform sector	Political	Economic
Clientele	Commercial sector	Precapitalist estates	Internal peasants	Family and upper subfamily peasants	Lower subfamily and landless peasants
Goals Primary	Economic: increase agricultural surplus	Economic: increase agricultural surplus	Political: create petty bourgeoisie	Political: create petty bourgeoisie	Economic: stabilize wages
Secondary				Economic: increase wage-food surplus	Political: social status quo
Instruments	Extension International capital	Threats of expropriation Change control of state Extension	Redistribution of land Incorporation	Neoextension Incorporation	Public amenities Integration

[a] See Figure 6.1.

Figure 7.1. Types of Agrarian Reforms

velopment programs have thus been the extension model applied to the diffusion of Green Revolution technology and encouragement of international
capital's penetration into agroindustry.[2]

The first instrument has led to rapid, if highly uneven, technological
changes: in Mexico some 95 percent of the wheat area is planted in high-
yielding varieties, while the spread of new wheat strains has been minor in
other countries; some 30 percent of the total Latin American rice area is
planted in high-yielding varieties.[3] The second instrument has implied increasing subordination of commercial agriculture to international agroindustry
on both the input side and the processing and marketing side, while domestic
producers continue to assume the risks of production.[4]

Although it has been effective in promoting the development of the forces
of production in agriculture, this strategy of agricultural development has had
two contradictory effects—one at the level of production and the other at the
level of poverty. Because unfavorable price conditions bind wage foods more
severely than exportables, inputs for industrial use, and luxury consumption
foods, the development of productive forces in the commercial sector has
been biased toward the latter three, thus eventually easing the balance-of-
payments crisis but worsening the deficit in the production of wage foods.[5]
Over the last ten years, a major agricultural revolution has taken place in the
production of exports, inputs for industry, and high-income-oriented commodities. Increasingly, land use has been diverted to the production of labor-
intensive (fruits and vegetables) and land-intensive (beef and soybeans)
exportables, as center capital has found more profitable production conditions
in Latin America, while the production of wage foods has fallen behind the
growth of effective demand and the deficit has been met by an increase in food
imports. As we saw in Chapter 2, there are also exceptions to this bias, such
as the production of rice in Colombia and the Dominican Republic and that of
wheat in Brazil, both of which are important wage foods.

This development of the forces of production in capitalist agriculture has,
however, been accompanied by the typical symptoms of unequal development: concentration of the land in commercial farms, expropriation of peasants, increasing semiproletarianization and landlessness, mechanization and
unemployment, increased regional disparities, etc.[6] To a large extent, the
social cost of the development of commercial agriculture has been borne by
the peasantry. The objective dimensions of the agrarian crisis (wage-food
prices and balance of payments) have been partially remedied at the expense
of an enhanced subjective crisis. And the crisis of peasant agriculture also
jeopardizes sustained accumulation in commercial agriculture as it destroys
the basis of functional dualism. Growth thus negates the reproduction of one
of its very sources. Faced with these new contradictions and given the end of
land reform, rural-development projects have acquired central importance in
agrarian reformism as both substitutes for land reforms and complements to
agricultural development programs.

Rural-development projects (RDPs) fall into two categories that are sharply contrasted in their clientele, goals, and instruments. We shall refer to these two types of projects as "political RDPs" and "economic RDPs," even though it will appear at first that the names given are exactly the reverse of what they should be. When both types are combined into a single project, we obtain what has been referred to as "integrated rural-development projects" (IRDPs).

"Political RDPs" are directed at a clientele located in the upper strata of the peasantry: family farms, modernized upper subfamily farms, the reform sector of redistributive land reforms, and peasant farms created by land settlement schemes. On all these farms, land resources are meager but are sufficient to provide a living to peasant families and a small surplus for sale on the market, which ensures the availability of cash for that part of necessary consumption which cannot be home-produced. Thus, the use of these resources can potentially be modernized through diffusion (down to the level of upper peasants) of the instruments of agricultural development that proved successful in commercial agriculture: land-saving technology (Green Revolution), access to institutional credit, and infrastructure development. Because access to public services has traditionally not been available to peasants, the institutional dimension of RDPs consists in managing the integration of peasants into the institutions of capitalist society: tailored technical assistance, supervised credit, informal education, and limited incentives for peasant organization. The extension-diffusion model applied to commercial agriculture needs to be modified here into tailored extensionism—managed diffusion and integration, termed "neoextension" in Table 7.1. When projects shift peasants from the category of upper subfamily farms (semiproletarians) to that of family farms (modernized upper subfamily farms), peasants join the ranks of the rural petty bourgeoisie and thus become socially incorporated as a politically effective fraction of a class.

Clearly, political RDPs can hardly apply to peasants internal to precapitalist estates since, in this case, peasant links to external institutions occur principally through the intermediation of the landlord, who in turn uses this dependency to maintain his hold on peasants and to extract a surplus from them—in particular, through the sale of their crops and through usury.[7] In this case a land reform that frees peasants from semifeudal bonds is an absolute prerequisite for RDPs: rural development cannot start to serve as a substitute for land reform until precapitalist estates have been eliminated. Beginning in the early 1970s with the liquidation of precapitalist social relations in agriculture and the "successful" end of land reform, this is precisely what has happened in Latin America.

Lower subfamily farms, where the large majority of peasants are found, are similarly excluded from the clientele of political RDPs. On these farms, the resource base is so small and the degree of semiproletarianization so high that the instruments of agricultural development, even if effectively tailored to peasants' needs, can have only negligible effects on their consumption or on income levels.

The potential clientele of political RDPs is thus only a small minority of peasant households. They belong principally to the upper strata of the peasantry and are characterized by privileged control over productive resources (farm size and ecologically favored areas) and by privileged access to effective demand (a location close to markets and good infrastructure).

The effectiveness of RDPs depends, as does agricultural development, on the nature of social control over the state. When the traditional landed elites dominate the state (capitalist estates), the instruments of agricultural development are severely limited. By contrast, when the bourgeoisie gains control of the state, the full potential of land-saving technology and infrastructure construction can be realized. It is then that RDPs can potentially be most effective.

Like land reforms, rural-development projects are, however, severely conditioned by two constraints that derive from the logic of dependent-disarticulated accumulation: unfavorable terms of trade for wage foods and the permanence of functional dualism.

The first constraint, in particular, proves to be a formidable obstacle to the modernization of peasant agriculture and to the stability of the petty bourgeoisie thereby created. Peasant agriculture tends to be less efficient than capitalist agriculture, with which it must compete in the product and land markets. This results from (1) small farm size (diseconomies of scale due, in particular, to lack of intermediate technology); (2) low capital investment (backward technology and lack of irrigation); (3) unfavorable access to markets (lack of transportation infrastructure and submission to monopolistic merchants and usurers); (4) unfavorable access to institutional services (institutional credit monopolized by commercial agriculture); and (5) low quality of natural resources (marginal areas and erosion). Higher production costs in modernized peasant agriculture result either in substantial differential rents for commercial agriculture or, more frequently, given the unfavorable terms of trade for wage foods, in the need for a considerable degree of intrafamilial self-exploitation.[8] In both cases, small farmers resist with great difficulty the encroachment of capitalist agriculture, which quickly forces differentiation and increasing semiproletarianization upon them.

Functional dualism also destabilizes the rural petty bourgeoisie as it specifically profits commercial agriculture. Limited resources and the low productivity of these resources do not permit peasants to hire significant quantities of labor and hence to benefit from functional dualism. While family farms must ensure the full subsistence cost of their members, commercial agriculture remunerates its hired semiproletarian labor at only a fraction of subsistence. Here, again, higher production costs can be offset only by severe self-exploitation of family labor within the farm.

This type of RDP thus aims at expanding and reinforcing a petty agrarian bourgeoisie. Upper subfamily peasants are transformed into family peasants, and family peasants are defended against competition from the commercial sector. The dominant objective is *political*—to buffer class conflict in the rural sector and to reduce the possibility of a class alliance between peasantry and urban proletariat. It is sought through the creation of a pampered conservative rural petty bourgeoisie of peasant origin. This fraction of a class is tied ideologically to the peasantry and economically to the rural bourgeoisie. It can consequently act as a stabilizing element in the growing conflict between actively expanding commercial agriculture and increasingly semiproletarianized peasants. The existence of this stabilizing class, on which the ideology of liberal capitalism has historically been based, helps reproduce the subjective basis (i.e., the political acceptability) of functional dualism. While these projects remove some semiproletarians from the labor market, in no case can their scope be sufficient to significantly reduce the role of the peasantry as a cheap labor reserve. Political acceptance of functional dualism is reinforced by creating expectations of vertical mobility among the bulk of the peasantry.[9] And such projects are also intended to reduce urban migration and hence the political threat and economic cost of urban unemployment.

This political objective implies that RDPs will tend to be promoted in instances where:

1. The peasant sector is numerically important and politically powerful. Political strength is related to the presence of indigenous communities as a means of mobilization, the history and activism of peasant organizations (agrarian leagues), and the magnitude of rural poverty.

2. Conflicts between bourgeoisie and proletariat are strong. As growing semiproletarianization tends to reinforce the power of the proletariat, creation of a petty bourgeoisie is seen as a means of discouraging a potential alliance between the rural and the urban proletariat. The proletariat's strategy, by contrast, is to encourage ideological identification of the rural semiproletarians with the working class at large and to foment worker-peasant alliances. The political economy of RDPs thus rests not only on the dialectic of functional dualism in the rural sector but, more globally, on the dialectic of all class relations at the national and international levels.

3. Social stability is obtained by means of reforms—that is, through negotiated settlements among social classes and not merely through the exercise of repression (economic repression and political and military suppression of peasant organizations). In this case, reforms aimed at alleviating rural poverty are important issues in electoral campaigns or in the legitimation of benevolent nondemocratic regimes.

4. The potential of using land reform programs against precapitalist estates has been exhausted either because (*a*) land reform programs have expropriated all of the traditional estates (transition reforms to the farmer road [Chapter 6]) or (*b*) the development of capitalism and threats of expropriation (transition reforms to the junker road) have fully transformed the precapitalist

estates into large-scale capitalist enterprises, and the landed elite has sufficient political power to retain its hegemonic position. Creation of a petty bourgeoisie at the expense of the precapitalist sector is no longer possible, and RDPs are the most politically workable alternative for doing so.

A secondary objective of political RDPs is *economic*—to increase delivery of wage foods to the market in spite of unfavorable prices. It can only be secondary since the bulk of productive land is held not by peasants but by the commercial sector, although it is obviously more important in some countries than in others—in particular, where commercial agriculture is highly export oriented and peasants have an important responsibility in food production (the Caribbean and Central America). This economic objective is severely constrained by the structural conditions of peasant agriculture, the terms of trade for wage foods, and functional dualism, from which upper peasants do not benefit. Yet these peasants have the capacity to supply cheaply a surplus of labor-intensive and delivery-intensive wage foods in spite of these unfavorable conditions, not as part of a stable division of labor with capitalist agriculture as Vergopoulos, Servolin, and the advocates of peasant modes of production have argued, but as part of a process of disequilibrium and differentiation. This is made possible both by surrendering any return to financial capital beyond the cost of credit and through severe "self-exploitation" of the family. With wage-food production increasingly marginalized into peasant agriculture by the logic of cheap food, destruction of peasant agriculture because of competition for land with capitalist agriculture further reduces the market delivery of wage foods.[10] The economic purpose of political RDPs is to slow down this process of collapse.

The second type of RDPs observed in Latin America are what we have named "economic RDPs." Their clientele exists throughout the ranks of the peasantry but is more specifically defined as the complement to the clientele of political RDPs—the bulk of external subfamily farms, which are highly semiproletarianized and constitute the foundation of functional dualism. Rural poverty is concentrated in this social group.

The methodology in this case is to integrate these marginalized strata into public institutions and thus to deliver public amenities to cover "basic needs": health, sanitation, school lunch programs, housing assistance, water supply, education, etc. While counteracting extreme poverty (political stabilization) is the openly advocated goal of these programs, the role of their clientele in supplying cheap labor implies that the dominant goal is, in fact, *economic*. Both a declining land base per household (demographic pressure, erosion, and expropriation by capitalist agriculture) and rising aspirations (the subjective component of subsistence) imply that subsistence agricultural production provides a declining fraction of household needs and thus puts upward pressure on wages. However, increasing the productivity of labor in the bulk of subsistence agriculture by inducing its modernization through the instruments of agricultural development is largely made impossible by the insufficiency of subsistence agriculture's resource base. A third component, beyond agricultural production (A) and income from wage work (W), can, however, be added to the sources of subsistence (S); it is the consumption of public amenities (P). As a result, $S = A + W + P$. The objective of economic RDPs is to perpetuate cheap labor under functional dualism. With W thus blocked as a goal and with A as a constraint, these programs increase P to make up for the fall in A (due to demographic explosion, marginalization, and erosion) and for the rise in S (the result of the changing moral and historical definition of subsistence). Economic RDPs thus aim at *reproducing the objective basis of functional dualism* by ensuring that "basic needs" are met through the distribution of public amenities within the confines of the budgetary capacity of the state. Their political purpose derives from this economic goal—to maintain the status quo in the social relations of agriculture.

Integrated rural-development projects (IRDPs), the archetypal programs of the World Bank and international aid agencies after the mid-1970s, combine the instruments and clientele of political and economic RDPs.[11] The economic programs reinforce the political impact of political programs by creating social acceptance for the modernization of peasant agriculture. In IRDPs, however, the lion's share of the budget involved has gone to production efforts. For this reason, this study concentrates principally on "political" projects. To return to a more intuitive terminology, we will call these projects "rural-development" projects; and we will call economic projects "basic-needs" projects.

CRITERIA FOR THE EVALUATION
OF RURAL-DEVELOPMENT PROJECTS

In the following section of this chapter, we turn to an evaluation of three rural-development projects: the Puebla project in Mexico, the Garcia Rovira project in Colombia, and the Cajamarca project in Peru.[12] All three projects follow a similar basic design that originated in Puebla and has become typical of rural-development projects promoted in the 1970s by the World Bank and international aid agencies. These projects consequently have strong analogies, and we refer to them as "Puebla-type" projects. Yet they occurred in markedly different structural, economic, and political contexts. A comparative analysis based on a set of established criteria would thus help us to better understand the achievements and limitations of this type of reform.

To make such an evaluation, we consequently first need to determine the criteria against which the success of these projects is to be judged. Choice of criteria depends, of course, on the specific purpose of the evaluation.

Fundamentally, two options are available. The first consists of taking at face value the explicit objectives set for a project by the sponsors at its inception and then comparing with them ex post facto the actual results obtained. In this case, evaluation is narrowly oriented toward improving the effectiveness of the project in reaching its explicit goals. In the case of RDPs, evaluation would tend to focus on whether the chosen clientele has been reached and whether the expected yield and income effects have been obtained. Emphasis would be given to an analysis of diffusion, to the determinants of adoption of project recommendations, as well as to the relative levels of costs and benefits of the program. This is the approach usually followed in economic project evaluation studies. While appearing to be objective, the method is not value free, since the explicit project objectives are tacitly endorsed by the evaluator as a normative standard. The evaluator does not question or rationalize the ends of the project, which are thus taken to be outside the realm of analysis, but rather concentrates exclusively on the means in order to improve project efficiency. This approach typifies neoclassical analysis, where the ends are taken to be exogenous to economics—for example, in the form of a set of subjective wants—and hence the means become the exclusive legitimate objects of an analysis confined to studying efficiency and "Pareto optimality."

The second procedure for evaluating a project is more demanding but also more comprehensive, for it scrutinizes ends and means jointly. A project is assumed to have both explicit (stated) and implicit (real) objectives. And some of the explicit objectives—especially the social and political ones, even though they may not actually be pursued—become implicit objectives merely by being advertised. Here lies the political art of reformism. Land reform programs that seek a transition from precapitalist estates to the junker road are a case in point: the simple threat of expropriation—the explicit objective—satisfied the implicit objective of inducing the transformation of semifeudal estates into large-scale commercial farms with capitalist social relations. In this manner, as we have seen, countries like Colombia have had an effective land reform without having one. Thus, evaluating a land reform project in terms of the stated redistributive objectives would be completely misleading, even though this is what has usually been done in the literature. The multiple implicit (real) objectives of a project may not only differ from the explicit ones but may even require the negation of some or all of the stated goals. This does not necessarily imply that all implicit objectives need to be fully conceptualized by the project sponsors in order to exist. Many are discovered by trial and error in the course of the project, while others, though undiscovered by project leaders, can be discerned by the evaluator through the relations of a particular project to the logic of the underlying economic and social processes into which it is inserted and relative to which it acquires consistency.

The purpose of this approach to project evaluation is thus not so much to analyze the internal efficiency of a project in achieving stated ends as it is to understand the global logic of the project (by identifying its implicit objectives) and the contradictions in the implementation of the project (by contrasting the implicit objectives to the use of a particular set of means). The difficulty with the approach, of course, lies in the identification of the implicit objectives against which the project is to be evaluated. We take the position that these objectives must be logically derived from the dominant characteristics and contradictions of the socioeconomic system in which it is to be implemented and from the way the state reacts to these contradictions to initiate a particular program of reforms. This consequently implies relying on a theory of the state. However, we also take the position that social phenomena cannot be understood purely externally as logical phenomena but are moved by individual and class agents whose particular internal vision of the contradictions and organizational capacity condition the way in which they react to these contradictions. It is in this sense that a class theoretic approach to the state is an essential complement to a capital logic approach, which alone would tend to infuse excessive rationality into the study of social phenomena.

The approach necessarily implies that the project be evaluated against a set of criteria that correspond to the evaluator's own interpretation of what the real objectives of the project are. As in the social sciences at large, any project evaluation is consequently an ideological statement, but no more so here than in the first method of evaluation, where the project sponsors' explicit objectives were taken as real objectives. And since there is no science without ideology,[13] scientific objectivity requires that the value premises on which an evaluation is made be fully explicated.

The criteria we choose here are derived from the objective and subjective forces that shape the laws of motion of capital in Latin American countries, from the resultant crises of accumulation and legitimacy, and from the associated logic of reformism. As we have explained, these laws of motion are characterized by two major contradictions in regard to agriculture: (1) the stagnation of food production and the consequent inflationary pressure, upward push on nominal wages, and deficit in the balance of payments (objective forces); and (2) the social pressures that originate in the massive impoverishment and increasing proletarianization of the peasantry (subjective forces).

In accordance with these contradictions, a whole set of interrelated reforms has been implemented, including land reform, agricultural development, and political and economic rural-development projects. Among these, RDPs have been seen to have two major objectives:

1. A production objective to increase the supply to the market of a low-cost food surplus originating in the peasant sector. This is obtained through increased production, which implies, in the absence of redistribution of the land and within a closed agricultural frontier, an increase in yields obtained from the diffusion of land-saving technological change (Green Revolution).

2. A political objective to create a politically stable and minimally organized petty bourgeoisie of peasant origin. This class serves as a social buffer between the expanding commercial sector and the mass of impoverished peasants and thus helps reproduce the subjective conditions of

functional dualism. Simultaneously, the prospects of vertical mobility and the distribution of public goods ("integrated" projects) stabilize the mass of semiproletarians and reproduce the objective conditions of functional dualism. Improved rural welfare also reduces urban migration and alleviates political pressures in the cities.

PUEBLA-TYPE RURAL-DEVELOPMENT PROJECTS

The Puebla Project

In 1967, responding to the widespread criticisms of the Green Revolution for its heavy social costs to the peasantry,[14] the International Maize and Wheat Improvement Center (CIMMYT) and the Graduate College of Agronomy at Chapingo initiated, with Rockefeller Foundation financing, an RDP in Puebla, Mexico. The purpose was to demonstrate that, adequately managed and promoted, the agricultural technology of the Green Revolution could indeed alleviate rural poverty and increase the marketable surplus of food produced by peasants.

The project was logical within the Mexican agrarian strategy of "contrived dualism:"[15] the land reform of Cárdenas had created an efficient commercial sector, concentrating the bulk of the land in commercial agriculture and assuring rapid growth in the production of wheat and exportables; at the same time, it had settled the mass of the peasantry in the *ejidos*, thereby creating a source of cheap food and the labor reserve for commercial agriculture. As erosion and demographic explosion increasingly threatened both the delivery of a corn surplus to the market and the social status quo obtained after the land reform, public policies directed at reproducing the conditions of functional dualism were sought. Given the political impossibility of initiating on any significant scale a new phase of land reform, which would this time have to be redistributive within the farmer road, rural development was considered as an alternative strategy. The project thus benefited from effective public support as well as from a relatively favorable price situation, an excellent infrastructure, and proximity to both product market and nonfarm employment opportunities. It also profited from a generally favorable natural environment, in spite of fluctuating rainfall and lack of irrigation, and from the presence of a relatively large number of upper subfamily and family farms that had been created by both the Spanish colonial settlement policy and land reform distributions.

Significant innovations were made in designing the Puebla project. An effective integration was achieved among agronomic research, technical assistance to peasants, socioeconomic analysis and evaluation, and linkage with external institutions (credit, insurance, etc.). Research was brought to the field and linked to extension services. Interdisciplinary barriers were weakened, and peasants were organized into "solidarity groups" in order to gain more effective access to credit and fertilizers.[16]

The explicit objective of the Puebla project was narrowly defined in terms of increased corn yields. Improved access to credit would enable peasants to buy fertilizers that increased corn yields. However, failure to identify new seeds and to define a profitable new technological package for peasant farming undermined the initial reasoning about the immediate significance of the Green Revolution for smallholders. With the consequent weakening of CIMMYT's participation, the project became increasingly oriented toward institutional change under the leadership of Chapingo, but this institutional change was defined in the narrow sense of access to credit and fertilizers by peasants who had previously been marginalized from those services.[17] Benefits of the project consequently accrued primarily to peasants who had enough land to make profitable use of fertilizers, but whose landholdings were small enough to have been previously excluded from access to public services. With a highly developed infrastructure in the region and favorable and stable corn prices relative to fertilizer prices, modest fertilizer doses applied to traditional seeds could indeed generate positive returns for these peasants. While the economic and nutritional benefits were thus quite small for peasants, the internal rate of return of the whole project was on the order of 14 percent, implying financial viability for this type of investment.[18]

By 1973, when the project came under the exclusive direction of the Mexican Ministry of Agriculture, the 553 solidarity groups that were in operation incorporated 8,700 families and represented some 20 percent of the households and 35 percent of the land in the area.[19] By then, the project had also become both a major training center for subprofessionals from other provinces in Mexico where the Puebla experience was to be repeated and a showcase for international agencies.

The Garcia Rovira Project

In addition to responsibility for doing agronomic research, the Instituto Colombiano Agropecuario (ICA) was assigned in 1968 the functions of extension and teaching—a combination typical of land-grant colleges in the United States but rare in Latin America. Extension was defined with respect to the peasant sector (family and subfamily farms), leaving technical assistance for the commercial sector in the hands of private consulting firms. As a way of making these three interrelated functions operational, and following the example of Plan Puebla in Mexico, ICA initiated in 1970 six rural-development programs. Three of the programs received major attention and developed into living laboratories for ICA's learning about the modernization of peasant agriculture: Caqueza, near Villavicencio (with substantial Canadian assistance);[20] Rio Negro, near Medellin; and Garcia Rovira, at the eastern tip of Santander Province. These projects were consequently very much at the core of ICA activities and were launched with strong support and enthusiasm. At the same time, though, almost everything specific to peasant agriculture was yet to be learned, for not only was the backlog of experience

ICA was bringing into the projects derived exclusively from dealing with commercial farming but often it was barely adapted to the Colombian context. By 1974, twenty-two IRDPs were in operation, and 47 percent of their budget was financed by the Inter-American Development Bank, the World Bank, and the Canadian International Development Agency. Through these programs it was expected that peasant pressure on the land held in commercial farms and deficits in the production of wage foods would be alleviated.

Garcia Rovira, a densely populated area, is predominantly characterized by family and subfamily farms. Larger farms on which labor needs cannot be met by a single family are generally subdivided and exploited by sharecroppers on a family basis. Relatively prosperous so long as the Colombian Orient was the main manufacturing area of the country, Garcia Rovira slowly regressed into backwardness after 1851, when free trade wiped out local manufacturers and eliminated the associated demand for food and textiles. Today, due to its remoteness, poor infrastructure, and marginal ecological conditions, it is an area in which poverty is fundamentally explained by a lack of effective demand for its products, which in turn blocks the development of commercial agriculture. In consequence, the local labor market is incipient, and archaic forms of labor relations, such as sharecropping and labor reciprocity among peasants, are maintained to ensure labor availability. Ironically, but also in response to the law of combined and uneven development, the ebullient development of capitalist agriculture and the creation of an active labor market in other areas of the country induce steady outmigration from Garcia Rovira and force the region to cling to archaic labor arrangements through which it ties its labor to the land and resists competition with other areas. Indeed, a difficult and heterogeneous natural environment and deficient effective demand (which jeopardize the profitability of technological change) proved to be major stumbling blocks for the project. And yet these conditions are typical of many areas in Colombia where large numbers of peasants are concentrated today.

The Garcia Rovira project was organized along the general lines of Plan Puebla, with ICA coordinating field experiments and managing extension and with the Agrarian Bank providing credit. However, Garcia Rovira differed from Plan Puebla in two significant respects: its technological focus was not narrowly commodity oriented, but at least in principle was to be directed at production systems; and its technology-credit thrust was integrated with social welfare programs in nutrition, family health, education, housing, and recreation.

In spite of the difficulty of the area and severe personnel instability in the project, technical assistance and credit were extended in 1974 and 1975 to some 660 families representing approximately 10–15 percent of the peasant households in the project area.[21] Lack of a sufficiently attractive new technological package, dubious profitability of the recommendations, and failure to use peasant organizations to increase outreach and reduce costs of delivery, however, left the project stagnating at this modest level of participation. With the initiation of the national program of IRDPs in 1974, of which Garcia Rovira is a part, the project clientele was more realistically defined: the upper limit for participation was set at 20 hectares or an endowment of U.S.$13,500, which in Garcia Rovira corresponds to farms of about 10 hectares; and a lower limit was defined by excluding farm households that derive less than two-thirds of their income from agricultural production. This lower limit effectively marginalized from the project 69 percent of the farms in the area, where the small land base implies high degrees of semi-proletarianization. It thus concentrated IRDP efforts on the family and upper subfamily farms, where the resource base is sufficient to permit receptivity to credit and technology.

The Cajamarca Project

The Cajamarca project was initiated in September 1971 as a collaborative endeavor between the Peruvian Ministry of Agriculture (wheat program), the National Agrarian University (corn program), the Institute of Agro-Industrial Research (product processing), and CIMMYT (technical assistance). Its declared purpose was to increase productivity and income among smallholders and members of land reform cooperatives through the dissemination of new technology in corn, wheat, and barley production. Its organization was also closely patterned after that of the Puebla Project, with a relatively small and autonomous interdisciplinary team combining the activities of field research, extension, institutional linkages, and evaluation.

The project was undertaken in an extensive northern valley of the Altiplano where large irrigated haciendas occupied the valley floors and engaged in highly capitalized dairy activities linked to the local Nestlé milk-processing plant. These haciendas coexisted with a huge number of subsistence farms devoted to the production of grains and other staple foods on the steep, dry, and eroded slopes of the valley's flanks. The bulk of these farms had sprung up in the 1950s when the opening of a road to the coast and the establishment of the Nestlé plant created a local market for dairy products and induced the haciendas to shift their activities from grains to cattle. As a consequence of sharply reduced labor needs, the haciendas expropriated their numerous *colonos* and sharecroppers and consolidated their lands into large-scale pasture operations. To finance the purchase of fine dairy cattle and ensure an adequate labor supply, the marginal lands of the haciendas were divided into numerous small plots and sold to the displaced peasants.[22] The development of capitalism in Cajamarca was thus typical of the junker road. Today these peasant farms are highly fragmented, use primitive technology, and are generally unable to provide the totality of family subsistence needs. Peasants are consequently increasingly forced into the labor market, both in the local commercial farms, mines, and towns and toward the coast and jungle.

The project was organized in an unfavorable national political context. Since 1969, the agrarian program of the military government had been dominated by the completion of an ambitious program of land reform. But until 1976, the central focus of the reform was on expropriations rather than on managing the production performance of either the reform or the nonreform sector. In Cajamarca the strength of the hacienda sector delayed the land reform, and the bulk of expropriations occurred only in 1974. The Cajamarca Project was thus initiated before successful achievement of the land reform program and in a context where the attention of government officials and peasants was directed not at technological change and the subsistence sector but at changing property relations to provide access to the land for the workers on the haciendas and some privileged peasants.

With virtual completion of the land reform in 1975 and a national crisis in food production, the agrarian program of the military government turned toward "consolidation of the process" by devoting attention to increasing food production in the land reform cooperatives.[23] In Cajamarca, the definition of the clientele of the RDPs was thus changed from independent smallholders to members of the labor cooperatives. The project's research activities were formalized in the shift from field experiments conducted by project personnel to the creation of a local experiment station with a stable scientific staff. And the extension program that had attempted to reach individual peasants was replaced by demonstrations for groups of specialized commercial producers. The project did not fail or disappear, although its initial institutional definition was canceled. Rather, as national political and economic priorities changed, it was transformed from a Puebla-type project directed at smallholders into an experiment station with research and extension programs oriented toward commercial production on the newly created land reform cooperatives.

In terms of its initial goal, the project met with serious difficulties that largely resulted from misconceptions about the nature of the peasant economy and from lack of experience with the management of rural development. Contrary to expectations, a new technological basis could not be developed, and the recommended package was of dubious profitability for adopting peasants. The project suffered from severe lack of leadership, inadequate planning of research and extension activities, and insufficient and unstable personnel. It also did not receive the necessary external institutional support. As a result, before being redefined, the project reached only 122 peasants, many of whom were actually the large commercial farmers of the area.[24]

ECONOMIC ACHIEVEMENTS OF RURAL-DEVELOPMENT PROJECTS

The effect of an RDP on production and net income is determined by three categories of factors: (1) the structural characteristics of the peasant economy, which condition the diffusion of new technologies; (2) the levels of profitability and risk associated with the recommendations made; and (3) the effectiveness of the diffusion methods used. The design of the Puebla-type approach to rural development was based on assumptions regarding these three categories of factors that were derived from received knowledge concerning the nature of the peasant economy and its position within broader society. This knowledge can be traced back principally to the "traditional agriculture" approach of Schultz,[25] Tax,[26] and Mosher;[27] to the dualistic interpretations of Lewis,[28] Ranis and Fei,[29] and Jorgenson[30] regarding the theory of economic growth; and to the diffusion-modernization literature in rural sociology exemplified by the work of Rogers.[31] The detailed benchmark studies conducted in the three project areas and the analyses of peasants' responses to the project initiatives are useful in arriving at a better understanding of the peasant economy and its patterns of transformation. These new observations suggest that some of the initial knowledge was indeed correct but that most of it was not. To contrast the conceptions of peasantry and rural development according to which the projects were initially defined to the knowledge derived from the ex post facto observations of the projects is very revealing. In evaluating the economic achievements of the three projects, we will consequently proceed by identifying the substantial discrepancies that exist between initial postulates and subsequent evidence.

STRUCTURAL CHARACTERISTICS OF THE PEASANT ECONOMY THAT CONDITION TECHNOLOGICAL CHANGE

Functional Dualism

Following the teachings of Schultz[32] and Lewis,[33] Puebla-type RDPs were designed in accordance with the assumptions that the peasant sector is *traditional* and *dual*. This vision implies that rural proverty can be analyzed as a phenomenon *sui generis,* unrelated to the process of growth in the rest of the economy. More specifically, this implies that the various mechanisms of surplus extraction to which peasants are subjected are not identified and that their transformation is not the aim of RDPs; consequently, neither is the transformation of the social relations that create and reproduce the patterns of surplus extraction the aim of RDPs. RDPs are specifically limited in scope to the development of the forces of production (through technological change, infrastructure construction, and the provision of credit) within a given set of internal and external social relations.

Detailed historical and empirical studies of the three project areas have demonstrated that the assumptions of traditionality and duality are untenable. In all three cases, as we saw in the previous section, the subsistence sector has been created by the development of capitalism in agriculture, is functionally related to the modern commercial sector to which it surrenders an economic surplus, and is subject to a rapid process of transformation and differentiation.

Indeed, students of peasantry who oppose the traditional dual approach have identified subordination to dominant classes and the resulting extraction of a surplus as the definitive characteristic of peasants.[34] Surplus is extracted via the product market (unfavorable prices due to lack of effective demand for wage foods, cheap-food price policies, monopolistic merchants, and poor infrastructure), the factor market (purchase of means of production at market prices that often include monopolistic margins and reflect industrial protectionism), the labor market (supply of semiproletarian labor at wages below the value of labor power), the land market (payment of rents in labor services, in kind, or in cash), the capital market (payment of interest often at usurious rates), and directly through the payment of taxes (tithes, sales taxes, and retentions). The consequence of this relation of domination is that peasants are incapable of capitalizing, not because they either do not want to (the behaviorist interpretation of folk culture according to which the peasant's objective is to ensure his survival year after year under the same material conditions) or do not generate any surplus (Schultz's and Tax's conceptualizations of traditional "penny capitalism"), but because the surplus they generate is siphoned out to the benefit of other social classes (functional dualism).

The peasant sector, from semiproletarians to family farms, is highly integrated into the capitalist economy through wages and the sale of products. Thus, in Cajamarca, while only 23 percent of the gross value of crops produced on the lower subfamily farms (less than 3.5 hectares) and a total of 40 percent of the gross value of all farm products are sold on the market, the important participation of wages (earned on the labor market) in total income implies that monetary income constitutes as much as 82 percent of total gross income. For family farms (11–30 hectares), monetary income is 81 percent of total gross income; but in this case, 76 percent of the gross value of all farm products is sold on the market. Yet this high degree of monetary integration is also a mechanism of extracting a surplus from the peasantry. During the 1973–75 period, when the project was effectively oriented toward peasants, the terms of trade for the commodities they bought and sold deteriorated at an annual rate of 8.6 percent. This deterioration of the terms of trade was part of an accelerating trend that began at least as far back as the early 1950s. Thus, the real price of wheat deteriorated by 12 percent between 1953–54 and 1960–64 and by 33 percent between 1960–64 and 1970–74. Similarly, the real price of potatoes deteriorated by 14 percent and 25 percent, respectively.[35]

Surplus extraction via the labor market is reflected in the 72 percent of peasant households that derive an average of 50 percent of their income from wages, while the average wage received is only on the order of 69 percent of the minimum legal rural wage. Although this minimum wage is only U.S. $1.00 per day, 89 percent of the peasants receive per day worked on their home plots a net return that is below this level, which clearly makes impossible either savings formation or investment.[36] In Garcia Rovira, 42 percent of the households pay rents in kind that are equal to half of their gross product, and the most extreme levels of poverty are found in that category of peasants.

In Puebla, the lower subfamily farms under 2 hectares (or 21 percent of the farms in the area) have a negative cash balance from farming activities: the cost outlays on purchased means of production exceed the gross income from sale of products. The deficit in the monetary balance is covered by other sources of cash income and in particular by wage earnings. It is indeed rational for these peasants to produce at a monetary loss as long as (1) the magnitude of this loss per unit of product is not greater than the price they would have to pay to acquire these consumption products on the market and (2) the total monetary loss does not exceed the net cash income from other sources, including credit. For semiproletarian peasants, the monetary accounting of farming activities appears as a net expenditure. Yet this is logical in the sense that it provides cheaper access to subsistence food than would reliance on the market.[37] For the whole category of subfamily farms (representing 58 percent of the farms in the area), the income from farming does not cover the opportunity cost of family labor and implies a negative rate of profit of −5.5 percent (Table 7.1). Clearly, these farms remain in production only because of the severe internal exploitation of family labor. And the low price of the products they deliver on the market is made possible only by the low implicit farm wage of semiproletarianized peasants. The differential rates of profit between commercial farms (+6.1 percent) and subfamily farms (−5.5 percent) are at the root of the process of social differentiation, which results in a tendency toward concentration of the land in commercial farms and increased proletarianization among subfamily peasants.

This interpretation of peasants as a dominated social group whose surplus is siphoned out has dramatic implications for the expected results of RDPs. If capital investment in peasant agriculture is jeopardized by surplus extraction, modernization schemes that aim at increasing surplus generation via technol-

Table 7.1.   Puebla: Profitability of Farm Activities by Farm Type, 1970

Farm type[a]	Net income without imputing labor (pesos)	Net income imputing labor costs (pesos)	Capital value[b] (pesos)	Profit rate[c] (percent)
I. Lower subfamily farms	1,503	−1,784	32,231	−5.5
II. Upper subfamily farms	2,254	1,104	36,104	3.1
III. Family farms	5,443	280	60,240	0.5
IV. Commercial farms	15,885	11,685	191,493	6.1

Source: Carlos Benito, "The Puebla Project," mimeographed (Berkeley: University of California, Department of Agricultural and Resource Economics, 1978).

[a] Farm types are defined as follows: I = 0–4 hectares and hired labor less than 33 percent of family labor, II = 0–4 hectares and hired labor more than 33 percent of family labor, III = 4–8 hectares, and IV = more than 8 hectares.

[b] Includes the value of the land.

[c] Ratio of net income imputing labor costs to capital value.

ogy and credit but that do not transform the channels of surplus extraction will likely result in increased surplus captured by the dominant groups and minimally improved economic conditions for the peasantry.[38] Any meaningful attempt at rural development would require that, first and foremost, the channels of surplus extraction be identified. The components of RDPs would then need to aim not only at increasing surplus generation but also at facilitating surplus retention. This would require introducing as integral components of RDPs the transformation of land tenure patterns (complementarity with land reform), the protection and stabilization of the terms of trade (ensuring a stable effective demand), the ensurance of minimum wages (so that increased farm incomes do not result in lower wages according to the logic of functional dualism), and the provision of institutional credit and new technological options. In general, the Puebla-type projects have concentrated only on these last components, credit and technology.

Semiproletarianization

Puebla-type RDPs were intended to reach the bulk of the rural poor. Rural poverty was believed to be found mainly among smallholders. As McNamara said in his 1973 Nairobi speech: "Clearly the bulk of the poor today are in the rural areas. . . . Within the rural areas the poverty problem revolves principally around the low productivity of the millions of small subsistence farms."[39] For this reason, the instruments of rural development consisted principally of credit, technology, infrastructure, extension, and access to public services.

This assumption has proven to be highly fallacious in all three areas studied. The bulk of the rural poor control a resource base that is so small and of such poor quality that agriculture can only ensure a fraction of subsistence needs (Tables 7.2 and 7.3). In Cajamarca, 72 percent of the households live on farms of less than 3.5 hectares, farms on which agriculture accounts for only 23 percent of net income; and on these smaller farms, corn, wheat, and barley, the crops toward which the project was oriented, generate only 5 percent of net income. Clearly, even the doubling of yields of these crops would have an insignificant effect on peasants' welfare. The bulk of nonfarm income derives from wages. In Cajamarca, 50 percent of the net income of the lower subfamily farms and 24 percent of that of the upper subfamily farms was obtained from employment on the labor market (Table 7.4). Only on family and commercial farms are farm activities a largely dominant source of net income, reaching 82 percent and 90 percent, respectively. Similarly, in Garcia Rovira, in spite of primitive development of the labor market, 32 percent of the peasant households earn an average of 48 percent of their net income from nonfarm sources.[40] And in Puebla, where the labor market is highly developed, 71 percent of the rural households in the project area also earn more than half of their income from nonfarming activities, in spite of the fact that average farm size for these households is relatively large (2.1 hectares).

Table 7.2. Cajamarca, Puebla, and Garcia Rovira: Distribution of Farms by Farm Type, 1970–73

Farm type[a]	Percentage of farms			Percentage of land area			Average farm size (hectares)		
	Cajamarca	Puebla	Garcia Rovira	Cajamarca	Puebla	Garcia Rovira	Cajamarca	Puebla	Garcia Rovira
I. Lower subfamily farms	72	58	32	6	32	6	1.1	2.1	1.0
II. Upper subfamily farms	17	13	38	7	7	22	5.8	2.2	2.8
III. Family farms	8	25	23	11	43	28	15.9	6.5	6.9
IV. Commercial farms	3	4	6	76	18	44	47.8	15.7	37.5

Sources: Cajamarca survey, 1973; Puebla survey, 1970; and Garcia Rovira survey, 1972.

[a] Farm types are defined as follows: in Cajamarca, I = 0–3.5 hectares, II = 3.5–11 hectares, III = 11–30 hectares, and IV = 30–100 hectares; in Puebla, I = 0–4 hectares and hired labor less than 33 percent of family labor, II = 0–4 hectares and hired labor more than 33 percent of family labor, III = 4–8 hectares, and IV = more than 8 hectares; in Garcia Rovira, I = 0–4 hectares, II = 4–10 hectares, III = 10–50 hectares, and IV = more than 50 hectares.

Table 7.3.   Cajamarca, Puebla, and Garcia Rovira:
Sources of Net Household Income by Farm Type

Farm type[a]	Farm income: percentage of total net income			Nonfarm income:[b] percentage of total net income		
	Cajamarca	Puebla	Garcia Rovira	Cajamarca	Puebla	Garcia Rovira
I. Lower subfamily farms	23	34	52	77	66	48
II. Upper subfamily farms	55	29	80	45	71	20
III. Family farms	82	65	78	18	35	22
IV. Commercial farms	90	64	100	10	36	0

Sources: Cajamarca survey, 1973; Puebla survey, 1970; and Garcia Rovira survey, 1972.

[a] Farm types are defined as follows: in Cajamarca, I = 0–3.5 hectares, II = 3.5–11 hectares, III = 11–30 hectares, and IV = 30–100 hectares; in Puebla, I = 0–4 hectares and hired labor less than 33 percent of family labor, II = 0–4 hectares and hired labor more than 33 percent of family labor, III = 4–8 hectares, and IV = more than 8 hectares; in Garcia Rovira, I = 0–4 hectares, II = 4–10 hectares, III = 10–50 hectares, and IV = more than 50 hectares.

[b] Nonfarm income includes income from the sale of labor power, artisan production, commerce, and remittances.

Clearly, despite its deceptive agrarian appearance, the bulk of today's peasantry is more *proletarian* than agricuturalist. Puebla-type RDPs can benefit only a small fraction of the peasants—those who are located on the family and upper subfamily farms, where the resource base is sufficient to make technological change economically meaningful. In Colombia, for example, this stratum constitutes a maximum of 19 percent of the rural families in all the IRDP areas.[41]

While the three projects started with a definition of their potential clientele that included all family and subfamily farms, this clientele was gradually redefined in Garcia Rovira (and in all the Colombian IRDPs) and Cajamarca to impose a lowe limit that left as eligible only the upper subfamily and family farms. This lower limit was set at about three hectares in Cajamarca when, in 1975, increased production became the thrust of government policy. This implied excluding from access to public research and extension services some 60–70 percent of the peasant families in the area. In Garcia Rovira, the lower limit for access to the agricultural services of the IRDP was redefined by stipulating that peasant households derive no less than two-thirds of their income from agriculture. If strictly enforced, this rule would have excluded 69 percent of the peasant households in the area. This "new realism" corresponded to identifying explicitly that stratum of farms endowed with a sufficient resource base for a Puebla-type project to have an impact on production levels. In Puebla, a more favorable natural environment and infrastructure and larger farm size among subfamily farms (2.1 hectares versus 1.1 hectares in Cajamarca and 1.0 hectare in Garcia Rovira) reduced the need for an equally stringent definition of clientele. While the clientele was thus spread over all

Table 7.4. Cajamarca: Sources of Net Household Income by Farm Type, 1973

Farm type[a]	Percentage of total net income									Median total net income (U.S.$)[b]
	Agricultural production	Agricultural processing	Animal production	Rental	Subtotal: all farm activities	Artisan production	Wage labor	Commerce	Remittance	
I. Lower subfamily farms	10.2	0.2	11.6	2.8	23.3	7.5	49.9	12.1	7.0	143
II. Upper subfamily farms	19.6	0.1	27.0	8.7	55.4	4.1	23.5	10.4	6.6	179
III. Family farms	42.0	0.2	24.4	15.4	82.0	2.1	11.4	3.6	0.9	292
IV. Commercial farms	26.1	0.1	62.1	1.3	89.6	0.7	5.7	3.3	0.7	356
Total	17.6	0.2	23.6	5.4	46.7	5.2	33.8	9.2	5.0	156

Source: Cajamarca survey, 1973.
[a] Farm types are defined as follows: I = 0–3.5 hectares, II = 3.5–11 hectares, III = 11–30 hectares, and IV = 30–100 hectares.
[b] In 1973 dollars.

farm sizes, the project nevertheless reached 38 percent of the commercial farms, 22 percent of the family farms, and only 18 percent of the subfamily farms in the area.

For the bulk of the rural poor, employment availability and wage levels are more important determinants of welfare than is agricultural productivity. The economic basis of the welfare of the rural poor is more akin to that of workers than to that of peasants and is sometimes in direct conflict with that of pure peasants (e.g., over the issues of food prices and rural wages). Welfare improvement requires a bettering of peasants' proletarian status or a drastic expansion in their control of resources in order to enable enhanced agricultural productivity to have a meaningful income effect. Puebla-type RDPs have neglected these two lines of action.

Labor Scarcity

The peasant sector was assumed to be characterized by surplus labor. This interpretation follows the assertions of Lewis, Ranis, and Fei, in their formulation of dual economy models, that the marginal productivity of labor in traditional agriculture is zero. Consequently, labor could be removed from agriculture with no loss in agricultural production. The consequent reduction in food-consumption needs in agriculture would permit the sustenance of this relocated population as industrial workers. Technological change in agriculture would be detrimental to economic growth: by increasing the productivity of labor in agriculture, it would also raise the opportunity cost of urban labor. The resulting wage increase would reduce the rate of capital accumulation and employment creation in the modern sector unless, of course, there existed a landlord class that was sufficiently powerful to fully tax away from peasants any extra product resulting from increased productivity. The presence of a landlord class is, in any case, essential to maintain constant wages in the face of the rising productivity of labor in agriculture that results from the absorption of surplus labor in industry. The classical dual economy models are thus of the same ideological bent as Malthus's two-sector models: they imply the need for a landlord class that reproduces rural poverty and creates effective demand for industry by the consumption of rents.[42] Hence, they are a scientific apology for disarticulated accumulation as a social structure for accelerated growth.

The controversy over surplus labor in agriculture that raged in the 1960s between "classical" (surplus labor) and "neoclassical" (no labor surplus) versions of dual economy models[43] is another typical example of misconceived debate resulting from the lack of specification of the mode of production and of the social class elements under discussion. The postulate of surplus labor is based on the empirical observation that labor availability far exceeds labor requirements in *commercial* capitalist agriculture, even while taking due account of the seasonality of labor use. In our opinion, this observation is correct, and we have cited the emergence of surplus labor in the late 1950s in

Latin America as an important factor in the liquidation of precapitalist social relations in agriculture and the rise of functional dualism.

Surplus labor relative to the needs of capitalist agriculture does not, however, imply that the marginal productivity of labor in peasant agriculture is zero. The many empirical studies of labor use in peasant agriculture by Schultz, Hopper, and others[44] led Schultz to conclude: "I know of no evidence for any poor country anywhere that would even suggest that a transfer of some small fraction, say, 5 percent, of the existing labor force out of agriculture, with other things equal, could be made without reducing its [agricultural] output."[45] This, of course, does not mean that the average productivity of labor is high. In Garcia Rovira, for example, the average employment of rural labor in peasant agriculture is only 57 percent of available labor. Yet it rises to 93 and 94 percent in the months of April and May, when corn and beans are seeded and weeded.[46] In Latin America today, the marginal productivity of labor in subsistence agriculture is not zero because of the high degree of semiproletarianization. In spite of the difficulty of finding employment and the low level of wages, external sources of income on the labor market establish a positive opportunity cost for labor.[47] To be adopted, the new technologies recommended by RDPs would need to increase the productivity of additional labor demands sufficiently for the income from this labor to exceed the opportunity cost at that particular time of the year. In Puebla, the new technology implied increased labor needs but did not sufficiently increase the productivity of labor to justify reallocation of labor between external work and farm work.[48] As a result, increased labor demands associated with the new technology constituted an effective bottleneck to adoption. And this bottleneck is likely to be more restrictive when, as in Puebla, the project concentrates on a single crop (the so-called "minimum package approach," in this case corn technology), which already constitutes the major activity in the area, than it is in projects that seek to increase labor demands in periods of slack, thereby increasing the average productivity of labor throughout the year instead of labor demand in the period of full employment. Determination of this opportunity cost is, however, complex. Some tasks can be performed only by adult males (e.g., plowing and participation in credit groups), while others can be distributed within the family among sexes and ages.[49] Furthermore, the opportunity cost of different family members varies widely throughout the life cycle and from region to region and season to season.

PROFITABILITY AND RISK

Given the structural characteristics of the peasant economy, its receptivity to new technology is conditioned by the economic worth of the change in terms of profitability (implicit wage effect) and risk. Profitability is determined physically by the nature of the technology offered and economically by the terms of trade for the peasant sector.

New Technologies for Peasant Agriculture

Turning first to the issue of technology, it is clear that the projects were organized in the belief that *new technological packages* did exist in experiment stations and that only local adaptation was needed to make them available for use in peasant agriculture. In all three projects, adaptive agronomic research was thus an integral part of the activities pursued. Definite methodological innovations were made, in particular by taking research into peasant fields and in this way linking research and extension.

In reality, new technologies that could be readily adapted to peasant agriculture proved to be unavailable. In Puebla, new corn varieties introduced by CIMMYT could not surpass the traditional varieties improved by local seed merchants (who cultivated them with the black waters of the city of Puebla, and hence under high fertility conditions, long before the era of the Green Revolution) and already widely used by peasants. As a result, technological recommendations essentially consisted of inducing peasants to use heavier fertilizer doses and greater plant densities with the same genetic material. In the process, the concept of "poor but efficient" was forgotten.[50] Peasants were told to increase the levels of factor use without introducing technological change and without carefully taking into account the features of peasant agricuture—ability to bear risk, labor constraints, symbiotic crop mixes, diet requirements, etc.—that had determined the current levels of factor use. As a result, those who followed the technological recommendations did not obtain better—and often obtained worse—economic results than those who remained with traditional technology. The poor but efficient often became inefficient and poorer. In addition, with the tremendous heterogeneity of peasant farms and households, global recommendations proved to be seriously unfit for the majority of customers.[51]

An overwhelming conclusion of the three projects is that, contrary to expectations, no significantly new technological packages capable of yielding increased net returns could be offered to peasants. The early withdrawal of CIMMYT's support from Puebla and Cajamarca was in recognition of this incapacity. Projects initiated to demonstrate that the Green Revolution, which had been developed to service commercial agriculture, could also benefit peasants could not fulfill this promise. Extensionists were reduced to observing what the best peasants in the area were doing and—rightly or wrongly—recommending to others to do the same. Consequently, the positive economic benefits from the projects derived not from technological change but from institutional change, whereby access to credit—and hence to existing technology for which cash purchases of fertilizers are needed—was made possible for groups previously excluded from access to institutional credit. As a result, a positive net income effect was derived in Puebla only by the subfamily farms.[52] For all the other social groups, the project had a negative economic effect. Similarly, in Garcia Rovira the net income effect of adopting the project's technological recommendations was generally negative.[53] And in Cajamarca, little peasant participation and a high turnover of participants reflected the unattractive economic benefits derived from the project's technological recommendations.[54]

Effective Demand

Profitability is a matter not only of technology but also of terms of trade and, in particular, of product versus fertilizer prices. In general, the projects were designed under the structuralist assumption that price conditions at the farm level are adequate to allow for profitable use of improved technology.[55] For this reason, the projects did not regard the terms of trade as an issue deserving particular attention and concentrated instead on technological and credit constraints.

Analysis of the three projects shows this assumption to be highly fallacious: the production of wage foods in peasant agriculture is characterized by highly unfavorable and often deteriorating terms of trade that block the penetration of capital and constitute an important mechanism of surplus extraction. Puebla was an exception in this regard, which largely explains the relative success of that project compared to the other two. In Mexico, corn prices are stabilized by law, and fertilizer prices are highly subsidized. The price ratio of nitrogen to corn at the farm level in Puebla was 5.6 in 1971 and 3.2 in 1975.[56] In Garcia Rovira and Cajamarca, by contrast, this price ratio was on the order of 7. As a general rule, application of fertilizer to corn is unlikely to be profitable and pass the acceptable level of risk when this ratio exceeds 5 or 6.[57]

In general, the problem of effective demand and price suppression for wage foods is one of the most serious constraints on rural-development efforts. The orientation of commercial agriculture toward the production of exportables, industrial inputs, and luxury foods and the relegation of many wage foods to peasant agriculture result precisely from unfavorable prices for the latter and the capacity of peasant agriculture to withstand those prices by forgoing rent, the return to financial capital, and decent living conditions. In this sense, rural proverty is the image of urban poverty. As Edward David, one of the leaders of the German Social Democratic party, said in 1894 in defense of the economic viability of peasant farming: "The problem of the worker is the problem of the peasant. . . . Who[ever] retains from the worker his full salary also retains it from the peasant."[58] Low urban wages and urban unemployment result in limited effective demand and suppression of wage-food prices. The consequence is functional dualism in agricuture and blockage of the farmer road to development. Clearly, the countervailing efforts of RDPs cannot be successful if they are guided by an agrarian strategy alone. On the contrary, they would require simultaneously (1) development of the productive forces in peasant agriculture (technological change and increased access to means of production and to public institutions); (2) surplus retention to permit accumulation and modernization; and (3) increased effective demand for wage foods to permit creation of a financial surplus. Successful rural development thus depends on a national strategy of development that attacks the whole logic of disarticulated accumulation.

Risk

The projects were designed with the explicit recognition that risk aversion is an important aspect of peasant behavior. High risks are indeed associated with adoption of recommended practices for the cultivation of rainfed crops. The new technological packages developed and field tested under adequate moisture conditions often performed worse than traditional technologies when subjected to rainfall deficiencies. And to implement the recommended technologies in Puebla, farmers experienced a 90 percent increase in costs, chiefly in the form of higher fertilizer outlays (166 percent increase) and expenditures for animal and labor power (16 percent increase).[59] In this case a crop insurance service was established, but it covered only the loan (the bank) and not the farmer's subsistence needs. Due to limited knowledge of the significance of risk for peasants, recommendations were not adequately tailored to attitudes toward risk.[60] As a result, recommended packages were rarely fully adopted; and peasants settled for levels of factor use that were intermediate between traditional and recommended.

DIFFUSION STRATEGY

Given the structural context of peasant farming and the availability of profitable new technologies, the diffusion of new technologies among the clientele of RDPs is conditioned by the extension model followed, the effectiveness of the management of the project, and the ability to remove institutional constraints.

Extension Model

Following the Puebla example, the Garcia Rovira and Cajamarca projects adopted an extension model that was definitely "top-down" and paternalistic.[61] Despite declared intentions to foster and use peasant organizations, existing organizations were systematically by-passed. In Puebla, new peasant associations (the "solidarity groups") were founded for the specific and restricted purpose of obtaining credit collectively. In the other projects, only individual relations were established between extension agent and peasant. Active participation of peasants in the resolution of their problems and, in particular, in the identification of constraints and priorities for change was not encouraged, nor was collective action to improve access to technology, institutions, and markets. The diffusion model followed (neoextension) was not significantly different from the traditional "banking" extension model; only this time it was applied to a clientele stretching downward to the family and upper subfamily farms.[62] As a result, the cost of delivery of recommended practices was extremely high and the outreach capacity of the projects was severely limited by personnel and budget constraints. The most significant innovation introduced was the linkage between research and extension obtained by conducting experiments in farmers' fields and using them for demonstration purposes (field days).

The reason farmer organizations were not used was, of course, a consequence of the history of peasant militancy and the political situation in each project area. In Cajamarca, the slow rate of implementation of the land reform had permitted the traditional power structure to mobilize many unorganized small and medium farmers against the reform and any public (e.g., SINAMOS) or private organization likely to be associated with it. With public and peasant organizations committed to the reform, use of these organizations by the project was impossible because rural development rightly appeared to them to be a substitute for land reform. In Garcia Rovira, radicalization of the peasant movement under the leadership of the Asociación Nacional de Usuarios Campesinos placed it in open opposition to ICA's rural-development effort which was denounced as reactionary, aimed at breaking the political power of the peasantry by creating a privileged minority, and economically infeasible due to urban poverty and lack of effective demand for wage foods.[63] Discrepancies between peasant and project objectives again blocked the possibility of collective action.

The effectiveness of the diffusion strategy cannot be judged in isolation from the political purposes of rural development. Since rural development was defined as a strategy of distributing credit and technology instead of land, and of using this as a means of political control of the peasantry, peasant organizations could not be simultaneously involved and kept in check. On the contrary, the projects were organized as autonomous or semiautonomous agencies to systematically by-pass and undermine peasant organizations and obtain direct control over a privileged stratum of peasants. In this sense, the dominant political purpose of rural development (control and co-option to prevent social change) negated its very effectiveness as an economic strategy (increased delivery of cheap wage foods).

Institutional Linkages

The projects were designed under the assumption that not only primitive technology but also lack of access to public institutions were effectively constraining the modernization of peasant agriculture. This interpretation of poverty corresponded to the theory of marginality that was so influential in the social programs of the Christian Democrats in Chile. The projects also followed this recommended line of action: that the incorporated should share with the poor some of their privileges by granting to those previously excluded some degree of integration with (access to) the institutions of society. It applied in this case to banking services; agronomic research and extension; and, in integrated projects, to the consumption of public goods and services such as health services, school lunch programs, education, infrastructure, etc.

Within their limited spheres of influence, Puebla-type projects have indeed increased the linkage of peasants with public services. And institutions have been induced to better coordinate their actions at the regional level and tailor some of their services to the needs of peasants. To a large extent, failure on the technological front has been compensated by institutional integration, which, for example, ensured the economic viability of the Puebla and Garcia Rovira projects.

However, the problem of organizing the public sector to permit integration of the peasantry raises serious conflicts. At the pilot stage, institutional linkage and coordination have been obtained on a voluntaristic basis; and the managerial capacity of the project director has been a major determinant of the successes obtained. Once the projects expand beyond that stage, the increased demands on institutions require explicit commitments, and coordination needs to be formalized. In Colombia, two alternative models have been tried, both of which involve difficulties. From 1970 to 1975, the Colombian Agricultural Institute was in charge of RDPs and of coordinating the participation of other supporting agencies. As a result, it was drawn into areas where it had no experience and had to deal with institutions over which it had no formal authority. After 1975, the coordination of the thirteen agencies participating in the IRDPs became the responsibility of the National Department of Planning. Since this agency has no field staff and no implementation capacity, coordination is ensured by budgetary appropriations for the participating agencies and by periodic critical evaluations. The Agrarian Bank distributes and certifies the use of the funds. Coordination is hence assured completely from above and by means of controls that are definitely quite weak. And since these agencies have traditionally been semiautonomous fiefs, actual coordination is minimal. This fragmentation of the public sector, which we have identified as one of the typical characteristics of the peripheral state, creates a major stumbling block to integrated rural development.

THE POLITICAL ECONOMY OF INTEGRATED RURAL DEVELOPMENT

It is clear that the economic effect of rural-development projects has been relatively minimal due to the combination of factors mentioned above. Some of these factors can be overcome within the economic and political context of disarticulated accumulation. This applies in particular to the development of an adequate technology for peasant farming and the organization of an effective diffusion strategy. Indeed, major efforts have recently been made in this direction, as the popularity of the search for "intermediate technologies" evidences. With sufficient resource funds from international assistance agencies and with enough time, there is every reason to expect that some technological breakthroughs can be made in peasant farming, but these breakthroughs will almost inevitably be accessible only to those peasants who are most favored in terms of control of resources and access to markets.

Other factors, however, can hardly be overcome without challenging the whole social structure associated with the logic of disarticulated accumulation in the post–land reform and post–Green Revolution period. This is the case with the extraction of surpluses from peasants via cheap food, with the appropriation of the land by commercial agriculture and the consequent marginalization of the peasantry on a minimal and deteriorating resource base, and with the lack of effective demand corresponding to urban poverty and unemployment.

The result is that the economic effect of rural-development projects will rarely be spectacular and will be systematically confined to the upper strata of accommodated peasants, a definition of clientele evidenced in the three projects we studied. With the bulk of the Latin American peasantry already highly differentiated, the large majority of peasants are more proletarian than producer and consequently are beyond the reach of rural-development projects. These projects thus focus on the creation of a pampered minority fringe of petty bourgeois who serve as an essential buffer between bourgeoisie and semiproletarianized and landless peasants: their economic interests are tied to those of the bourgeoisie while their ideological identification lies with the bulk of peasants, who recognize them as political patrons. In situations where social disarticulation negates the possibility of co-opting labor under social democratic arrangements and where sheer repression is not possible or sufficient, the petty bourgeoisie becomes a politically stabilizing element: separation replaces co-option and complements repression.

There exists, however, a contradiction between the political end of rural development (political stabilization) and the economic instruments used for this purpose (credit, new technologies, infrastructure investments, and information). If rural development is indeed successful in developing among upper subfamily and family peasants the ability to accumulate capital, the development of capitalism would then follow the farmer road and lead inevitably to social differentiation and to the negation of the petty bourgeois character of these peasants. Disseminated, the instruments of modernization would lead to concentration of the land at the expense of the medium and lower subfamily farms and to accelerated dispossession and proletarianization of the mass of peasants. This is inevitable since those peasants who successfully modernize need to expand the scale of their operations and make use of hired labor to

meet higher costs and effectively compete against the well-established commercial sector. And land is available to them only from worse-off peasants.
As a result, successful implementation of rural-development projects effectively negates their very purpose. Agricultural development projects directed
at commercial agriculture developed the forces of production at the political
cost of increased landlessness, proletarianization, and immiserization of peasants, and thus also developed a need for rural development to yield a harvest
of legitimating results. Inevitably, the very same process will be repeated
here, but this time among the rural poor themselves. As Feder puts it, "The
'small green revolution' which the [World] Bank wants to carry out in the
smallholder sector will have consequences similar to those of the big Green
Revolution, except that it will be still more disastrous in terms of greater
poverty, unemployment, landlessness, and hopelessness."[64]

This contradiction can be overcome only through serious political control of
social differentiation within the peasantry. This requires close state control
over the access to credit, the mechanisms of surplus extraction, and the
circulation of land in order to maintain a check on the displacement of peasants. Today, only in Mexico does the *ejido* system offer some check—though
quite an imperfect one—on peasant differentiation, and only in Mexico is
rural development being implemented on a large and increasing scale. This
also requires the severe repression of peasant organizations and movements in
order to prevent the frustrated expectations of vertical mobility among the
majority of semiproletarian peasants excluded from the projects from turning
into destabilizing political forces. The contradiction of rural-development
projects is thus both overcome and re-created at the level of the state in the
form of increased direct state control over the sphere of production and in the
fiscal, legitimacy, and administrative limits of the state.

For the bulk of the semiproletarianized and landless peasantry, further
"depeasantization" leads to an upward pressure on wages to meet subsistence
needs which contradicts the objective logic of functional dualism under socially disarticulated accumulation. To counteract this tendency, "basic-
needs" programs have been initiated through which public amenities are
distributed to the rural poor. By thus putting the world's poor on welfare, they
constitute the last card of the disarticulated alliance in attempting to reproduce
the objective possibility of functional dualism. Today, they are at the core of
the programs of international agencies.[65] And here again their limits are
defined by the fiscal, legitimacy, and admistrative crises of the state.

8

The Agrarian Question
and Change in Latin America:
Conclusions

Having analyzed the two components of the agrarian question—unequal
agricultural growth and rural poverty—we now turn to the policy and political
implications of the analytical conclusions we have reached. In this chapter,
we will briefly survey the most recent policy-oriented thought on economic
and agrarian underdevelopment, then criticize this thought in terms of our
analysis—thus providing a summary of the analysis itself—and, finally, explain some of the policy and political implications of our perspective.

POLICY PROPOSALS FOR GROWTH WITH EQUITY

It is clear that there has been, since the early 1970s, a marked shift in mainstream development economics. This shift was motivated by recognition that
the "Development Decade" strategy of accelerating economic growth, while
generally successful in its effect on gross national product, failed to improve
the welfare of the poor through the expected "trickle-down" effects on employment and wages. As we have seen, the relative position of the poor in most
countries of the periphery has worsened. There is also substantial evidence of
absolute deterioration in the living standards of the poorest groups in many
countries. Given this evidence, and given the need (for political or humanitarian reasons, or both) to do something about poverty, Western development
economists have proposed a series of alternative programs for equitable
growth.[1] The most significant of these programs are summarized in the following sections.

Employment Creation

In studying unemployment in several countries, the International Labour Organization observed that the high rate of growth of the 1960s had been extremely capital intensive.[2] In fact, growth had been so capital intensive in some countries that it resulted in an inverse relation between accumulation and employment creation. This finding, when coupled with the obvious fact that the poor are unemployed, and vice-versa, naturally led to a call for labor-intensive growth as a policy for equitable growth. This, in turn, has led to the recommendation of policies that would encourage cottage industries and the "informal sector," promote the development of efficient labor-intensive "intermediate" technologies, and eliminate market "distortions" that artificially cheapen capital goods and increase labor costs.

Integrated Rural Development

The observation, especially by agricultural economists, that the growth of the 1960s was concentrated in the urban industrial sector, while agriculture lagged behind, has led to a renewed emphasis on the need to foment development of the rural sector.[3] However, simultaneous observation of the disparity-increasing consequences of mere agricultural growth, such as that fomented by the Green Revolution, made it impossible simply to recommend agricultural growth via support prices, improved infrastructure, technological innovations, and extension programs. Instead, the promotion of technical change was to be specifically oriented toward small holders. And it was to be accompanied by the provision of public amenities such as health, nutrition, and education programs. These proposals are behind the strategy of integrated rural development launched by the World Bank and the U.S. Agency for International Development in 1973.[4]

Redistribution with Growth and Basic Needs

Both employment creation and integrated rural development would be means of redistributing income through a redirection of growth. Economists at the World Bank and the Overseas Development Council have argued, however, that income redistribution via changes in orientation of investment or changes in the target groups of growth programs is itself too indirect a way of approaching the problem of the living standard of the poor.[5] They therefore suggest a basic-needs approach that calls essentially for direct state provision of the components of an improved standard of welfare to the poor. Thus, Paul Streeten claims that "the essence of the case for basic needs is that it enables us to achieve a widely agreed upon, high-priority objective in a shorter period, and with fewer resources, than if we took the roundabout route of only raising employment and incomes."[6] In that sense, "implementing basic needs is a more operational goal than equality.''[7] The classic example of this approach is that of Sri Lanka, where basic needs were covered (in spite of low per capita income levels) through public subsidies to the poor in the form of free grain deliveries, food subsidies, and cheap health and educational services.[8]

New International Economic Order

Aware of the imperfections in the economic relations among nations, some economists have called for a new international economic order as at least a component of the strategy to improve the income position of the poor in the underdeveloped countries. This would involve:

Greater access to the markets of the developed nations, especially for labor-intensive industrial products of the periphery.

Improved access to world capital markets and debt relief, since it is clear that the austerity programs demanded of Third World governments as conditions for access to capital under current arrangements imply onerous loads for the poor.

Stabilization of primary commodity markets, which would make it easier for the periphery to reemphasize the growth of primary-sector exports.

Greater volumes of foreign aid.

These demands were spelled out at the Seventh Special Session of the U.N. General Assembly and have been the subject of protracted negotiations between countries of the North and South since then.[9]

Redistribution Before Growth

The previous propositions all imply that redistribution of income should occur either after or concurrently with growth. Instead of growth with redistribution, Irma Adelman questions the structural context within which growth occurs and proposes a strategy of redistribution before growth.[10] This approach, which is based on the historical examples of Taiwan and South Korea, implies that as a precondition for equitable and rapid growth, assets must be redistributed, especially through extensive land reform, and massive educational and human capital formation programs must be organized. It is also presumed to require authoritarian governments to muster the necessary political power for at least the redistributive and take-off phases of this process.

Obviously, several aspects of these proposals for equitable growth overlap. For example, much of the normative literature on integrated rural development presumes the prior equitable distribution of land and hence is linked with the redistribution-before-growth approach.[11] Yet this categorization of proposals is useful for purposes of analysis and discussion.

The broadest criticism that can be, indeed must be, leveled at all these reformist positions is their theoretical poverty. Either they approach the problem of policy prescription in an ad hoc way or they lack an adequate theory of poverty upon which to base action on poverty. This is more blatant in some of the positions than in others. The basic-needs approach, for example, has absolutely no theoretical foundation; nor does it really need one, being, as it is, nothing more than institutionalized charity based on evident presumptions such as its "operationality" (to use Streeten's term) vis-à-vis the more abstract goal of reducing inequality. The advocates of basic needs themselves admit this theorectical indigence: "We are ignorant about the conditions that lead to an effective and determined basic needs approach to development."[12]

This lack of an adequate theory of poverty has a clear cause. In all the above cases, the inequitable growth that is deemed undesirable is conceptualized in the framework of neoclassical growth theory. In this context, the condemnation of poverty can lead to only one of the following three positions:

1. If growth does not alleviate poverty, it is simply because it has not been rapid enough or because increasing inequality is the necessary cost of the early stages of economic growth. The first interpretation is sustained by economists like Walter Galenson, who claims that "growth has not 'failed'; there has simply not been enough of it in the great majority of less developed nations."[13] The implication is that growth must be systematically accelerated, while the reforms advocated by international agencies to promote equity should be opposed: "It is distinctly unhelpful to call for 'massive, wide-ranging attacks' on the maldistribution of income without any evidence that such policies have even worked, or are likely to be anything but a shortcut to disaster."[14]

The second interpretation is defended by advocates of the divergence-convergence (or "Kuznets U") hypothesis, according to which one inescapable law of economic development is that relative income inequality increases during the early stages of growth before ultimately decreasing at later stages of industrialization.[15] This law implies that greater equity is only a matter of patience, that redistributive measures would only slow down growth, and that the best way of helping the poor is to grow as fast as possible.

Yet while strongly entrenched in the economic profession, it is this grow-or-bust position which the advocates of equitable growth denounce, in spite of their neoclassical affinities, for both political and humanitarian reasons.

2. The other logical condemnation of poverty in the context of neoclassical theory derives from exposing the existence of distortions that prevent the free operation of markets and the consequent equalization of inequalities through efficient factor reallocation. As we have seen, this is at the heart of the monetarist position, and its principal policy implication is the need to eliminate government economic interventions so as to restore perfect competition.[16]

Again, the neoclassical advocates of growth with equity denounce this interpretation as being correct but insufficient. They do so principally because the distribution of income would remain highly unequal even if maximal efficiency in resource use were obtained. And as recent comprehensive econometric modeling has demonstrated for the Philippines and South Korea, even substantial policy interventions within the existing structure affect the size distribution of income only marginally.[17] These simulation studies thus lead to the conclusion that "only a massive, wide-ranging, balanced, and continued attack on poverty and maldistribution of income has much chance of succeeding; lesser modifications to existing strategies will fail."[18] For this purpose, "fundamental changes in social structure and institutions are likely to be needed."[19]

3. At this point, the limits of neoclassical theory in dealing with the issue of poverty have been reached. Political and structural changes are deemed important in reconciling growth and equity; yet politics and structures are outside the realm of neoclassical theory, which deals with efficiency questions only within a given political and structural context. Strategies for equitable growth are consequently advanced on an ad hoc and voluntary basis.

THE LIMITS OF REFORMISM

Any proposal to eliminate poverty and improve the distribution of income within and among nations needs to originate in a positive analysis of the sources of unequal development. In this study, we chose the perspective of political economy to develop a theory of the laws of motion of capital in the center-periphery structure that would explain unequal growth and poverty and, consequently, the nature of the agrarian question in Latin America.

Taking the political economy approach means basing one's analysis on the concept of social classes as contradictory components of the social whole. The nature of this contradiction and the pattern of its development reveal the dynamics of the social system. The state, in particular, is seen as both an objective and an instrument of class struggle. Specific policies, especially those that institutionalize and reinforce inequitable growth in the case in point, are thus understood as key links between contradictory class relations and the dynamics of the social whole. That is, policies are the outcome of the attempted resolution, at the level of the state, of crises that arise from class contradictions; and it is policies that condition the development of the economic and social system, in particular its performance in terms of growth and distribution. Our analysis is therefore centered on the study of the policy expression of class relations and the influence of these policies on development.

The theory of underdevelopment we have developed in this book is based on the changing nature of the internal class structure of Third World nations and of international class alliances. The key concepts we have used are, on the one hand, mode of production, which permits us to locate class positions, and, on the other, surplus generation, extraction, and use, which allows us to understand both the sources of growth or stagnation and the pattern of income distribution.

On the basis of these criteria, we distinguished between two broad periods in the recent social transformations of Latin America: (1) the period that, generally speaking, comprised the 1950s and included the development of import-substitution industrialization, a time when there still were significant remnants of noncapitalist social relations in agriculture (semifeudal and petty-commodity); and (2) the period of the 1960s and 1970s, when the capitalist mode of production defined essentially all class positions, including that of peasants.

The class structure in the first period still largely corresponded to the social relations established by the colonizers for the purpose of generating an extractable surplus. Based on strong relations of extraeconomic coercion over labor—mandated by labor scarcity and implemented by powerful agrarian oligarchies—the surplus generated was of an absolute nature and investment took place largely for the purpose of expanding commodity production aimed at satisfying foreign demand or the consumption of luxuries by precapitalist elites and the comprador class. Import-substitution industrialization itself— while initially oriented toward satisfying both wage-goods and luxury demands—increasingly found its dynamics in the association with foreign capital and the expansion of a domestic market for luxuries.

As surplus labor emerged and political pressures against coercive labor relations intensified, the transition to capitalism in agriculture occurred following one of two broad roads. One was the transformation of social relations without change in the social and geographical location of the market, in the distribution of assets, or in control over the state. In the large majority of cases, it was this *junker road* that occurred. And the antifeudal land reforms of the 1960s fundamentally served to ratify this form of transition. The other road implied that the power of the landed elites and comprador classes would be greatly curtailed and that capitalists of a petty, rather than a semifeudal, origin would participate in the control of the state. Along this *farmer road,* land reform against the landed elites resulted in redistribution of the land and in a more egalitarian growth process. In Latin America, however, land reforms that supported the transition to the farmer road (in Mexico and Chile) or shifts between junker and farmer roads (in Peru) never constituted full-scale national bourgeois revolutions.[20] These reforms were always too limited, too unequal, and too late relative to urban-industrial development. As a result, they were unable to counteract dependency relations and break class alliances between dependent bourgeoisies and foreign capital.

As a positive science, neoclassical growth theory and the associated ideology of pluralist democratic political science were predicated on the assumption that the underlying structural conditions were those of a petty bourgeois society. Therefore, the only countries in which the theory explained the occurrence of solid, equitable growth were at best those where modernizing national bourgeois revolutions had occurred. But in areas such as Latin America, this assumption does not hold.

Advocates of dependency theory and the development-of-underdevelopment school similarly began with an incorrect and ahistorical characterization of the underlying socioeconomic structure. By focusing on the sphere of circulation, they assumed that Latin American countries have been thoroughly capitalist from the beginning. By basing their arguments largely on empirical evidence about a period when the social relations of capitalism had not yet developed thoroughly but were still in a process of transition, they were forced to conclude that the lack of autonomous growth observed was due not to the nature of surplus generation and its appropriation and disposition by landed elites and comprador oligarchies but to the withdrawal of the investable surplus in favor of center nations; hence, their emphasis on pillage, repatriation of superprofits, and unequal exchange in trade.

A perspective from which capitalist development is seen as the development of capitalism (using the concepts of modes of production and their associated social relations and class positions) and which recognizes that there have been different, historically specific roads in this development overcomes the shortcomings of both of the above theories. It can explain why there is inequitable growth in terms of the social and geographical location of the sphere of circulation and in terms of authoritarian relations between capital and labor, both of which are typical of countries in which capitalist development is based on a class structure that is not radically different from that of the precapitalist period and where external class alliances are important determinants of internal class positions. Unlike dependency theory, it admits to an interpretation of the law of unequal development whereby rapid growth and industrialization can occur in the periphery, even though this growth is precarious and systematically accompanied by worsening income distribution.

The crucial elements of the perspective we have developed involve the notions of social disarticulation and (contradictory) functional dualism. The first refers to a structure where socially and geographically the final-goods market is located principally in profits and rents (luxury goods) and abroad (exports). This structure dissociates market expansion from real wage increases and leaves the determination of real wages to the balance of political forces. It is the image of a class structure dominated by an associated dependent import-substituting bourgeoisie, which is the direct descendant of a landed elite and a merchant oligarchy.

Functional dualism is the contradictory mechanism whereby the disarticulated economy satisfies its need for cheap labor by taking advantage of the large masses of semiproletarianized peasants created by the dissolution of precapitalist relations. This mechanism of primitive accumulation, which allows wages to be driven below the cost of maintenance and reproduction of labor power, is itself contradictory because it simultaneously functionalizes peasants to the needs of disarticulated capital accumulation and negates their reproduction as agriculturalists by differentiating them into the essential classes of the capitalist mode. The destruction of peasant and artisan production (the "informal sector"), which occurs prematurely relative to the absorptive capacity of the modern sector, is thus an important contribution to poverty. Under these conditions, absolute poverty can be seen as the dialectical counterpart of disarticulated growth: it is the social image of cheap labor obtained through functional dualism and a mechanism of social control (ignorance and malnutrition). And so are authoritarian states, which act as the guarantors of cheap labor and favorable "investment climates" for the disarticulated alliance. Inequality also is a counterpart of disarticulated growth: the expansion of the domestic market for luxuries depends on the increasing regressivity of income distribution, while the market for wage goods only widens through proletarianization.

On the basis of this perpective, we can make a critical assessment of the recent policy proposals for equitable growth.

The changes advocated by proponents of the New International Economic Order (NIEO) clearly have the potential of perfecting the internationalization of capital and enhancing the global efficiency of the world capitalist system. They can, on this basis, further accelerate growth in the periphery. But if they refuse to consider the social and structural foundations of this growth, their welfare impact on the world's poor can only be insignificant. In the few countries where there have been extensive redistributive reforms (e.g., Taiwan and South Korea), the poor may benefit from accelerated growth. But in the majority of others, where social disarticulation and functional dualism are the engines of accumulation, the welfare impact on the poor can only be negligible. As William Cline thus observes in his extensive empirical study of the potential impact of NIEO propositions, "The extent of world poverty is so massive that even if virtually *all* of the changes advocated by the developing countries could be enacted, the result still would be only a moderate increase in per capita income of the poor countries."[21] Even for advocates of the NIEO, this implies the sobering conclusion that redistribution of income on a world scale and equitable growth cannot be entrusted to eventual successful NIEO negotiations.

The employment-creation, integreated-rural-development, redistribution-with-growth, and basic-needs strategies can all be understood in either one of two contrasted ways. Either they can be seen as constraints on growth imposed fundamentally for purposes of political legitimation—itself legitimized as humanitarian concern—and hence to reproduce class positions, or they can be seen as the objectives of social and structural changes aimed at reconciling growth and distribution.

The validity of these diametrically contrasted interpretations stresses the obvious fact that economic policy without political economy is a useless and utopian exercise. To the extent that policies are perceived as the expression, at the level of the state, of specific contradictions and of the attempted resolutions of those differences, policy recommendations cannot be understood without a theory of the state. And it is indeed the purpose of political economy to help clarify which class (and fraction-of-a-class) interests are at stake in different policies and why the state may act on their behalf.

As we have shown in this book, the programs of integrated rural development implemented within current agrarian structures can have only an extremely narrow clientele of upper peasants. This is due to the advanced process of social differentiation whereby the large majority of rural poor are highly proletarianized and more dependent on employment and wages for their subsistence than on agricultural production. For the minority of upper peasants for whom rural development is potentially meaningful, successful programs hinge crucially on the availability of an adequate technology and on remunerative terms of trade. The latter is a particularly difficult policy variable to manipulate because unfavorable terms of trade are directly linked to the structure of disarticulated accumulation through cheap-food policies and the lack of effective demand: one is a prerequisite for cheap labor, and the other is its immediate consequence.

For the majority of semiproletarianized peasants, rural development could be effective only after implementation of massive redistributive land reforms. Yet as we have seen it, while land reform remains an active political issue, it is no longer a policy issue: antifeudal land reforms have been successfully completed; the domination of agriculture by capitalist farmers implies a growing trade-off between equity and efficiency; and dominance of the disarticulated alliance dissociates income redistribution from the need for markets created out of improved peasant incomes. As for the minority of upper peasants who could benefit from rural-development projects, the fact that they constitute a fraction of a class with a contradictory location under capitalism implies that their differentiation and elimination are accelerated by rural development. Thus, the objective of political stabilization via class separation (by means of a petty bourgeoisie) is negated when rural development is effective economically, for it further enchances class polarization.

The idea of redistribution before growth is the most progressive of the proposals reviewed because it allows us to question the distribution of assets and hence the existing social class structure. What it proposes, however, is to re-create the type of petty bourgeois society that has allowed equitable growth in the past. As a policy prescription, it is of dubious value. First, appealing to the "political will" of the elites as a prerequisite for policy implementation is idealistic and utopian. As such a prescription, redistribution before growth is another example of policy without political economy. Second, there are few, if any, countries in Latin America where an antifeudal alliance between liberal and radical forces could promote a successful national bourgeois revolution.

This is because, as we have seen, precapitalist social relations have by now essentially disappeared. Consequently, a land reform against the landed elite could no longer be organized as a political mobilization to transform social relations. Third, the process of disarticulated capitalist accumulation is already so advanced and powerfully backed by international alliances that a national bourgeois revolution capable of displacing the disarticulated class alliance has proved illusory for the last fifty years in Latin America. Nevertheless, where the process of capitalist disarticulated accumulation has become such a grotesque parody of itself, a class alliance between capitalists and the popular classes against the elite could form, as it did in Nicaragua in 1979. There, it was the miniscule size of the elite in comparison to the lands and assets it controlled, the consequent lack of investment opportunities for the nonelite capitalists, and the government's lack of legitimacy in its exercise of severe repression that made possible a capitalist-supported national revolution.

To be a meaningful proposition, the strategy of redistribution before growth thus begs a theory of transition. And such a theory can derive only from political economy.

THE POLITICAL ECONOMY OF EQUITABLE GROWTH

It is clear that at this stage of development of the world capitalist system—with massive poverty, malnutrition, and extraordinarily unequal distribution of income among and within nations—only a basic-needs approach can deal with world poverty. Even if growth is not immiserizing, resource and environmental limits imply that the growth rates in agricultural and industrial production required to satisfy basic needs within a lifetime under the current national and international distribution of income simply could not be sustained.[22] Yet this strategy of basic needs is not to be understood as an income constraint on growth, as proposed by Streeten and others, whereby minimum income levels have to be ensured for all via the distribution of public amenities while growth is stimulated. On the contrary, it should be understood as an effort to achieve the structural changes needed to reconcile growth and distribution and to make the satisfaction of basic needs the essential purpose of economic growth. As growth occurs and personal incomes increase, basic needs are continuously redefined beyond mere subsistence and are met in accordance with the rising productivity of labor.

The structural criterion of social articulation provides an effective guideline for policy making aimed at satisfying basic needs. It gives us a theory of planning and the choice of technique: what to produce and how to produce it should always be assessed in terms of contributions to social articulation. It also gives us the basis for a theory of international trade that goes beyond both the static Ricardian theory of comparative advantage and Emmanuel's and Amin's theory of comparative advance (according to which new investments should always be in those activities where relative productivity gains are greatest). Clearly, social articulation does not imply autarky, self-reliance, and delinking.[23] Japan, with its resource and energy poverty and its consequent need to export in order to import, is a good proof of this. What social articulation gives us is a set of guidelines as to how to manage trade in such a fashion that it sustains, not opposes, the relation between growth and distribution. In particular, it permits us to define the optimal balance between food self-sufficiency and comparative-advantage strategies in each specific situation.

An important question at this stage, and possibly one of the most controversial issues for development economists, is whether growth itself is articulating: does growth in disarticulated export enclaves or in import-substitution industrializing countries lead (through the creation of employment and hence through a growing domestic market for wage goods) to gradual changes in the production structure that result in social articulation? The divergence-convergence $\cup$ hypothesis is in point of fact a reduced-form law that is based on this structural hypothesis. The theoretical existence of a "Lewis turning point" in dual economy models, where an economy evolves, under the thrust of growth and the consequent resorption of surplus labor, from a disarticulated classical model to an articulated neoclassical model is the formalization of the same hypothesis.

As we have argued in this book, the structures of social articulation and disarticulation are the economic images of sharply contrasted patterns of social class alliances. Each of these alliances, when dominant, has its own laws of reproduction and, in particular, makes use of its control of the state to attempt perpetuation of the social status quo. As a result, there is no mechanistic reason why the contradictions of disarticulated accumulation, originating in the process of growth, should necessarily be resolved through subsequent articulation: the resolution of these contradictions can just as well be postponed (and, hence, the contradictions enhanced) through the call on foreign capital and food; concentration in the distribution of income; greater extroversion of the economy; and the use of co-option, segmentation, separation, and repression—all of which reproduce and deepen social disarticulation. The ultimate resolution of these contradictions is a matter of social change and hence of class struggle and is by no means guaranteed to occur, as in the $\cup$ hypothesis and at the Lewis turning point, evolutively and under the capitalist order. Some recent work by Charles Wright has, in fact, shown that there is no empirical support for the $\cup$ hypothesis in less-developed countries.[24] And except in Japan, the quest for historical Lewis turning points has indeed proved illusory.[25] Wright's results, by contrast, show that it is not stages of growth but institutional structures and governmental policies that determine the distribution of income at any income level.

Since growth does not articulate, structural change needs to occur as a product of social change: economic policies for articulation obtain via the politics of articulation. And the politics of articulation is essentially that of mass mobilization toward the establishment of mass-based democratic regimes.

Clearly the strategy of transition toward social articulation and mass-based democratic participation has hardly been traced out. But it is here that the debates on the law of unequal development and the peasantry provide useful political guidelines.

For those who have argued that the law of unequal development implies stagnation in the periphery, either because the surplus produced there is extracted to the benefit of the center (the *Monthly Review*, development-of-underdevelopment, and dependency schools) or because of lack of surplus generation (Bettelheim, Mandel, Kay, Weeks, and Dore), the inevitable conclusion is that the proletariat is incipient and that the relevant social base for change must be sought in the peasantry. At the same time, the associated ideas of peasant mode of production, articulation of modes of production, and permanent primitive accumulation imply that peasants have to be mobilized in terms of their own demands: the protection and modernization of their land plots through rural development and increased access to land through redistributive land reforms.

In Mexico, where the debate on peasants is quite active and highly politicized, this position has been argued by Fernando Rello and Gustavo Esteva.[26] As Harris explains, this leads to the position that "the peasantry must develop its own political organizations and seek the support of the urban working class for the protection and rapid modernization of this small-scale production of basic commodities for the national market.... This would serve the interests of both the rural and urban wage earners since it would increase the production of basic commodities, stop the flow of peasants into the towns and cities, in search of employment, reduce the surplus population and the reserve army, and take the pressure off the wage workers caused by the huge national population of unemployed persons standing in line to replace them."[27] This agrarian populist position was, at least at the level of rhetoric, the official policy in Mexico from 1940 to the end of the Echeverria administration in 1976. And peasant support has been an essential element of political stability during that period.

The opposite interpretation of the law of unequal development is supported in particular by Warren, Philips, Cardoso, and Tavares. It originates in the observation that since the 1960s the main characteristic of Latin American economies has not been stagnation but rapid industrialization and unequal development in agriculture, which have led to the formation of an urban proletariat, rapid urbanization, extensive semiproletarianization in agriculture, and the emergence of an itinerant and temporary rural labor force that is largely urban based.[28] The peasantry itself is seen as a rapidly differentiating fraction of a class, and those who still retain the status of peasant producers are viewed as having been transformed into workers working at home and hence as nothing other than workers for capital.[29] The implication is that the significant force for social change should be sought in the urban sector and in the promotion of an alliance between the proletarianized segments of the peasantry and workers. Programs of rural development and redistributive land reform that have as their purpose the strengthening of the petty bourgeoisie and thus the preservation of the social status quo through separation are seen as reactionary. To counter the populism of the state and parts of the Left in Mexico, Bartra thus suggests formation and adoption of "proletarian strategies": "For the exploited classes, the problem consists in guiding the process of disintegration of peasants, not toward an attempt at recovering their former status but toward the organization of forms of proletarian struggle directed at the most modern forms of capitalist exploitation."[30]

This proletarian position, while objectively correct, is fraught with serious contradictions: even though peasants have indeed become rapidly proletarianized, they have not, for all that, acquired class consciousness as proletarians. This is due to the fact that, for them, poverty has come as a gradual loss of peasant status, which they consequently seek to reverse, however glorified and fictional the past may have been. This is also due to the extreme insecurity and low remuneration of wage employment, which forces peasants to cling to land plots for survival. As Silvia Terán observes in her study of peasant consciousness in Mexico: "The struggles in the countryside—even those of the wage earners—have an essentially peasant character due to the incapacity of the dependent capitalist system to provide salaried employment as a viable alternative for economic survival. It is for this reason that the peasants and workers seek refuge in the peasant situation."[31] And the collective struggles for land have in fact strengthened their class consciousness as peasants. Lygia Sigaud similarly finds that in Brazil not only peasants but also plantation wage workers define their demands in terms of landownership.[32]

It is clear that the locus of class struggle is increasingly being displaced away from the countryside and into the cities. And it is indeed for this same reason that most Latin American governments can so fully neglect rural poverty and push for agricultural development and comparative advantages in agroexports. In Mexico, for example, the Lopez Portillo administration has shed much of the agrarian rhetoric of the previous forty years and is pushing for changes that will undoubtedly rapidly undermine the remaining productive basis and political platform of peasants, in part counting on migration to the United States as a substitute for rural development and for redistributive land reform in its handling of rural political pressures. And food deficits are likely to increase rapidly as disarticulation and cheap-food policies reinforce the bias against the production of wage foods. Thus, the contradictions of the agrarian question—unequal development against food and massive rural poverty—can only be expected to deepen. At this stage, the agrarian question is fundamentally nonagrarian, and its solution lies in social and structural changes at the level of the total social formation.

Displacement of the locus of class struggle toward the proletariat, however, also implies that this is where the potential for mass mobilization toward articulation and democracy exists. In agriculture, the political program should thus be one of fomenting an alliance between workers and those segments of the peasantry that can be mobilized for this purpose. It is consequently essential to carefully distinguish between different strata of rural producers in terms of class consciousness: some strata can be drawn into such an alliance, while the demands of others should be opposed. And it is important to create a state of consciousness among peasants that allows them to see beyond petty bourgeois demands. For this purpose, redistributive land reforms and rural development programs conducted *by* (and not *for*) peasants can be useful departing points in a struggle for democracy and articulation. If their goal is the creation of ideas and organizations, and not merely the diffusion of technology or the reinforcement of petty bourgeois ideals, these programs can serve as instruments of social change. Indeed, seen in this perspective, land reform and rural-development programs that foment collective action and class consciousness can be effective mechanisms in the creation of social articulation and mass-based democratic regimes.

Notes

Chapter 1

1. T. W. Schultz, *Economic Growth and Agriculture* (New York: McGraw-Hill, 1968); Harry G. Johnson, *Economic Policies Toward Less Developed Countries* (Washington, D.C.: Brookings Institution, 1967).

2. Solon Barraclough, ed., *Agrarian Structure in Latin America* (Lexington, Mass.: Heath, Lexington Books, 1973); Ernest Feder, *The Rape of the Peasantry* (Garden City, N.Y.: Doubleday, Anchor Books, 1971); Matthew Edel, *Food Supply and Inflation in Latin America* (New York: Praeger Publishers, 1969).

3. George Foster, "Peasant Society and the Image of Limited Good," *American Anthropologist* 67, no. 2 (April 1965): 293–315; Oscar Lewis, *Tepoztlan, Village in Mexico* (New York: Holt, Rinehart & Winston, 1960); T. W. Schultz, *Transforming Traditional Agriculture* (New Haven: Yale University Press, 1964).

4. Hollis Chenery, "Patterns of Industrial Growth," *American Economic Review* 50, no. 4 (September 1960): 624–54; W.W. Rostow, *The Stages of Economic Growth* (Cambridge: Cambridge University Press, 1960).

5. Everett Rogers, *The Diffusion of Innovations* (New York: Free Press of Glencoe, 1962).

6. Samir Amin, *Accumulation on a World Scale* (New York: Monthly Review Press, 1974).

7. We characterize here two schools of thought that have addressed the problems of economic development: modernization theory, which derives from neoclassical economics; and the classical theories of imperialism, radical structuralism, and Neo-Marxian theories, all of which derive from dialectical and historical materialism. A third approach, which was influential in the 1950s and 1960s with the contributions of Rosenstein-Rodan, Hirschman, Myrdal, Nurkse, Gerschenkron, and Leibenstein, is "development economics." It defined itself by rejecting both the idea of linearity of history in modernization theory and the concept of exploitation in the materialist approach. As Hirschman recently argued, however, this third approach has failed to account adequately for the course of history and to overcome the attacks of the other two schools. See Albert O. Hirschman, "The Rise and Decline of Development Economics," mimeographed (Princeton: Institute for Advanced Study, March 1980).

8. Robert Brenner, "The Origins of Capitalist Development: A Critique of Neo-Smithian Marxism," *New Left Review*, no. 104 (July–August 1977), pp. 25–92.

9. Karl Marx, *Capital*, vol. 1 (New York: Vintage Books, 1977), p. 91.

10. See V. G. Kierman, "Marx on India," in *Socialist Register, 1967* (London: Merlin Press,

1967); Gabriel Palma, "Dependency: A Formal Theory of Underdevelopment or a Methodology for the Analysis of Concrete Situations of Underdevelopment?" *World Development*, 6 (1978): 881-924.

11. Rosa Luxemburg, *The Accumulation of Capital: An Anti-Critique* (New York: Modern Reader, 1972).

12. Paul M. Sweezy, *The Theory of Capitalist Development* (New York: Modern Reader, 1942); Samir Amin, *Unequal Development* (New York: Monthly Review Press, 1976); Meghnad Desai, *Marxian Economic Theory* (London: Gray-Mills Publishing, 1974).

13. Barbara Bradby, "The Destruction of Natural Economy," *Economy and Society* 4, no. 2 (May 1975): 127-61.

14. V. I. Lenin, *Imperialism: The Highest Stage of Capitalism* (Peking: Foreign Languages Press, 1973); Nikolai Bukharin, *Imperialism and World Economy* (New York: Monthly Review Press, 1973).

15. Lenin, *Imperialism*, pp. 73-74.

16. Ibid., p. 73.

17. This is in opposition to Kautsky's thesis of "ultraimperialism," according to which the internationalization of capital gives hope for peace among nations under capitalism; ibid., p. 88. Lenin also opposes Kautsky by showing that imperialism is a necessity for monopoly capital, while Kautsky considers imperialism to be a policy that can be reformed.

18. Ibid., p. 76.

19. Ibid., p. 117.

20. Otto Kuusinen et al., *Fundamentals of Marxism-Leninism* (Moscow: Foreign Language Publishing House, n.d.), pp. 247-48.

21. Sweezy, *The Theory of Capitalist Development*.

22. Paul A. Baran and Paul M. Sweezy, *Monopoly Capital* (New York: Monthly Review Press, 1966).

23. Ibid., p. 193.

24. Ibid., p. 105.

25. Paul A. Baran, *The Political Economy of Growth* (New York: Prometheus Paperbacks, 1960), pp. 163-64.

26. Andre Gunder Frank, *Capitalism and Underdevelopment in Latin America* (New York: Modern Reader, 1969); Ruy Mauro Marini, "Dialectica de la Dependencia," *Sociedad y Desarrollo*, no. 1 (January-March 1972), pp. 5-31; Theotonio Dos Santos, "The Structure of Dependence," *American Economic Review* 60, no. 2 (May 1970): 231-36; Paul Prebisch, "Commercial Policy in Underdeveloped Countries," ibid., 49, no. 2 (May 1959): 251-73; Osvaldo Sunkel, "National Development Policy and External Dependence in Latin America," *Journal of Development Studies*, October 1969; Celso Furtado, *Obstacles to Development in Latin America* (Garden City, N.Y.: Doubleday, Anchor Books, 1970).

27. Philip O'Brien, *A Critique of Latin American Theories of Dependency*, Institute of Latin American Studies, Occasional Paper no. 12 (Glasgow: University of Glasgow, 1974).

28. Theotonio Dos Santos, "La Crisis de la Teoria del Desarrollo y las Relaciones de Dependencia en America Latina," in *La Dependencia Politico Economica de America Latina*, ed. Helio Jaguaribe et al. (Mexico City: Siglo XXI, 1970), pp. 163, 164, and 176.

29. Frank, *Capitalism and Underdevelopment*, pp. 14-15.

30. For the debate on the transition to capitalism, see Paul M. Sweezy et al., *The Transition from Feudalism to Capitalism* (London: Verso, 1978).

31. D. Hodges, *The Latin American Revolution* (New York: W. Morrow & Co., 1974).

32. Emmanuel Wallerstein, *The Modern World System* (New York: Academic Press, 1974).

33. Arghiri Emmanuel, ed., *Unequal Exchange* (New York: Modern Reader, 1972).

34. A. A. Dadone and L. E. Di Marco, "The Impact of Prebisch's Ideas on Modern Economic Anlysis," in *International Economics and Development*, ed. L. E. Di Marco (New York: Academic Press, 1972).

35. Charles Bettelheim, "Theoretical Comments," in *Unequal Exchange,* ed. Arghiri Emmanuel (New York: Modern Reader, 1972), appendix I; Samir Amin, *Imperialism and Unequal Development* (New York: Monthly Review Press, 1977), part IV ("The End of a Debate"); Oscar Braun, *Comercio Internacional e Imperialismo* (Buenos Aires: Siglo XXI, 1973); Ernest Mandel, *Late Capitalism* (London: New Left Books, 1976); Geoffrey Kay, *Development and Underdevelopment: A Marxist Analysis* (New York: St. Martin's Press, 1975); John Weeks and Elizabeth Dore, "International Exchange and the Causes of Backwardness," *Latin American Perspectives* 6, no. 2 (Spring 1979): 62-87.

36. Amin, *Imperialism and Unequal Development;* Kay, *Development and Underdevelopment.*

37. Bettelheim, "Theoretical Comments"; Amin, *Imperialism and Unequal Development;* Braun, *Comercio Internacional e Imperialismo.*

38. Alain de Janvry and Frank Kramer, "The Limits of Unequal Exchange," *Review of Radical Political Economy* 11, no. 4 (Winter 1979): 3-15.

39. Mandel, *Late Capitalism.*

40. Several other aspects of the debate are of a more technical, though equally important, nature: in particular, (1) whether the rate of surplus value is greater in the center (where both labor productivity and real wages are higher) or in the periphery (Bettelheim, "Theoretical Comments"); and (2) whether or not the postulate of the internationalization of value holds (Mandel, *Late Capitalism*).

41. Amin, *Unequal Development,* p. 75.

42. Ibid., p. 188.

43. Ibid.

44. Ibid., p. 259.

45. This same model was applied to Latin America by Ruy Mauro Marini in *Dialectica de la Dependencia* (Mexico City: Ediciones Era, 1973).

46. Amin, *Imperialism and Unequal Development,* p. 352.

47. Frank, *Capitalism and Underdevelopment.*

48. Paul M. Sweezy, "A Critique," in Paul M. Sweezy et al., *The Transition from Feudalism to Capitalism* (London: Verso, 1978); Wallerstein, *The Modern World System.*

49. Maurice Dobb, *Studies in the Development of Capitalism* (New York: International Publishers, 1947); Robert Brenner, "Agrarian Class Structure and Economic Development in Preindustrial Europe," *Past and Present,* no. 70 (February 1976), pp. 30-75.

50. Pierre Jalée, *The Pillage of the Third World* (New York: Modern Reader, 1968).

51. Baran, *The Political Economy of Growth;* Frank, *Capitalism and Underdevelopment;* Harry Magdoff, *The Age of Imperialism* (New York: Modern Reader, 1969); Stephen Hymer, "The Multinational Corporation and the Law of Uneven Development," in *Economics and World Order from the 1970's to the 1990's,* ed. J. Bhagwati (New York: Macmillan, Collier, 1972), pp. 113-40.

52. Prebisch, "Commercial Policy in Underdeveloped Countries."

53. Braun, *Comercio Internacional e Imperialismo.*

54. Emmanuel, ed., *Unequal Exchange;* Amin, *Imperialism and Unequal Development.*

55. Brenner, "The Origins of Capitalist Development," p. 67.

56. Weeks and Dore, "International Exchange"; Kay, *Development and Underdevelopment.*

57. Kay, *Development and Underdevelopment.*

58. Ann Phillips, "The Concept of 'Development,'" *Review of African Political Economy,* no. 8 (1977), pp. 7-20; Ira Gerstein, "Theories of the World Economy and Imperialism," *The Insurgent Sociologist* 7, no. 2 (Spring 1977): 9-12.

59. Emmanuel, ed., *Unequal Exchange.*

60. Amin, *Unequal Development.*

61. Bettelheim, "Theoretical Comments"; Kay, *Development and Underdevelopment;* Mandel, *Late Capitalism.*

62. Baran, *The Political Economy of Growth;* Frank, *Capitalism and Underdevelopment;* Wallerstein, *The Modern World System.*

63. Amin, *Unequal Development.*

64. Pierre Philippe Rey, *Les Alliances de classes* (Paris: Maspéro, 1976); Claude Servolin, "L'Absorption de l'agriculture dans le mode de production capitaliste," *L'Univers politique des paysans dans la France contemporaine* (Paris: Armand Colin, 1972); Kostas Vergopoulos, "El Capitalismo Disforme," in *La Cuestión Campesina y el Capitalismo,* ed. Samir Amin and Kostas Vergopoulos (Mexico City: Editorial Nuestro Tiempo, 1975); Rodolfo Stavenhagen, *Social Classes in Agrarian Societies* (Garden City, N.Y.: Doubleday, Anchor Books, 1975).

65. Bill Warren, "Imperialism and Capitalist Industrialization," *New Left Review,* no.. 81 (September-October 1973), pp. 3-44.

66. Ibid., p. 37.

67. Cardoso made the fact of stagnation the starting point of his best-known early work on dependency. See Fernando E. Cardoso and E. Faletto, *Dependencia y Desarrollo en America Latina* (Mexico City: Siglo XXI, 1969).

68. Fernando E. Cardoso, "Associated-Dependent Development: Theoretical and Political Implications," in *Authoritarian Brazil: Origins, Policies, and Future,* ed. A. Stepan (New Haven: Yale University Press, 1973).

69. Bettelheim, "Theoretical Comments"; Weeks and Dore, "International Exchange."

70. Karl Marx, *Capital,* vols. 2 and 3 (New York: International Publishers, 1967); idem, *Grundrisse* (New York: Vintage Books, 1973).

71. An excellent interpretation of Marx's theory of the essence of crises is found in M. Lebowitz, "Marx's Falling Rate of Profit: A Dialectical View," *Canadian Journal of Economics* 9, no. 2 (May 1976): 223-54.

72. Marx, *Capital,* 1 (1977 ed.): 592.

73. Ibid., 2 (1967 ed.): 316.

74. Marx, *Grundrisse,* p. 419.

75. Michael Kalecki, *Essays in the Theory of Economic Fluctuations* (London: Allen & Unwin, 1939), p. 26.

76. As is well known, there is no automatic relationship between technological change and the organic composition of capital; see, for example, G. Hodgson, "The Theory of the Falling Rate of Profit," *New Left Review,* no. 84 (1974). Yaffe implies a rising organic composition on the grounds that even if technological change economizes on fixed capital, it will increase the use of intermediate goods and raw materials, which are also component parts of constant capital; see David Yaffe, "The Marxian Theory of Crisis, Capital, and the State," *Economy and Society* 2, no. 7 (May 1973): 209-11. Only secondary importance is here attributed to this possible source of a falling rate of profit.

77. The correspondence between these two tendencies under atomistic and monopoly capital has been shown by Baran and Sweezy, *Monopoly Capital.*

78. Amin, *Accumulation on a World Scale.*

79. Mao Tse-tung, *Four Essays on Philosophy* (Peking: Foreign Language Press, 1968), pp. 27-28.

80. Nathan Rosenberg, "Capital Goods, Technology, and Economic Growth," *Oxford Economic Papers,* n.s., 15, no. 15 (November 1963): 217-27; Albert O. Hirschman, *The Strategy of Economic Development* (New Haven: Yale University Press, 1958). The manipulation of forward and backward linkages in economic planning is thoroughly explored by Hirschman.

81. Donald J. Harris, "Theory of Economic Growth: A Critique and Re-formulation," *American Economic Review* 65, no. 2 (May 1975): 329-37.

82. In this simple model we assume that workers do not save (hence the derived demand for capital goods is fully determined by the return to capital) and that capitalists do not consume (hence the final demand for consumption goods is fully determined by the return to labor).

83. Robert M. Solow, "A Contribution to the Theory of Economic Growth," *Quarterly*

Journal of Economics 70, no. 1 (February 1956): 65–94; T. W. Swan, "Economic Growth and Capital Accumulation," *Economic Record* 32 (November 1956); 334–61. Hirofumi Uzawa, "Neutral Inventions and the Stability of Growth Equilibrium," *Review of Economic Studies* 28, no. 76 (February 1961): 117–24. At the limit, however, the neoclassical "golden age" implies that growth becomes independent of the rate of savings.

84. Piero Sraffa, *Production of Commodities by Means of Commodities* (Cambridge: Cambridge University Press, 1960).

85. Thomas Weisskopf, "Marxist Perspectives on Cyclical Crisis," in URPE, *U.S. Capitalism in Crisis* (New York: URPE, 1978), p. 242.

86. Mandel, *Late Capitalism;* John Gurley, "Unemployment and Inflation," *Monthly Review* 29, no. 7 (December 1977): 23–28; R. Boddy and J. Crotty, "Food Prices: Planned Crisis in Defense of the Empire," *Socialist Revolution* 5, no. 1 (April 1975): 101–9; Weisskopf, "Marxist Perspectives," p. 257.

87. Erich Fromm, *The Sane Society* (New York: Holt, Rinehart & Winston, 1955); Vance Packard, *The Hidden Persuaders* (New York: D. McKay, 1957); John Kenneth Galbraith, *The New Industrial State* (Boston: Houghton Mifflin, 1967); Philip Slater, *The Pursuit of Loneliness* (Boston: Beacon Press, 1970).

88. Amin, *Imperialism and Unequal Development,* pp. 187 and 188.

89. Lenin addressed this question as follows in his study of the formation of a domestic market in Russia:

For capitalism, therefore, the growth of the home market is to a certain extent "independent" of the growth of personal consumption, and takes place mostly on account of productive consumption. But it would be a mistake to understand this "independence" as meaning that productive consumption is entirely divorced from personal consumption: the former can and must increase faster than the latter (and there its "independence" ends), but it goes without saying that, in the last analysis, productive consumption is always bound up with personal consumption.

See V. I. Lenin, *The Development of Capitalism in Russia* (Moscow: Progress Publishers, 1964), pp. 54–55.

90. Sweezy, *The Theory of Capitalist Development,* chap. X.

91. James O'Connor, *The Fiscal Crisis of the State* (New York: St. Martin's Press, 1973).

92. John Weeks, "The Sphere of Production and the Analysis of Crisis in Capitalism," *Science and Society* 41, no. 3 (Fall 1977): 281–320.

93. Marx, *Grundrisse,* p. 420; Samir Amin, "Accumulation and Development: A Theoretical Model," *Review of African Political Economy,* no. 1 (August–November 1974), pp. 9–26.

94. Lenin, *The Development of Capitalism in Russia,* pp. 68–69.

95. Here wage goods are defined as commodities for which demand originates in wages, while luxury goods are commodities for which demand originates in profits and rents; see Sweezy, *The Theory of Capitalist Development,* p. 109.

96. Both the role of wages in creating a market for the modern sector and the role of the modern sector in producing wage goods are discussed in the section entitled "Market-Widening and Market-Deepening."

97. Albert Berry and Miguel Urrutia, *Income Distribution in Colombia* (New Haven: Yale University Press, 1976), pp. 114–16.

98. Enrique Hernandez Laos and Jorge Cordova Chavez, "Estructura de la Distribución del Ingreso en México," *Comercio Exterior* 29, no. 5 (May 1979): 507.

99. These data are discussed and presented in E. Bacha and L. Taylor, "Brazilian Income Distribution in the 1960s: 'Facts,' Model Results, and the Controversy," *Journal of Development Studies* 14, no. 3 (April 1978): 277.

100. Raymundo Arroyo, "Relative and Absolute Pauperization of the Brazilian Proletariat in the Last Decade," *Latin American Research Unit Studies* 1, no. 1 (October 1976): 23–40.

101. Bacha and Taylor, "Brazilian Income Distribution," p. 287.

102. The terms "modern" and "traditional" are used here provisionally. The sectors are characterized in terms of modes of production in Chapter 2.

103. For this purpose, Amin relies on the concept of the articulation of modes of production, according to which the peasantry is thought to constitute a noncapitalist mode, while Bartra writes of "permanent primitive accumulation." See Amin, *Unequal Development*, and Roger Bartra, *Estructura Agraria y Clases Sociales en México* (Mexico City: Ediciones Era, 1974).

104. ILO, *Yearbook of Labor Statistics, 1973* (Geneva: ILO, 1973).

105. James Wilkie, ed., *Statistical Abstract of Latin America* (Los Angeles: UCLA Latin American Center, 1977), pp. 204 and 324.

106. ILO, *Urban Development and Employment in São Paulo* (Geneva: ILO, 1976).

107. United Nations, *Yearbook of National Accounts Statistics, 1976* (New York, 1976), vol. 1, table 1B.

108. Amin, *Unequal Development*, p. 361.

109. World Bank, *World Tables, 1976* (Baltimore: The Johns Hopkins University Press, 1976).

110. World Bank, *World Debt Tables* (Washington, D.C.: World Bank, September 1977).

111. United Nations, Economic Commission for Latin America, *El Desarrollo Economico y Social y las Relaciones Externas de America Latina* (Santo Domingo, Dominican Republic, February 1977).

112. M. C. de Tavares and J. Serra, "Beyond Stagnation: A Discussion on the Nature of Recent Development in Brazil," in *From Dependence to Revolution*, ed. James Petras (New York: John Wiley & Sons, 1973), p. 95.

113. A low rate of saving and a deficit in the balance of payments are the two fundamental constraints to growth that are singled out in the "two-gap" models. See H. B. Chenery and A. M. Stout, "Foreign Assistance and Economic Development," *American Economic Review* 56, no. 4, pt. 1 (September 1966): 679-733; and V. Joshi, "Savings and Foreign Exchange Constraints," in *Unfashionable Economics*, ed. P. Streeten (London: Weidenfeld & Nicolson, 1970).

114. C. Moser, "Informal Sector or Petty Commodity Production: Dualism or Dependence in Urban Development?" *World Development* 6, no. 9/10 (September-October 1978): 1041-64; P. Souza and V. Tokman, "The Urban Informal Sector in Latin America," *International Labor Review* 114, no. 3 (November-December 1976): 355-65.

115. B. Roberts, *Cities of Peasants: The Political Economy of Urbanization in the Third World* (London: E. Arnold, 1978).

116. Alejandro Portes, "The Informal Sector and the Capital Accumulation Process in Latin America," mimeographed (Durham, N.C.: Duke University, February 1980).

117. Ed McCaughan, "1968-1978: Contours of Crisis," *NACLA* 12, no. 5 (September-October 1978): 2-7.

118. Brenner, "The Origins of Capitalist Development."

119. Amin, *Imperialism and Unequal Development*, p. 279.

120. Fernando E. Cardoso, "Dependency and Development in Latin America," *New Left Review*, no. 74 (1972), pp. 83-95.

121. As Mao Tse-tung observed:
In capitalist society, the two forces in contradiction, the proletariat and the bourgeoisie, form the principal contradiction. The other contradictions, such as those between the remnant feudal class and the bourgeoisie, between the proletariat and the peasant petty bourgeoisie, between the non-monopoly capitalists and the monopoly capitalists, between bourgeois democracy and bourgeois fascism, among the capitalist countries and between imperialism and the colonies, are all determined or influenced by this principal contradiction.
Four Essays on Philosophy, p. 51.

122. Albert O. Hirschman, "The Political Economy of Import-Substituting Industrialization in Latin America," *Quarterly Journal of Economics* 82, no. 1 (February 1968): 1-32.

123. Cardoso, "Dependency and Development."

124. Guillermo O'Donnell, "State and Alliances in Argentina, 1956–1976," *Journal of Development Studies* 15, no. 1 (October 1978): 3–33.

125. Tom Nairn, *The Break-up of Britain* (London: New Left Books, 1977).

126. A complete model would allow for a supply of capital goods both through imports (as in the present model of sectoral disarticulation) and through domestic production. Sectoral disarticulation is maintained here to simplify the exposition.

127. F. Fajnzylber and T. Martinez, *Las Empresas Transnacionales: Expansión a Nivel Mundial y Protección en la Industria Mexicana* (Mexico City: Fondo de Cultura Economica, 1976).

128. Amin, for example, argues that "the process of resource allocation is distorted to such an extent as to undermine all possibility of decisive progress in the sectors producing mass consumer goods" (Amin, *Unequal Development*, p. 352).

129. OAS, *Basic Working Documents for Discussion at the VII Inter-American Conference on Agriculture, Tegucigalpa, Honduras, September 1977* (Washington, D.C.: OAS, 1977).

130. Robert Fox, *Urban Population Growth Trends in Latin America* (Washington, D.C.: Inter-American Development Bank, 1975).

131. Maria Conceicao de Tavares, "The Growth and Decline of Import Substitution in Brazil," *Economic Bulletin for Latin America* 9, no. 1 (March 1964): 1–59.

132. Healy calculated that for the period 1950–68, 75 percent of the growth in industrial product in Latin American countries was explained by growth in productivity; only 25 percent was explained by increased employment. See Derek Healy, "Development Policy: New Thinking About an Interpretation," *Journal of Economic Literature* 10, no. 3 (September 1972): 757–97; see also David Turnham, *The Employment Problem in Less Developed Countries: A Review of Evidence* (Paris: OECD, 1971), and David Morawetz, "Employment Implications of Industrialization in Developing Countries: A Survey," *Economic Journal* 84, no. 335 (September 1974): 491–542.

133. This model has the same fundamental dynamic properties as that of Kalecki. See Michael Kalecki, "The Marxian Equation of Reproduction and Modern Economics," *Social Science Information* 7, no. 6 (December 1968): 73–79.

134. Anibal Pinto, "Styles of Development in Latin America," *CEPAL Review*, 1976, first half, pp. 99–130.

135. Ibid., p. 117.

136. Nora Lustig, "Distribución del Ingreso, Estructura del Consumo y Características del Crecimiento Industrial," *Comercio Exterior* 29, no. 5 (May 1979): 535–43.

137. Francisco de Oliveira, "A Economica Brasileira: Critica a Razao Dualista," *Estudos CEBRAP*, no. 2 (October 1972), pp. 5–82.

138. Vivianne Ventura Dias, "Small and Large Enterprises in the Brazilian Textile Industry: The Modernization of a Traditional Industry" (Ph.D. diss., University of California, Berkeley, 1979).

139. Arroyo, "Relative and Absolute Pauperization," p. 37.

140. J. Mathieson, *The Advanced Developing Countries: Emerging Actors in the World Economy*, Development Paper no. 28 (Washington, D.C.: Overseas Development Council, November 1979), p. 15.

141. In particular, see Magdoff, *The Age of Imperialism;* Dos Santos, "The Structure of Dependence"; Ronald Müller, "The Multinational Corporation and the Underdevelopment of the Third World," in *The Political Economy of Development and Underdevelopment*, ed. C. Wilber (New York: Random House, 1973); Mandel, *Late Capitalism*.

142. Richard Newfarmer and Willard Mueller, "Multinational Corporations in Brazil and Mexico" (Report to the Subcommittee on Multinational Corporations, U.S. Senate, Washington, D.C., 1975), p. 11.

143. Magdoff, *The Age of Imperialism*, p. 198.

144. Newfarmer and Mueller, "Multinational Corporations."

145. Michael Kalecki, *Theory of Economic Dynamics* (New York: Rinehart & Co., 1954); Baran, *The Political Economy of Growth*.

146. Amin, *Imperialism and Unequal Development*, chap. 2.

147. Celso Furtado, "The Brazilian 'Model' of Development," in *The Political Economy of Development and Underdevelopment*, ed. C. Wilber (New York: Random House, 1973).

148. Emmanuel, ed., *Unequal Exchange;* Amin, *Imperialism and Unequal Development*.

149. This result obtains when (*a*) the products exchanged are specific to each country (Emmanuel's case) and the countries' productivities are consequently not comparable, or (*b*) the products exchanged are nonspecific (Amin's case) and the difference in wages is greater than the difference in productivities.

150. Bettelheim, "Theoretical Comments"; Amin, *Imperialism and Unequal Development*.

151. Braun, "Comercio Internacional e Imperialismo."

152. Kay, *Development and Underdevelopment*.

153. Braun, "Comercio Internacional e Imperialismo."

154. Mandel, *Late Capitalism*, chap. 11.

155. URPE, *U.S. Capitalism in Crisis*, p. 344.

156. U.S. President, *Economic Report of the President, 1979* (Washington, D.C.: Government Printing Office, 1979).

157. U.S. Department of Commerce, *Statistical Abstract of the United States* (Washington, D.C.: Government Printing Office, 1978).

158. Paul M. Sweezy, "The Crisis Within the Crisis," *Monthly Review* 30, no. 7 (December 1978): 7–11.

159. U.S. Department of Labor, consumer price index for 1974 and 1978; see U.S. President, *Economic Report of the President, 1979*.

160. Harry Magdoff, "The U.S. Dollar, Petrodollars, and U.S. Imperialism," *Monthly Review* 30, no. 8 (January 1979): 1–13.

161. URPE, *U.S. Capitalism in Crisis*, pp. 344 and 345.

162. Private U.S. assets, direct investments abroad at book value; see U.S. President, *Economic Report of the President, 1979*, p. 298.

Chapter 2

1. Stanley and Barbara Stein, *The Colonial Heritage of Latin America* (New York: Oxford University Press, 1970).

2. For example, see Edmundo Flores, *Tratado de Economía Agrícola* (Mexico City: Fondo de Cultura Económica, 1961), pp. 267–99.

3. Horacio Ciafardini, "Sur la Question du mode de production en Amérique Latine," *Etudes rurales* 47 (July–September 1972): 148–62.

4. According to Bartolomeo de las Casas, the population of the island of Hispaniola declined from 1,100,000 in 1492 to 10,000 in 1530 and that of Cuba declined from 600,000 inhabitants in 1492 to 270 households in 1570. See Pierre Vilar, *Oro y Moneda en la Historia, 1450–1920* (Barcelona: Ariel, 1969), p. 69; and Keith Griffin, *Underdevelopment in Spanish America* (London: George Allen & Unwin, 1969), pp. 42–50.

5. Ernesto Laclau, "Feudalism and Capitalism in Latin America," *New Left Review*, no. 67 (1971), pp. 19–38.

6. Mario Gongora, "Origen de los Inquilinos de Chile Central," in *Estructura Social de Chile*, ed. H. Godoy (Santiago de Chile: Editorial Universitaria, 1971).

7. V. I. Lenin, *Imperialism: The Highest Stage of Capitalism* (New York: International Publishers, 1939), pp. 76–87.

8. John Gerassi, "Violence, Revolution, and Structural Change in Latin America," in *Latin American Radicalism*, ed. Irving L. Horowitz, Josue de Castro, and John Gerassi (New York: Vintage Books, 1969), p. 474.

9. Eduardo Galeano, *Open Veins in Latin America* (New York: Modern Reader, 1973), p. 102.

10. U.S. Congress, Joint Committee on Foreign Affairs, *Background Information on the Use of U.S. Armed Forces in Foreign Countries,* 91st Cong., 2d sess., 1970.

11. Celso Furtado, *Economic Development of Latin America* (Cambridge: Cambridge University Press, 1970), p. 40.

12. IIA, *The Agricultural Situation in 1932–1933* (Rome: IIA, 1934).

13. Furtado, *Economic Development,* p. 166.

14. Enrique Iglesias, "The Great Tasks of Latin American Development," *CEPAL Review,* 1977; United Nations, Department of International, Economic, and Social Affairs, *World Economic Survey, 1977* (E/1978/70/Rev. 1, ST/ESA/82) (New York, 1978).

15. Food and Agriculture Organization of the United Nations, *Yearbook of Food and Agricultural Statistics,* various issues; and idem, *Production Yearbook,* various issues.

16. World Bank, *World Bank Tables, 1976* (Baltimore: The Johns Hopkins University Press, 1976), p. 393.

17. James Wilkie, ed., *Statistical Abstract of Latin America,* vol. 18 (Los Angeles: UCLA Latin American Center, 1977), table 2209, p. 315.

18. Food and Agriculture Organization of the United Nations, "Population, Food Supply, and Agricultural Development," *Monthly Bulletin of Agricultural Economics and Statistics* 23, no. 9 (September 1974): 1–13.

19. United Nations, ECLA, "Cuestiones Principales Sobre el Desarrollo Social Rural en America Latina," mimeographed (Santiago de Chile, October 1978).

20. IFPRI, *Meeting Food Needs in the Developing World: The Location and Magnitude of the Task in the Next Decade,* Research Report no. 1 (Washington, D.C., February 1976).

21. Food and Agriculture Organization of the United Nations, *Production Yearbook, 1970* (Rome, 1970); see also idem, *Production Yearbook, 1976* (Rome, 1977).

22. U.S. Department of Agriculture, *Agriculture in the Americas: Statistical Data,* FDCD Working Paper (Washington, D.C., 1976), p. 28.

23. Wollman indicates that "the main conclusions reached by investigations of Chilean irrigation are that water is used with a prodigality that can only mean great waste" (see N. Wollman, *The Water Resources of Chile* [Baltimore: The Johns Hopkins Press, 1968], p. 43). This waste is quantified in an analysis of the efficiency of water used in the Maipo basin: "Field losses of 60% (farm efficiency 40%) and canal conveyance losses of 30% would together give an overall efficiency of only 28%" (see Chile, Ministry of Public Works, Irrigation Directorate, *Investigation of the Water Resources of the Maipo Basin* [Santiago de Chile, January 1970]).

24. Carlos Diaz-Alejandro, *Essays on the Economic History of the Argentine Republic* (New Haven: Yale University Press, 1970), p. 144.

25. M. Ballesteros, "Desarrollo Agrícola Chileno, 1910–1955," *Cuadernos de Economía* 5 (1965): 4–70.

26. U.S. Department of Agriculture, *Agriculture in the Americas,* p. 23.

27. United Nations, ECLA, *Economic Survey of Latin America, 1969* (New York: United Nations, 1970), p. 267.

28. G. Sahota, *Fertilizer in Economic Development: An Economic Analysis* (New York: Frederick A. Praeger, 1968).

29. IICA-OAS.

30. Omitting cases where the crop is insignificant.

31. Brazil, national agricultural census, 1970.

32. Peter Knight, *Brazilian Agricultural Technology and Trade: A Study of Five Commodities* (New York: Praeger Publishers, 1971); and R. Paiva, S. Schattan, and C. Trench de Freitas, "Brazil's Agricultural Sector: Economic Behavior, Problems, and Possibilities" (Paper presented at the Fifteenth International Conference of Agricultural Economists, São Paulo, Brazil, 1973).

33. U.S. Department of Agriculture, *Changes in Agricultural Production and Technology in Colombia,* Foreign Agricultural Economic Report no. 52 (Washington, D.C., June 1969).

34. D. Adams et al., *Public Law 480 and Colombia's Economic Development* (East Lansing: Michigan State University, Department of Agricultural and Resource Economics, 1964).

35. G. Scobie and R. Posada, *The Impact of High-Yielding Rice Varieties in Latin America, with Special Emphasis on Colombia* (Cali, Colombia: CIAT April 1976).

36. Cristobal Kay, "Comparative Development of the European Manorial System and the Latin American Hacienda System," *Journal of Peasant Studies* 2, no. 1 (October 1974): 69–98.

37. Andrew Pearce, *The Latin American Peasant* (London: Frank Cass, 1975).

38. Gongora, "Origen de los Inquilinos."

39. Furtado, *Economic Development,* chap. 23.

40. The *price* of labor power is the price of subsistence needs for the worker and his family. It is equal to the sum of (1) the cost of reconstituting the laborer from the effort of work; (2) the cost of maintaining the laborer in periods of sickness, unemployment, and old age; and (3) the cost of reproducing the labor force (cost of maintaining women in periods of bearing and attending children and of feeding and rearing children until working age). As for other commodities, the price of labor power is its price of production calculated in accordance with the prevailing social relations of production. The *cost* of labor is the outlay that the employer incurs in exchange for labor power; see C. Meillassoux, *Femmes, greniers, et capitaux* (Paris: Maspéro, 1975). In the case of "semiproletarian servile" labor, for the serf, income (the price of labor power) can be defined as follows:

Price of labor power = payments in kind + payments in cash + value of production generated on land plot in usufruct.

Cost of labor power = payments in kind + payments in cash + opportunity cost of land plot for the landlord

= price of labor power − (value of production of use values on plot − opportunity cost of plot).

41. For the political aspects of servile relations, see Patricia Garrett, "Some Economic and Political Aspects of Subsistence Production: The Landlord's Perspective" (Paper presented at the Society for the Study of Social Problems, San Francisco, Calif., September 1978).

42. This includes an estimate of imputed income from home-produced subsistence crops; see ECLA, *Agriculture in Latin America* (Santiago de Chile: ECLA, 1966).

43. World Bank, *The Assault on World Poverty* (Baltimore: The Johns Hopkins University Press, 1975), pp. 79 and 80.

44. D. Altimir, *La Dimensión de la Pobreza en America Latina* (Santiago de Chile: ECLA, 1978).

45. Keith Griffin, "Increasing Poverty and Changing Ideas About Development Strategies," *Development and Change* 8 (1977): 491–508.

46. Carlos Samaniego, "Movimiento Campensino o Lucha del Proletariado Rural en El Salvador," mimeographed (Madison: University of Wisconsin, Department of Rural Sociology, 1978).

47. Keith Griffin, *Land Concentration and Rural Poverty* (New York: Macmillan Co., 1976), pp. 164 and 177.

48. Richard Webb, *Government Policy and the Distribution of Income in Peru, 1963–1973* (Cambridge, Mass.: Harvard University Press, 1977), p. 38.

49. Albert Berry and Miguel Urrutia, *Income Distribution in Colombia* (New Haven: Yale University Press, 1976), p. 68.

50. Griffin, "Increasing Poverty," p. 495.

51. United Nations, ECLA, *La Distribución del Ingreso en America Latina* (New York: United Nations, 1970).

52. P. Scandizzo, "Land Distribution, Tenancy Systems, and Target Populations in Northeast Brazil," mimeographed (Washington, D.C.: World Bank, Development Research Center, 1974).

53. M. Ponce, "Reforma Agraria y Reconstrucción Nacional Dentro del Plan Nacional de

Desarrollo," mimeographed (Tegucigalpa: Universidad Nacional Autonoma de Honduras, 1974).

54. Erik Eckholm, *Losing Ground: Environmental Stress and World Food Prospects* (New York: W. W. Norton & Co., 1976).

55. Environmental Fund, *World Population Estimates, 1979* (Washington, D.C.: Environmental Fund, 1979).

56. Wilkie, ed., *Statistical Abstract of Latin America*, vol. 18, table 101a, p. 29.

57. U.S. Department of Commerce, Bureau of the Census, *A Statistical Portrait of Women in the United States, Current Population Reports*, Special Studies Series, no. 58 (Washington, D.C.: Government Printing Office, 1976), p. 23.

58. Leibenstein has identified three possible types of utility for which an additional child might be wanted: (1) consumption utility, (2) work or income utility, and (3) security utility. See H. Leibenstein, *Economic Backwardness and Economic Growth* (New York: John Wiley & Sons, 1957), p. 161.

59. H. Leibenstein, "An Interpretation of the Economic Theory of Fertility: Promising Path or Blind Alley?" *Journal of Economic Literature* 12, no. 2 (1974); and G. Becker, "An Economic Analysis of Fertility," in *Demographic Changes in Developed Countries*, ed. National Bureau of Economic Research (Princeton: Princeton University Press, 1960).

60. CIDA, *Tenencia de la Tierra y Desarrollo Socio-Economico del Sector Agrícola, Chile* (Santiago de Chile: CIDA, 1966).

61. Leibenstein, *Economic Backwardness and Economic Growth*.

62. M. Mamdani, *The Myth of Population Control* (New York: Monthly Review Press, 1972), p. 14.

63. Barbara de Janvry, "Natural Fertility in Rural Areas of Latin America," mimeographed (Santiago de Chile: CELADE, March 1974).

64. CELADE, "La Fecundidad Rural en Latino America," ser. A, no. 56 (Santiago de Chile: CELADE, December 1970), p. 1.

65. H. Elkins, "Cambio en la Fecundidad en Colombia," in *La Fecundidad en Colombia* (Bogotá: Asociación Nacional de Medicina, Division de Medicina Social y Población, November 1973), p. 31.

66. C. Miro and W. Mertens, "Influencia de Algunas Variables Intermedias en el Nivel y en las Diferencias de Fecundidad Urbana y Rural en America Latina," CELADE, ser. A, no. 92 (Santiago de Chile: CELADE, August 1962), p. 16.

67. Elkins, "Cambio en la Fecundidad en Colombia."

68. A. Conning notes in this respect: "Since anthropologists suggest that nearly all primitive groups understand the interrelation between sexual intercourse and childbearing, it is difficult to accept *a priori* that methods such as abortion and withdrawal were unknown to most Latin American populations, even if they were not normally practiced or practiced efficiently" (A. Conning, "A Framework for Considering Social and Economic Processes Affecting Fertility in Latin America," mimeographed [Santiago de Chile: CELADE, August 1973]).

69. This implies the existence of a negative relationship between farm size and desired family size. However, because fertility declines with poverty (due to malnutrition, poor health and hygiene, and overwork) and because infant mortality increases, actual completed family size is usually found first to increase with farm size and then to decrease in accordance with desired family size.

70. Solon Barraclough, ed., *Agrarian Structure in Latin America* (Lexington, Mass.: Heath, Lexington Books, 1973), p. 10.

71. D. Turnham, *The Employment Problem in Less Developed Countries: A Review of Evidence* (Paris: OECD, 1971); see also Derek Healy, "Development Policy: New Thinking About an Interpretation," *Journal of Economic Literature* 10, no. 3 (September 1972): 757–97.

72. IICA-OAS, *Basic Working Documents for Discussion at the VII Latin American Conference on Agriculture, Tegucigalpa, Honduras, September 1977* (Washington, D.C.: OAS, 1977), p. 5.

73. Shlomo Reutlinger and M. Selowsky, *Malnutrition and Poverty: Magnitude and Policy Options* (Baltimore: The Johns Hopkins University Press, 1976), p. 22.

74. F. Monckeberg et al., "Condiciones de Vida, Medio Familiar y Examen Clínico y Bioquímico de Lactantes y Preescolares de la Provincia de Curicó," *Revista Chilena de Pediatría,* July 1967.

75. F. Monckeberg, "Effect of Early Marasmic Malnutrition on Subsequent Physical and Psychological Development," in *Malnutrition, Learning, and Behavior,* ed. N. Scrimshaw and J. Gordon (Cambridge, Mass.: MIT Press, 1968).

76. F. Monckeberg, "Reflexiones Sobre la Desnutrición en México," *Comercio Exterior* 28, no. 2 (February 1978).

77. Wilkie, ed., *Statistical Abstract of Latin America,* vol. 18, pp. 95–114.

78. In 1970, the rural illiteracy rate was 10 percent in Uruguay, 15 percent in Costa Rica, 24 percent in Chile, 25 percent in Paraguay, 35 percent in Colombia, 36 percent in Panama, 42 percent in Ecuador (1960) and the Dominican Republic, 47 percent in Mexico (1960) and Peru, 57 percent in El Salvador, 59 percent in Brazil, 61 percent in Honduras (1960), and 66 percent in Guatemala. See ECLA, "Cuestiones Principales."

Chapter 3

1. The concepts of mode of production and social formation are defined in L. Althusser and E. Balibar, eds., *Reading Capital* (New York: Pantheon Books, 1970). The concept of articulation of modes of production is defined in Pierre Philippe Rey, *Les Alliances de classes* (Paris: Maspéro, 1976). See also Aiden Foster-Carter, "The Modes of Production Controversy," *New Left Review,* no. 107 (January–February 1978), pp. 47–77.

2. Karl Marx, *Theories of Surplus Value* (Moscow: Progress Publishers, 1968), pt. 1, p. 408.

3. Karl Marx, *The Eighteenth Brumaire of Louis Bonaparte* (New York: International Publishers, 1963), p. 124.

4. "The independent peasant or handicraftsman is cut up into two persons. As owner of the means of production he is capitalist; as labourer he is his own wage-labourer. As capitalist he therefore pays himself his wages and draws his profit on his capital; that is to say, he exploits himself as wage-labourer, and pays himself, in the surplus-value, the tribute that labour owes to capital" (Marx, *Theories of Surplus Value,* pt. 1, p. 408).

5. Karl Marx, *Capital,* vol. 3 (New York: International Publishers, 1967), pp. 806–8. The differentiation and disappearance of peasants as capitalism develops are referred to explicitly by Marx in *Theories of Surplus Value,* pt. 1, p. 409: "It is also a law that economic development distributes functions among different persons; and the handicraftsman or peasant who produces with his own means of production will either gradually be transformed into a small capitalist who also exploits the labour of others, or he will suffer the loss of his means of production and be transformed into a wage labourer."

6. M. Morishima and G. Catephores, "Is There an 'Historical Transformation Problem'?" *Economic Journal* 85, no. 338 (June 1975): 309–28.

7. Karl Marx, *Capital,* vol. 1 (New York: Vintage Books, 1977).

8. R. Meek, "Some Notes on the Transformation Problem," *Economic Journal* 66, no. 261 (March 1956): 94–107; E. Nell, "Marx's Economics: A Dual Theory of Value and Growth, by M. Morishima" (book review), *Journal of Economic Literature* 11 (December 1973): 1369–71.

9. F. Engels, "Supplement to Capital, Volume Three," in *Capital,* 3: 900.

10. Karl Kautsky, *La Cuestión Agraria* (Bogotá: Editorial Latina, 1976).

11. Ibid., pp. 16 and 101.

12. Ibid., p. 179.

13. Ibid., p. 259.

14. Ibid., p. 175.

15. V. I. Lenin, *Collected Works,* vol. 4 (Moscow: Progress Publishers, 1972), pp. 96 and 97.

16. Ibid., 3: 173.

17. Ibid., p. 174.

18. Ibid., p. 177.

19. Ibid., p. 178.

20. E. Preobrazhensky, *The New Economics* (Oxford: Clarendon Press, 1965).

21. Mark Harrison, "The Peasant Mode of Production in the Work of A. V. Chayanov," *Journal of Peasant Studies* 4, no. 4 (July 1977): 323–36.

22. A. V. Chayanov, "On the Theory of Non-Capitalist Economic Systems," in *The Theory of the Peasant Economy*, ed. D. Thorner et al. (Homewood, Ill.: Richard D. Irwin, 1966), p. 44.

23. Daniel Thorner, "Peasant Economy as a Category in Economic History," in *Peasants and Peasant Societies*, ed. T. Shanin (Baltimore: Penguin Books, 1971); Rodolfo Stavenhagen, *Social Classes in Agrarian Societies* (Garden City, N.Y.: Doubleday, Anchor Books, 1975).

24. Claude Servolin, "L'Absorption de l'agriculture dans le mode de production capitaliste," *L'Univers politique des paysans dans la France contemporaine* (Paris: Armand Colin, 1972), p. 41.

25. Ibid., p. 50.

26. Rey, *Les Alliances de classes*.

27. Samir Amin and Kostas Vergopoulos, eds., *La Question paysanne et le capitalisme* (Paris: Editions Anthropos, 1974); Kostas Vergopoulos, "Capitalism and Peasant Productivity," *Journal of Peasant Studies* 5, no. 4 (July 1978): 446–65.

28. H. Mouzelis, "Capitalism and the Development of Agriculture," *Journal of Peasant Studies* 3, no. 4 (July 1976): 483–92.

Beyond the problem of whether a peasant mode as defined by Vergopoulos does or does not exist, the analysis is clearly inconsistent in that it makes a dynamic prediction (the elimination of capitalists by peasants) on the basis of a static accounting of production costs. In particular, it fails to identify how the fact that peasants do not retain an investable surplus (profits) does not eventually lead their labor productivity to fall far behind productivity on capitalist farms. Even admitting zero profit and lower wages in peasant agriculture, a productivity gap greater than the cost gap between capitalist and peasant farms would lead to the elimination of peasants.

29. This mode is also referred to as "parcel mode of production" (*modo de producción parcelario, mode de production parcelaire*). See Hector Diaz-Polanco, *Teoría Marxista de la Economia Campesina* (Mexico City: Juan Pablos Editor, 1977); Michel Gutelman, *Structures et réformes agraires* (Paris: Maspéro, 1974); and Fernando Rojas and Victor Moncayo, *La Producción Parcelaria y el Modo de Producción Capitalista* (Bogotá: ASIAS, 1978).

30. Diaz-Polanco, *Teoría Marxista*, p. 86; Gutelman, *Structures et réformes agraires*, pp. 53 and 54.

31. In the subsequent discussion, peasant and petty commodity modes are considered indistinctively.

32. For a specification of the interrelationships between production, consumption, and reproduction functions in peasant households, see Carmen Diana Deere and Alain de Janvry, "A Conceptual Framework for the Empirical Analysis of Peasants," *American Journal of Agricultural Economics* 61, no. 4 (November 1979): 601–11.

33. Samir Amin, *Unequal Development* (New York: Monthly Review Press, 1976), p. 15.

34. S. Cook and Martin Diskin, eds., *Markets in Oaxaca* (Austin: University of Texas Press, 1975).

35. Vergopoulos, "Capitalism and Peasant Productivity."

36. Samir Amin and Kostas Vergopoulos, eds., *La Cuestión Campesina y el Capitalismo* (Mexico City: Editorial Nuestro Tiempo, 1975), p. 234.

37. William Roseberry, "Peasants as Proletarians," *Critique of Anthropology* 3, no. 11 (1978): 3–18; J. Banaji, "Modes of Production in a Materialist Conception of History," *Capital and Class*, no. 3 (Fall 1977): 1–43; Baudel M. N. Wanderley, "O Campones: Un Trabalhador para o Capital," mimeographed (São Paulo: State University of Campinas, Agrarian Studies Group, 1979).

38. Servolin, "L'Absorption de l'agriculture."

39. Marx, *Capital*, 3 (1967 ed.): 805.

40. Ibid., p. 804.

41. Amin and Vergopoulos, eds., *La Cuestión Campesina*, pp. 36, 37, 42, and 165.

42. Chayanov, "On the Theory of Non-Capitalist Economic Systems," pp. 1–5; B. Kerblay, " 'Chayanov' and the Theory of Peasantry as a Specific Type of Economy," in *Peasants and Peasant Societies*, ed. T. Shanin (Baltimore: Penguin Books, 1971), chap. 12; Mark Harrison, " 'Chayanov' and the Economics of the Russian Peasantry," *Journal of Peasant Studies* 2, no. 4 (1975).

43. James O'Connor, *The Fiscal Crisis of the State* (New York: St. Martin's Press, 1973).

44. Thus, Wolf defines peasants as "rural cultivators whose surpluses are transferred to a dominant group of rulers," while for Shanin, "the political economy of peasant society has been, generally speaking, based on expropriations of its 'surpluses' by powerful outsiders through corveé, tax, rent, interest, and terms of trade." See E. Wolf, *Peasants* (Englewood Cliffs, N.J.: Prentice-Hall, 1966), pp. 3–4; and T. Shanin, "Peasantry: Delineation of a Sociological Concept and a Field of Study," *European Journal of Sociology* 12 (1971): 289–300.

45. J. Ennew, P. Hirst, and K. Tribe, " 'Peasantry' as an Economic Category," *Journal of Peasant Studies* 4, no. 4 (July 1977): 295–322.

46. Rojas and Moncayo, *La Producción Parcelaria*.

47. E. Balibar, "The Basic Concepts of Historical Materialism," in *Reading Capital*, ed. L. Althusser and E. Balibar (New York: Pantheon Books, 1970).

48. Gutelman, *Structures et réformes agraires*, p. 60.

49. Servolin, "L'Absorption de l'agriculture"; Markos Mamalakis, "The Theory of Sectoral Clashes," The University of Wisconsin, Center for Latin American Studies, Reprint no. 9 (Madison, 1970); Michael Lipton, *Why Poor People Stay Poor: A Study of Urban Bias in World Development* (Cambridge, Mass.: Harvard University Press, 1977).

50. Marx, *Capital*, 3 (1967 ed.): 799.

51. V. I. Lenin, "The Agrarian Programme of Social-Democracy in the First Russian Revolution," in *Selected Works*, vol. 3 (London: Lawrence & Wishart, 1936), pp. 159–286.

52. The presumed superiority of large farms over small ones in terms of labor productivity, which is the essence of the classical studies of social differentiation in agriculture, was most fully argued by Kautsky.

53. Lenin's description of the farmer road is more fully developed in V. I. Lenin, "New Data on the Laws of the Development of Capitalism in Agriculture," in *Selected Works*, 12: 190–282.

54. Ibid., p. 181.

55. Ibid., p. 281.

56. V. I. Lenin, "The Development of Capitalism in Russia," in *Collected Works*, vol. 3 (Moscow: Progress Publishers, 1964), p. 32.

57. Lenin, "The Agrarian Programme," p. 280.

58. Cristobal Kay, "Comparative Development of the European Manorial System and the Latin American Hacienda System," *Journal of Peasant Studies* 2, no. 1 (October 1974): 69–98.

59. K. Duncan and I. Rutledge, eds., *Land and Labour in Latin America* (Cambridge: Cambridge University Press, 1977); M. Murmis, "El Agro Serrano y la Via Prusiana de Desarrollo Capitalista," in FLACSO-CEPLAES, *Ecuador: Cambios en el Agro Serrano* (Quito: Editores Asociados, 1980).

60. James Petras, *Critical Perspectives on Imperialism and Social Class in the Third World* (New York: Monthly Review Press, 1978).

61. Typologies of social classes and farm enterprises in Latin America based on alternative criteria to the above have been developed by: Stavenhagen, *Social Classes;* R. Pozas, *Los Indios en las Clases Sociales de México* (Mexico City: Siglo XXI, 1971); Roger Bartra, *Estructura Agraria y Clases Sociales en México* (Mexico City: Ediciones Era, 1974); and David Lehmann, "A Theory of Agrarian Structure: Typology and Paths of Transformation in Latin America," unpublished paper (Washington, D.C.: World Bank, Development Center, 1978).

62. The Inter-American Committee for Agricultural Development was organized jointly by the United Nations Food and Agriculture Organization, the United Nations Economic Commission for Latin America, the Organization of American States, the Inter-American Institute for Agricultural Sciences, and the Inter-American Development Bank to collect data on land tenure and rural development in seven countries. The results of this work are summarized in Solon Barraclough, ed., *Agrarian Structure in Latin America* (Lexington, Mass.: Heath, Lexington Books, 1973).

63. Ibid., p. xviii.

64. Dividing the percentage of total agricultural land held in LMF and MMF farms by the percentage of rural families holding those farms provides the following indexes of concentration: Brazil, 6.4; Chile, 9.8; Argentina, 10.0; Colombia, 14.6; Ecuador, 26.8; Peru, 29.4; and Guatemala, 45.2.

65. CIDA, *Tenencia de la Tierra y Desarrollo Socio-Económico del Sector Agrícola, Chile* (Santiago de Chile: CIDA, 1966), chap. 12.

66. Barraclough, ed., *Agrarian Structure in Latin America*. See, in particular, the chapters on Ecuador, Brazil, and Colombia.

67. Solon Barraclough and J. A. Fernandez, *Diagnóstico de la Reforma Agraria Chilena* (Mexico City: Siglo XXI, 1974).

68. Carlos Samaniego, "Movimiento Campesino o Lucha del Proletariado Rural en El Salvador?" mimeographed (Madison: University of Wisconsin, Department of Rural Sociology, 1978).

69. ECLA, "Cuestiones Principales Sobre el Desarrollo Social Rural en America Latina," mimeographed (Santiago de Chile, October 1978), pp. 26 and 29. See also the data in Table 2.4 above.

70. PREALC, "The Employment Pattern in Latin America: Facts, Outlook, and Policies," mimeographed (Santiago de Chile, 1976).

71. Peter Peek, "Agrarian Change and Rural Emigration in Latin America," ILO Working Paper, World Employment Programme Research (Geneva: ILO, 1978), p. 22.

72. Emilio Klein, "Diferenciación Social: Tendencias del Empleo y los Ingresos Agrícolas," mimeographed (Santiago de Chile: ILO, March 1980).

73. Jose Graziano da Silva, "A Mao de Obra Volante em São Paulo," *Contexto,* no. 5 (March 1978), pp. 71–88.

74. These data are reported in William Saint, "The Wages of Modernization: Temporary Labor Arrangements in Brazilian Agriculture," mimeographed (Rio de Janeiro: Ford Foundation, March 1979).

75. Juarez Lopes, "Aspects of Adjustments of Rural Migrants to Urban-Industrial Conditions in São Paulo, Brazil," in *Urbanization in Latin America,* ed. Philip Hauser (Paris: UNESCO, 1961).

76. David Goodman and Michael Redclift, "The 'Boias Frias': Rural Proletarianization and Urban Marginality in Brazil," *International Journal of Urban and Regional Research* 1, no. 2 (1977): 348–64.

77. Floyd and Lillian Dotson, "Mexico's Urban-dwelling Farmers," *Rural Sociology* 43, no. 4 (Winter 1978): 691–710.

78. Verena Martinez-Alier, "As Mulheres do Caminhao de Turma," in *Capital e Trabalho no Campo,* ed. Jaime Pinsky (São Paulo: Editora Hucitec, 1977).

79. These three countries have been chosen because they are the locations of the rural-development projects analyzed in Chapter 7 below.

80. Rodolfo Stavenhagen, *Neolatifundismo y Explotación* (Mexico City: Editorial Nuestro, 1968).

81. Clark W. Reynolds, *The Mexican Economy: Twentieth-Century Structure and Growth* (New Haven: Yale University Press, 1970).

82. Cynthia Hewitt de Alcantara, *Modernizing Mexican Agriculture* (Geneva: UNRISD, 1976), p. 459.

83. Reed Hertford, *Sources of Change in Mexican Agricultural Production, 1940–1965*, U.S. Department of Agriculture, Foreign Agricultural Economic Report no. 13 (Washington, D.C.: Government Printing Office, 1971); Hewitt de Alcantara, *Modernizing Mexican Agriculture*.

84. Barbara Tuckman, "The Green Revolution and the Distribution of Agricultural Income in Mexico," *World Development* 4, no. 1 (1976): 17–24.

85. Ibid., p. 22.

86. *V Censo Agrícola-Ganadero y Ejidal* (Mexico City, 1970).

87. Kirsten de Appendini and Vania Almeida Salles, "Algunas Consideraciones Sobre los Precios de Garantía y la Crisis de Producción de los Alimentos Básicos," *Demografía y Economía*, no. 33 (1979).

88. DEGA-SARH, "Consumos Apparentes de Productos Agropecuarios para los Años de 1925 al 1976," *Econotecnia Agrícola* 1, no. 9 (1977).

89. Arthur Domike and Gonzalo Rodríguez, "Agroindustria en México: Estructura de los Sistemas y Oportunidades para Empresas Campesinas," mimeographed (Mexico City: CIDE, 1976).

90. NACLA, "Bitter Fruits," *Latin America and Empire Report* 10, no. 7 (1976): 14.

91. David Barkin, "Mexican Agriculture and the Internationalization of Capital," Report no. 68 (Irvine: University of California, School of Social Sciences, May 1980), p. 15.

92. Roger Bartra, "Campesinado y Capitalismo en Mexico" (Paper presented at the meeting of the Latin American Studies Association, Pittsburgh, Pa., 1979).

93. Ibid.

94. CIDA, *Estructura Agraria y Desarrollo Agrícola en México* (Mexico City: Fondo de Cultura Economica, 1974), p. 482.

95. Carlotta Botey, J. L. Herida, and M. Zepeda, "Los Jornaleros Migratorios: Una Solución Organizada," mimeographed (Mexico City: Secretaria de la Reforma Agraria, 1975).

96. CIDA, *Estructura Agraria;* Botey, Herida, and Zepeda, "Los Jornaleros Migratorios"; Hewitt de Alcantara, *Modernizing Mexican Agriculture*.

97. Barkin, "Mexican Agriculture."

98. Hewitt de Alcantara, *Modernizing Mexican Agriculture*, p. 123.

99. Luis Gómez Oliver, "Crisis Agrícola, Crisis de los Campesinos," *Comercio Exterior* 28, no. 6 (June 1978): 714–27.

100. *V. Censo Agrícola-Ganadero y Ejidal* (Mexico City, 1970).

101. CIDA, *Estructura Agraria*, p. 587.

102. Ibid., p. 274.

103. Hewitt de Alcantara, *Modernizing Mexican Agriculture*, pp. 131–33.

104. Jorge A. Bustamante, "More on the Impact of the Undocumented Immigration from Mexico on the U.S.-Mexican Economies: Preliminary Findings and Suggestions for Bilateral Cooperation" (Paper presented at the Forty-sixth Annual Conference of the Southern Economic Association, Atlanta, Georgia, November 17–19, 1976), table 8.

105. James Parsons, *Antioqueño Colonization in Western Colombia* (Berkeley: University of California Press, 1949).

106. Absalon Machado, *El Café: De la Aparcería al Capitalismo* (Bogotá: Punta de Lanza, 1977).

107. Victor Moncayo, "La Ley y el Problema Agrario en Colombia," *Ideología y Sociedad* 14–15 (July–December 1975): 7–46.

108. DANE, *La Agricultura en Colombia, 1950–1972* (Bogotá: DANE, 1977).

109. Salomon Kalmanovitz, *Desarrollo de la Agricultura en Colombia* (Bogotá: Editorial la Carreta, 1978).

110. World Bank, *World Tables, 1976* (Baltimore: The Johns Hopkins University Press, 1976).

111. Kalmanovitz, *Desarrollo de la Agricultura*, p. 37.

112. Albert Berry, "Land Distribution, Income Distribution, and the Productive Efficiency of Colombian Agriculture," mimeographed (New Haven: Yale University, Economic Growth Center, 1971).

113. José Carlos Máriategui, *Siete Ensayos de Interpretación de la Realidad Peruana* (Lima: Biblioteca Amauta, 1976), p. 84; see also Mariano Valderrama, *Siete Años de Reforma Agraria Peruana, 1969–1976* (Lima: Fondo Editorial, Pontificia Universidad Católica, 1977).

114. Colin Harding, "Land Reform and Social Conflict in Peru," in *The Peruvian Experiment,* ed. Abraham Lowenthal (Princeton: Princeton University Press, 1975), p. 231.

115. Douglas K. Horton, "Comparative Study of Land Reform in Latin America: Peru Case Study," *Studies in Employment and Rural Development,* no. 22 (Washington, D.C.: World Bank, June 1975).

116. Harding, "Land Reform and Social Conflict."

117. Even as harsh a critic as Aníbal Quijano gives this assessment, although he denounces the actual thrust of the land reform movement. See his "La Reforma Agraria en el Perú," in *La Lucha de Clases en el Campo,* ed. Ernest Feder (Mexico City: Fondo de Cultura Economica, 1975).

118. Julio Cotler, "The New Mode of Political Domination in Peru," in *The Peruvian Experiment,* ed. Abraham Lowenthal (Princeton: Princeton University Press, 1975), p. 63.

119. Douglas K. Horton, "Land Reform and Group Farming in Peru," in *Cooperative and Commune,* ed. Peter Dorner (Madison: University of Wisconsin Press, 1977), p. 236.

120. Harding, "Land Reform and Social Conflict," p. 238.

121. Cotler, "The New Mode of Political Domination in Peru," p. 63.

122. Thomas Carroll, "Land Reform in Peru," *AID Spring Review on Land Reform,* 1970, p. 7.

123. A. Figueroa, "La Economia Rural de la Sierra Peruana," in *Distribución del Ingreso en America Latina,* ed. O. Muñoz (Buenos Aires: Editorial El Cid, 1979).

124. José Maria Caballero, "Sobre el Caracter de la Reforma Agraria Peruana," *Latin American Perspectives* 4, no. 3 (Summer 1977): 146–59.

125. ILO, "Peru: Estrategia de Desarrollo y Grado de Satisfacción de las Necesidades Básicas," mimeographed (Santiago de Chile: PREALC, 1978).

Chapter 4

1. G. Hardin, "Living on a Lifeboat," *Bio Science* 23, no. 10 (October 1974): 561–68. For Malthus, while death rates increase with poverty due to malnutrition and hunger, birth rates remain largely unaffected.

2. P. Ehrlich, *The Population Bomb* (New York: Ballantine Books, 1968); D. Meadows et al., *The Limits to Growth* (New York: Universe Books, 1972).

3. G. Borgstrom, *The Food and People Dilemma* (North Scituate, Mass.: Duxbury Press, 1973), p. 14.

4. A Coale and E. Hoover, *Population Growth and Development in Low Income Countries* (Princeton: Princeton University Press, 1958). In Latin America, 45–55 percent of the population is comprised of youth under fifteen years of age; see World Bank, *Population Policies and Economic Development* (Washington, D.C.: World Bank, 1975).

5. L. Brown, *By Bread Alone* (New York: Praeger Publishers, 1974).

6. Barry Commoner, "How Poverty Breeds Overpopulation (And Not the Other Way Around)," *Ramparts,* 1975.

7. F. Oechsli and D. Kirk, "Modernization and the Demographic Transition in Latin America and the Caribbean," *Economic Development and Cultural Change* 23, no. 3 (April 1975): 391–420.

8. P. Bairoch, "Agriculture and the Industrial Revolution, 1700-1914," in *The Fontana Economic History of Europe: The Industrial Revolution,* ed. C. Cipolla (London: Fontana Books, 1973). See also Ernest Mandel, "Revolución Agrícola y Revolución Industrial," *Críticas de la Economía Política,* no. 5 (October-December 1977), pp. 39-55.

9. Exceptions are Argentina and Uruguay, which had agricultural revolutions in the nineteenth century and which developed very much as center nations until the 1930s, when the collapse of the world food market destroyed the basis of their insertion into the international economy.

10. S. Wortman and R. Cummings, *To Feed This World* (Baltimore: The Johns Hopkins University Press, 1978).

11. Everett Rogers, *The Diffusion of Innovations* (New York: Free Press of Glencoe, 1962).

12. Y. Hayami and V. Ruttan, *Agricultural Development: An International Perspective* (Baltimore: The Johns Hopkins University Press, 1971), p. 59.

13. Steve Marglin, "What Do Bosses Do? The Origins and Functions of Hierarchy in Capitalist Production," *Review of Radical Political Economics* 6, no. 2 (Summer 1974): 60-112.

14. In particular, development of technology that permits substitution of renewable energy for fossil energy and biological control or genetic resistance for chemical control of pests and diseases.

15. Frances Moore Lappé and Joseph Collins, *Food First* (Boston: Houghton Mifflin, 1977).

16. C. Wallace, "After the Green Revolution," *The Sciences* 13, no. 8 (October 1973): 6-12.

17. T. W. Schultz, *Economic Growth and Agriculture* (New York: McGraw-Hill, 1968); Harry G. Johnson, *Economic Policies Toward Less Developed Countries* (Washington, D.C.: Brookings Institution, 1967).

18. Michael Lipton, *Why Poor People Stay Poor: A Study of Urban Bias in World Development* (Cambridge, Mass.: Harvard University Press, 1977).

19. Markos Mamalakis, "Public Policy and Sectoral Development: A Case Study of Chile, 1940-1958," in *Essays on the Chilean Economy,* ed. M. Mamalakis and C. Reynolds (Homewood, Ill.: R. Irwin, 1965), p. 148.

20. T. W. Schultz, *Transforming Traditional Agriculture* (New Haven: Yale University Press, 1964).

21. Schultz, *Economic Growth,* p. 188.

22. See, for example, the summary of results in Raj Krishna, "Agricultural Price Policy and Economic Development," in *Agricultural Development and Economic Growth,* ed. H. Southworth and B. Johnston (Ithaca, N.Y.: Cornell University Press, 1967).

23. I. Little, T. Scitovsky, and M. Scott, *Industry and Trade in Some Developing Countries: A Comparative Study* (New York: Oxford University Press, 1970); and B. Balassa, "Effective Protection in Developing Countries," in *Trade, Balance of Payments, and Growth,* ed. J. Bhagwati et al. (Amsterdam: North-Holland Publishing Co., 1970), pp. 300-323.

24. This committee was sponsored by the United Nations, the Organization of American States, and the Inter-American Development Bank. Its findings are summarized in Solon Barraclough, ed., *Agrarian Structure in Latin America* (Lexington, Mass.: Heath, Lexington Books, 1973), p. 101; see also Ernest Feder, *The Rape of the Peasantry* (Garden City, N.Y.: Doubleday, Anchor Books, 1971).

25. Barraclough, ed., *Agrarian Structure,* p. xxiv.

26. In general, the enormous literature on economies-of-scale in farm size does conclude that there are virtually no internal economies beyond very small farms. See, for example, Albert Berry and William Cline, *Agrarian Structure and Productivity in Developing Countries* (Baltimore: The Johns Hopkins University Press, 1979), p. 6.

27. Edith Obschatko and Alain de Janvry, "Factores Limitantes al Cambio Tecnológico en el Sector Agropecuario," *Desarrollo Económico* 11, no. 44 (March 1972): 263-85.

28. Solon Barraclough, "Agricultural Production Prospects in Latin America," *World Development* 5, nos. 5-7 (1977): 459-76.

29. Frances Moore Lappé, *Diet for a Small Planet* (New York: Ballantine Books, 1971), p. 6.

30. Brown, *By Bread Alone,* p. 197.

31. One of the resolutions adopted at the 1974 World Food Conference in Rome was phrased to this effect.

32. W. Paddock and P. Paddock, *Famine—1975!* (Boston: Little, Brown & Co., 1967).

33. As Earl Butz, U.S. Secretary of Agriculture, said, "food is a weapon." See NACLA, *U.S. Grain Arsenal* 9, no. 7 (October 1975).

34. P. Svedberg, "World Food Sufficiency and Meat Consumption," *American Journal of Agricultural Economics* 60, no. 4 (November 1978): 661–66.

35. Wyn Owen, "The Double Developmental Squeeze on Agriculture," *American Economy Review* 56, no. 1 (March 1966): 43–70.

36. Frances Moore Lappé, "Fantasies of Famine," *Harper's*, January 1975.

37. S. Rosenfeld, "The Politics of Food," *Foreign Policy*, no. 14 (Spring 1974), pp. 17–29.

38. N. Eberstadt, "Myths of the Food Crisis," *New York Review of Books* 23, no. 2 (February 1976): 32–37.

39. For example, see R. Weisskoff, "Income Distribution and Economic Growth in Puerto Rico, Argentina, and Mexico," *Review of Income and Wealth* 16, no. 4 (December 1970): 303–32; and A. Fishlow, "Brazilian Size Distribution of Income," *American Economic Review* 62, no. 2 (May 1972): 391–402.

40. Keith Griffin, "Increasing Poverty and Changing Ideas About Development Strategies," *Development and Change* 8 (1977): 491–508.

41. Brown, *By Bread Alone*, p. 210.

42. Schultz, *Transforming Traditional Agriculture*, chap. 4.

43. Vekemans, Desal Institute, Santiago de Chile. See F. Hinkelhammert, *Dialéctica del Desarrollo Desigual* (Santiago de Chile: CEREN, 1972).

44. Pierre Philippe Rey, *Les Alliances de classes* (Paris: Maspéro, 1976); Samir Amin and Kostas Vergopoulos, eds., *La Question paysanne et le capitalisme* (Paris: Editions Anthropos, 1974); Victor Moncayo, "Es Capitalista la Renta de la Tierra?" *Ideología y Sociedad* 17–18 (April–September 1976): 36–64.

45. Victor Moncayo, "La Ley y el Problema Agrario en Colombia," *Ideología y Sociedad* 14–15 (July–December 1975): 7–46.

46. Salomon Kalmanovitz, *Desarrollo de la Agricultura en Colombia* (Bogotá: Editorial la Carreta, 1978).

47. V. I. Lenin, "The Agrarian Program of the Social Democracy in the First Russian Revolution of 1905–1907," in *Collected Works*, vol. 12 (Moscow: Foreign Language Publishing House, 1962), pp. 238–42.

48. World Bank, *Economic Growth of Colombia: Problems and Prospects, 1970* (Baltimore: The Johns Hopkins Press, 1972), p. 241.

49. CIDA, *Tenencia de la Tierra y Desarrollo Socio-Económico del Sector Agrícola, Colombia* (Washington, D.C.: Pan-American Union, 1966), p. 193.

50. Ibid., p. 181.

51. Albert Berry and Miguel Urrutia, *Income Distribution in Colombia* (New Haven: Yale University Press, 1976).

52. Ibid., p. 270.

53. CIDA, *Tenencia de la Tierra . . . Colombia*, p. 173.

54. Berry and Urrutia, *Income Distribution in Colombia*, p. 240; see also Wayne Thirsk, "Income Distribution Consequences of Agricultural Price Supports in Colombia," mimeographed (Houston: Rice University, Program of Development Studies, 1973).

55. Berry and Urrutia, *Income Distribution in Colombia*, p. 234.

56. For small borrowers, the corresponding rates were 7–8 percent and 11 percent.

57. Berry and Urrutia, *Income Distribution in Colombia*, p. 213.

58. Ibid., p. 209.

59. Ibid., p. 236.

60. Kalmanovitz, *Desarrollo de la Agricultura*.

61. OAS, *Basic Working Documents for Discussion at the VII Inter-American Conference on*

Agriculture, Tegucigalpa, Honduras, September 1977 (Washington, D.C., 1977), pp. 17 and 18. In Brazil, agricultural credit was as much as 89 percent of the gross value of agricultural production in 1975; see Gervasio Castro de Rezende, "Subsidized Credit Policy and Capital Accumulation in Brazilian Agriculture, 1969–79," mimeographed (Rio de Janeiro: IPEA, October 1979).

62. Ibid., p. 20.

63. NACLA, "Agribusiness Targets in Latin America," *Report on the Americas* 12, no. 1 (January–February 1978); Ernest Feder, *Strawberry Imperialism* (The Hague: Institute of Social Studies, 1978).

64. *Latin America,* October 22, 1976, p. 326.

65. Lappé and Collins, *Food First,* pp. 199–200.

66. Cheryl Payer, *The Debt Trap: The International Monetary Fund and the Third World* (New York: Monthly Review Press, 1974); NACLA, *Public Debts and Private Profits* 12, no. 4 (July–August 1978).

67. Little, Scitovsky, and Scott, *Industry and Trade,* p. 417.

68. The effective rate of protection measures the percentage difference between the value added in production valued at domestic prices and the value added at world market prices, taking into account differences between domestic and world prices of inputs as well as products. Using the equilibrium value of the rate of foreign exchange instead of the official rate of exchange, the net effective rate of protection or the effective rate of protection at the shadow value of the national currency can be calculated. See Harry G. Johnson, *Economic Policies Toward Less Developed Countries* (Washington, D.C.: Brookings Institution, 1967), pp. 90 and 91.

69. A. Valdés, "Trade Policy and Its Effect on the External Agricultural Trade of Chile, 1945–1965," *American Journal of Agricultural Economics* 55, no. 2 (May 1973): 154–64.

70. Balassa, "Effective Protection in Developing Countries."

71. Fernando Homem de Melo, "Agricultura de Exportacão e o Problema da Producão de Alimentos," mimeographed (São Paulo: University of São Paulo, IPE, January 1979).

72. J. Gasques et al., "A Forca de Trabalho Volante na Agricultura Paulista," *Agricultura en São Paulo* 24, nos. 1–2 (1977): 83–94.

73. J. Bengoa, J. Crispi, M. E. Cruz, and C. Leiva, "Capitalismo y Campesinado en el Agro Chileno," Grupo de Investigaciones Agrarias, Academia de Humanismo Christiano, Report no. 1, mimeographed (Santiago de Chile, November 1979).

74. NACLA, "Agribusiness Targets," p. 32.

75. PREALC, "The Problem of Employment in Latin America and the Caribbean: Diagnosis, Perspectives, and Policies," mimeographed (Santiago de Chile, November 1975), p. II-24.

76. Lappé and Collins, *Food First.*

77. NACLA, "Agribusiness Targets," p. 28.

78. UNCTAD, *The Marketing and Distribution System for Bananas* (December 1974).

79. Arghiri Emmanuel, ed., *Unequal Exchange* (New York: Modern Reader, 1972), chap. 6.

80. Lappé and Collins, *Food First,* pp. 381 and 382.

81. Derek Healey, "Development Policy: New Thinking About an Interpretation," *Journal of Economic Literature* 10, no. 3 (September 1972): 757–97.

82. Fund Stall, "The Resurgence of Protectionism," *Finance and Development* 15, no. 3 (September 1978): 14–19.

83. ILO, *Towards Full Employment: A Programme for Colombia* (Geneva: ILO, 1970), p. 338.

84. Shlomo Reutlinger, *Food Insecurity: Magnitude and Remedies,* World Bank Paper No. 267 (Washington, D.C.: World Bank, July 1977).

85. Willard Cochran, *Farm Prices: Myth and Reality* (Minneapolis: University of Minnesota Press, 1958); Owen, "The Double Developmental Squeeze on Agriculture."

86. Ashok Mitra, "The Terms of Trade, Class Conflict, and Classical Political Economy," *Journal of Peasant Studies* 4, no. 2 (January 1977): 181–94.

87. CIDA, *Tenencia de la Tierra y Desarrollo Socio-Económico del Sector Agrícola, Chile* (Santiago de Chile: CIDA, 1966), p. 246.

88. E. Venezian and W. Gamble, *The Agricultural Development of Mexico* (New York: Frederick A. Praeger, 1969), p. 117.

89. G. E. Schuh, *The Agricultural Development of Brazil* (New York: Frederick A. Praeger, 1970), p. 97.

90. Miguel Teubal, "Policy and Performance of Agriculture in Economic Development: The Case of Argentina" (Ph.D. diss., University of California, Berkeley, 1975).

91. Carlos Diaz-Alejandro, *Essays on the Economic History of the Argentine Republic* (New Haven: Yale University Press, 1970), p. 89.

92. A. Saleh, "Disincentives to Agricultural Production in Developing Countries: A Policy Survey," U.S. Foreign Agricultural Service, *Foreign Agriculture* 13, supp. (March 1975): 107.

93. Little, Scitovsky, and Scott, *Industry and Trade*.

94. Alain de Janvry, "Optimal Levels of Fertilization Under Risk: The Potential for Corn and Wheat Fertilization Under Alternative Price Policies in Argentina," *American Journal of Agricultural Economics* 54, no. 1 (February 1972): 1–10.

95. Willis Peterson, "International Farm Prices and the Social Cost of Cheap Food Policies," *American Journal of Agricultural Economics* 61, no. 1 (February 1979): 12–21. Peterson's terms-of-trade data are, however, biased against the periphery, since they fail to allow for lower wage costs there.

96. Valdés, "Trade Policy."

97. A. Valdés, "Protección de la Industria de Fertilizantes y su Efecto en la Producción Agrícola y en el Ahorro Neto de Divisas: El Caso del Salitre," mimeographed (Santiago de Chile: Catholic University of Chile, Department of Agricultural Economics, 1973).

98. G. E. Schuh, "Effects of Some General Economic Development Policies on Agricultural Development," *American Journal of Agricultural Economics* 5, no. 5 (December 1968): 1283–93.

99. Peterson, "International Farm Prices," p. 21.

100. S. Mann and J. Dickinson, "Obstacles to the Development of a Capitalist Agriculture," *Journal of Peasant Studies* 5, no. 4 (July 1978): 466–81.

101. G. Scobie and R. Posada, "The Impact of Technical Change on Income Distribution: The Case of Rice in Colombia," *American Journal of Agricultural Economics* 60, no. 1 (February 1978): 85–92.

102. F. Diaz et al., "Costs and Use of Inputs in Cassava Production in Colombia: A Brief Description" (Cali, Colombia: CIAT, 1974).

103. G. Scobie and R. Posada, *The Impact of High-Yielding Rice Varieties in Latin America, with Special Emphasis on Colombia* (Cali, Colombia: CIAT, April 1976) p. 119.

104. Lana Hall, "Food Aid and Agricultural Development: The Case of P.L. 480 Wheat in Latin America" (Ph.D. diss. University of California, Berkeley, 1978).

105. Barraclough, "Agricultural Production Prospects in Latin America."

106. Barraclough, ed., *Agrarian Structure*, p. 14.

107. For example, see Marglin, "What Do Bosses Do?"

108. Hayami and Ruttan, *Agricultural Development*.

109. Alain de Janvry, "Inducement of Technological and Institutional Innovations: An Interpretative Framework," in *Resource Allocation and Productivity of National and International Agricultural Research*, ed. T. Arndt, D. Dalrymple, and V. Ruttan (Minneapolis: University of Minnesota Press, 1977).

110. "In the dynamics of growth this phenomenon gives the nonfarm sector, under the conditions of the Mill-Marshallian model [i.e., yield-increasing technological change and inelastic demand] a perpetual advantage in respect to its claim on the total income stream vis-à-vis the farm sector, which really amounts to a dynamic form of intersectoral taxation expertly administered by the invisible hand" (Owen, "The Double Developmental Squeeze," p. 55).

111. F. Dovring, "Land Reform and Productivity in Mexico," *Land Economics* 46 (August 1970); and Reed Hertford, *Sources of Change in Mexican Agricultural Production, 1940-1965,* U.S. Department of Agriculture, Foreign Agricultural Economic Report no. 13 (Washington, D.C., August 1971). In the Magdalena Valley of Colombia, rice is produced in the context of the farmer and merchant roads, for large estates were divided and sold in the process of constructing irrigation networks.

112. In Brazil, for instance, credit for mechanization in agriculture provided by the Bank of Brazil had an average negative real rate of interest of 27 percent between 1961 and 1971. Analyzing the factors that determine tractor sales, J. Sanders ("Mechanization and Employment in Brazilian Agriculture, 1950-1971" [Ph.D. diss., University of Minnesota, 1973]) demonstrates that availability of subsidized credit, not the market price of tractors, is the major explanatory variable. A similar situation is found in Colombia. See Wayne Thirsk, "The Economics of Colombian Farm Mechanization" (Ph.D. diss., Yale University, 1972); and J. Araya and C. Ossa, *La Mecanización en la Agricultura Colombiana* (Bogotá: Adimagro, 1977).

113. Food and Agriculture Organization of the United Nations, *Production Yearbook,* 1952, 1972, and 1975.

114. ECLA/FAO, "Evolución de la Agricultura y la Alimentación en America Latina: Notas Sobre el Desarrollo de America Latina," no. 210, mimeographed (Santiago de Chile, March 1976).

115. CIDA, *Tenencia de la Tierra... Colombia,* p. 212.

116. PREALC, "The Problem of Employment in Latin America and the Caribbean."

117. OAS, *America en Cifras: Situación Económica* (Washington, D.C.: OAS, 1974).

118. Keith Griffin, *The Political Economy of Agrarian Change: An Essay on the Green Revolution* (London: Macmillan & Co., 1975), chap. 5.

119. R. Boddy and J. Crotty, "Food Prices: Planned Crisis in Defense of the Empire," *Socialist Revolution* 5, no. 1 (April 1975): 102.

120. D. Morgan, *Merchants of Grain* (New York: Viking Press, 1979).

121. G. E. Schuh, "The New Macroeconomics of Agriculture," *American Journal of Agricultural Economics* 58, no. 5 (December 1976): 802-11.

122. J. Grant, "The Trilateral Stake: More Food in the Developing Countries or More Inflation in the Industrial Democracies," *Trilogue* 17 (1978): 3-13.

123. U.S. Commission on International Trade and Investment Policy, *United States International Economic Policy in an Interdependent World,* report prepared for the President (Washington, D.C.: Government Printing Office, 1971).

124. Two authors who discuss the Williams Report in this context are James Petras, *Critical Perspectives on Imperialism and Social Class in the Third World* (New York: Monthly Review Press, 1978): and E. Havens, "The Political Economy of Food," mimeographed (Madison: University of Wisconsin, 1978).

125. S. Forman and W. Saint, "Agricultural Production, Distribution, and Consumption: An Interim Program Document for Agriculture and Rural Development in Brazil, 1978-80," mimeographed (Rio de Janeiro: Ford Foundation, June 1978).

126. NACLA, "Harvest of Anger: Agro-Imperialism in Mexico's Northwest," *Latin American and Empire Report* 10, no. 6 (July-August 1976): 11.

127. The peripheral countries, which were exporting 12 million tons of grain a year in the 1930s, were importing 63 million tons in 1976. See IFPRI, *Food Needs in Developing Countries: Projections of Production and Consumption to 1990* (Washington, D.C.: IFPRI, 1977).

128. Grant, "The Trilateral Stake."

129. Feder, *Strawberry Imperialism;* NACLA, "Agribusiness Targets"; G. Arroyo, "Modelos de Acumulación, Clases Sociales y Agricultura," mimeographed (Paris: University of Paris, November 1977); Susan George, *How the Other Half Dies* (Montclair, N.J.: Allanheld, Osmun & Co., 1977).

130. NACLA, "Agribusiness Targets."

Chapter 5

1. For recent surveys of theories of the state, see Bob Jessop, "Recent Theories of the Capitalist State," *Cambridge Journal of Economics* 1, no. 4 (1977): 353-73; and J. Holloway and S. Picciotto, "Introduction: Towards a Materialist Theory of the State," in *State and Capital: A Marxist Debate*, ed. J. Holloway and S. Picciotto (Austin: University of Texas Press, 1979).

2. D. Gold, C. Lo, and E. Wright, "Recent Developments in Marxist Theories of the State," *Monthly Review* 27, nos. 5 and 6 (October and November 1975): 29-43 and 36-51.

3. Paul A. Baran and Paul M. Sweezy, *Monopoly Capital* (New York: Monthly Review Press, 1966).

4. N. Poulantzas, *Political Power and Social Classes* (London: New Left Books, 1973).

5. J. O'Connor, *The Fiscal Crisis of the State* (New York: St. Martin's Press, 1973).

6. Holloway and Picciotto, eds., *State and Capital.*

7. This category is used by Holloway and Picciotto to include a variety of theorists, but especially Engels, Gramsci, Poulantzas, and Miliband.

8. On the displacement of crises, see Jurgen Habermas, *Legitimation Crisis* (Boston: Beacon Press, 1975), pt. 2. For a critical review, see Tony Woodiwiss, "Critical Theory and the Capitalist State," *Economy and Society* 7, no. 2 (May 1978): 175-92.

9. A good explanation of this abstraction is given by Margaret Fay in "Review of Holloway and Picciotto, eds., *State and Capital: A Marxist Debate,*" *Kapitalistate,* no. 7 (1978), pp. 130-52.

10. The seminal article on this issue is W. Muller and C. Weususs, "The Illusion of State Socialism and the Contradiction Between Wage Labor and Capital," *Telos,* no. 25 (Fall 1975), pp. 13-90.

11. This question was first raised by E. B. Pashukanis in an article translated as "The General Theory of Law and Marxism," in *Soviet Legal Philosophy,* ed. H. W. Babb and J. N. Hazard (Cambridge, Mass.: Harvard University Press, 1951), pp. 111-225.

12. E. Altwater, "Some Problems of State Interventionism: The 'Particularization' of the State in Bourgeois Society," in *State and Capital: A Marxist Debate,* ed. J. Holloway and S. Picciotto (Austin: University of Texas Press, 1979); B. Blanke, U. Jurgens, and H. Kastendiek, "On the Current Marxist Discussion on the Analysis of the Form and Function of the Bourgeois State," ibid.

13. J. Hirsch, "The State Apparatus and Social Reproduction: Elements of a Theory of the Bourgeois State," ibid.

14. H. Reichelt, "Some Comments on Sybille von Flatow and Freerk Huisken's Essay, 'On the Problem of the Derivation of the Bourgeois State,'" ibid.

15. Jessop, "Recent Theories of the Capitalist State," p. 36.

16. Holloway and Picciotto, eds., *State and Capital,* p. 29.

17. Karl Marx, *The Eighteenth Brumaire of Louis Bonaparte,* in K. Marx and F. Engels, *Selected Works,* vol. 1 (Moscow: Progress Publishers, 1969), p. 398.

18. Holloway and Picciotto, eds., *State and Capital.*

19. The archetypal expression of this ideology is found in Milton Friedman, *Capitalism and Freedom* (Chicago: University of Chicago Press, 1962).

20. Douglas Kellner, "Ideology, Marxism, and Advanced Capitalism," *Socialist Review* 8, no. 6 (November-December 1978): 37-65.

21. Antonio Gramsci, *Prison Notebooks* (New York: International Publishers, 1971), p. 328.

22. Herbert Gintis, "The Nature of Labor Exchange and the Theory of Capitalist Production," *Review of Radical Political Economics* 8, no. 2 (Summer 1976): 36-54.

23. Michael Reich and Richard Edwards, "Political Parties and Class Conflict in the United States," *Socialist Review* 8, no. 3 (May-June 1978): 37-57. In 1970, Singleman and Wright distributed the U.S. population among social classes as follows: workers, 46 percent;

semiautonomous employees, 11 percent; managers and supervisors, 34 percent; petty bourgeoisie, 4 percent; and employers, 5 percent. For further discussion, see Joachim Singleman and Erik Olin Wright, "Proletarianization in Advanced Capitalist Economies," mimeographed (Madison: University of Wisconsin, Center for Class Analysis, 1978).

24. Samuel Bowles and Herbert Gintis, "The Invisible Fist: Have Capitalism and Democracy Reached a Parting of the Ways?" *American Economic Review* 68, no. 2 (May 1978): 358–63.

25. Reich and Edwards, "Political Parties and Class Conflict."

26. C. Wright Mills, *The Power Elite* (New York: Oxford University Press, 1956).

27. Harry Boyte, "Building the Democratic Movement: Prospects for a Socialist Renaissance," *Socialist Review* 8, nos. 4–5 (July–October 1978): 17–41.

28. Harry Braverman, *Labor and Monopoly Capital* (New York: Monthly Review Press, 1974).

29. Richard Edwards, Michael Reich, and David Gordon, eds., *Labor Market Segmentation* (Lexington, Mass.: D.C. Heath & Co., 1975).

30. Erik Olin Wright, "Class Boundaries in Advanced Capitalist Societies," *New Left Review*, no. 98 (July–August 1976), pp. 3–39.

31. Nicos Poulantzas, *Classes in Contemporary Capitalism* (London: New Left Books, 1975), p. 291.

32. Ibid., p. 292.

33. Quoted in Arthur Blaustein and Geoffrey Faux, *The Star-Spangled Hustle* (Garden City, N.Y.: Doubleday, Anchor Books, 1972), p. 18.

34. Ibid., pp. 249–61; Earl Ofari, *The Myth of Black Capitalism* (New York: Modern Reader, 1970).

Franklin Frazier gives a good description of the contradictory class location of the black bourgeoisie:

> In escaping from identification with the masses, the black bourgeoisie has attempted to identify with the white propertied classes. Since this has been impossible, except in their minds, because of the racial barriers, those identified with this class have attempted to act out this role in a world of make-believe. In the world of make-believe they have not taken over the patterns of behavior of white-collar and professional white workers but the values and as far as possible the patterns of behavior of wealthy whites. With their small earnings, their attempt to maintain the style of living of the white propertied classes has only emphasized the unreality of their way of life. Faith in the myth of Negro business, which symbolizes the power and status of white America, has been the main element in the world of make-believe that the black bourgeoisie has created.

See Franklin Frazier, *Black Bourgeoisie* (New York: Macmillan, Collier, 1970), p. 141.

35. Kellner, "Ideology, Marxism, and Advanced Capitalism," pp. 52–53.

36. Fernando E. Cardoso, "Associated-Dependent Development: Theoretical and Political Implications," in *Authoritarian Brazil: Origins, Policies, and Future*, ed. A. Stepan (New Haven: Yale University Press, 1973); Guillermo O'Donnell, *Modernization and Bureaucratic Authoritarianism: Studies in South American Politics* (Berkeley: University of California, Institute of International Studies, 1973); Octavio Ianni, *Crisis in Brazil* (New York: Columbia University Press, 1970); Philippe Schmitter, *Interest Conflict and Political Change in Brazil* (Stanford: Stanford University Press, 1971); David Collier, ed., *The New Authoritarianism in Latin America* (Princeton: Princeton University Press, 1979).

37. Sherry Girling, "Comments on Hamza Alavi," *Kapitalistate*, no. 2 (1973), p. 49; N. Hamilton, "Dependent Capitalism and the State: The Case of Mexico," ibid., no. 3 (1975), p. 75; W. Hein and K. Stenzel, "The Capitalist State and Underdevelopment in Latin America— The Case of Venezuela," ibid., no. 2 (1973), p. 31.

38. Hein and Stenzel, "The Capitalist State and Underdevelopment," p. 31.

39. Hamilton, "Dependent Capitalism and the State," p. 75.

40. Ibid.

41. Ian Gough, "State Expenditures in Advanced Capitalism," *New Left Review*, no. 92 (July–August 1975), pp. 53–92; Bill Warren, "Capitalist Planning and the State," ibid., no. 72 (March–April 1972), pp. 3–29.

42. Pierre Philippe Rey, *Les Alliances de classes* (Paris: Maspéro, 1973).

43. Nicos Poulantzas, *Political Power and Social Classes* (London: New Left Books, 1973); Antonio Gramsci, *Selections from the Prison Notebooks* (London: Lawrence & Wishart, 1971).

44. O'Connor, *The Fiscal Crisis of the State*.

45. C. Offe and V. Ronge, "Theses on the Theory of the State," *New German Critique*, no. 6 (Fall 1975), pp. 137–47; Jessop, "Recent Theories of the Capitalist State."

46. Fred Block, "The Ruling Class Does Not Rule: Notes on the Marxist Theory of the State," *Socialist Revolution* 7, no. 3 (May–June 1977): 6–28.

47. The role of the International Monetary Fund in dictating policy to nation-states plagued by balance-of-payment crises has been documented by Cheryl Payer in *The Debt Trap: The International Monetary Fund and the Third World* (New York: Monthly Review Press, 1974).

48. J. Cockcroft et al., *Dependence and Underdevelopment* (Garden City, N.Y.: Doubleday, Anchor Books, 1972), p. 34.

49. Ibid., p. 40; M. Pompermayer and W. Smith, "The State in Dependent Societies: Preliminary Notes," in *Structures of Dependency*, ed. F. Bonilla and R. Girling (Stanford, Calif., 1973).

50. Albert O. Hirschman, *Journeys Towards Progress* (New York: Twentieth Century Fund, 1963).

51. Clodomir Moraes, "Peasant Leagues in Brazil," in *Agrarian Problems and Peasant Movements in Latin America*, ed. R. Stavenhagen (Garden City, N.Y.: Doubleday, Anchor Books, 1970); Solon Barraclough, ed., *Agrarian Structures in Latin America* (Lexington, Mass.: Heath, Lexington Books, 1973).

52. J. Boyce and R. Evenson, *Agricultural Research and Extension Programs* (New York: Agricultural Development Council, 1975), pp. 25 and 35.

53. D. Dalrymple, *Measuring the Green Revolution*, U.S. Department of Agriculture, Foreign Agricultural Economic Report no. 106 (Washington, D.C., July 1975), p. 8.

54. Robert McNamara, "Address to the Board of Governors, Nairobi, Kenya" (Washington, D.C.: World Bank, 1973).

Chapter 6

1. The expropriation of indigenous lands by republican elites occurred throughout Latin America, reaching its most massive dimensions in Mexico. There, between 1877 and 1910, over 72 million hectares of land were appropriated under the Porfirio Diaz regime (see R. E. Smith, *The United States and Revolutionary Nationalism* [Chicago: University of Chicago Press, 1972], p. 3). By 1910, fully 90 percent of the rural population could not subsist on the land, while real wages had fallen to about 25 percent of the level of the early 1800s (see F. Tannenbaum, *The Mexican Agrarian Revolution* [Washington, D.C.: Brookings Institution, 1930], p. 372).

2. By contrast to Asian countries like Taiwan and South Korea, there is as yet no Latin American country where the land tenure system is dominated by family farms.

3. Figure 6.1 is to be read as a matrix of transitions among states of the agrarian structure before and after land reform. A particular country can thus reenter the matrix more than once as land reform programs are redefined over time; but it must always reenter the matrix in the state to which it was transformed by the previous land reform.

4. Ernest Feder, *The Rape of the Peasantry* (Garden City, N.Y.: Doubleday, Anchor Books, 1971), p. 247.

5. Luis Crouch, "The Development of Capitalism in Dominican Agriculture" (Ph.D. diss., University of California, Berkeley, 1981).

6. Angel Jemio Ergueta, "La Reforma Agraria en Bolivia" (Paper presented at the Seminar on Experiences and Evaluations of Land Reform in Latin America, United Nations Economic Commission for Latin America, San José, Costa Rica, March 1973), p. 68.

7. The survival of the landowning class has been treated by P. Graeff, "The Effects of Continued Landlord Presence in the Bolivian Countryside During the Post-Reform Era: Lessons to Be Learned," Land Tenure Center Reprint no. 103, mimeographed (Madison: University of Wisconsin, 1974); Dwight Heath, Charles Eramus, and Hans Buechler, eds., Land Reform and Social Revolution in Bolivia (New York: Frederick A. Praeger, 1969); R. J. Clark, "Landholding Structure and Land Conflicts in Bolivian Cattle Regions," Inter-American Economic Affairs 28, no. 2 (Autumn 1974):

8. D. Heyduck, "The Hacienda System and Agrarian Reform in Highland Bolivia: A Re-Evaluation," Ethnology 13, no. 1 (January 1974); M. Burke, "Land Reform in the Lake Titicaca Region," in Beyond the Revolution: Bolivia Since 1952, ed. J. M. Mallory and R. S. Thorn (Pittsburgh: University of Pittsburgh Press, 1974); W. Carter, Aymora Communities and the Bolivian Agrarian Reform, Monograph no. 24 (Gainesville: University of Florida, 1964); Heath, Eramus, and Buechler, eds., Land Reform and Social Revolution.

9. Heath, Eramus, and Buechler, eds., Land Reform and Social Revolution; see also Clark, "Land-holding Structure and Land Conflicts."

10. Food and Agriculture Organization of the United Nations, "Economic and Social Aspects in Developing Countries, with Special Reference to Food and Agriculture," Country Background Information (Rome), August 1968.

11. Solon Barraclough and J. A. Fernandez, Diagnóstico de la Reforma Agraria Chilena (Mexico City: Siglo XXI, 1974).

12. Michel Gutelman, Réforme et mystification agraires en Amérique Latine: Le Cas du Mexique (Paris: Maspéro, 1971).

13. José Maria Caballero, "Sobre el Caracter de la Reforma Agraria Peruana," Latin American Perspectives 4, no. 3 (Summer 1977): 146–59.

14. Clark, "Land-holding Structure and Land Conflicts."

15. Hugo Fazio, "El 'Plan Kelly' y la Inestabilidad de la Economía Chilena," Comercio Exterior 28, no. 9 (September 1978): 1077–84.

16. Ricardo Fenner, "La Política Agraria de la Junta Militar Chilena: Un Intento de Involución Histórica," Cuadernos Agrarios 2, no. 5 (September 1977): 3–15.

17. Keith Griffin, The Political Economy of Agrarian Change: An Essay on the Green Revolution (London: Macmillan & Co., 1975), chap. 5; Andre Gunder Frank, Latin America: Underdevelopment or Revolution? (New York: Modern Reader, 1969), chap. 17; Solon Barraclough, "Latin American Land Reform in Action" (Paper presented at the Rehovoth Conference on Economic Growth in Developing Countries, Rehovoth, Israel, September 1973); D. Warriner, "Results of Land Reform in Asian and Latin American Countries" (Paper presented at the Conference on Strategies for Agricultural Development in the 1970s, Stanford, California, 1971); Edmundo Flores, "La Teoría Económica y la Tipología de la Reforma Agraria," Lecturas Sobre Desarrollo Agrícola (Mexico City: Fondo de Cultura Económica, 1972), pp. 297–317; Ernest Feder, "When Is a Land Reform a Land Reform? The Colombian Case," American Journal of Economics and Sociology 24, no. 2 (1965): 113–34.

18. CIDA, Tenencia de la Tierra y Desarrollo Socio-Económico del Sector Agrícola, Chile (Santiago de Chile: CIDA, 1966).

19. CIDA, Tenencia de la Tierra y Desarrollo Socio-Económico del Sector Agrícola, Ecuador (Washington, D.C.: Pan-American Union, 1965).

20. CIDA, Tenencia de la Tierra y Desarrollo Socio-Económico del Sector Agrícola, Peru (Washington, D.C.: Pan-American Union, 1966).

21. David L. Bayer, "Reforma Agraria Peruana: El Problema de la Descapitalización del Minifundio y la Formación de la Burguesía Rural," mimeographed (Lima, Peru, 1975), pp. 33, 34, and 53.

The negative employment effects of land reform are often magnified by the reaction of landowners to new labor codes commonly contained in the land reform laws. For instance, in the Peruvian Sierra, landowners expelled the permanent workers and rehired them as temporary workers, to whom the minimum wage and social security legislation did not apply. Another example is the reaction of landowners to the increase of the minimum wage contained in the reform law in Colombia (1961/P1); see CIDA, *Tenencia de la Tierra y Desarrollo Socio-Económico del Sector Agrícola, Colombia* (Washington, D.C.: Pan-American Union, 1966), chap. 6 and app. 5.

22. Colin Harding, "Agrarian Reform and Agrarian Struggles in Peru," Center of Latin American Studies, Working Paper no. 15 (Cambridge: Cambridge University, September 1973), pp. 5 and 6; Barraclough and Fernandez, *Diagnóstico de la Reforma Agraria Chilena*.

23. CIDA, *Tenencia de la Tierra . . . Ecuador*, p. 451.

24. Ibid., p. 450.

25. Piedad Costales and Alfredo Costales, *Historia Social de Ecuador*, vol. 4, *Reforma Agraria* (Quito: Editorial Casa de la Cultura, 1971), pp. 64 and 282.

26. Douglas K. Horton, "Comparative Study of Land Reforms in Latin America: Peru Case Study Volume," *Studies in Employment and Rural Development* no. 22 (Washington, D.C.: World Bank, June 1975).

27. Hugo Zemelman and James Petras, *El Campesino y Su Lucha por la Tierra* (Santiago de Chile: Empresa Editorial Nacional Quimantu Limitado, 1972), p. 138.

28. Between 1970 and 1972, the importation of machinery increased 306 percent while the importation of fertilizers declined 29 percent; see Barraclough and Fernandez, *Diagnóstico de la Reforma Agraria Chilena*, p. 132. This rapid mechanization in the reform sector was permitted by a massive inflow of subsidized credit.

29. Harry Wing, *Land Reform in Venezuela: Spring Review*, U.S. Agency for International Development (Washington, D.C., June 1970), p. 46.

30. Ibid., p. 50.

31. J. Kirby, "Venezuela's Land Reform: Progress and Change," *Journal of Inter-American Studies and World Affairs* 15, no. 2 (May 1975).

32. Eleanor Howard, "The Approach to Agrarian Reform in Colombia and the Role of External Lending Agencies," mimeographed (n.p., 1976).

33. R. J. Clark, "Land Reform and Peasant Market Participation in the Northern Highlands of Bolivia," in *The Political Economy of Development*, ed. N. Uphoff and U. F. Ilchman (Berkeley: University of California Press, 1972), pp. 309 and 313.

34. Douglas K. Horton, *Haciendas and Cooperatives: A Preliminary Study of Latifundist Agriculture and Agrarian Reform in Northern Peru*, Land Tenure Center, Research Paper no. 53 (Madison: University of Wisconsin, 1973), p. 69.

35. For Chile, see Barraclough and Fernandez, *Diagnóstico de la Reforma Agraria Chilena*, p. 43; for Peru, see Bayer, "Reforma Agraria Peruana," p. 9; for Colombia, see INCORA, "Reforma Agraria Colombiana," mimeographed (Bogotá, 1972). See also Wing, *Land Reform in Venezuela*, p. 44; and O. D. Soto, *La Empresa y la Reforma Agraria* (Mérida: Instituto Ibero Americano de Direcho Agrario y Reforma Agraria, 1973), p. 80.

36. Centro de Investigaciones Agrarias, *Estructura Agraria y Desarrollo Agrícola en México* (Mexico City: Fondo de Cultura Económica, 1974).

37. Barraclough and Fernandez, *Diagnóstico de la Reforma Agraria Chilena*, pp. 134 and 135.

38. Ibid., p. 39.

39. Food and Agriculture Organization of the United Nations, "Economic and Social Aspects in Developing Countries," p. 13.

40. Potatoes and cereals are produced mainly in the Altiplano, where most of the land reform activity took place, while sugarcane and cottonseed are produced mainly in the Santa Cruz region, which was relatively unaffected by expropriations. It is true, of course, that the disparate produc-

tion performances in these commodities could be due to factors other than a "plan" designed to favor the nonreform sector. However, the design of government programs with respect to agricultural development did indeed systematically favor the nonreform sector; see, for instance, Heath, Eramus, and Buechler, eds., *Land Reform and Social Revolution*, p. 290; Luis Antezano, *El Feudalismo de Melgraejo y la Reforma Agraria* (La Paz, Bolivia, 1970), pp. 157-62; Mark Ruhl, "Santa Cruz: A Study of Economic Growth in Eastern Bolivia," *Inter-American Economic Affairs* 29, no. 2 (Autumn 1975); Clark, "Land-holding Structure and Land Conflicts in Bolivia's Cattle Regions," ibid. 28, no. 2 (Autumn 1974).

41. For cottonseed, the figures cover the 1961-65 to 1974 period; see Food and Agriculture Organization of the United Nations, *Production Yearbook* (Rome), 1961 and 1975.

42. As we saw in Chapter 3, Table 3.7, there are essentially three sectors in Mexican agriculture: the *ejido*, the private capitalist sector, and the private smallholder sector.

43. NACLA, "Harvest of Anger: Agro-Imperialism in Mexico's Northwest," *Latin America and Empire Report* 10, no. 6 (July-August 1976): 18.

44. D. T. Nguyen and M. L. Martinez Saldivar, "The Effects of Land Reform on Agricultural Production, Employment, and Income Distribution: A Statistical Study of Mexican States, 1959-1969," *Economic Journal* 89 (September 1979): 624-35; see also M. Mueller, "Changing Patterns of Agricultural Output and Productivity in the Private and Land Reform Sectors in Mexico, 1940-1960," *Economic Development and Cultural Change* 18, no. 2 (January 1970): 252-66.

45. Reed Hertford, *Sources of Change in Mexican Agricultural Production, 1940-1965*, U.S. Department of Agriculture, Foreign Agricultural Economic Report no. 13 (Washington, D.C., August 1971); see also Table 3.5 above.

46. U.S. Department of Agriculture, *Western Hemisphere Agricultural Situation*, Foreign Agricultural Economic Report no. 136 (Washington, D.C., 1977), p. 22.

47. Food and Agriculture Organization of the United Nations, *Production Yearbook* (Rome), various years.

48. World Bank, *Economic Growth of Colombia: Problems and Prospects, 1970* (Baltimore: The Johns Hopkins University Press, 1972), p. 235.

49. Paul Cox, *Venezuela's Agrarian Reform at Mid-1977*, Land Tenure Center, Research Paper no. 71, (Madison: University of Wisconsin, February 1978), table 27.

50. Ibid., pp. 54 and 55.

51. Dominican Republic, Secretary of State for Agriculture, "Diagnóstico del Sistema de Mercadeo Agrícola en Republica Dominicana," mimeographed (Santo Domingo, 1977).

52. This problem has been particularly acute in Mexico. For example, see Centro de Investigaciones Agrarias, *Estructura Agraria y Desarrollo Agrícola en México;* and Iván Restrepo Fernández and José Sanchez Cortés, *El Arrendamiento de Tierras Ejidales: El Caso de Apatzingan,* Land Tenure Center Reprint no. 86-5 (Madison: University of Wisconsin, n.d.).

53. David Lehmann, "A Theory of Agrarian Structure: Typology and Paths of Transformation in Latin America" unpublished paper (Washington, D.C.: World Bank, Development Center, 1978).

54. José Gimeno, *Agricultura Socialista: Chile y Dieciséis Países* (Santiago de Chile: Editorial Universitaria, 1972).

55. INCORA, *Agrarian Reform and Development in Colombia: Spring Review,* U.S. Agency for International Development (Washington, D.C., June 1970).

56. Criteria for selection of those to be benefited by land reforms are usually that they be internal peasants and/or possess some education, "management skills," etc. Internal peasants are generally the better-off segment of the peasantry due to the stability of their employment and their access to the resources (pasturage, and sometimes schools, medical attention, kindling, etc.) of the estates.

57. Chile, *Mensaje Presidente Allende ante Congreso Pleno,* May 21, 1973, p. 272.

58. Emilio Klein, *Antecedentes para el Estudio de Conflictos Colectivos en el Campo* (San-

tiago de Chile: ICIRA, 1972); A. Affonso et al., *Movimiento Campesino Chileno* (Santiago de Chile: ICIRA, 1970).

59. José Maria Caballero, "Reforma y Restructuración Agraria en Peru," mimeographed (Cambridge: Cambridge University, March 1976), p. 11.

60. Kirby, "Venezuela's Land Reform," p. 207.

61. Ibid., p. 209.

62. Ibid., p. 219.

63. Rodolfo Stavenhagen, "Land Reform and Institutional Alternatives in Agriculture: The Case of the Mexican Ejido," Occasional Paper no. 9 (Vienna: Institute for Development, 1973).

64. Fernando Rello and Rose Elena de Oca, "Acumulación de Capital en el Campo Mexicano," *Cuadernos Politicos,* no. 2 (October–December 1974), p. 70.

65. Stavenhagen, "Land Reform and Institutional Alternatives in Agriculture."

66. For a similar conclusion arrived at through different reasoning, see David Lehmann, "The Death of Land Reform: A Polemic," *World Development* 6, no. 3 (1978): 339–45.

Chapter 7

1. The concepts of integration and incorporation are clearly defined in David Lehmann, "Political Incorporation Versus Political Stability: The Case of the Chilean Agrarian Reform, 1965–1970," *Journal of Development Studies* 7 (1971): 365–96.

2. Everett Rogers, *Communication of Innovations* (New York: Free Press, 1971). For a discussion of the different models of agricultural and rural development, see also Philip H. Coombs and Manzoor Ahmed, *Attacking Rural Poverty: How Nonformal Education Can Help* (Baltimore: The Johns Hopkins University Press, 1974). These authors distinguish four types of models: the extension model, the training model, the self-help model, and the integrated-development model.

3. D. Dalrymple, *Development and Spread of High-Yielding Varieties of Wheat and Rice in Developing Nations,* U.S. Department of Agriculture, Foreign Agricultural Economic Report no. 95, 5th ed. (Washington, D.C., August 1976).

4. NACLA, "Agribusiness Targets in Latin America," *Report on the Americas* 12, no. 1 (January–February 1978); Ernest Feder, "The New Penetration of the Agricultures of the Underdeveloped Countries by the Industrial Nations and Their Multinational Concerns," University of Glasgow, Institute of Social Studies, Occasional Papers no. 19 (Glascow, 1975).

5. Frances Moore Lappé and Joseph Collins, *Food First* (Boston: Houghton Mifflin, 1977).

6. The uneven social impact of the Green Revolution has been amply described in the literature. See, in particular, Keith Griffin, *The Political Economy of Agrarian Change: An Essay on the Green Revolution* (London: Macmillan & Co., 1974); T. Byres, "The Dialectic of India's Green Revolution," *South Asian Review* 5, no. 2 (January 1972): 99–116; H. Cleaver, "The Contradictions of the Green Revolution," *American Economic Review* 62, no. 2 (May 1972): 177–86; and Carl Gotsch, "Technical Change and the Distribution of Income in Rural Areas," *American Journal of Agricultural Economics* 54, no. 2 (May 1972): 326–41.

7. P. Scandizzo, "Resistance to Innovation and Economic Dependence in Northeast Brazil," mimeographed (Washington, D.C.: World Bank, 1975); A. Badhuri, "Agricultural Backwardness Under Semi-Feudalism," *Economic Journal* 83, no. 239 (March 1973): 120–37.

8. Chayanov's terminology is used here even though the determinant of exploitation postulated is contrary to his theory. For Chayanov, the peasant household self-exploits itself to a degree that is *internally* determined by the subjective equilibrium between the drudgery of labor and family-demand satisfaction. Here self-exploitation is part of a reactive survival strategy designed by the peasant household in response to *external* coercive forces that are determined by the form of articulation of the peasant class with the dominant mode of production. For Chayanov's theory,

see A. V. Chayanov, *The Theory of Peasant Economy*, ed. D. Thorner et al. (Homewood, Ill.: Richard D. Irwin, 1966), esp. pp. 5-7.

9. As Silvia Terán observes, even the landless and semiproletarian peasants who earn their subsistence principally on the labor market define their political objectives in terms of a return to the status of peasant and not improvement of employment and wage conditions; see Silvia Terán, "Formas de Conciencia Social de los Trabajadores del Campo," *Cuadernos Agrarios* 1, no. 4 (October-December 1976): 20-36.

10. In Mexico, the area in corn production declined by 20 percent between 1966 and 1975, implying the need to import 2.6 million tons of corn in 1976 in order to counteract upward pressures on the price of this essential wage food. Luis Gómez Oliver attributes this crisis principally to the collapse of peasant agriculture as a supplier of commodities; see Luis Gómez Oliver, "Crisis Agrícola, Crisis de los Campesinos," *Comercio Exterior* 28, no. 6 (June 1978): 714-27.

11. A. T. Mosher, *Projects of Integrated Rural Development* (New York: Agricultural Development Council, December 1972); D. Adams and E. W. Coward, *Small Farmer Development Strategies: A Seminar Report* (New York: Agricultural Development Council, July 1972).

12. We had the opportunity to observe these projects on repeated occasions and had access to the farm survey data collected in each area. The Puebla data were collected by Leobardo Gimenez and Heliodoro Diaz of the National School of Agriculture in Chapingo; the Garcia Rovira data were compiled by Diego Londoño and Fernando Bernal of the Colombian Agricultural Institute in Bogotá; and the Cajamarca data were obtained by Efrain Franco of the National Agrarian University in La Molina and by Carmen Diana Deere of the University of Massachusetts at Amherst.

13. See, for example, D. Harvey, "Population, Resources, and the Ideology of Science," *Economic Geography*, July 1974, pp. 256-77; see also M. Agosin, "Economic Welfare and Alternative Views of Man," *Alternatives* 2 (1976): 1-12. This interpretation stands in opposition to Harberger's philosophy on the objectivity of project evaluation; see A. Harberger, "Three Basic Postulates for Applied Welfare Economics: An Interpretative Essay," *Journal of Economic Literature* 9, no. 3 (September 1971): 785-97.

14. W. Falcon, "The Green Revolution: Generation of Problems," *American Journal of Agricultural Economics* 52, no. 5 (December 1970): 698-710; Griffin, *The Political Economy of Agrarian Change*.

15. Wyn Owen, "The Double Developmental Squeeze on Agriculture," *American Economic Review* 56, no. 1 (March 1966): 43-70; idem, "Absorbing More Labor in LDC Agriculture: A Comment," *Economic Development and Cultural Change* 19, no. 4 (July 1971); 652-56.

16. By extending credit to a "solidarity group" of ten to 20 peasants instead of to individuals, the banks were able to reduce transaction costs significantly. The group members then informally organized among themselves the distribution of the loan and the collection of principal and interest for repayment; see Heliodoro Diaz-Cisneros, "An Institutional Analysis of Rural Development Projects: The Case of the Puebla Project in Mexico" (Ph.D. diss., University of Wisconsin, 1974).

17. Ibid.

18. CIMMYT, *Plan Puebla: Seven Years of Experience* (El Batan, Mexico, 1974).

19. Ibid.

20. K. Swanberg and E. Shipley, "The Nutritional Status of the Rural Family in East Cundinamarca, Colombia," *Food Research Institute Studies* 14, no. 2 (1975): 111-26.

21. F. Bernal, J. Jaramillo, and L. Agudelo, *Evaluación del Proyecto Garcia Rovira* (Bogotá: ICA, División de Estudios Socioeconómicos, 1976).

22. Carmen Diana Deere, "Changing Social Relations of Production and Peruvian Peasant Women's Work," *Latin American Perspectives* 4, no. 1 (Winter-Spring 1977): 48-69.

23. Mariano Valderrama, *Siete Años de Reforma Agraria Peruana, 1969-1976* (Lima: Fondo Editorial, Pontificia Universidad Católica, 1977).

24. F. Franco, T. Haller, and E. Gonzales, *Diagnóstico del Area de Influencia del Proyecto Cajamarca-La Libertad* (Cajamarca, Peru: Ministerio de Agricultura, 1976).

25. T. W. Schultz, *Transforming Traditional Agriculture* (New Haven: Yale University Press, 1964).

26. Sol Tax, *Penny Capitalism: A Guatemalan Indian Community,* Smithsonian Institute of Social Demography, no. 16 (Washington, D.C., n.d.).

27. A. T. Mosher, *Creating a Progressive Rural Structure* (New York: Agricultural Development Council, 1969).

28. Arthur Lewis, "Economic Development with Unlimited Supplies of Labor," in *The Economics of Underdevelopment,* ed. A. Argarwala and S. Singh (New York: Oxford University Press, 1958).

29. G. Ranis and J. Fei, "A Theory of Economic Development," in *Agriculture in Economic Development,* ed. C. Eicher and L. Witt (New York: McGraw-Hill, 1964).

30. Dale Jorgenson, "The Role of Agriculture in Economic Development: Classical Versus Neo-Classical Models of Growth," in *Subsistence Agriculture and Economic Development,* ed. C. Wharton (Chicago: Aldine Publishing Co., 1969).

31. Everett Rogers, *The Diffusion of Innovations* (New York: Free Press of Glencoe, 1962).

32. Schultz, *Transforming Traditional Agriculture.*

33. Lewis, "Economic Development."

34. E. Wolf, *Peasants* (Englewood Cliffs, N.J.: Prentice-Hall, 1966); J. Ennew, P. Hirst, and K. Tribe, " 'Peasantry' as an Economic Category," *Journal of Peasant Studies* 4, no. 4 (July 1977): 295–322; T. Shanin, "Peasantry: Delineation of a Sociological Concept and a Field of Study," *European Journal of Sociology* 12 (1971): 289–300.

35. O. Flores, E. Grillo, and C. Samaniego, "Caso de la Papa en el Peru," mimeographed (Lima: ISCA-OEA, 1979).

36. Full employment is defined here as 250 days worked per year; see Carmen Diana Deere and Alain de Janvry, "A Conceptual Framework for the Empirical Analysis of Peasants," *American Journal of Agricultural Economics* 61, no. 4 (November 1979): 601–11.

37. Roger Bartra, *Estructura Agraria y Clases Sociales en México* (Mexico City: Ediciones ERA, 1974).

38. In an early seminar of the Agricultural Development Council on RDPs, the conclusion was similarly reached that in "bimodal societies"—what we call here functional dualism—"most growth stimulating programs... resulted in deterioration in the position of the small farmer." See Adams and Coward, *Small Farmer Development Strategies,* p. 22.

39. Robert McNamara, "Address to the Board of Governors, Nairobi, Kenya" (Washington, D.C.: World Bank, 1973).

40. D. Londoño, "Economic Analysis of Subsistence Agriculture in Garcia Rovira, Colombia" (Ph.D. diss., Oklahoma State University, 1975).

41. Colombia, National Department of Planning, "Bases para la Evaluación del Programa de Desarrollo Rural Integrado" (Bogotá, December 1976).

42. John Weeks, "The Political Economy of Labor Transfer," *Science and Society* 35, no. 4 (Winter 1971): 463–80.

43. C. Kao, K. Anschel, and C. Eicher, "Disguised Unemployment in Agriculture: A Survey," in *Agriculture in Economic Development,* ed. C. Eicher and L. Witt (New York: McGraw-Hill, 1964), chap. 7.

44. Schultz, *Transforming Traditional Agriculture;* David Hopper, "Allocative Efficiency in Traditional Indian Agriculture," *Journal of Farm Economics* 47, no. 3 (August 1955): 611–24.

45. T. W. Schultz, "The Role of Government in Promoting Economic Growth," in *The State of the Social Sciences,* ed. L. White (Chicago: University of Chicago Press, 1956), p. 375.

46. German Escobar and Kenneth Swanberg, "Uso de la Mano de Obra en Dos Zonas Rurales: Pleno Empleo Estacional?" mimeographed (Tibaitatá, Colombia: ICA, División de Estudios Socioeconómicos, September 1976).

47. This is in contrast to Georgescu-Roegen, who conceptualizes peasants as disconnected from the labor market and hence as having a zero opportunity cost for labor outside the home plot. See N. Georgescu-Roegen, "Economic Theory and Agrarian Economics," in *Agriculture in Economic Development*, ed. C. Eicher and L. Witt (New York: McGraw-Hill, 1964).

48. Manuel Villa Issa, "El Mercado de Trabajo y la Adopción de Tecnología Nueva de Producción: El Caso del Plan Puebla" (M.S. thesis, Colegio de Postgraduados, Centro de Economía Agrícola, Chapingo, Mexico, 1977).

49. Carmen Diana Deere, "The Development of Capitalism in Agriculture and the Division of Labor by Sex: A Study of the Northern Peruvian Sierra" (Ph.D. diss., Department of Agricultural and Resource Economics, University of California, Berkeley, 1978).

50. Schultz, *Transforming Traditional Agriculture*.

51. In Puebla, tailoring recommendations to different types of farms and households leads to widely divergent optimum levels of fertilizer use; see E. Moscardi and A. de Janvry, "Attitudes Toward Risk Among Peasants: An Econometric Approach," *American Journal of Agricultural Economics* 59, no. 4 (November 1977): 710–16.

52. Carlos Benito, "The Puebla Project," mimeographed (Berkeley: University of California, Department of Agricultural and Resource Economics, 1978).

53. Bernal, Jaramillo, and Agudelo, *Evaluación del Proyecto Garcia Rovira*.

54. Franco, Haller, and Gonzales, *Diagnóstico del Area de Influencia*.

55. This is the general assumption that underlies the work of the Economic Commission for Latin America. See Chapter 4 above and Solon Barraclough, ed., *Agrarian Structures in Latin America* (Lexington, Mass.: Heath, Lexington Books, 1973).

56. D. Winkelmann, "The Adoption of New Maize Technology in Plan Puebla, Mexico" (El Batan, Mexico: International Center for Wheat and Corn, 1976).

57. Alain de Janvry, "Optimal Levels of Fertilization Under Risk: The Potential for Corn and Wheat Fertilization Under Alternative Price Policies in Argentina," *American Journal of Agricultural Economics* 54, no. 1 (February 1972): 1–10.

58. Ernst Schraepler, Prologue to the German edition of *La Cuestión Agraria*, by Karl Kautsky (Bogotá: Editorial Latina, 1976).

59. Huntley Biggs, "New Technologies for Small Farmers: The Puebla Project," in *Small Farmer Agricultural Development Problems*, ed. H. Biggs and R. L. Tinnermeier (Fort Collins: Colorado State University, 1974).

60. Moscardi and de Janvry, "Attitudes Toward Risk Among Peasants."

61. For a useful contrast of alternative diffusion models, see Eric Miller, *Desarrollo Integral del Medio Rural* (Mexico City: Fondo de Cultura Económica, 1976).

62. Paulo Freire, *Pedagogy of the Oppressed* (New York: Seabury Press, 1970).

63. Asociación Nacional de Usuarios Campesinos, "DRI: Nueva Estrategia de Lopez," *Carta Campesina*, no. 31 (October 1975), p. 8.

64. Ernest Feder, "The New World Bank Program for the Self-Liquidation of the Third World Peasantry," *Journal of Peasant Studies* 3, no. 3 (1976): 343–54.

65. ILO, Overseas Development Council, *Employment, Growth, and Basic Needs: A One-World Problem* (New York: Praeger Publishers, 1977).

Chapter 8

1. J. Weaver, K. Jameson, and R. Blue, "A Critical Analysis of Approaches to Growth and Equity," in *The Political Economy of Development and Underdevelopment*, ed. C. Wilber, 2d ed. (New York: Random House, 1979), chap. 28.

2. ILO, *Towards Full Employment: A Programme for Colombia* (Geneva: ILO, 1970). See also D. Turnham, *The Employment Problem in Less Developed Countries: A Review of Evidence*, Employment Series, no. 1 (Paris: OECD, 1976); and David Morawetz, "Employment Implica-

tions of Industrialization in Developing Countries: A Survey," *Economic Journal* 84, no. 335 (September 1974): 491–542.

3. Michael Lipton, *Why Poor People Stay Poor: A Study of Urban Bias in World Development* (Cambridge, Mass.: Harvard University Press, 1977).

4. World Bank, *The Assault on World Poverty* (Baltimore: The Johns Hopkins University Press, 1975); Uma Lele, *The Design of Rural Development* (Baltimore: The Johns Hopkins University Press, 1975); John Mellor, *The New Economics of Growth* (Ithaca, N.Y.: Cornell University Press, 1976).

5. H. Chenery et al., *Redistribution with Growth* (London: Oxford University Press, 1974); ILO, Overseas Development Council, *Employment, Growth, and Basic Needs: A One-World Problem* (New York: Praeger Publishers, 1977).

6. Paul Streeten, "From Growth to Basic Needs," *Finance and Development* 16, no. 3 (September 1979): 31; see also idem, "Basic Needs: Premises and Promises," *Journal of Policy Modeling* 1, no. 1 (1979): 136–46.

7. Streeten, "From Growth to Basic Needs," p. 30.

8. Frances Stewart, "Country Experiences in Providing for Basic Needs," *Finance and Development* 16, no. 4 (December 1979): 23–26.

9. R. Hansen, *Beyond the North-South Stalemate* (New York: McGraw-Hill, 1979); Geoffrey Barraclough, "Waiting for the New Order," *New York Review of Books* 25, no. 16 (October 1978): 45–53.

10. Irma Adelman, "Growth, Income Distribution, and Equity-Oriented Development Strategies," *World Development* 3, nos. 1 and 2 (February–March 1975).

11. This is the case in particular for S. Wortman and R. Cummings, *To Feed This World* (Baltimore: The Johns Hopkins University Press, 1978); and A. Waterson, "A Viable Model for Rural Development," *Finance and Development* 11, no. 4 (December 1974): 22–25.

12. Stewart, "Country Experiences," p. 26.

13. Walter Galenson, "Economic Growth, Poverty, and the International Agencies," *Journal of Policy Modeling* 1, no. 2 (March 1979): 251–69.

14. Ibid., p. 268.

15. Simon Kuznets, "Economic Growth and Income Inequality," *American Economic Review* 45, no. 1 (March 1955): 1–28; Felix Paukert, "Income Distribution at Different Levels of Development," *International Labor Review* 108 (August–September 1973): 97–125; M. Ahluwalia, "Inequality, Poverty, and Development," *Journal of Development Economics* 3 (December 1976): 307–42.

16. Harry G. Johnson, *Economic Policies Toward Less Developed Countries* (Washington, D.C.: Brookings Institution, 1967); T. W. Schultz, *Economic Growth and Agriculture* (New York: McGraw-Hill, 1968).

17. I. Adelman, M. Hopkins, S. Robinson, G. Rodgers, and R. Wery, "A Comparison of Two Models for Income Distribution Planning," *Journal of Policy Modeling* 1, no. 1 (January 1979): 37–82.

18. Ibid., p. 81.

19. Ibid., p. 82.

20. Table 6.1 above.

21. William Cline, *Policy Alternatives for a New International Economic Order* (New York: Praeger Publishers, 1979), p. 52.

22. Lyle Schertz, "World Needs: Shall the Hungry Be with Us Always?" in *Food Policy,* ed. P. Brown and H. Shue (New York: Free Press, 1977).

23. Carlos Diaz-Alejandro, "Unshackled or Unhinged? On Delinking North and South," unpublished paper (Yale University, October 1976); Thomas Wiesskopf, "Self-Reliance and Development Strategy" (Paper presented at the International Conference on Alternative Development Strategies and the Future of Asia, United Nations Institute for Training and Research, New Delhi, October 1979).

24. Charles Wright, "Income Inequality and Economic Growth: Examining the Evidence," *Journal of Developing Areas* 13, no. 1 (October 1978): 49-66.

25. J. Fei and G. Ranis, "Innovation, Capital Accumulation, and Economic Development," *American Economic Review* 53, no. 3 (June 1963): 283-313.

26. Fernando Rello, "Modo de Producción y Clases Sociales," *Cuadernos Políticos* 8 (April-June 1976): 100-105; Gustavo Esteva, "Y Si los Campesinos Existen?" *Comercio Exterior* 28 (June 1978): 699-732.

27. Richard Harris, "Marxism and the Agrarian Question in Latin America," *Latin American Perspectives* 5, no. 4 (Fall 1978): 2-26.

28. Floyd and Lillian Dotson, "Mexico's Urban-dwelling Farmers," *Rural Sociology* 43, no. 4 (Winter 1978): 691-710; David Goodman and Michael Redcliff, "The 'Boias Frias': Rural Proletarianization and Urban Marginality in Brazil," *International Journal of Urban and Regional Research* 1, no. 2 (1977): 348-64.

29. William Roseberry, "Peasants as Proletarians," *Critique of Anthropology* 3, no. 11 (1978): 3-18; Maria de Nazareth Baudel Wanderly, "O Campones: Um Trabalhador para o Capital" (São Paulo: Agrarian Studies Group, State University of Campinas, 1979).

30. Roger Bartra, *Estructura Agraria y Clases Sociales en México* (Mexico City: Ediciones Era, 1974), p. 78; see also idem, "Y Si los Campesinos se Extinguen . . .," *Historia y Sociedad,* no. 8 (1975), pp. 71-83.

31. Silvia Terán, "Formas de Conciencia Social de los Trabajadores del Campo," *Cuadernos Agrarios* 1, no. 4 (October-December 1976): 20-36.

32. Lygia Sigaud, "A Idealizacão do Passado numa Area de Plantation," *Contraponto* (Rio de Janeiro), 2, no. 2 (November 1977): 115-26.

Selected Bibliography

Adelman, Irma. "Growth, Income Distribution, and Equity-Oriented Development Strategies." *World Development* 3, nos. 2 and 3 (February–March 1975).

Amin, Samir. *Unequal Development*. New York: Monthly Review Press, 1976.

_____. "The End of a Debate." Part IV of *Imperialism and Unequal Development*. New York: Monthly Review Press, 1977.

Bacha, E., and Taylor, L. "Brazilian Income Distribution in the 1960s: Facts, Model Results, and the Controversy." *Journal of Development Studies* 14, no. 3 (April 1978): 271–97.

Banaji, J. "Summary of Selected Parts of Kautsky's 'The Agrarian Question.'" *Economy and Society* 5, no. 1 (1976): 5–29.

Baran, Paul A. *The Political Economy of Growth*. New York: Prometheus Books, 1957.

Baran, Paul A., and Sweezy, Paul M. *Monopoly Capital*. New York: Monthly Review Press, 1966.

Barraclough, Solon. "Agricultural Production Prospects in Latin America." *World Development* 5, nos. 5–7 (1977): 459–76.

Barraclough, Solon, ed. *Agrarian Structure in Latin America*. Lexington, Mass.: Lexington Books, 1973.

Barraclough, Solon, and Fernandez, J. A. *Diagnóstico de la Reforma Agraria Chilena*. Mexico City: Siglo XXI, 1974.

Bartra, Roger. *Estructura Agraria y Clases Sociales en México*. Mexico City: Ediciones Era, 1974.

Berry, Albert, and Urrutia, Miguel. *Income Distribution in Colombia*. New Haven: Yale University Press, 1976.

Bradby, Barbara. "The Destruction of Natural Economy." *Economy and Society* 4, no. 2 (May 1975): 127–61.

Braun, Oscar. *Comercio Internacional e Imperialismo*. Buenos Aires: Siglo XXI, 1973.

Brenner, Robert. "The Origins of Capitalist Development: A Critique of Neo-Smithian Marxism." *New Left Review*, no. 104 (July–August 1977), pp. 25–92.

Cardoso, Fernando E. "Associated-Dependent Development: Theoretical and Practical Implications." In *Authoritarian Brazil,* edited by Alfred Stepan. New Haven: Yale University Press, 1973.

————. "Dependency and Development in Latin America." *New Left Review,* no. 74 (1972), pp. 83–95.

Chayanov, A. V. "On the Theory of Non-Capitalist Economic Systems." In *The Theory of the Peasant Economy,* edited by D. Thorner et al. Homewood, Ill.: Richard D. Irwin, 1966.

Cockcroft, J., et al. *Dependence and Underdevelopment.* Garden City, N.Y.: Doubleday, Anchor Books, 1972.

Collier, David, ed. *The New Authoritarianism in Latin America.* Princeton: Princeton University Press, 1979.

Deere, Carmen Diana, and de Janvry, Alain. "A Conceptual Framework for the Empirical Analysis of Peasants." *American Journal of Agricultural Economics* 61, no. 4 (November 1979): 601–11.

Dos Santos, Theotonio. "The Structure of Dependence." *American Economic Review* 40, no. 2 (May 1970): 231–36.

Duncan, K., and Rutledge, I. *Land and Labour in Latin America.* Cambridge: Cambridge University Press, 1977.

Emmanuel, Arghiri. *Unequal Exchange.* New York: Modern Reader, 1972.

Ennew, J.; Hirst, P.; and Tribe, K. " 'Peasantry' as an Economic Category." *Journal of Peasant Studies* 4 (1977): 295–322.

Feder, Ernest. *The Rape of the Peasantry.* New York: Anchor Books, 1971.

Foster-Carter, Aidan. "The Modes of Production Controversy." *New Left Review,* no. 107 (January–February 1978), pp. 47–77.

Frank, Andre Gunder. *Capitalism and Underdevelopment in Latin America.* New York: Modern Reader, 1969.

Furtado, Celso. *Economic Development of Latin America.* Cambridge: Cambridge University Press, 1970.

Galeano, Eduardo. *Open Veins in Latin America.* New York: Modern Reader, 1973.

George, Susan. *How the Other Half Dies.* Montclair, N.J.: Allanheld, Osmun & Co., 1977.

Griffin, Keith. "Increasing Poverty and Changing Ideas About Development Strategies." *Development and Change* 8 (1977): 491–508.

————. *The Political Economy of Agrarian Change: An Essay on the Green Revolution.* London: Macmillan & Co., 1975.

Hewitt de Alcantara, Cynthia. *Modernizing Mexican Agriculture.* Geneva: UNRISD, 1976.

Hodges, D. *The Latin American Revolution.* New York: W. Morrow & Co., 1974.

Holloway, J., and Picciotto, S. *State and Capital: A Marxist Debate.* Austin: University of Texas Press, 1979.

Hymer, Stephen. "The Multinational Corporation and the Law of Uneven Development." In *Economics and World Order from the 1970's to the 1990's,* edited by J. Bhagwati, pp. 113–40. New York: Collier-Macmillan, 1972.

Jessop, Bob. "Recent Theories of the Capitalist State." *Cambridge Journal of Economics* 1, no. 4 (1977): 353–73.

Kalmanovitz, Salomon. *Desarrollo de la Agricultura en Colombia.* Bogotá: Editorial la Carreta, 1978.

Kay, Cristobal. "Comparative Development of the European Manorial System and the Latin American Hacienda System." *Journal of Peasant Studies* 2, no. 1 (October 1974): 69–98.

Kay, Geoffrey. *Development and Underdevelopment: A Marxist Analysis.* New York: St. Martin's Press, 1975.

Laclau, Ernesto. "Feudalism and Capitalism in Latin America." *New Left Review,* no. 67 (1971), pp. 19–38.

Lappé, Frances Moore, and Collins, Joseph. *Food First.* Boston: Houghton Mifflin, 1977.

Lebowitz, M. "Marx's Falling Rate of Profit: A Dialectical View." *Canadian Journal of Economics* 9, no. 2 (May 1976): 223–54.

Lehmann, David. "The Death of Land Reform: A Polemic." *World Development* 6, no. 3 (1978): 339–45.

Lenin, V. I. *The Development of Capitalism in Russia.* Moscow: Progress Publishers, 1964.

_____. *Imperialism: The Highest Stage of Capitalism.* Peking: Foreign Languages Press, 1973.

Magdoff, Harry. *The Age of Imperialism.* New York: Modern Reader, 1969.

Mandel, Ernest. *Late Capitalism.* London: New Left Books, 1976.

Marini, Ruy Mauro. "Dialectica de la Dependencia." *Sociedad y Desarrollo,* no. 1 (January–March 1972), pp. 5–31.

Newfarmer, Richard, and Mueller, Willard. "Multinational Corporations in Brazil and Mexico." Report to the Subcommittee on Multinational Corporations, U.S. Senate, Washington, D.C., 1975.

North American Congress for Latin America (NACLA). "Agribusiness Targets in Latin America." *Report of the Americas* 10, no. 1 (January 1978).

O'Connor, James. *The Fiscal Crisis of the State.* New York: St. Martin's Press, 1973.

O'Donnell, Guillermo. "State and Alliances in Argentina, 1956–1976." *Journal of Development Studies* 15, no. 1 (October 1978): 3–33.

Palma, Gabriel. "Dependency: A Formal Theory of Underdevelopment or a Methodology for the Analysis of Concrete Situations of Underdevelopment?" *World Development* 6 (1978): 881–924.

Pearce, Andrew. *The Latin American Peasant.* London: Frank Cass, 1975.

Petras, James. "The Latin American Agro-Transformation from Above and Outside." *Critical Perspectives on Imperialism and Social Class in the Third World.* New York: Monthly Review Press, 1978.

Phillips, Ann. "The Concept of 'Development.'" *Review of African Political Economy,* no. 8 (1977), pp. 7–20.

Portes, Alejandro. "The Informal Sector and the Capital Accumulation Process in Latin America." Mimeographed. Durham, N.C.: Duke University, February 1980.

Rey, Pierre Philippe. *Les Alliances de classes.* Paris: Maspéro, 1976.

Stein, Stanley, and Stein, Barbara. *The Colonial Heritage of Latin America.* New York: Oxford University Press, 1970.

Stavenhagen, Rodolfo. *Social Classes in Agrarian Societies.* Garden City, N.Y.: Doubleday, Anchor Books, 1975.

Tavares, M. C. de, and Serra, J. "Beyond Stagnation: A Discussion on the Nature of Recent Development in Brazil." In *From Dependence to Revolution,* edited by J. Petras. New York: John Wiley & Sons, 1973.

Terán, Silvia. "Formas de Conciencia Social de los Trabajadores del Campo." *Cuadernos Agrarios* 1, no. 4 (October–December 1976): 20–36.

Valderrama, Mariano. *Sieta Años de Reforma Agraria Peruana, 1969–1976.* Lima: Fondo Editorial, Pontifica Universidad Católica, 1976.

Vergopoulos, Kostas. "El Capitalismo Disforme." In *La Cuestión Campesina y el Capitalismo,* edited by S. Amin and K. Vergopoulos. Mexico City: Editorial Nuestro Tiempo, 1975.

Warren, Bill. "Imperialism and Capitalist Industrialization." *New Left Review,* no. 81 (September–October 1973), pp. 3–44.

Wright, Charles. "Income Inequality and Economic Growth: Examining the Evidence." *Journal of Developing Areas* 13, no. 1 (October 1978): 49–66.

Index

307